FAITH IN DOUBT

Praise for *Faith in Doubt*

A priest in an emptying church asks vital questions about life and faith in a secular age.

Join the pilgrimage with Harold (the priest), John (a believer) and Rosalind (a non-believer) as they encounter challenges that re-interpret their world and themselves.

In a blend of memoir, romance, and intellectual enquiry drawing on science, theology and other disciplines, the author proposes a human relationship with God that is continuously evolving (as relationships do). Such a relationship, he explains, requires us to test our assumptions and withdraw our projections:

> *"The underlying process of projections being embraced and then being integrated is the central dynamic of full human life. In a culture like ours when the projection of God is being withdrawn, religion's new role will be to support awareness of, and participation in that process by which the God projection is integrated into our lives."*

Faith in Doubt takes a courageous and honest approach to existential questions you may have been afraid to ask. It offers a breakthrough to deep joy and purpose beyond the noisy breakdowns of modernity.

KATHLEEN GIBSON, *agriculture and science journalist based in Victoria, B.C.*

This book is about 'sharing, astonishment, awe and wonder.' An adventure in a love story that invites you to think. Worth the risk of reading! Science or Faith? Which makes most sense to you? Harold's book discovers the distance between science and faith is imaginary. This 'love story' invites us on an amazing journey.

RT. REV. KENNETH GENGE, *retiree bishop of Edmonton and former director of the Sorrento Centre.*

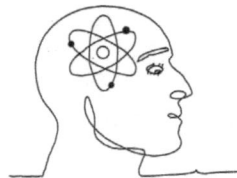

A bold and insightful book! The author proposes a challenging conciliation between religious faith and secular science—not an easy sell, by any means. A collaborative effort between conscientious scientists and courageous committed persons of faith just might offer hope to a burning and violence-torn planet. Warning: if the reader identifies with either group, don't peek at the ending!

...I cannot remember reading anything on science and faith as stimulating and enjoyable as this.

> DR. WILLIAM CLOSE, MA (CANTAB) DR THEOL *(Basel, Switzerland). Former Dean and Director, Doctor of Ministry Program, St Stephen's College, Edmonton, and retired President, Atlantic School of Theology, Halifax, ordained minister, United Church of Canada.*

God does not exist! The proof is all around us. God exists! The proof is all around us! Munn applies mediation tools like deep listening to surface a third truth calling on each camp to meet the challenge of preserving life on Earth by leaning on the other, not to meet each other halfway, but to deepen their own perspective.

> PATRICIA LANE LAWYER, *Mediator, and doubtful church goer.*

What if the world of faith and the world of science and secularism both point to the same underlying structure of reality? Munn is convinced they do, and argues that the time has come for each to see how their respective insights have also found expression in the other's language, an encounter that he maintains will bring wholeness and vitality to a culture siloed by lines of faith and disbelief. The candor with which Munn shares his own faith journey and his patent interest in the connections to be made from a willingness to learn a new language make for an engaging read, but if this is not enough he weaves his argument through a delightful story of improbable but almost necessary love!

> NICHOLAS MAY, PHD, *historian of Nisga'a Christianity, Department of History, Simon Fraser University*

The content presented herein is based on the author's perspective and interpretation of the subject matter. The author has tried to recreate events, locales and conversations from the author's memories of them. In some instances the names of individuals and places and identifying characteristics have been disguised.

This book represents the opinions of the author and does not necessarily reflect the positions or opinions of any organization or individual with which the author is or has been affiliated. Neither the publisher nor any associated parties shall be held responsible for any consequences arising from the opinions or interpretations expressed within this book.

◆ FriesenPress

One Printers Way
Altona, MB R0G 0B0
Canada

www.friesenpress.com

Copyright © 2024 by Harold Munn, M.Div, D.Min., DD.
First Edition — 2024

Original drawings by Lena Lenz.
DOUBJLE
-design-
Cover image from Adobe Stock.

ISBN
978-1-03-919602-5 (Hardcover)
978-1-03-919601-8 (Paperback)
978-1-03-919603-2 (eBook)

1. Religion, Religion & Science

Distributed to the trade by The Ingram Book Company

For Miriam.

FAITH *in* DOUBT

How My Dog Made Me an Atheist
and Atheism Made Me a Priest

An Experiment in Faith

With best wishes on your journey in Faith.

HAROLD MUNN

Harold Munn.

Table of Contents

DEDICATION

My life partner met me when I was struggling with whether God is real, and her patience in listening to my endless agonized questions enabled me to find my way to trust again. Her own experiences of life and death in the high-pressure work of emergency medicine and as head nurse of Canada's first transplant unit, as well as in her own life, were experiences of great courage which pressed me to face more deeply the issues of life and death and to find unexpected life within both.

Her loyalty to me and her courage in refusing to accept any of my projections about her or about myself opened me to a new depth of understanding about how to be in relationship. That truth turned out to apply equally to the faith. Without her I would have hardly come alive either in the faith or in our marriage.

Some of the stories in this book are my way of returning her love and her faithfulness in accompanying me on this journey.

No wonder within an hour of first meeting her I held her hand. In that short time, I'd already fallen in love with Claire. Nothing and everything has changed in the half century since. Her love for me became the womb in which the seminal ideas in this book could be nurtured and come to fruition. I'm honoured to have had such a life partner whose commitment to the truth about each of us made possible this project and our love.

ACKNOWLEDGEMENTS

There are more people to thank than I can count, but these have provided special assistance. Bill and Lanna Kelly supported and encouraged my doctoral research at St. Stephen's College at the University of Alberta, Edmonton into secular disbelief right from the beginning, and Lanna provided invaluable feedback on the text. Dr. William Close, then director of the Doctor of Ministry program at St. Stephen's College at the University of Alberta Edmonton, guided and challenged me through the research process, and unstintingly shared his time and insights subsequently. Without his inspiration and trust in the importance of this project, it would never have been completed. Thank you, Bill. Dr. Clair Woodbury, my thesis advisor shepherded me through the complexities of the degree program. Dr. Lynne Van Luven, former professor of creative non-fiction at the University of Victoria challenged me to make the original dry version far more personal—an invaluable challenge that transformed my vision of what I was attempting to do and made the argument so much more forceful by being grounded in personal experience. Thanks so much, Lynne.

Harold Coward, Founding Director of the Centre for Studies in Religion and Society at the University of Victoria, provided sabbatical support for studies related to this project. Margot Boland generously shared her professional experience in the publishing business as I first put a toe into that world; without her patient explanations of the publishing geography I would have floundered in that unfamiliar territory.

Susan McCaslin and Kate Braid generously shared their time and experience as published authors. Their enthusiasm and wisdom gave me the courage to move from tentative hope to serious commitment.

Bishop Ken Genge continued through the years nudging me without respite to actually get the book done. Friends read early versions and provided invaluable responses and insights: members of a discussion group at St. John the Divine, Victoria, including especially Jim Field and Bob Carey, and others. Other early supporters were Gwen Bright, Malcolm Maclure and Patricia Lane,

Susan Findlater, Joyce Bainbridge, Timothy Cheek, Jennifer Gerwing, John and Jasmine Kramer, Jamie Lawson, Pitman Potter, and John Stephens—their comments and insights immensely improved an early version of the text. The parishes of Christ Church and All Saints' Cathedral, both in Edmonton, of St. John the Divine, Victoria, and of St. Anselm's, Vancouver, have all been generous with their time and support as I worked at this project. Barbara Mitchell, who applied her skills as editor, correcting errors large and small and challenging me to write more clearly in my first full draft, ensured I had a solid basic text from which to work.

Pushing through the last lap to the finish line of actually submitting a fair text to FriesenPress were Joy Gibson, Kathleen Gibson, Nicholas May, Alisdair Smith and Sam Zhai all of whom were of immense assistance in clarifying my writing and challenging my assumptions.

The support of all these wonderful people has been invaluable. Nevertheless any imperfections and mistakes are my responsibility alone.

Finally, the editors and consultants at FriesenPress have been unflaggingly helpful and encouraging. Without their professional expertise in every area of the publishing process the actual text would never have seen the light of day. Thanks to you all.

My father, born just after the end of the nineteenth century grew up and was trained as a priest in a world more different from mine than can be imagined. Yet his extraordinary awareness of God, and especially his calm acceptance of the call of love at whatever the cost, influenced me profoundly and continued to give me hope that the faith might mean something until such time as it did. He appears occasionally in the text but his influence is throughout.

My wife, Claire, has supported me through endless re-writes. That has been an extraordinary act of patience and love. Mark and Eric, our sons, have taught me so much about the world in which they live, and their children about the secular world in which they live and what it's like to have known no other.

To all these people and so many more, I owe immense gratitude. Thank you all.

Harold Munn

Introduction

In every congregation in which I've served, sooner or later some version of the following conversations takes place. "You've got a couple of babies. There used to be dozens of babies in the nursery in this congregation. I remember when we needed eight or ten adults every Sunday just to look after all the babies. Now we don't have any babies besides yours. You've been with us a year now, so why haven't you filled the nursery with babies?" Or, "Your kids are in their teens. I grew up in a teen group here that was so large we had to have three separate meeting places every Sunday night. You've been here a year and there are only two kids in their teens. Why haven't you got three youth groups going yet, like we used to have?" Or, "We used to be a big successful congregation. Not so much now. What are you going to do about it?"

They were right about two things. The numbers of people of all ages in church began to decline around the time I was ordained, and I never reversed that trend. However, I doubt that my ordination was the cause of the decline. Those concerned members were also right in longing that the faith again become the centre of many people's lives, and they were mourning the fact that it wasn't.

I share their longing and their mourning.

But they were wrong in thinking that I could do something about it by dreaming up some new program or becoming a "kid magnet."

There is bad news and good news about this decline in church attendance. In the pages ahead we'll look at both.

First, the bad news.

The situation is much worse than it seems.

There are no programs or charismatic leaders who are about to turn it all around. I can assure readers that if there were some program that would make all the difference in church attendance, clergy would be flocking to it, taking the right courses, and before long everything would go back to the way it was, with overflowing numbers. If there were a way for clergy to turn themselves into such highly effective leaders that people would again flock to church, we clergy would mortgage our homes to learn how. Despite all the hopeful mythology about how much greener the grass is on the other side of some theological or denominational fence, it's just not happening. Not anywhere in the secular West.

It's not that clergy suddenly are incompetent or that congregations suddenly are boring. The truth is much more disturbing than that. We could do something about fixing programs or leadership styles. The difficult truth is our entire western culture no longer thinks church-going is normal and no amount of leadership training or program innovation is going to change that. At best, our culture considers going to church to be an eccentric hobby or a way of proving one is a good, upstanding citizen, or worse, a haven for people who want to avoid the real world and remain immersed in a long-outdated illusion.

That's the bad news.

The good news is there's a way to do a judo move on the culture of disbelief. Judo philosophy describes how you can take your opponent's superior weight and momentum, and with a quick movement, turn it to your advantage. In other words, society's widespread disbelief may have within it the seeds of a revitalized, relevant expression of faith.[1]

All we need to do is learn the moves. With a certain kind of judo move, we'll uncover a profound and energizing expression of faith at the very core of the secular experience.

That sounds counter-intuitive. But rather than resisting disbelief with persuasive argument, attractive programming, or impressive social action, the only effective approach to our society's secularism will be to take disbelief seriously. That's about the only move we haven't tried yet.

It amounts to believing in disbelief.

That may sound not only counter-intuitive, but frankly, absurd. But then we must never forget Christianity is founded on the counter-intuitive and absurd idea that God, in the form of Jesus, was determined to follow priorities which were guaranteed to get himself executed by torture. Many in the first century thought that was absurd. We have precedent for pursuing the absurd.

There is also precedent within Canadian missionary history.

A nineteenth-century Canadian missionary in the western Arctic, Archdeacon Robert McDonald, took the local culture and language so seriously he literally married into it; he married a Gwich'in woman Julia Kutuq. His

---

1   Terms such as 'faith', 'God' or 'consciousness' are discussed in the glossary.

deep immersion in the culture and language of the Dene peoples in the Arctic and northern Yukon, enabled him and his wife to translate religious texts, to invent a syllabary with which to write the unique Gwich'in vocal sounds, and to produce a grammar and a dictionary of those Athapaskan languages. So deeply did he embed Christian faith inside those cultures, that during modern land claims negotiations those First Nations required federal government ministers to engage in public prayer as the first agenda item in their formal meetings to settle their claim to the land. A century later, his translations are still in active use. The Archdeacon's influence would have been far less if he had preached an English-only version of his faith, staunchly insisting on placing it within his own childhood Scottish culture.

Faith in Doubt invites people of faith to follow the Archdeacon's example and journey into the strange, and at first incomprehensible, language and culture of secularism. The book proposes that people of faith will not only experience delight in entering this new culture and will find learning the secular language fascinating, but that their faith will be clarified and deepened by that exposure. It will take courage and humility to go on this journey, immersing ourselves in the secular worldview, but we will find it to be a modern version of the journey Jesus made through the cross to resurrection. Like Archdeacon McDonald, we may have something of value to say to the modern secular world, and when that world hears people of faith speaking their language fluently, we may find secular people not only have ears to hear, but have things of value to say to us about faith in return. Wouldn't that be fun!

Not to take such a journey into deeply understanding our secular culture will result in our faith becoming more and more the esoteric hobby of people who enjoy religion,[2] or a backwater for people who irrationally deny the factual foundations of the modern world. If that happens, faith will have proved the secular world is correct after all—faith isn't about anything important.

Archdeacon McDonald fell so in love with the Gwich'in caribou culture that he married into it. This book invites people of faith to do the same and fall in love with modern secular culture.

The journey of falling in love with secular culture is told by three characters. One is myself, describing turning points on my own journey as a person of faith in the land of secular atheism which I have come to love and in which I have found Christ to be powerfully present. Two imaginary characters, John

2   See glossary.

and Rosalind, represent the cultures of faith and science[3] and demonstrate how those two ways of looking at the world might engage in a creative conversation.

That conversation has been underway for far longer than we usually think.

In 1851, Matthew Arnold, a British nineteenth-century poet, was honeymooning at Dover in the UK. Listening to the waves roaring in and out over the gravel as the tide ebbed, he wrote the following lines in his poem *On Dover Beach*:

> *"The Sea of Faith was once, too, at the full, and round earth's shore lay like the folds of a bright girdle furl'd. But now I only hear its melancholy, long, withdrawing roar...."*[4]

In the mid-nineteenth century, eight years *before* Darwin published his discovery of evolution, Arnold was aware that faith was ebbing, and that loss felt melancholic. Now, one hundred and sixty years later, he would be astonished at how far the tide of faith has receded—so far that only occasional tide-pools remain, and even those are drying up. As did Matthew Arnold, religious people in our day experience melancholy and nostalgia at this receding tide of faith, and because the tide of faith has nearly vanished over the horizon, many congregations live with a sense of impending disaster. For many, closure seems one financial statement away.

But don't forget, Arnold was at Dover on his honeymoon.

Despite the melancholy in his outer world, he was no doubt celebrating a new relationship and new joy with his beloved Frances. That can be our experience as well, as we follow his example and look unblinkingly at why the faith is receding so dramatically in our time. Then we may be surprised by joy and to our astonishment discover faith at the very centre of secular culture.

We might even find ourselves in the delight of a honeymoon with secularism.

Our three characters are setting out on an adventure of conversation, and with them we will find ourselves in a new ship of faith being raised by an incoming, but different tide than that about which Arnold wrote. If our churches are prepared to embark on such a journey, we may find ourselves as delighted as were the disciples of Jesus in a boat in a different storm on another sea, in which voyage the outcome was not death by drowning, but amazement and wonder at the calming of that storm and the discovery of new hope and joy that changed the world.

---

3   See glossary.
4   On Dover Beach, Matthew Arnold, 1867.

I invite you to join this twenty-first-century voyage of discovery on the incoming tides of secularism that have the power to carry faith to new shores we once thought were terrifying but which may turn out to be experiences of deeper faith and more fulfilling joy.

Bon voyage!
Harold Munn
April 2024, Vancouver

PART ONE

Why Religion Must Learn to Speak Secular

CHAPTER 1

Growing up with Disbelief

My dog told me there was no God[1]

At eight years old I did a theological experiment on my dog.

Bumble was my pet terrier, a birthday gift from my father when I was six.

I sat down on the living room carpet with Bumble to find out if God exists or not.

Because my father was a priest, I grew up surrounded by faith,[2] hearing about God and Jesus, and being subjected to interminably boring church services.

The night of my experiment I had been left alone. With my parents out of the house, doubtless attending yet another boring service, I could finally find out if God was real.

My plan went like this.

Since God had made everything, including Bumble, I could test that belief by whispering the word 'God' into Bumble's ear. God being so big and Bumble being such an intelligent dog, she would respond with recognition and I would

1   See glossary.
2   See glossary.

have confirmation that it was all true.

But I knew whispering anything into her ear would produce a response, no matter what I said. If you have ever whispered into a dog's ear, or better, blown into a dog's ear, you know you can get quite a satisfying reaction.

So, I had to choose carefully what I would whisper. After whispering 'God,' I would have to whisper a second, unimportant, word so I could compare Bumble's responses to the two words to be sure it wasn't just my whispering that caused her reaction. I knew I would need to whisper the two words in the same neutral tone of voice, otherwise Bumble's response might be to my tone of voice and not to the meaning of the words.

Even at age eight I was aware of the rudiments of the scientific method.

Since the word 'God' was one syllable, the other word would also have to be a single syllable. I settled on 'chair' as being suitably neutral.

Surely, I thought, if God was real and the creator of Bumble, there would be a significant difference between her response to the word for the creator of the universe and to the word for a chair.

Sitting on the floor with Bumble, I carefully held up her ear with one hand, and whispered the two words, leaving a pause between them, with my mouth as close as I could get to the inside of her ear.

But after saying the two words, I couldn't discern any difference in Bumble's response.

She looked alert, even expectant, with her big brown eyes gazing quizzically at me. Perhaps expecting a dog biscuit. Her tail wagged. But to each of the words equally. This was disappointing. I hadn't learned anything.

So, I waited until she got bored and tried again. Still no special response to the word 'God.'

Surely Bumble must sense a connection to God, her creator.

Perhaps the word 'God' was too distant, too far removed from her everyday life.

So, I tried 'Jesus' and 'chair.' I whispered both, carefully using the same tone of voice.

Still no discernible difference in her response.

She was an intelligent dog—she could beg and went wild when I returned home after being away. So, either she was unintelligent, which obviously wasn't true, or else God's reality was less certain than everyone thought. At least to Bumble. And Bumble wasn't capable of dissembling.

That was the end of the experiment.

No profound dark night of the soul followed. It wasn't the demise of my faith. But it was my first inkling that I lived in two incompatible worlds—the world of faith that was so obvious to my parents, and the world of investigation in which God seemed absent.

Even at eight years old, I felt sure my parents wouldn't understand the world I lived in—the world of figuring out how things worked. In that world, my electric train, magnets, science fiction novels, and the truths available through scientific experiment were all open to investigation. So why not God?

Because I was sure this latter world was foreign territory to my parents, I never told them about my experiment with Bumble. In my parents' world, God was utterly obvious. I was sure that to them it would be incomprehensible that anyone would want to demonstrate the obvious.

Nevertheless, my parents were well aware of science. My father knew a little about physics—he was intrigued that atoms, and therefore all physical things, are mostly empty space. He had figured out, on his own, that the entire mighty Fraser River, on which we lived, must also be flowing upstream twenty-four hours a day in the form of clouds. Otherwise, that great river would dry up.

My father's idea of scientific knowledge was that scientists had discovered some fascinating facts that were like new toys but none of that really mattered. In his world, religious faith was the central dynamic through which all life was experienced. Scientific discoveries might be interesting and might elicit a sense of awe, but they held no special significance in themselves.

This belief, that the physical world is of little importance in comparison with the non-physical spiritual world, originated in ancient Greek philosophy, and has become the normative assumption of Christianity. But in contrast, the ancient Jews thought the physical world was the *centre* of God's activity, not a special spiritual world somewhere else. Their belief will be transformative for us as we explore a new faith relationship with our culture now grounded in scientific knowledge of the physical world.

I suspect that attitude of my father's about faith and science seemed obvious to him because being born ten years before the First World War, he had never played with an electric train when he was a child. No one made electric trains then. However, after the Second World War, when I was born, military factories were re-tooled to produce consumer goods such as electric trains for curious little boys like myself. So, unlike my father, I never knew a time when science and electric trains weren't a normal part of everyday life.

My experiment on Bumble was the product of the scientific culture that had even then become normative in our society.

So pervasive was that scientific culture that, for me, its assumptions seemed simply obvious. That's what was remarkable about my experiment on Bumble: not that an eight-year-old child did a theological experiment on his dog, but having had no instruction in science, the child knew he had to include controls in his experiment. The word 'God' had to be tested in the same tone of voice against another one-syllable word or the experiment wouldn't be valid. That's a remarkably sophisticated insight for an eight-year-old, and it demonstrates the immense power our scientific culture had exerted upon me and everyone of my generation. It didn't matter that we were entirely unconscious of its influence.

The implication is that at that tender age I already had one foot firmly planted in the scientific culture of our time. More than half a century later, most people in the West, and in much of the rest of the world, have been so immersed in the products of science all their lives that they have adopted the investigative assumptions of science as simply obvious—that's just the way the world works. Indeed, as we shall see later, contrary to popular opinion, scientific assumptions are so deeply ingrained in our culture that members of faith communities long for affirmation from science to confirm their faith.

For those of us who participate in mainline religious communities, the two worlds of religion and science seem to coexist more or less peacefully. However, those two worlds have little understanding of or even curiosity about one another, and they engage in virtually no significant conversation. Science is ignored in sermons and services, while science studies religious faith as a cultural phenomenon but not as a source of truth as religion claims to be. Scientists who attend church report to me they take a risk of placing their professional credibility in question if they let it be known they are people of faith. Likewise, church attenders who publicly affirm evolution report having their faith called into question by their religious friends. The quiet toleration between science and faith papers over cracks of mutual misunderstanding, ignorance, distrust, and assumptions of superiority.

It's long past due that the two communities of faith and science, both experiencing awe and both seeking truth, come to understand each other more deeply and discover themselves to be partners. Sometimes that conversation will be as naïve and delightful as a young boy whispering 'God' into his puppy's ear. Sometimes it will be more difficult and challenging. Just as is any mature relationship.

Before long the conversation between faith and science did indeed become more difficult and challenging. Within five years of his Bumble experiment that young boy encountered a world in which the drip, drip, drip, of disbelief became a steady stream.

My friends knew there was no God — shame in the dormitory

I had just turned thirteen when I went to boarding school. At night in the dormitory, I would wait until the restless sounds and surreptitious whispers of my dozen dormitory mates settled down to steady breathing. I knew then there was a chance of my not being caught.

I would lie in the dark filled with shame at what I was about to do. I was afraid as well as ashamed. I even felt shame about being afraid. I was determined that no one would see or hear. So I would lie motionless until everyone else was asleep.

Shameful as it was to do what I was about to do, it felt even more shameful not to do it. To do it beneath the sheets would be the act of a coward. Knowing I was a coward, I was determined not to go down that path. The certain shame of proving to myself that I was a coward by staying in bed would be worse than the merely possible shame of being caught.

When there were no more sounds, I would loosen the covers, slide silently out of my bed, and kneel on the bare wood dormitory floor in the pitch dark and say my prayers.

I would feel huge relief. It was done. There was no turning back. I hadn't taken the coward's way out by accidentally succumbing to sleep. Even if I was caught now and laughed at, at least I'd done what was right.

But far better if nobody ever found out that I was on my knees saying my prayers.

Saying my prayers wasn't simple. My prayers consisted of an exhaustive list of everyone I knew, and all my various relatives. Everyone I could think of. Including my dog Bumble. The scheme and the prayers had to be memorized because in the pitch dark I couldn't read them. The prayer cycle was long. I said a group of set formulaic prayers at the start and, in careful reverse order, repeated them at the end. My family and friends and Bumble were prayed for in the middle.

When this marathon prayer cycle was completed, I would crawl back under the sheets and drift off into blessed safety and sleep. I had done my duty and nobody had caught me. That was doubly pleasurable.

However, the remarkable thing was not only the gritty determination of that young boy just entering his teens. The more remarkable thing was where it happened.

The dormitory was in a church-related school of my father's denomination, a school that employed a full-time chaplain, and had its own chapel complete with pipe organ. Daily worship in the chapel was compulsory for all the students.

How could it be that enormous courage was required to pray within that religious context?

Despite being religiously affiliated, the school was deeply immersed in the surrounding culture, that as early as the late 1950s was already well along the road of becoming secular. In the world from which most of my fellow students came, there was still outward support for religion but because of the growing cultural secularism nobody was expected to take religion seriously as a personal activity of daily life.

All of us students shared the boarding school world of intellectual stimulation, the team experience of sports (there was a team for every skill level or lack thereof which was a boon to kids not gifted in athletics), the challenging cultural activities, and the sense of community and accomplishment. But one thing we didn't share was whether God was real and significant and whether, therefore, daily prayer was normal.

My thirteen-year-old self was becoming uncomfortably aware of the dissonance between my family experience in which religious practice was normative and our society's declining engagement with religious belief. Despite the remnants of official respect for faith, in the world of my fellow students religion was starting to become irrelevant and those who took it seriously enough to kneel down and pray were eccentric.

Eccentric is the last thing a young teenager wants to be.

When I was eight, experimenting with my dog showed me that animals seem unaware of the God who has created them. That discovery seemed merely odd. But at thirteen I found myself painfully torn between the cultural assumptions of faith and the cultural assumptions of secularism. This was no longer oddity. This was agony.

I was experiencing a gulf emerging between a world centred upon faith into which I had been born and the world of practical disbelief centred on science in which my fellow students and their families lived. These two worlds collided with emotional pain every night in the dark on that bare dormitory floor.

However, the pain was about more than my fear of possible embarrassment at being found kneeling in prayer. The deeper pain was that I felt torn between loyalties. I felt at home in both worlds and didn't want to deny the reality of either. Yet the two worlds seemed incompatible. So, night after night I placed my body in the centre of that excruciating dis-junction.

Was it wise to have subjected myself to such pain? Was it healthy to express loyalty at such cost? Perhaps not. But it was an act of courage which continues to impress the more experienced person of faith I later became.

Although I didn't know it at the time, my determination to pray in that ostensibly religious but actually secular context was also a determination to find a connection between the mutually antagonistic worlds of science and of faith. Choosing to remain in that painful tension was an important and creative act, despite my not being aware of its wider significance.

Without being aware of why he was doing it, that young boy refused to take the easy way out. He didn't succumb to joining the majority because it was more popular, he didn't become fanatically religious and retreat into religious isolation believing the other students were doomed to hell, he didn't deny the fascinating world opening up through high school science, and he didn't pretend there was no issue. He tried to live in both worlds with integrity and, for doing so, paid the price on that hard wooden floor.

That young boy's private struggle to hold together those contradictory experiences was more significant than he knew; it was a local manifestation of a much wider cultural tension. Like two tectonic plates grinding up against each other, the religious worldview and the secular worldview were, and still are, in profound conflict. That global conflict, acted out on a local scale, is what gave rise to the young boy's experiment on his dog, and his later decision as an adult to abandon faith in favour of the certainty of science.

In response to this enormous change, religious organizations have come to believe the decline in church attendance arises from individuals making their own personal decisions to abandon faith in favour of secularism. The hopeful implication of this assumption is that if religious communities can identify what they are doing wrong, such as not being friendly enough, or advertising enough, or using enough popular music, or being too conservative, or being too liberal, they will make themselves more attractive, and then people will make the same private individual decisions to return to church.

But the reality is much more threatening than that. The conflict between the two worldviews is deeply embedded in our culture and the decision to retain or abandon faith is seldom made by each person privately after carefully weighing the options. It's a decision being taken by an entire culture and it sweeps its members along with it. Individuals seldom think they have made a profound life-changing decision. Instead people perceive their changing practice and abandonment of active faith to be simple common sense.

As far as I could tell, all of my fellow students in the dormitory and all but one of the teachers at that religious school, appeared to consider it perfectly obvious that daily personal prayer wasn't something normal people do.

In order to respond to this challenge in which the active practice of faith is no longer normative in our society, churches need to learn what lies behind this profound cultural shift.

It didn't just happen. There's a reason for the change. If faith doesn't understand that reason, faith's responses to secularism will continue to be ineffective.

Science proved there was no God — Occam's razor

By the time I was in grade eleven, the rising stream of disbelief had become a raging torrent.

Dr. C.A.C. Porter was our chemistry teacher in grade eleven. We boys knew him as "Doc Cac." He knew everything. Except his nick-name. At least we hoped he didn't.

In one chemistry class, Doc Cac waxed philosophical and explained Occam's razor to us: if there are two equally plausible explanations for the same phenomenon, the simpler explanation will probably be the correct one. William Occam was a Franciscan scholar living in the 1300s who developed this logical technique to distinguish credible explanations from less credible. His idea was God wouldn't waste time creating unnecessary causes for things. So if we examine some phenomenon and there are two possible explanations, the explanation which is the more complicated is likely to be wrong. The image of a straight razor suggested how this technique can shave away unnecessary explanations from the face of an argument when deciding between competing reasons for something. Thus, Occam's razor.

The disturbing implication was immediately obvious to me.

God was an unnecessary complication for explaining things.

I already knew there were two explanations of the universe—the religious one in which I had grown up, in which God is the loving origin and continuing creator of the universe, and the scientific one that doesn't need God to explain how the universe emerged in the big bang or how it unfolded subsequently. I couldn't see how the two explanations could be compatible, but until Doc Cac's presentation I wasn't worried. Up to that moment I had assumed the contradiction would be resolved when I learned more about science or more about faith.

But Doc Cac's observation about the power of simplicity struck me as so self-evidently true that I didn't need to wait for further information to resolve the conflict between the religious and scientific explanations of the world. Simpler explanations are always going to be the right ones. God is an unnecessary complication in explaining anything.

I realized, the very moment he finished the explanation, that if I ever had to choose between the scientific explanation of the universe and the religious one, I would choose the scientific. I consciously decided to put off that choice hoping I wouldn't ever be forced to choose. But with a sinking feeling, I knew I already had.

It was eight more years before integrity forced me to put that choice into action. But when the choice came, it's no wonder I chose science and rejected faith in a superfluous God.

Occam's razor inflicted a deeper wound than the hard dormitory floor. Much of the time, I could come to terms with my emotions of shame and fear about being an eccentric believer, but there was no way to come to terms with this discovery of the total irrelevance of God. God was an unnecessary complication, irrelevant for everything I found fascinating—my electric train, my puppy, chemistry and physics, and fascination and awe about the way the universe works. This was no longer a matter of personal courage resisting social rejection. This was the dismantling of the entire world of faith, and when the time came, I gave it my full support. I agreed with this rejection of faith because it was so self-evident that simpler explanations are going to be correct.

But that didn't make the problem go away. I had grown up in a religious world to which I felt deep loyalty and for which I held deep respect. In my home, religion was gentle, healthy, and well integrated into everyday life. Faith was simply the natural fabric of mature adult life. In my family, religion was not a private preference but was a deeply integrative perspective by which to understand the world and by which to become a mature person. The most mature, balanced, and deeply generous person I'd ever known, who had no illusions about himself, was my father. And he was a priest. There was no question his intimate and constant awareness of the reality of God, and his desire to obey the command to love no matter what the personal cost, lay at the basis of his remarkable character and wide influence.

Faith wasn't a deep personal conviction for him, the way one might choose to put energy into becoming skilled at music or mechanics, or becoming passionate about hockey or a hobby. For him, faith was a way of viewing the world, living in it, and becoming mature. It wasn't an activity one did. It was the way one lived and became fully, deeply and intensely human. So regular daily prayer was simply obvious. That's how one remained aware of God.

So, I trusted faith. I'd seen its goodness, integrity and reality first hand.

The problem was I also trusted science.

It wasn't just that I was intrigued about the way things work, such as my electric train. I trusted science because by my teens, science had saved my life, not once, but several times.

From early childhood I had heard stories about my extremely premature birth. The tale had been told over and over by friends and family. By the age of eight, I knew I was alive only because there were incubators, and because science had learned how to produce and store oxygen so extremely premature babies, such as I had been, could be kept alive. Then when I needed prescription glasses in grade five, without which I would have become incapable of learning in a classroom and might have become a social outcast, I knew it was science, not prayer, which underlay the study of optics so lenses could be made to improve my vision. So, by grade five, I knew science could be trusted, and science couldn't be dismissed in the way some religious people did, as an interesting hobby uncovering curiosities of no significance. Science had given me back my life and then had given me my vision and my social place in the world. That was pretty impressive. That deserved my loyalty.

It happened again in my teen years. Upon being offered communion the night before a surgery, I refused. Not because I didn't believe in the faith, but because I wanted to take no chance that my religious practice might somehow disturb the delicate scientific and surgical skill in which I would put my trust the next morning. I wasn't sure faith could help, but I knew science and a surgeon could. And there was no way I wanted to take a chance religion might muck things up. It was clear which one I really trusted.

Despite my growing up in a profoundly mature religious home, our culture had utterly transformed my attitude toward religious faith. Faith could be trusted for some things, but others, particularly involving my physical body, were better left to science. You could trust science to work, religion wasn't so reliable when it came to physical problems.

While my culture's influence on me as a child was enormous, our culture has had an even more dramatic effect on the next generation. I came to atheism in my early twenties. My own children lost their faith when they were six.

At six years old my children devised an experiment similar to my experiment on Bumble thirty years earlier. On Christmas morning, my children compared the evidence of cookie crumbs left by Santa to the total absence of a bicycle under the tree following intense prayer to God for a bicycle the night before. The conclusion, based on the evidence, was obvious: Santa Claus existed and God didn't. Just like my eight-year-old self, they kept that experiment a secret from my wife and me until they were in their thirties. They were sure we wouldn't understand. Sounds familiar.

Were our children rebellious toward faith? No. They were simply normal members of their culture who, by their early childhood had become far more secular than I had been in my own childhood a generation before.

If faith is to have a fruitful conversation or anything to share with the secular culture in which we live and move and have our being, people of faith will need to understand this world-changing transformation which secular western culture has wrought upon us all.

Summary

I grew up in a world in which religion was a mature, solid, life-affirming, natural part of life. But as I entered the wider world, I discovered that a great many of my school friends and my teachers had no serious interest in religious faith. In fact, anyone who did was considered eccentric. Science had a lot to do with my new attitude toward faith because of the impressive things science had invented and had provided for me, all without reference to God.

My own children had the same experience but had it earlier in life than I had. God had become an optional belief, almost a hobby; something that has no deep significance.

So, what's going on?

The first step in finding out what's going on is to meet people who don't believe and find out what's going on for them. Like learning a new language, that won't be easy at first, but it will pay off in spades when we become fluent in the language of secularism. That will be the next stage of our journey of finding faith inside the doubt of secularism.

CHAPTER 2
Deluged by Disbelief

What happened to belief in God?

Our secular society is infused with religious symbols. Whether it is the names of the days of the week, common expletives of frustration, the subject-matter of great art and music, or the social custom of the weekend, western civilization is steeped in religion.

Yet growing numbers of people aren't interested in and don't know the first thing about the religion that for two thousand years has been the foundational identity of our society.

A seven-year-old boy was brought to my Edmonton church by his mother for the first time in his life, as we prepared for his baptism. He asked me why there was a "plus-sign" on top of the church roof, and more "plus-signs" on the furniture inside the building. He was very proud of knowing his arithmetic. He had no idea what a cross was. Despite his mother wanting him to be baptized clearly he'd had no exposure to the faith at home.

Justin Welby, the Archbishop of Canterbury, recounts a conversation in a jewellery store overheard by his wife.[1] A customer had asked to see a small pendant cross on a chain. The salesperson explained, "We've got two sorts of crosses: we've got a plain one and we've got one with a little man on it."

For the salesperson in a jewellery store to think that the little man on a pendant cross was simply decorative would have been inconceivable a generation ago. But in our day, ignorance about the basics of the faith that has been the foundation of western culture has become commonplace.

A television quiz show offered the following choices in answer to the question, "Who betrayed Jesus?" The options were Joshua, Moses, Judas, or Paul.

A university graduate watching the show was puzzled. "Moses?" she wondered.

"Judas!" declared her boyfriend who had a church background.

"How'd you know that?" she asked. "Did Jesus get betrayed?"

For many people the foundational Christian story has come to have the same significance as trivia questions like who won the World Series in 1931.

While taking my order in a restaurant one day, the waitress asked me about my black clergy shirt with the wrap-around white clergy collar. She wondered if it meant something. She thought it was a great fashion statement and asked me where she could buy one for her boyfriend.

A local store recently had eighty different sets of Easter cards on display for that festival. I checked all of them. Only three sets had a religious theme and not one of them mentioned Jesus' death or resurrection, the entire point of Easter. I checked with people in other Canadian cities and did the same investigation in a major department store on Oxford Street in London, England. The same proportion held true everywhere. Not one card mentioned Jesus' death and resurrection. Easter cards portray Easter as a celebration of chocolate eggs, bunnies, and springtime. The meaning of Easter, the foundation of Christianity and western society, has virtually disappeared from public consciousness. At least for people who buy Easter cards.

A painting displayed for sale in a kiosk at an art fair in Port Angeles, Washington, parodied Leonardo da Vinci's *Last Supper* by depicting various birds seated at each of the places of the disciples, with body positions matching the originals'. In the place of Jesus is an owl gazing upward to heaven with wings

1   Justin Welby, Sermon, 17th September 2014, Bristol Cathedral, http://archive. archbishop.canterbury.brix.fatbeehive.com/articles.php/5410/ this-cross-is-for-all-of-us-archbishop-justins-sermon-at-bristol-cathedral

raised in prayer. The painting was entitled *Birds of Prey*, and was offered for sale as an amusing pun. The painting deliberately mimicked the original which presents Jesus' betrayal and self-offering death that has been the foundational symbol of western society for the past two thousand years. This parody was displayed in the most religious of all western countries, the United States, as if it were but an innocuous pun, the entire painting a joke.

Neil MacGregor, the former director of the British Museum, who hosts the BBC TV series *Living with the Gods* was quoted in the *Telegraph* saying, "Britain is trying to become the first society to function without religious belief at its core."[2] He could have said the same of many European countries and of Canada.

Consider the text of an ad in a middle-class homemaker's magazine dedicated to upholding traditional values: "Cozy Sunday mornings were made for Duralex carpet. That first sip of hot coffee. The Sunday paper. A good book. And the sun streaming across the floor." The ad shows dad in jeans, slouched in a comfortable chair, reading the paper and mom playing on the floor with the baby; all on the comfort of a Duralex carpet. We might ask why the ad writer picked Sunday morning? Why not a cozy Saturday morning? Because Saturdays are about rushing around getting chores done and kids driven to soccer practices, while Sunday is the day to be free of obligations, to be yourself and to relax at home *doing nothing of importance*. "That's the point of life," the ad seems to say. The last thing this traditional family magazine suggests that a comfortable, happy middle-class American family would do on a Sunday morning is go to church. Even religious America, despite its reputation, turns out not to be very religious at all. Indeed, despite the reputation, religious attendance in the United States is in rapid decline.

The transition from faith as normative to faith as the exception can be seen in the family of a couple who married during the Second World War. Babies arrived in the years following, and every Sunday, without fail, the whole family attended church, received communion, contributed to their congregation, and were unfailingly faithful in this weekly religious practice. In the 1970s when the three children of that family left home as young adults, not one of them had any desire to attend church again. All three children married and now the original church-going couple have five grandchildren and five great-grandchildren. Including their various spouses, there are now nineteen descendants

2   Anita Singh, *The Telegraph*, 11 October, 2017, 7:00 a.m. https://www.telegraph.co.uk/news/2017/10/11/neil-macgregor-britain-stands-alone-comes-religion/

of the original weekly church-attending couple. Of those nineteen, only three have a regular religious practice or attend church. Of the five grandchildren, only two have been baptized and only one attends church; and of the five great-grandchildren, only one is baptized and none attend. In that family with highly religious roots, within the lifetime of the original parents, there has been an eighty-five percent reduction in the practice of religious faith, and nobody thinks that's odd.

Why did so many of this family leave active faith? All three adult children of the original couple were well-educated and held responsible careers in public service. They weren't mad at church, they weren't reacting to having been forced to attend church during their childhood, and they didn't convert to some other faith. *They just didn't see any point in religion.* On a Sunday morning, the only quiet day of the week, they'd rather have a leisurely breakfast with their friends at Tim Horton's. For them religion is rather like golf—an optional hobby. If you like it, you do it; but if you aren't interested, and there's no reason or social expectation to do so, going to church would just be a waste of time.

So, what happened?

The entire culture, of which they are part, shifted from religious to secular without their noticing it; they were simply carried along by that cultural shift. When you live inside a culture, changes in its priorities seem unremarkable and are barely noticed. The abandonment of faith by most of the descendants of the original couple is due to their being normal members of a culture in which weekly church-going is no longer normal.

Not only are there many people in our culture who don't believe in God, the number of people who don't believe is growing far more rapidly than are the adherents to any religious community. StatsCanada indicates the number of people reporting no religious affiliation is doubling every ten years. No religious group is growing at anything like that rate. In light of this trend, it is no wonder Canadians who declare they have no religious affiliation now outnumber churchgoers of all denominations and all faiths put together.

The speed of the decline in church involvement is astonishing. In the middle of the twentieth century, two-thirds of Canadians attended church weekly, but seventy years later only one-seventh attend regularly. Recent statistics suggest three quarters of our national population has no church connection.

Surveys report that between 11% and 19% of British Columbians claim to worship weekly. However, we know from other research that when people who are being interviewed feel the behaviour being investigated is socially desirable, they will over-report their activity.[3] This bias means it is likely that less than one-tenth of Canadians actually attend any place of worship weekly. That means over ninety percent do not.

That is an average across Canada. One specific example is Victoria, the capital of British Columbia.

In 2006, I asked the members of an adult study group in Victoria, a city generally regarded as fairly traditional, to telephone the office of every place of worship in that city, of all faiths, to ask what the attendance had been the week before. We discovered twenty-one thousand people had attended some place of worship the preceding week. It sounds like a lot, but it amounts to just seven percent of Victoria's population. Two hundred eighty thousand—93%—of the people in that capital city had not attended any place of religious worship during the previous week.

In Victoria, the number of attendees may have decreased even further since my survey of fifteen years ago. Perhaps it is no coincidence that Victoria is the capital city of the most secular province in the country.[4]

In Europe, the decline has been even more dramatic.

This is an astonishing development in western culture.

For most of human history, almost everyone believed in some god. The god people believed in might have been the God of the universe or the god of their city or simply a local spirit who helped them get a fire started. However they imagined it, most people throughout history have always been sure there is an unseen world populated with spiritual beings with whom we need to be in active relationship. Everyone took it for granted that the spirits, or the God, of that unseen world are of overwhelming importance in both this life and the next.

Before our modern age, it was not unusual for the sociology, economy, and technology of entire civilizations to be organized for the sole purpose of relating to the spiritual world of divine beings. The civilization of ancient Egypt, for example, existed to prepare the Pharaoh for the next life. Whether by growing rice to feed the labourers who hauled those enormous blocks of stone to construct the pyramids, or by inventing the engineering, mathematics, construction technology, and administrative skills required by such a monumental project, or by carrying out the intricate embalming processes that made possible the Pharaoh's journey to the next life, in ancient Egypt every personal

---

3   Public Opinion Quarterly, Volume 72, Issue 5, 1 December 2008, Pages 847–865.
4   StatsCan 2021.

act and every monetary transaction was ultimately intended for the purpose of relating to the gods who ruled the universe.

Our own European civilization has been focused for centuries on similar gigantic construction projects. In medieval Europe, it was not uncommon for every person in a city, over several generations, to spend their entire life building an enormous religious structure—a medieval cathedral. Religion was what made sense of life and what life was about.

While there have been times in the history of western civilization when people were not very active about their religious belief—in the medieval world not everyone went to church or carried out religious obligations in ways their faith required—there has never been a time before ours when an entire society treated religious beliefs and practices as irrelevant. Never before in history, in any culture, have there been such substantial numbers of ordinary people who have no interest in, or knowledge of, any religion.

Where once a loving God had been present at every moment of life, almost overnight there is no God. Humanity has gained the ability to figure things out and understand how the world and the universe work without any need for God as an explanation. For some of us, this abandonment of outmoded religious belief is experienced as freedom from superstition and hope for a wonderful future unfettered by oppressive religious beliefs. For others, this new direction is a descent into darkness and disaster as humanity loses its way without the underpinnings of any foundation more secure than the profit motive. But perhaps for most of us, the move toward secularism is neither a new freedom nor a descent into disaster, because for many in our culture, there is no memory of there ever having been a cultural norm other than modern secularism.

This is an extraordinary development.

It's as if our culture leapt off a cliff into disbelief and no one noticed. After that leap most people in our culture float contentedly in these non-religious assumptions without a second thought.

No wonder church leaders and members live with anxiety, denial, and dread as awareness of this new social attitude toward religion sinks in and attendance dwindles.

Anybody concerned with the decline in church attendance should be asking why this is happening. It's fruitless to passively hope that secularism will just go away. If churches are to find an effective response to secularism they need to understand what secularism is.

Secularism is more than religion not being popular.[5] Secularism is the belief that religion is not only irrelevant, but probably detrimental, to the management of communities from towns and cities to countries and the planet. It's not just that no denomination or religion should receive preferential treatment over any other; the secular assumption is that religion is an unwelcome and inappropriate partner when decisions are being made about our social, economic or political priorities.

That's despite the fact that it was an ordained Baptist minister, Tommy Douglas, who spearheaded the adoption of the Canadian universal access to health care because he understood that was an implication of his religious faith.

Secular society understands religion to be an activity that individual people are free to participate in or not as they choose. Secularism takes pride in this policy of fairness—being an active participant in a religion is neither advantageous nor detrimental for citizens of a secular society. Religious people sometimes mistakenly take comfort in this policy, feeling safe that faith isn't under attack by our secular government. But that's a misleading interpretation.

Despite appearances, secular society isn't neutral about religion. Secularism is clear that religion is a privately chosen optional activity for one's spare time. Religion is not the way in which a society might learn about any underlying God whose wisdom is essential for setting priorities for our culture and country and for the earth. Whatever God is, God has nothing to do with how we organize our society and set its direction. Secularism treats religion as a voluntary activity motivated by desire for its own advancement and power, and not for the public good.

People of faith need to recognize that secularism denies faith's central claim. Faith's central claim is that humanity's meaning arises from encountering the foundation of the cosmos, deepening our relationship with the ultimate source of everything and thereby enabling us to build a mature and fulfilled world and a global community. That's religion's point, to discover the meaning and purpose of being human. Faiths have always understood that to be their lifeblood, their very purpose. Secularism denies that purpose.

Secular society says that religious claims about what God might want are irrelevant, misleading, and quite likely selfish and very possibly destructive. Members of faiths need to clearly understand that what secular society calls

---

5   I acknowledge with gratitude the contribution in conversation with the religious historian, Dr. Nicholas May, Simon Fraser University, to my understanding of these distinctions.

tolerance is in fact an attack on the heart of religion.

It's worth noting that this secular attitude to religion is very different from that of a Marxist society which understands religion to be evil, the enemy of justice and fairness, a tool by which permission and blessing is given to the wealthy and powerful to oppress and exploit the less powerful for the sake of making more money. In Marxism, for the health of everyone, religion must be removed so people are no longer exploited. Secularism, in contrast, isn't interested in removing religion. Instead, secularism declares religion to be irrelevant and consigns it to the private sphere of hobbies.

Curiously however, authoritarian states which have outlawed religion have been less successful at accomplishing that goal than has secularism. Our secular society has seen a rapid and widespread growth of irreligion without the need for legal prohibitions, so much so that irreligion has become normative in our society. Indeed, in the secular west, active religious practice is withering away. Secularism has accomplished what Marxism couldn't.

That's powerful.

And churches need to understand the source of that power.

It's widely assumed that science, which has found no evidence for the existence of God, and which questions many religious beliefs, must be the underlying cause of secularism. Science holds great credibility in our society because it has revealed so many ways in which the physical world operates, and provides the basis for our everyday life. So it is easy to conclude that science has given rise to secularism. However, the secular policy of excluding religion from conversations about the direction of our society and the priorities of our world isn't based on any scientific research. No government mandated research on the role of religion in determining public policy. Secularism simply declared religion to be irrelevant.

One source of this attitude to religion may be that secular leaders can accrue the leadership power formerly held by faith. Indeed, it's easy for them to claim moral superiority when churches are blamed for the damage done by residential schools, while conveniently ignoring the uncomfortable fact that politicians and media and the general public were virtually unanimous in their affirmation of residential schools at the time. But science had nothing to do with the decision to declare religion irrelevant. Science is about truth, and presumably if science discovered evidence for the reality of God, then science would affirm that truth and be opposed to the sidelining of faith to the realm of individual private preference.

As we will soon see, science may turn out to be far more supportive of faith than religion can yet imagine.

Faith's response to secularism: self-blame, denial, and wishful thinking

If churches are to respond to this challenge of secularism, they must start by understanding the culture of disbelief and how it has transformed our formerly religious culture.

The fundamental issue that few people of faith dare to ask is: How is it that the God of the universe has been so easily trumped by commercial entertainment and social expectation? Is it that the vast majority of modern people have become selfishly self-absorbed? Or immature? Or more likely, is it that something fundamental has changed in our culture? And if so, what? And how can faith respond to that change?

Sadly, religious communities avoid that central challenge, and instead focus their efforts on trying to reinvent their past relationship with our culture. Instead of trying to understand why this changed attitude to faith has arisen, churches desperately try to find a quick fix.

The first fix churches try is to blame themselves for society's abandonment of faith. If churches can change themselves in some way, so this hopeful analysis goes, and tweak their advertising or worship or programs or leadership, religion will regain its central role in society. But this approach is like a child blaming their own behaviour for their parents' divorce. That mistaken blame seems to work because self-blame provides hope. The child thinks, "It's up to me to change something I did wrong and then mommy and daddy will love each other again." So churches put immense effort into discovering how they themselves have caused our culture's abandonment of faith.

Churches first assume the cause of secularism is that churches aren't welcoming enough, so they try to present themselves as welcoming as possible. "Everyone is welcome!" is the nearly universal message on church signboards. Churches imagine secular people will respond, "Finally, we found a welcoming church!" But this response is based on the unlikely assumption that secular people have been desperately searching for a welcoming church and not finding one. But that's to miss the entire point. Secular people aren't looking for a church at all.

In another version of "It's our fault," many churches advertise their positive

contributions to the wider society. Such churches sponsor social programs or
rent their under-used facilities to childcare centres as a way of proclaiming their
value to society. But this response to secularism assumes secular people have
been desperately looking for church-run social programs! They haven't.

A third type of fix that many churches use is closer to the real issue, which
is to focus on encouraging faith. Churches have embarked on evangelistic
programs such as "A Decade of Evangelism" or "Wonder Café" or "Alpha"
or "Catholics Come Home." Liturgical churches, for whom worship is the
prime path by which to experience God, hope the awe and mystery of their
liturgy will communicate the reality of God. But none of these evangelical
approaches have made any difference to the steady decline in attendance. All
these approaches assume secular people share our basic assumptions about
faith and simply need encouragement to return to worship. But secular
people don't share the assumption that faith is important. That's the point.
They just aren't interested.

A fourth fix that mainline churches attempt is to critique themselves by
looking across some theological fence where they think the grass is greener on
the other side, accepting the widespread belief that conservative evangelical
churches are growing exponentially because of their clarity and self-confidence
and perhaps because of their conservative views. Perhaps, many mainline
churches wonder, we should act more like conservative evangelicals.

But statistics don't bear that out.

Conservative evangelical churches are losing numbers, most dramatically in
the United States.[6] The Crystal Cathedral, once a colossus in the American
religious scene, went bankrupt and the building was sold to a Roman Catholic
diocese. Despite the establishment of mega-churches and enormous publishing
businesses among conservative traditions, their numbers are declining. In the
past fifteen years, evangelicals in the USA declined from almost a quarter of the
population to 14%. During the same fifteen years, people with no religious affiliation grew from 16% to more than a quarter of the population,[7] almost exactly
changing places. The decline in church affiliation may be even more dramatic
than that because people with little or no church affiliation are likely to

6   Jones Robert, Daniel Cox, Public Religion Research Institute (PRRI),
     (Washington D.C. 2003, 6 September 6, 2017).
7   https://www.nytimes.com/2023/07/05/opinion/biden-trump-2024.html

over-report the frequency of their attendance.[8] Thus the numbers of non-affiliated people are likely to be growing even more rapidly and to be substantially larger than the self-reported quarter of the American population.

A fifth fix churches have tried is to identify a widespread, although inarticulate, longing for faith within secular people. That longing could imply there is a fruitful source of new members within secular culture. Surveys report up to thirty percent of Canadians who don't belong to any faith do believe in God.[9]

However, this may not be the hopeful news churches think it is.

Combined with the tendency to affirm socially approved attitudes when being surveyed, it may also be such people have no other vocabulary with which to describe their experiences of harmony and unity with the cosmos. The term often used in surveys is to ask about belief in God, and so the concept of 'God' is likely fed back to the interviewers, albeit unconsciously, by respondents who don't believe in an existing God but who want to affirm they have some sense of goodness behind things, and that deep goodness is significant to them.

It's important for churches to understand that spirituality among the "spiritual but not religious" and among the "nones" (people who report having no religious affiliation) are very different from the experiences religions have traditionally commended. Religiously unaffiliated people typically describe their spiritual experiences as, "relating to our inner soul," "peace of mind," "the beauty of nature," "being accepting of others and one's self."[10] These people describe their spirituality as having feelings of inner peace or of respect for others—but not as a desire to communicate with a divine being, 'God.' Yet God is understood by communities of faith, particularly in the Abrahamic religions, to be more present, more personally challenging, more other, yet more involved and more intimate, than the spiritual experiences reported by many 'spiritual but not religious' people. Churches' hopeful expectation of attracting secular people who have an inarticulate longing for God may simply be wishful hoping for new members. Churches are grasping at straws which will turn out simply to be further evidence of the all-embracing secularism of our society.

If any of these approaches had really worked, it would have spawned headlines and every congregation would be adopting the formula.

---

8   Presser Stanley, Stinson Linda, Data Collection Mode and Social Desirability Bias in Self-Reported Religious Attendance, (American Sociological Review, 1998), vol. 63 (pg. 137-45).

9   Angus Reid, April 2017.

10   Angus Reid, April 2017.

Whether churches diagnose the problem as their own fault for being too liberal, too conservative, too accepting of secular culture, too critical of secular culture, too demanding of faith, or too irrelevant to the world's needs—nothing has stemmed the tide of declining attendance.

It's time churches face the fact that the decline in church attendance isn't the fault of churches, or church leaders, or unimaginative church programming, nor some fault in secular people who have lost interest in religious faith.

So, if there is no easy fix to put things back where they were when everyone went to church, what's the path ahead?

The proposal: take secularism seriously

In order to respond to this new and threatening culture of disbelief in which churches find themselves, religious communities must give up trying to push the river of secularism backwards.

Instead, churches need to immerse themselves in the river of secular assumptions. Churches must take those secular attitudes seriously, *not in order to refute them, but in order to know the experience of secularism from the inside.* How else could the religious community know how to function and what to say to people who live within secular culture?

People of faith must have the courage to undergo total immersion in what secular society is saying when it rejects faith and belief in an explicit God. That immersion could turn out to be a baptism for faith.

Counter-intuitive as it seems, the experience of disbelief is where churches, along with secular culture, will encounter God.

To religious people, this proposal may feel like embracing atheism and the death of faith. But strangely, the dying and rising God is central to the Christian faith, and by trusting in that process which Christ himself underwent, people of faith may find themselves experiencing a renewed and powerful faith that will also have credibility within secular culture.

In the next chapters we will take a journey into the heart of secularism to find what makes that heart beat.

We may discover there the beating of our own heart, and the beating of God's heart, too.

To access the heart of secularism, a culture in which God and religion are optional, we must become fluent in the idea-language spoken by the secular world. In the next chapter we will begin by listening closely to secular language and learning to understand and speak it.

We may be astonished and delighted by what we hear.

In the chapters ahead, we will look at what caused this sea change to happen, we will examine what disbelief looks like from the inside, and if we have courage not to turn away from disturbing discoveries, we will find unexpected resources that will be revelatory to believers and unbelievers alike as we encounter a faith and God already fully present at the centre of both science and secularism.

Summary

Although Western society has been steeped in religious experience for at least the past five thousand years all the way back to ancient Egypt, an astonishing change has recently happened. In the past fifty years, more and more people in the West have no connection with any religion. The idea of getting up on Sunday morning to go to a specific building to connect with a divine being strikes increasingly large numbers of people as meaningless. Churchgoers and their leaders are puzzled and worried about why so few new members are joining churches and why attendance is declining. Denominations and local congregations develop programs to attract people but experience little success.

Communities of faith need to look more deeply at this widespread emergence of disbelief. No longer can they hope for a return to the virtually universal affirmation of faith that was normative only a couple of generations ago. Being nice and welcoming just isn't enough.

Instead, people of faith need to understand what is going on behind this cultural transformation. When we do, we may find a whole new experience of God opening up for us in the very centre of the secular culture of disbelief.

CHAPTER 3
The Language of Disbelief

Foreign languages are always gibberish

I graduated from high school, the one with the hard dormitory floors and the sharp Occam's razor; earned a degree, got reasonable marks, and had no idea what to do with my life. Adventure and travel beckoned, as well as a desire to be helpful; so I joined CUSO and was assigned to teach in Malawi, East Africa. The language training for East Africa was held in Montreal, and there I encountered my very first social gathering in French.

Being from the west coast, I had hardly ever heard French spoken by anyone other than my Scottish French teacher.

I was invited to a party in downtown Montreal. As the evening progressed, the event grew larger and louder, and as new people were introduced around the room the French became more raucous by the minute. I was astonished to see that without any explanation, each newcomer to the party knew all the requisite grammar and vocabulary and could joke and tease instantly with people they had never met before.

How did they do that? I was amazed.

Clearly, out there in Quebec was an invisible, but very real, matrix of French vocabulary and grammar in which everyone but I had been immersed without even noticing. Only then did I realize I too had grown up in an equivalent English matrix that enables me to enter any English-speaking room and immediately speak fluently with complete strangers. It happens for every language in the world and hardly anyone notices they are immersed in a language, embedded in its invisible matrix of vocabulary and grammar. Until we encounter a foreign language matrix, our own remains invisible to us.

At first, the unfamiliar language sounds simply like gibberish. My hostess was kind enough to translate some of the more outrageous jokes going around, comments about the shape of some buildings at the World Expo that the party-goers were hilariously comparing to certain body parts, conversational topics unimaginable in the context of my proper English upbringing.

I was discovering that a language matrix has two levels of shared understanding. Grammar and vocabulary are one level, but there is also a shared assumption about what topics are possible in conversation. Both were utterly foreign to me, but fascinating. I was very attracted.

No wonder half a dozen years later I married someone of French background.

From Montreal, our CUSO contingent flew to Malawi, East Africa, where people speak many languages, but the main one is Chichewa, a language related to Swahili. We received some instruction in Chichewa before leaving Canada, and upon arrival at the airport in Malawi I could say to the customs officials in their language, "Are all these chickens yours?" It was one of those clever sentences which illustrate a number of grammatical rules and exceptions. No, I didn't try it on the customs officials. But over time I delighted in learning enough Chichewa to be able to get by in simple conversations. When I was at that French party, I could pick out occasional words such as '*extraordinaire!*' and even some sentences, but in Malawi, I could listen all day and not recognize or even guess at one single word. There are no cognates with English. Not one.

For example, in Chichewa the word for dog is *garu*. When I returned to Canada after three wonderful years teaching science to Malawian high school students, I'd get people in Canada to guess what *garu* means. People would find it frustrating after trying "garage" and being told they weren't even close. The longer I refused to reveal the meaning the more frustrated people would become. But when I told them *garu* means *dog* people were intrigued.

One last discovery about a foreign language. Not only are there strange sounds, there are sounds one cannot even hear. In Chichewa the word for *plate* and the word for *brother* sound identical to me. They both sound like 'm-bah-lay.' When I asked my students to say the two different words, no matter how carefully I listened I could hear no difference at all. It was a source of great amusement to my students that I couldn't tell the difference between my brother and a plate! Whatever the distinguishing sound is, it doesn't exist in English, and never having heard it, my brain insists on ignoring it as irrelevant to understanding speech. I just don't hear the sound. Even though it's actually there. Hard to believe but true.

The same is true of learning the secular language. It has its own grammar and vocabulary. We can expect certain nuances of meaning may be nearly impossible for non-secular speakers to grasp. But with time and patience and determination, we may start to hear more than we thought possible.

That's the position churches are in as they seek to learn the secular language. At first, that language will feel equally as foreign and just as challenging as learning a language which has no cognates with English. But in time, learning this secular language will be fascinating and supportive for people of faith.

But, first, it will be frustrating.

One source of frustration will likely be that for people of faith it is meaningless to live in a world without God, yet secular people aren't going around moaning about living in a meaningless world. That fact in itself is challenging for religious people—the godless assumptions of secularism seem meaningless and sound like gibberish, but don't bother secular people. *How can that be?* wonder religious people. *What are you talking about?* secular people respond.

Like a unilingual English person suddenly immersed in French or Chichewa, people of faith won't know the vocabulary, the grammar, or even what topics of conversation are possible in the secular language matrix. That can be very uncomfortable. But discomfort is unavoidable when we encounter something utterly unfamiliar. But it can also become a delight and a revelation.

Meet the characters

For the remainder of this book, we'll listen in on three people who are journeying into foreign languages—secular and religious. One you have already met—myself. You've met me as the child who performed a religious experiment on my dog and who found few of my school mates took faith seriously. But you'll also meet me in adulthood as I continue to experience the absence of God in a variety of situations in my own life and ordained ministry. Maybe because I liked mechanical toys as a kid, I always had a feel for the secular language. So, I will be your guide as we journey into this unfamiliar secular language.

You may already know the second and third people—one of them may even be yourself or someone close to you. The first is a faithful church-goer who finds the language of secularism to be gibberish. The second is a person for whom going to church would be the last thing she'd do. For her, the language of faith is meaningless gibberish.

We'll be listening in on these three—myself in various real-life experiences, and our two imaginary fellow-travellers, a believer and an atheist—while together we encounter the discomfort and challenge of learning the other's language.

So, let's meet John, our imaginary church-goer.

On any Friday, Saturday or Sunday, John and nicely-dressed families gather in their local mosque, synagogue, or church, to sing, pray, and commune with the God whom they experience as their ultimate source. For them, God provides meaning and direction for their lives, and indeed, for the whole universe. They are committed to living in accordance with God's loving will, and to loving their neighbours as themselves. They care about the poor and needy in their city and around the world. John and others like him have a living sense of history; they know their faith has ancient roots and deep wisdom and are concerned about the superficiality of so many cultural priorities in our day. These religious people, like John, also know not everyone shares their perspective. They know there are other faiths as well as people of no faith.

After Sunday worship, John returns home and waves pleasantly across the back fence to his neighbour. He knows she doesn't go to church and he feels slightly uncomfortable about that, and he doesn't understand why she doesn't believe in God. He himself has the role of holding the cup of holy wine from which people in the congregation drink each Sunday, and he finds that to be a mysterious and deeply moving experience. He can't explain it, but he is sure that each time, he's being pressed up against something true and profound. On those occasions, his experience of God is immediate and all-surrounding. Sometimes he thinks it's the only thing in life that makes sense.

Rosalind is the next person I'd like you to meet.

She lives in a world in which science, not religion, is the foundation upon which our entire culture functions.

Like John, Rosalind gathers with groups of friends, and like the believers, she dresses up when they gather. But her gatherings are mid-week in a research facility—she and her colleagues wear lab coats and find their community at universities and research institutes because all their lives they have been fascinated by the universe in which they find themselves. Just like the religious people, she and her colleagues experience awe and wonder in the face of a magnificent and seemingly infinite universe. They, too, care about the quality of life for the poor in their city and around the world; they are deeply moved at symphonies; they are well aware of their small place in history; and they take energetic part in community organizations and volunteer in food banks and are concerned about social justice. But religious faith? That's not a hobby that appeals to Rosalind or her colleagues. To start going to church would be as peculiar as taking up competitive dog-grooming, but with the dark underside of embracing ignorance and superstition.

Rosalind waves back to her neighbour John across the fence, but although she respects him and knows he goes to church every Sunday and, she suspects, even prays on other days, she feels sad for him because he hasn't yet grown out of his childhood illusion about having to please an imaginary supreme being.

These two neighbours remain in two solitudes. They never talk about anything important. Just like faith and science.

So, John, the religious believer, goes off to worship on Sunday morning and feels vaguely sorry for the atheist scientist next door who is going to her lab and doesn't know the loving God behind it all. On her way to the lab on Monday, Rosalind feels vaguely sorry for her neighbour who has so little awareness of being caught up in a long-debunked illusion.

When they talk over the back fence, John dares not share the encouragement he has experienced through faith that morning at worship because he cannot bear to face the polite responses from the scientist. Rosalind dares not share the wonders she has discovered in her lab that week nor the immense sense of freedom disbelief in God brings her, because she cannot face the judgement she will see in the face of her believing neighbour.

At best, the relationship between faith and science will remain tolerant and polite but superficial. Sadly, the deep and significant truths in both these worldviews remain unavailable to the other and both will be the poorer.

Until either faith or science takes the initiative to talk more deeply.

Somebody has to take the first step.

The urge to talk

John has begun to feel silly about the polite standoff between himself and the atheist next door. There had been times when he would have liked to have asked her to keep an eye on his house when he was away, but he couldn't bring himself to entrust his home to someone he didn't know well. It would be great if he could get to know her a little. But, with their profound differences, he isn't sure that would be possible. Besides, he isn't entirely sure you can really trust an atheist.

What he doesn't know is a similar conundrum has been emerging in Rosalind's mind. Like many of her colleagues at work, she attends Handel's *Messiah* every Christmas and has often wanted to tell her neighbour how much she enjoys the music she knows is a central part of his religious tradition. But she anticipates he would think he'd found a crack in her commitment to atheism. So, she hasn't risked sharing her thoughts about the *Messiah* for fear of getting into a conversation from which she would need to politely withdraw. In her experience, religious people want to make everything religious, including herself. Better not to open up that can of worms. But she wishes she could share her delight in the *Messiah* with him.

Each has been wondering about how to get a conversation started.

Something inside our religious friend was nudging him to take the risk. It would take courage to ask, because he knew he would find himself on secular turf, immersed in a culture that has little respect for his faith. But something about her intrigued him. Of course, that was just the fact that she was a scientist. Maybe it was that he'd enjoyed playing with a chemistry set and electric trains as a kid. They were sort of scientific, weren't they? His religious parents had named him "John" after the writer of John's gospel, and that John had opened his gospel with a cosmic perspective. Wouldn't that be a link with science?

He decided to take the risk.

Over the back fence, after they'd talked about the weather, John screwed up his courage and told his neighbour he'd be interested in knowing more about her work. Maybe a tour?

His first surprise was her response to his interest.

"I'd be delighted to show you around. Want to come later this week?"

This was already going better than he could have hoped. He was so glad he'd asked.

Without understanding what he was doing, John had volunteered to undergo total immersion in another language. Even though the outward language of her world is English he was about to discover that beneath the layer of familiar individual words, lay another layer of meaning that was to prove incomprehensible.

He knew her world would look different.

What he didn't anticipate was how different.

That would be his second surprise.

It was going to be a very interesting conversation.

A crash course in disbelief-speak

A few days later, off they go in Rosalind's car to her research institute. She explains she has been in touch with a couple of her colleagues to tell them who John is and that he is interested in what they do, and that she's made appointments for him to meet them. "I think you'll enjoy them," she said.

But John is starting to feel apprehensive because he never could do math, and he wonders, *will they all look down at me for my ignorance? They'll think I'm an idiot: I failed out of the only science course I ever took. Will this be the beginning of the end of my faith? Is my host secretly gleeful at the prospect of convincing me to become the atheist she is?* The closer they get to her work, the more he thinks this might be a really bad idea.

He steals a glance at her as she drives. There is something disturbing about her calmness and her honesty. *And something attractive*, he thinks. Then he doubts himself. *It could be all a plot into which I am walking, the willing, innocent victim, the lamb about to be slain on the altar of godless science.* He steals a second glance to be sure. Even in his fear there is something very attractive about her.

He'd never done anything this risky before.

At least that felt good.

When they arrive at her office, Rosalind introduces John to three of her colleagues. He is pleasantly surprised by what a good sense of humour they have, and how gracious they are to him. Not a hint of superiority. It was as if it were the most normal thing in the world to have a religious believer in their research institute. Somehow, he hadn't expected it all to be so human, so respectful. *Odd,* he thinks, *when all they do is study how mechanical stuff works.*

Andy the Church-Attending Atheist[1]

The first person John meets is Andy. Andy's interest is in the engineering applications of research. Andy lives with his family in the suburbs of a large city and is active in community affairs, including his local church. He goes to the opera and is concerned about social justice for the poor and countries suffering from extreme poverty. But he doesn't believe in God.

Andy invites our religious friend into his office and they get to talking about science and religion. Andy says the idea of God doesn't make any sense to him.

"Sometimes I sit there in church on the verge of hysterics," he says. "I look around the building and I know nobody believes a word of what is going on."

"So why do you go to church?" asks John, astonished.

"I think it's the best place my kids have to meet other kids with similar interests. And I like the atmosphere the church provides in supporting me as I bring up my kids. It's a good thing. Like scouts. In fact, I volunteer with our church's scout group."

John wonders if Andy has had a particularly unhappy past encounter with a church. One hears a lot about that lately. But it soon becomes clear that Andy's disbelief in God doesn't arise from a bad experience. For Andy, quite the opposite is true—he values the church as a social group that provides a healthy community for his children. But he can't make sense of the religious beliefs. Believing in God is ludicrous.

Andy explains. "I know lots of people get something out of it, but for the life of me, I can't figure out what it is! We are just sitting there and we are sort of worshipping an unknown being, whatever it is, an unseen being, that is professed to be perfect but requires this worship. Having never really done it, it seems funny to me. I sit there in church and I'm often on the verge of hysterics. Then, looking at my children, I think, I don't want them to absorb this. There's no need: it's just a big waste of time. I understand how all-encompassing religion is. There must be some value to it. I'm enough of a pragmatist to understand that the fact that I can't participate in it doesn't mean that it's not kinda there for a reason. But Lord if I can understand what it is."

John tries to pull his thoughts together. He'd never imagined anything like

---

[1] Except where indicated otherwise, the quotes from Rosalind's three colleagues are taken verbatim from interviews the author recorded with non-believing respondents during his doctoral research in 1993. *Why People Don't Believe in God and What it Means to the Church*, St. Stephen's College, University of Alberta. Names and identifying details have been disguised.

this. Andy is so much fun to be with. Not at all the aggressive atheist he had been anticipating—Andy can laugh at himself, scratch his head, and say with a wry smile that he just didn't get the stuff about God. But he hopes someone can make sense of religion. A very generous thought from an atheist.

It all seemed so bizarre.

The secular language was already starting to sound strange.

It was going to sound very much stranger by the time this day was over.

Maybe John would have better luck with Beverly, the next person to whom Rosalind introduced him.

Beverly the Beagle Biologist[2]

Beverly is involved in biological research, studying disease-causing organisms. *What an admirable life's project*, thinks John. *Here indeed I will find a scientist who will appreciate the necessity of a divine creator to originate life.* John asks her, expectantly, what she thinks about God.

"I don't believe in God," she says, "because there just isn't any evidence. Show me some evidence—but nobody ever has."

John points out that biology has still not been able to explain the origin of life, and that surely would be a good reason to believe in God as the cause of life getting started.

But even though it means accepting an ongoing contradiction in her fundamental research, Beverly says that contradiction is preferable to adopting religious belief as an explanation. She describes how she came to this opinion.

"Well, I think it's a lot easier to try and speculate on how that jump from non-living chemicals to life occurred using natural models of biology and chemistry than it is to try and explain the presence of a deity. In research, you have *something*—you have starting materials and you have an end point you have to get to. You can speculate as to how it might have happened, with fairly reasonable hypotheses.

"But I just don't know how to even begin speculating on a deity. I don't know where to start. Where is he? I think of the size of the universe and I can't think of a deity that would rule that entire universe. It's not comprehensible to

---

2   Except where indicated otherwise, the quotes from Rosalind's three colleagues are taken verbatim from interviews the author recorded with non-believing respondents during his doctoral research in 1993. Names and identifying details have been disguised.

me. I could think of some power out there that might organize our solar system but not some person who is in our image who's floating around out in space somewhere, or in some imaginary place called heaven, which I can't imagine. I can't imagine such a being."

John is taken aback at her clarity in dismissing what he so deeply believes. As he remembers it later, he raises some contrary facts, and the conversation might have continued somewhat as follows.

John points out that the mysterious processes of life—the breath, the warmth of the blood, the energy evident in living bodies—is so different from that of inanimate objects like rocks that living things must come from a different source than does inanimate matter. That source, whatever you call it, must itself be living—a spirit, or God, who breathes life and warmth into inanimate matter to make it alive. Inanimate objects don't suddenly become alive, warm and breathing. Living things always arise from other living things. Rocks don't just turn into mice or birds. In some way, the origin of the first life must have been the original living thing—that's what religion calls God.

But Beverly would have responded that the warmth of bodies is the result of purely chemical processes; breath is the assimilation of oxygen so its energy can be transferred to those physical processes; movement happens by tiny mechanical ratchet-shaped molecules in our muscles latching onto each other; bodily development is governed by physical and chemical genetic processes; and so on. At no point is an external divine agency required to make things be alive, to give them warmth and movement. Oxygen and carbon aren't alive. Warmth and movement are the outcome of the way in which inanimate chemicals interact. There's no need for an intermediary spiritual being to make life happen.

John isn't particularly disturbed by this. A generation ago, religions might have found such discoveries threatening, but today most mainline religious believers accept these explanations of biological processes as interesting technical descriptions that do not impinge on their faith. People of faith hardly notice that religion has come to accept what was very recently considered heresy. Mainline religion is almost unaware that little by little biological research is pushing God off the stage of life.

But John hopes to find a place for God at some point in the emergence of life. It is easy enough, he suggests, to understand that one living thing can give life to another, and that there are physical mechanisms underlying life processes, but surely God must be required to give life to the very first living thing. "It cannot be," he says to Beverly, "that life can arise out of non-living mechanical matter all by itself."

Beverly might have responded, "I expect you've heard of the DNA 'double helix' that is the shape in which our genetic inheritance molecules are arranged. Each half of the double helix makes a copy of itself which contains the blueprint for a new living creature. That creature in turn follows the instructions encoded in its copy, including the blueprint of how to make copies of the instructions. The question you pose is how the very first DNA molecule got into that particular helix shape by which copies of the blueprint could be made and passed on. How did that first helix-shaped, self-copying molecule arise when there were no prior helix-shaped molecules from which to copy itself? A very good question. I can see how religious people might think God is required to explain how that first DNA molecule arose.

"However, there are ways in which that first self-copying molecule could have arisen without requiring any external divine being to construct the first DNA molecule.

"One possibility is since ordinary clay has some of the right shapes, parts of previously non-living molecules could have become attached to each other by accidentally lying near the correctly shaped clay and by chance falling into the shape of DNA which then had the ability to duplicate itself. Another possibility is that hot water geysers on the ocean bottom may have provided both the energy and the chemicals needed for the assembly of the first DNA molecule. Still another possibility is that alternating wet and dry periods around natural geysers may have provided a way of sorting chemicals from which the basic elements of life developed. We also know bio-chemical molecules exist in outer space, having been put together there by natural processes, and from them may have come the first molecules with the correct shape to form DNA. The fact that we do not yet know for certain how the first genetic molecule acquired the helix shape doesn't mean we aren't going to find out. And even if we never find out, we can be confident some physical mechanism such as those I just described gave rise to the very first life. No need for an external being called 'God' to put the pieces together."

John objects, pointing out that there has been insufficient time for these enormously complex processes to have occurred just by chance all by themselves. The complexity of even the simplest living thing is staggering and couldn't possibly have just arisen by random changes happening to random non-living molecules. It would take far longer than the entire time the universe has existed for a group of accidentally appropriate molecules to form themselves into a spiral helix and then combine with millions of other helices to form a microscopic functioning living cell, let alone a human. Surely that proves God must have had a role. It couldn't possibly have happened by purely random collisions of molecules within the time the universe has existed.

John was relieved he could propose this defence of faith so persuasively. It was so obviously true.

To his surprise, Beverly agrees. She might have explained, "You're right! At least as far as that goes. That argument holds true if there had been one single original molecule and it had to go through a series of extremely complex steps from the earliest pre-living molecule to something as complex as a human. You're correct, that would have taken longer than the universe has existed to have happened purely by chance. I totally agree with you, and who knows, I might become a believer if that were the only route to the first living thing!

"But what actually happened is that uncountable billions of pre-living molecules were thrashing around together in the primordial oceans, and all that was required was for just one of those thousands of billions of molecules just once to fall into an accidental arrangement capable of passing on genetic information. The chances of life happening, if there was only one original molecule, are infinitesimally small. You are right about that. But if there were billions of inanimate molecules, as there were, then the chances of one of them accidentally falling into a shape that allowed life to happen are billions of times more likely. The time required for that accidental arrangement is billions of times shorter than the scenario you had in mind, and that's likely what actually happened. It only needed to happen once among those billions of inanimate molecules, and from there the copying process would have spread with exponential speed, each molecule copying themselves into further molecules. Soon they would have been everywhere. There's no mystery that needs to be solved by an imaginary divine being starting the process.

"Darwin, in his trip on the Beagle, had figured out there must be some mechanism by which units of information are passed from parents to offspring. But without modern technology he had no way to determine what those units were. But he realized some such process must be operating, and not an arbitrary God arranging the designs of bodies. I'm so proud to hold the Beagle chair of this department—Darwin's daring insights, courage, and tenacity are qualities I deeply admire."

For John, this is more challenging than just learning the unfamiliar vocabulary of a new language. He has begun to feel uncomfortable with the core assumptions of this language.

That's a good thing, because it means John is taking the secular, new-to-him language seriously.

John hardly has time to absorb this disturbing information when Rosalind drops by Beverly's office and invites him to meet her third colleague. At least that provides a way out of his growing discomfort. "Charles belongs to a faith," Rosalind tells John. "You might enjoy that." Maybe this colleague will be more sympathetic to faith, John hopes. That hope would prove to be true, but not in the way John was expecting.

Charles the Cultured Cosmologist[3]

Charles puts John at ease with his gracious manners and willingness to take John's elementary questions utterly seriously. Charles, it turns out, is an international figure in the physical sciences, having written many highly technical books about the origin of the universe.

During the conversation, John discovers Charles is deeply interested in and knowledgeable about the humanities—he is as familiar with music, art, theatre, opera and the literary classics of western culture as with the mathematical intricacies of four-dimensional space-time. Charles does indeed have a strong religious background. In Charles, John finds someone who has already thought deeply about the puzzling relationship between science on the one hand, and the world of the humanities and religious faith on the other.

This, John thinks, *is going to be a much more enjoyable conversation. He knows and appreciates so much of what faith is about.*

"You continue to be part of a religious community," John says. "Tell me what you think about science and faith."

Charles' proposal for understanding the problem between science and faith is startlingly simple.

"You really have to believe in two gods—one is the god of physical matter, and the other is the god of human relationships. These gods are quite separate

---

3 Except where indicated otherwise, the quotes from Rosalind's three colleagues are taken verbatim from interviews the author recorded with non-believing respondents during his doctoral research in 1993. Names and identifying details have been disguised.

and really have nothing to do with one another."

Of course, Charles does not literally believe there are two gods. What he means is that as far as he can tell, the principles that lie behind human relationships seem to have no connection with the principles that lie behind the operations of the physical world. He knows religious beliefs have always claimed the principles behind human relationships are embodied in a personal God and the physical universe is created by the same God. But he cannot see how those two activities by God are connected. Charles has the honesty and integrity to acknowledge that he is forced into this fundamental contradiction by speaking of there being two gods.

Charles explains, "They're two completely different concerns—there is the god who's the categorical imperative[4] and there is the external universe that may or may not have been created by some sentient and kindly entity. My own beliefs are really split into two completely separate compartments. In one, I can carry on with my day-to-day living without worrying about how the universe was created. The only practical way to live one's life is to have a scientific world and a day-to-day everyday human world and not to try to reconcile the two. But I think for a believer it is a very important question. The trouble is I don't have an answer to it, and I don't think any scientist would have an answer either."

Charles' idea that there are two unrelated worlds, one of science and another of faith, is taken for granted by a large proportion of churchgoers as well as scientists, even if they haven't put it into words. The idea is that in everyday life—such as getting your car fixed, or paying your bills, or going to the doctor—it is best to operate on the assumption that cause and effect—the basic scientific assumptions—are the underlying foundation for the physical world, and belief in God doesn't come into those aspects of life in any significant way. But when we go to church or consider religious or personal matters such as ethics or morality or beauty, we switch over to the idea that there must be a personal God who is basic to all reality.

The attraction of Charles' solution of two gods is that religion and science can then remain at peace, each secure in their own world. We, the denizens of that double world, get to choose which God is the more relevant in any given situation. That's why religion has so often become something we do on a holy

4   Charles' is likely referring to the 'Categorical Imperative' described by the philosopher Kant as the experience of an undeniable demand for ethical behaviour which everyone experiences, and which could be an argument for the existence of God as the source of that experience.

day or at holy times, but isn't very significant during the rest of the week.

For many mainline believers who don't have a problem with science or evolution, this demarcation, whether they are conscious of it or not, provides a workable solution for how to live in both religious faith and in a scientific world without the two colliding. Stephen Jay Gould, the late paleontologist and science author, proposed this solution in his book, *Rocks of Ages.*[5]

Although Gould's division of life into two domains—or two *Magisteria* as he calls them—appears to be a workable solution, in the end it is not satisfactory. There can't be two gods or two basic principles behind the universe. If there were, something else must determine which area each of these gods or principles is responsible for. That 'something else' determines the realms of the two gods and would precede them and govern them and so would be the real God.

This two-god solution is a stop-gap measure, equivalent to agreeing not to talk. But agreeing not to talk is a clear recipe for a relationship to fall apart. Beginning to talk with his neighbour was the whole point of John coming on this visit.

NOTE TO THE READER: If the following conversation becomes difficult to follow, Charles and John will be happy for you to take a break and rejoin them at a social occasion by going directly to the next chapter. They promise you won't miss anything essential.

So, John poses some questions to Charles. The conversation might have gone like this.

"In one regard," John says, "my faith isn't terribly threatened by the scientific details of how the universe operates—religion once believed angels were required to push the planets around, but nobody today finds their religious faith threatened by the concepts of gravity and trajectories and geometry determining the paths of the planets. Faith has quietly adjusted to this kind of knowledge about the universe in much the same way as it has adjusted to the discoveries about biological processes enabling life. Except in poetic images, faith no longer needs God to physically intervene in the details of the cosmos to keep it running."

John then presents the central claim of his argument. "Surely the universe

---

5 Stephen Jay Gould, *Rocks of Ages* (Random House, 2002).

must have ultimately been caused by something, and whatever that something is, would be God. The origin of the universe, the origin of everything, is the ultimate problem to which science can never provide a logical answer. But religion can. Here's how.

"No matter what physical process science proposes as the origin of the universe, we can always ask, 'But what caused that process?' Then it does not matter if the details of life, or of cosmic origins, can be explained without the intervention of God. That's no threat since God lies behind it all and is ultimately needed to start the universe, or start whatever caused the universe."

It felt courageous to say it and good to know God had to exist behind it all, and science could never question that necessity.

Charles might have responded, "I understand. But I have to say that for my research, not finding the ultimate origin of the universe is not an insurmountable problem. Let me share with you the following suggestion, which although only one example among many, has been proposed by Stephen Hawking in collaboration with his colleague Jim Hartle. Hartle and Hawking called their proposal for how the universe could start without something to start it, the 'No-boundary proposal.'

"The traditional religious argument you raise is there must be an ultimate cause for everything. Traditional religion then calls that primary cause 'God.' The place (or contradictorily, the moment!) when time starts, is the beginning of the universe, but because by definition there isn't anything before that, something must have started or created time in the first place. Religion calls whatever caused time, 'God'. God is the prime mover. This argument has been used for many centuries and was first developed in detail by Thomas Aquinas in the Middle Ages."

John feels quite sure Charles is entirely capable of giving an impromptu lecture on Thomas Aquinas, the prolific medieval scholar whose ideas still provide the basis for modern philosophy, theology, and ethics.

"However," Charles continues, "Aquinas' attempt to demonstrate that God is needed to start the universe relies on the idea that time is a straight line which has a definite starting point. If that is true, then indeed something is needed to get time started, and that would indeed be 'God,' who lives outside of time. If that were the case then I would be persuaded that something, such as God, is needed to get time going and start the universe.

"However, what if time can be understood not as a straight line, but as a sphere?"

John blinked. "Time could be a sphere?"

"Imagine it like this," says Charles. "For all practical purposes when we drive along a straight road, we treat the earth as if it were a flat table-top, ignoring the fact that the earth is actually a sphere. Yes? For all practical purposes the road is completely flat. But on the large scale your flat road is always going downhill in front of you, and, strangely, downhill behind you. No matter how far you drive you are always at the summit of a hill. It's true. But in everyday life nobody drives their car with that awareness. On our small scale it doesn't matter. Unless, of course, you live on the prairies where I do, and the round earth forces you to drive around right-angled 'correction jogs' just to keep the road straight. Curious, eh? Just as an aircraft flying a level course must constantly curve downward to stay close to the earth's curving surface. Otherwise, the airplane would fly off into space.

"So, for most purposes we can live our lives on the common assumption that the world is flat. You'd be crazy to walk to the grocery store trying to calculate how much of the curvature of the earth you'd gone around!

Now, what if the same thing is true of time? For normal purposes we live as if time were a straight line from past to future without needing to be aware that on a larger scale, time may be spherical, just like the earth is. After all, Einstein is famous because he discovered time and space can bend, so the idea of spherical time is not as crazy as we might think. We have all heard of black holes. They are places where time and space have bent so far that they become a sphere so tiny their centres actually move out of time and space. So, it's entirely possible time could be a sphere on the large scale.

"On the small scale, there's no problem treating time as if it were a straight line from the past to the future. But when we are considering the large scale with long stretches of time, such as back to the beginning of the universe and on into the deep future, our assumption that time is a straight line may not be accurate.

"There are implications if time is indeed spherical. If so, then, like a sphere, time has no point of beginning or ending, just as there is no point on the earth which can be said to be the beginning or ending of the planet. Since in that sense time doesn't have a point at which it starts, there is no need for an external push by God or anything else to 'cause' it. This is what Stephen Hawking and John Hartle were proposing. While such an idea of spherical time has not yet been proven, it is taken seriously by researchers—it has physical and math-ematical consequences that can be tested.

"If time is actually shaped like a ball, then the straight-line idea of time with which we are familiar would be like an optical illusion, a mistaken image of actual time."

Charles could see that John was having trouble thinking of time as spherical.

Charles explained. "Think of a beach ball being slowly lifted out of a pool. At first there is a tiny dot of the ball sticking out above the water, but as the ball is lifted a little higher the single dot grows to become a small circle where the top of the ball is out of the water. As the ball is raised further, that circle gets larger and larger until the ball is half-way out of the water, after which the circle, where the water meets the ball, gets smaller and smaller again until it becomes a dot at the bottom of the ball, after which the dot simply disappears when the ball is lifted out of the water. From the point of view of someone living on the ball, and not being able to see the ball from outside, it would look as if that dot at the top of the ball starts from nothing, and then gets bigger and bigger, and eventually winks out into nothing at the bottom of the ball. That's how we have traditionally thought about time—it appears to start at some specific moment in the past, and then proceeds in a straight line, and at some time in the future it will end. But from a perspective outside the ball, there's nothing mysterious about how the circle starts and ends. If that's how time actually functions, there's no 'before' in which a God would be needed to start things.

Charles might have gone on to say this proposal wasn't developed as a handy trick to think up objections to God. It was developed by Hawking and Hartle for the purpose of explaining some of the mysterious processes near the origin of the universe that are currently being investigated.

Charles added that Hawking and Hartle had been developing alternate proposals because some of the four-dimensional mathematics, which show how four-dimensional spherical time might work, didn't work! Indeed, before his death, Hawking had been working on another solution to the problem of time not having to be started at some definite time, and he felt his new solution was far better than his previous proposal of spherical time.[6] But that wouldn't provide a way out for traditional religious belief wanting to demonstrate that a God is required to start time.

Charles went on to describe a second way in which the universe could have emerged without any prior cause.

---

6   For Hawking's subsequent proposal, see Thomas Hertog, *On the Origin of Time: Stephen Hawking's Final Theory* (Random House, 2023).

"Although not widely known outside of scientific circles, the following facts have been established beyond doubt for over eighty years. Strange as it may seem—and even we scientists agree it is exceedingly strange—" Charles said, smiling, "every physical thing in the entire universe is composed of nothing but tiny particles, called 'quantum particles.'[7] All of them, every single one, are constantly coming in and out of existence for no reason. So peculiar is this discovery that Einstein himself doubted this to the end of his life and hoped that there would be some alternate explanation. However, there wasn't an error. That's just the way all physical things are.

"Sometimes these quantum particles, of which all physical matter consists, are in two places at once. Sometimes they just cease existing for no reason. Sometimes they end up where they are going *before* they move away from where they started. Furthermore, there is no reason for any of the movements they make. This behaviour, called 'quantum mechanics,' seems bizarre, but has been conclusively demonstrated. It's not a theory or an illusion. It is really happening. Every single physical thing that exists in the entire universe consists of nothing but these peculiar particles that come in and out of existence for no reason. If all these tiny particles, out of which every atom of your shirt button, for example, is made, were all to go out of existence at the same moment, your shirt button would simply disappear. The button wouldn't explode or go anywhere. It would simply stop existing. Your body could do the same. So could the whole universe. Fortunately, all the tiny particles don't normally get themselves organized like that so we never see that happen on the large scale. But that's what's actually going on at every moment, 24/7/365, in every place in the entire universe.

"I know it seems unbelievable," Charles continued, "but everything that exists is composed of stuff that's constantly disappearing into nothingness. And randomly reappearing some where and some time else. Or not reappearing at all. It's so weird we scientists say that anyone who thinks they've understood it hasn't understood it! One explanation, called 'String Theory,' suggests that what's happening is that these particles are moving in eleven or even more dimensions simultaneously but we don't have the ability to track that many dimensions. But that's only one of many attempts to understand why these tiny bits making up everything that exists, behave the way they do."

Charles went on. "One aspect of this discovery has implications for your question about the origin of the universe. It turns out that anything that is

---

7   See glossary.

smaller than a billionth of a billionth of a centimetre (known as the Planck[8] distance, after the German researcher Max Planck who first measured it) will emerge into existence and disappear out of existence and behave in these very strange ways without any cause. Such particles are called 'quantum particles' because they exist only in a single size and speed. Which is curious when you think the entire universe is made of nothing but such particles.

"Now on almost every occasion, when such a particle appears literally out of nowhere, it disappears back into nothingness almost instantaneously. You may have heard of 'virtual particles'—that's what they are. Planck also measured how long these virtual particles can stay in this sort of semi-existence before they return to nothingness. Naturally we call it the Planck time and it is a billionth of a billionth of a second.

"It's as if time exists only in tiny chunks—a billionth of a billionth of a second—and between the chunks of time there is nothing—not even time. So, between the chunks of time anything can happen to these particles. And does. Another way of imagining this is to think of each particle existing literally in every place and at every time while it is in the quantum crack between chunks of real time.

"As long as these virtual particles remain in the tiny gap between the chunks of time there is nothing stopping them from coming into and out of existence in any way whatever. But if a quantum particle ended up lasting too long and survived past the end of a Planck chunk of non-time, then it could not return to nothingness. Instead, it would enter real time, but it would have all the energy it had when it was in the crack between segments of time. In such a situation, the minute particle would have no constraints to remain small, and it could explode into an entire universe. Which is what may have actually happened at the origin of our universe."

Charles went on to tell John that we know from other research that at the big bang our universe was indeed smaller than the Planck size. It is entirely possible our universe is just one of these minute particles which overstayed its normal time in virtual existence and so exploded to become the universe of the enormous size we see today. In this way, there is no need to explain why the early but very tiny universe began existing any more than we need to explain why such particles continue to do exactly the same thing in our transistors and computer chips and everywhere else in the universe. Emerging from nothing turns out to be the norm. That's the basis of the new idea Stephen Hawking

---

8   See glossary.

was working on when he died. He realized that when the universe began it was a quantum particle and so contained everything that could ever possibly happen. Since what actually happened was you and me and everybody else, time, which we require to exist, was in there, too. And that's why time had to come into existence.

John thinks about this and sees a problem with this explanation. "These discoveries simply move God back a step. Surely something had to be there to make time into a spherical shape in the first place, or to create the processes of how tiny objects can arise from nothing. Even the discovery about how tiny they have to be surely suggests a pre-existing underlying order which we should then refer to as God."

Charles smiles. "If that sounds like looking for the God of the ultimate gaps, it is!" They both chuckle. "If there is a cause behind these originating processes, that cause will turn out to be pure mathematics. Then the patterns of spherical time, or the behaviour of quantum particles, will be the way they are because any other way would be self-contradictory. They don't need a preceding cause to be the way they are any more than the fact that two plus two equals four needs a preceding cause. Or, as Hawking was suggesting, we are the cause! So no need for a God.

"Researchers in these matters accept that there might have been pre-existent mathematical patterns, but that does not convince them that therefore there had to be a pre-existent creator God to invent mathematics. The mathematical conditions that brought about the universe can perfectly well be pure chance. Indeed, it is possible that an unending variety of types of time all exist, but only spherical time and Planck-sized particles end up making an actual universe. Which is where we live, and is the only place we can live and observe a universe."

John tries putting forward another objection he had heard. "In recent years," he says, "it has been discovered that if gravity had been even the tiniest bit stronger, the universe would have collapsed long before any planets could have formed. If gravity had been even the tiniest bit weaker the universe would long ago have evaporated into a cold vacuum where no living thing could ever have existed. How is it the strength of gravity is so exquisitely precise that the universe could exist long enough for us to evolve? This discovery of the precision of gravity seems like a tailor-made proof for the existence of God. Such precise balance couldn't have happened just by accident."

Charles agrees and notes there are other such strange facts. "Not only does gravity turn out to be exactly the right strength for the universe to exist, but so do other things. If the forces that hold atoms together had been the slightest bit stronger than they are, the whole universe would have remained forever the size of one atom. Sub-microscopic. But if those same forces within atoms had been the slightest bit weaker than they actually are, all the particles atoms are made of would have wandered off and nothing solid, not even air, would ever have existed. If other forces had been just slightly different no stars could ever have formed to make planets and keep them warm. And so on."

"Exactly," exclaims John. "How is it all these unrelated forces are at exactly the strengths required for people to exist in the universe? It does indeed look as if we have caught a glimpse of the designer God behind the universe adjusting all these things so as to make our universe just right. It can't be just coincidence. Everything is adjusted too carefully."

Charles again says he understands. "But like all such hopeful religious solutions that attempt to find a God in the gaps, this one has alternate solutions that don't need the extra complication of a God. First, it is obvious that we can only exist in a universe that has exactly this strength of gravity. Any universe that had stronger gravity would cease to exist almost immediately because it would fall into a single lump. There'd be no planets and no people could ever exist in it. In a universe with weaker gravity everything would immediately fly apart and there'd be no planets. In a strange reversal, you could say because we exist, we demonstrate gravity must be at exactly the strength it is! Perhaps you have heard of the 'Anthropic Principle'[9], which is the study of these possibilities?" John thinks it sounded vaguely familiar.

"The problem with that hopeful religious argument for the existence of a divine engineer to adjust the dials correctly," Charles continues, "is that the exquisitely adjusted levels of all these forces does not prove anything. The fact is humans can never find themselves living in a universe that doesn't have these exact forces. There could be a large number of universes with every conceivable combination of strengths of gravity and forces inside atoms, but only a universe with this exact strength of gravity will ever have people in it, because only when gravity is at this exact strength will a universe last longer than a fraction of a second and contain solid places for life to live in. All the universes that have other strengths of gravity can never have any life in them. Those universes may be out there, but life can only ever find itself in a universe with the exact strength of gravity that makes planets possible. It doesn't require a creator to get

9   John D. Barrow, Frank J. Tipler, *The Anthropic Cosmological Principle* (Oxford University Press, 1986).

it right. There may be billions of universes and all that is required is that one, purely by accident, has the strength of the various forces just right for life. And that's the only kind we can exist in or ever experience. That's why this is the universe we do live in and experience!"

"Could there really be large numbers of universes?" John asked.

"Nobody knows for sure, yet," said Charles, "but the suggestion, strange as it sounds, isn't dismissed as impossible by my colleagues. Indeed, multiple universes could also be a solution to the problem of how those strange quantum particles keep coming in and out of existence. Perhaps what is really happening is that the quantum particles are moving in quite ordinary ways through a whole foam of universes all in their own dimensions, so in each universe the quantum particles seem to appear out of nowhere. You've heard of the particle accelerator in Europe called 'CERN?' That's where we hope to be able to find out if indeed there are these other dimensions, and if we do find them, then these multiple other universes may indeed exist. Sorry, you won't be able to visit them because your trip would have to last less than the Planck time—a billionth of a billionth of a second, and you'd have to be smaller than the Planck distance—a billionth of a billionth of a centimetre to get through to the other side; but nevertheless, the other universes may indeed be there. The ones with gravity the same as ours may have people in them asking how strange it is that their gravity is adjusted just right. The universes in which gravity is different may never come into existence and certainly will never have any people in them to ask why the gravity isn't right! So for people who ask why gravity is just right, the gravity has to be just right for them to exist and ask the question!"

John had never heard of spherical time, or that the universe had once been smaller than a billionth of a billionth of a centimetre, and he'd never heard of particles that arrived where they were going before they left from where they started. He wonders if all this really matters.

What John wants to say is, "It's so weird! Nobody in the real world is going to take spherical time or simultaneous universes seriously. It's all so far beyond ordinary understanding, and anyway, to really understand it you have to know a lot of mathematics. Besides, next week they'll think up something else. It's a lot simpler to believe in God."

It was like listening to gibberish. As it always is, when we encounter an unfamiliar language.

Because these ideas about the origin of the universe have not yet had time to become widely known in our culture in the way biological knowledge has, and because issues about the origin of the universe feel more remote and technical than do biological discoveries, and because technical issues about the origin of the universe don't appear in scripture or in discussion of the faith, it was easy for John to dismiss this origin of the universe research as esoteric and irrelevant. But that would be to refuse to enter into the conversation with science and to learn its language. That would be like giving up when foreign words are hard to pronounce.

But without conversation there's no relationship. Just as with Rosalind.

John is hoping for some way out of this difficult conversation. He knows that while scientists will have new ideas next week, he worries that sooner or later one of them will be proved correct, just as the once-outlandish idea that the earth orbited around the sun, or the fact that our entire bodies are planned by microscopic molecules called genes, are now unquestioned facts. John realizes that sooner or later he will have to decide whether or not to keep on defending the idea of an external being called God who physically started the universe and who makes life happen, or to allow these uncomfortable discoveries to challenge his faith and his belief in God.

But John wasn't ready to give up yet. He had some ideas that he was pretty sure couldn't be refuted by scientists. He had three arguments up his sleeve, trump cards, he hoped. Consciousness can't be measured, it is beyond scientific understanding; mystical experiences of being one with God were certainly not scientific experiences that could be examined in a lab; and the power of prayer was real and couldn't be explained away. It would take courage to pose these positions, but it would be worth it. He'd save his faith and be reassured of its foundational role in human life.

It's good he was still hoping to challenge the scientific interpretation of the world by using the language of faith. Because if he'd given up now, he would have dismissed the irreligion of secularism and science as ultimately meaningless, and he would have missed the profound experience of God that he will encounter if he takes secular language seriously. But for the moment, he was determined to prove his religious language meaningful and the worldview of secularism and science gibberish. Just the way it still sounded.

To present his three arguments would take courage, and he would soon need it.

Summary

In this chapter, we met the second and third main characters in this book, John and Rosalind. John represents people who believe in God and attend church, and Rosalind represents people who don't. It would be good if those two ways of looking at the world began to talk to each other. From a religious perspective, it's essential that this conversation happen if faith is to contribute its gift to our modern secular world and receive gifts in return.

But talking with someone who has very different ideas about what is real is as challenging as learning a new language. If churchgoers are to understand and communicate with those who don't find God to be real, they need first to learn how to listen to why God doesn't seem real to such people.

The first necessary step will be to talk seriously with someone who doesn't believe. And then to really listen.

That won't be easy.

John finds himself in conversation with articulate non-believers. One by one, they disprove everything he used to think would demonstrate that God exists.

John finds this threatening. Readers may also find this threatening. I did. I can only say that it will likely get worse. In the next couple of chapters, we will push through to the core of disbelief.

But after that, it will get better. Very much better. Because in the centre of that disbelief we will discover God in a new and even more powerful form than before we began to learn this foreign language. But only if we press through to the centre of what secularism is saying.

I invite you to journey on. If we do, it means we have the courage to enter deeply into another language, just as Archdeacon McDonald did in the Canadian Arctic a century ago. This British missionary literally married into the Gwich'in society, learned their language and culture, and with his wife translated the Bible and hymns into Gwich'in. See the Introduction for more about the Archdeacon.

NOTE TO THE READER: As we explore faith in a secular context, Rosalind and John, being fictional characters, naturally share my personal experience with the Christian faith. Although I've had significant conversations with members of the other two Abrahamic religions, Judaism and Islam, and conversations with Buddhists, and have participated in public and private First Nations ceremonies, the only faith with which I have deep experience is Christianity. For that reason, from this point onwards I and the two characters pay special attention to the secular implications for the Christian faith. That focus arises from my perspective and isn't intended to exclude other faiths from the implications of this approach.

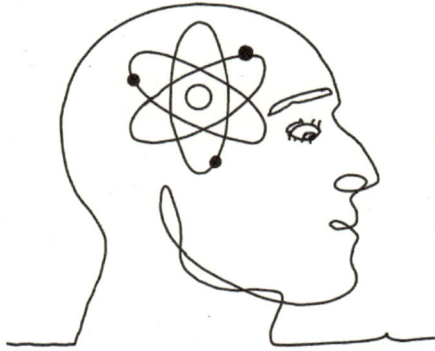

CHAPTER 4
Disoriented by Disbelief

The chemistry of consciousness

I wasn't feeling well. I'd stopped at a mall to buy a pair of running shoes and as I walked out of the store, I had the strangest sensation. It was as if I wasn't really there. I felt weak and clammy.

Of course, I thought, low blood sugar. Get a quick snack in the food court, and all will be well.

But it wasn't. I ate the snack and still felt weird. I decided to walk back to my car. At least I could sit there in quiet and let the strange feeling pass. As I was about to cross the busy traffic lane in the parking lot, I had a sensation of not knowing exactly where the lane was or if I was still standing on the curb or walking into traffic.

Suddenly I was standing beside my car on the far side of the lot with no memory of how I got there. I knew this was not normal. I sat down in my car and waited to feel better. But nothing changed. I decided to drive myself to my doctor's office which was not far away, willing total attention to my driving and my mental condition. I determined I would get into the curb lane and stop as soon as I noticed I was feeling too odd to drive, hoping it wasn't illegal to do so. I drove to my doctor's office without incident but still feeling just as strange.

My doctor had me lie down on the examining table and left the room for a moment.

Alone in the room, I became aware of how dangerous it is to lie on an examining table, four feet off the ground. The ticking of a wall clock became terrifying. I lowered myself carefully onto the floor and lay there quietly. It was a relief to finally feel safe on the floor.

The door opened and my doctor looked very startled to find me lying on the examining room floor. Did I have vertigo? No. Did I feel dizzy? No. Why was I lying on the floor? Because it was too dangerous up there on the examining table and much safer here on the floor. That was perfectly obvious. Why would he need to ask?

The doctor called an ambulance and I was transferred to a nearby hospital emergency ward. I became increasingly terrified of falling off the stretcher even with the paramedic next to me, and I hung on for dear life to a coat rack above my head. The paramedic explained to me it was only a light-weight coat rack that would collapse under my weight. I understood him, but I knew that what he said was of no significance in the face of my overwhelming need to hold on to something to prevent myself falling off the stretcher. It was important to breathe rapidly. Time passed in strange jumps. The paramedic asked me to breathe more slowly and not hold on so tightly to the rails of the stretcher. A moment later, the paramedic told me not to breathe so rapidly and not to hold on so tightly, and I had a vague feeling he had told me the same thing a long time ago. I determined I would do my best to not hang on so tightly. And then it happened again—he encouraged me to stop hanging on and I vaguely remembered this had all happened some other time long ago. But overriding my desire to be cooperative was the absolute desperate necessity to hang on to the stretcher with every ounce of my strength. Nobody could tear my fingers from their death-grip on the stretcher rails.

It turned out to be a temporary potassium imbalance, easily corrected.

Who found that out? Not the hospital chaplain and not a community of religious people praying for me. The problem with my consciousness was identified by a lab technician doing standardized tests developed on purely scientific principles. My consciousness was healed by an adjustment to my body chemistry using molecules designed to do that, developed by people researching biochemistry.

The implications are alarming. More alarming than physical disorientation. I had just experienced that the absence of a simple potassium atom could utterly transform my consciousness and awareness of reality. This did not make sense.

What has an atom of potassium to do with consciousness? What indeed?

Doesn't consciousness prove God exists?

The research institute was closing up for the day and John's three new acquaintances invited him to join them for drinks at the University Club. The five of them walked together, his atheist neighbour and her colleagues happily chatting about university politics.

As they walked, John became more aware of Rosalind. He noticed, for the first time, a kind of grace in her movements. It seemed as if just by walking she was the embodiment of poise and confidence. He realized it was a pleasure to watch her and to be near her. There was also something delightful in the way she engaged her colleagues as an equal; respected by them, expressing respect in turn. He was seeing a depth to their relationships he'd never expected from people studying the mere mechanics of physics and biology. The equality among them was like fresh air. How much there was about their life he didn't know. How human they all seemed. How at home and at ease she was in that world without God.

Something in him urged him to walk a little closer to her. He resisted at first, then caught up just enough so as not to be obvious, as he listened in on the issues of who might be the next chair of the department and why that person should never consider it. Suddenly he felt as if he was a part of this wonderful and mysterious world. When she glanced at him with a smile, he knew he was. He was so glad he came. This was going to be a wonderful evening.

With Rosalind seated beside him at the University Club, he was sure he'd have no problem holding up his side of the discussion. He knew there were those three topics—consciousness, mysticism, and the power of prayer—about which his new scientist friends had said nothing, experiences that were clearly beyond the reach of their research. This convivial social time seemed the right occasion to raise the unique insights of religious faith that make sense in an area of life closed to science but central to human experience.

Consciousness: the missing link between science and faith?

"I've been thinking more about this question of the relationship between science and faith," John began, as their drinks arrived and they settled down around the table. "It seems to me that consciousness is the central concern of religion. The purpose of faith is to deepen our sense of awe and wonder which is the experience of God. Religions do that through worship, a way of directly experiencing awe and wonder—the experience of God. Scientists, too, are full of awe and wonder—I've seen that in my conversations with each of you. Surely that means science has a fair bit in common with religion—awe and wonder and the deepening of consciousness are basic experiences in science. Our two communities share that, don't we?

"Religion should therefore be considered an equal partner in this conversation because awe and wonder are what drive people of faith just as they drive scientists, and faith has millennia of experience with those realities. Science has only been around a couple of hundred years in its modern form, and only examines physical objects but religion has been immersing people in the experience of awe and wonder and consciousness of God for millennia. Wouldn't that be a good reason for our two disciplines to work together in cooperation and mutual support and for science to take religion seriously?"

There was a pause. Rosalind could tell her three colleagues were hesitant to say what they really thought, so she decided it was up to her to affirm that this conversation was worth taking seriously.

"You're right, John," Rosalind said. "Religion has been around far longer than the discipline we now call science. The criterion for modern science is whether something can be shown to be true by repeating observations—if we get the same result as do others, we can be pretty sure what we are seeing is real. But with religion, it seems there is no way to repeat observations—groups of people can come up with whatever description of God they want. I've never heard of religions sitting down to work together to decide which religion's idea of God is the right one. None of us would want to disparage the genuine desire by religious people to experience awe and wonder." She looked around at her three colleagues and all were nodding in agreement. "But to call that sense of wonder 'God' as if that were a disembodied spiritual person we could relate to, well, that doesn't make sense to me. Yes, indeed, there is awe and wonder in the work of science, a great deal of it, but as Beverley has said, there's no evidence of a God."

John wasn't surprised by her answer. He'd thought she would say something like that. But he had a really good argument up his sleeve, and now was the time to pull out one of his trump cards and explain why religion's contribution is essential to science. He knew there was an experience where science couldn't go and where religion is right at home.

"I think there is more to it than that. I agree we can't just experience feelings of awe and simply call them 'God.' But to have feelings of awe and wonder, or even of ethics, a person has to have consciousness. I know science studies the mechanisms in our brains that take place when we are conscious, but I think religion has a foundational insight about consciousness that science doesn't have but science needs. Religion can supply that insight.

"Religion's unique contribution is to point to the ultimate origin of consciousness. That origin can't just be mechanistic. Consciousness isn't just a bunch of complex billiard balls bumping into one another. Religion doesn't need to concern itself about the mechanical processes in the brain—we are happy to leave that to science—but religion does have experience in describing where consciousness ultimately comes from. Consciousness must have a source that's beyond simple mechanics. We could also call it 'the origin of consciousness,' or the 'ultimate consciousness.' It seems to me that's a pretty important contribution to understanding the awe and wonder and consciousness that science studies. Religion contributes the insight that there must be an ultimate origin of consciousness. For convenience we call that 'God.'"

Beverly responded. Her biological research included a fair knowledge of brain functions. "I understand what you are saying, but I don't see how that proposal can fit into our scientific work. It seems to me that the religious approach to consciousness implies that a non-physical God has to reach into our brains non-physically and manipulate the physical neural processes in the brain to make us conscious. Religion might argue that the first external manipulation happened long ago when brains first became conscious and doesn't need to be repeated every moment to every brain since then. But that doesn't make sense to me. If God is a non-physical reality, then you'll have to explain how something that's not physical can non-physically manipulate the physical processes which we study in the lab. It's a lot simpler to leave out this imaginary idea of God."

John hadn't thought of that. But he had an answer. "If God made everything, then surely God could arrange for physical neural processes to be conscious." But he already had an inkling what the response would be.

"Certainly, that's possible," said Andy. "But it's pure speculation. There's no evidence at all for that. Anyone can imagine whatever explanation they want to explain anything, but the ability to test it and see if it works every time is the only way to be sure any particular explanation is true. I suppose we could test religious people to see if they are more conscious than non-religious people, but so far nobody has been able to find any difference between those groups. You could argue," he laughed, "that because scientists resist the idea of God, we are resisting God's consciousness and therefore are automatically more likely to be mistaken about the importance of religion! I'm open to that hypothesis!"

There were chuckles, and John realized he was being included as an equal in a warm self-deprecating community.

John appreciated being cared about, but wasn't about to abandon his clarity about the existence of God.

"I think there's another way religion can make a significant contribution to the scientific understanding of consciousness. We all know science is discovering an intimate relationship between consciousness and matter, but religions have had that insight for far longer, and religion's long experience with that relationship may be an important and unique contribution to scientific research.

"Let me explain. Many religions have stories about gods entering the physical world. In the ancient mid-East creation myth of Gilgamesh, the physical world is crafted from a dead god's physical body. Medieval Christian scholars built a sophisticated philosophical system by which to describe how the eternal Son of God can be simultaneously a physical human, fully present in the physical body of Jesus, as well as simultaneously fully and infinitely and eternally God who isn't physical. Their need to carry out disciplined systematic thinking on the problem of how divine consciousness could be united with a physical body gave rise to the medieval universities that in turn are the foundation of modern universities and research centres. Even yours, if you'll forgive me saying so!

"I propose that science is discovering the same connection between consciousness and physical matter that religious experience has been describing for millennia. Perhaps science and faith are more closely aligned than we usually think and religion should be welcomed by science to provide its foundational insights about the connections between consciousness and the physical world."

John was making a serious attempt to engage in a conversation with a partner who is speaking a different language. He is hoping to find the equivalent of a cognate word, an idea that both languages could agree on. He was counting on finding that consciousness and wonder might be the parallel concepts that could connect their two worlds. If he could establish a common experience both communities could agree on, then word by word he could build a way of understanding and translating their strange language of unbelief.

Surely, he thought, there must be parallel ideas in the secular language that have the same meaning as in religious experience.

But that's the error people make when they think *garu* must mean *garage*. It can be very misleading to assume there's always a simple one-to-one correspondence between similar sounding words in different languages.

John summed up his proposal for a deep connection between science and faith. "It is almost as if science, in its study of consciousness arising from physical processes, is studying the process that is also central to religious faith. Perhaps," he suggested wryly, "science is thereby affirming the central concern of religion!" He enjoyed the sense that he could return the tease. There were smiles from the others. But not affirmation.

Rosalind had been listening carefully. John had not been unaware of that.

She turned to him, "But I thought," she said, "that you Christians believe that when you die, you go to a non-physical heaven? Don't you believe the most important part of you is your non-physical soul that will live forever and join other souls in heaven? Doesn't religion believe your soul, your essential consciousness, is only temporarily connected to your physical body? If that's so, then science is studying something quite different from what religion is interested in, and much as it would have been nice to find a connection, it may be there isn't one. There's no credible evidence to support the idea of disembodied consciousness, which is what religion believes God is and souls are. If disembodied consciousness is what religion is ultimately about, science can't follow you there. So, I'm sorry, but I'm not so sure there is any such potential connection in the way you suggest."

That possibility disturbed him more than he wanted to admit. He was aware of an urgent desire to find a connection. Even if just with her.

"You're partly right," he responded, hoping to find some other way of connecting. "There is an ambivalence in Christianity about the relationship between the physical and the spiritual. Long before Christianity, Greek thought assumed a fundamental split between matter and consciousness and that has profoundly influenced Christianity. But Christianity originated in Jewish culture, not Greek, and Jewish culture could not imagine a split between the physical and the spiritual. The result is an ambivalence—sometimes Christianity affirms the unity of God with physical matter—for example in the incarnation of Jesus—and sometimes it denies that union in the belief that God makes souls that are inserted into physical bodies, and leave our bodies at death to enter an eternal non-physical realm. Just as you said."

He went on. "Although contemporary Christianity may be ambivalent about the relation between matter and the soul, a foundational Christian understanding remains: that God is en-fleshed in Jesus. The fact that the physical incarnation of God in the human person of Jesus persists as a central Christian affirmation, in the face of the ancient Greek idea that souls and bodies are entirely separate, shows how deeply the Christian religion is committed to an underlying connection between consciousness and physical matter. In spite of the popular notion of the disembodied soul, Christianity maintains there is a fundamental connection between matter and consciousness. Don't you think this shows that religion long ago anticipated the modern neurological discoveries of science? Shouldn't science and faith seek a deep connection between our two worlds because both our worlds affirm the connection between consciousness and matter? And then religion could make its contribution as the guide to experiencing the origin of consciousness."

John was working hard to find a connection between their languages.

But it wasn't working.

Rosalind didn't seem impressed. She pointed out that religions may indeed have some incoherent idea that consciousness has to be inserted into physical matter as happened in the story of the non-physical Holy Spirit initiating Mary's physical pregnancy, but this has nothing to do with actual research and hasn't been confirmed by any experiments designed to observe disembodied consciousness being inserted into physical brain matter.

Whatever he said to them, they didn't get it, and whatever they said back to him made no sense. This was getting frustrating. The existence of God was obvious. Why didn't they get it?

With a sinking feeling, he decided to ask what Rosalind thought. He'd gone this far and maybe he'd find something new that he could use to bolster his faith and find a connection in which faith is central to science. It was a courageous decision.

And, after all, she was a very nice person.

So, he took the risk of asking her what science is learning about consciousness. Maybe he'd find a new crack in her argument that would give him, and his faith, a way in.

Rosalind was delighted to be asked. That was what she was passionate about. She launched into a quick tour of her area of interest.

"Scientific attempts to understand the origin and nature of consciousness range from research on artificial intelligence that ultimately hopes to construct consciousness on a computer chip, to understanding the physical processes that led to the evolution of the human brain.

"Consciousness on a chip presupposes that if it were technically possible to replace each cell in someone's brain with a chip that performed exactly the same function as the replaced cell, the result would be a fully conscious human mind in the physical form of a computer. That means theoretically it would be possible to create a human mind from scratch, using physical material, on a computer chip. That's what one aspect of Artificial Intelligence research is about: discovering how we would program the chip so it would, in essence, be a person."

She didn't need to point out the obvious. God would then be an unnecessary complication.

It was Occam and his razor all over again.

"Many people are thinking through the implications of that possibility," Rosalind explained. "Stephen Pinker in his *How the Mind Works*[1] proposes a purely mechanical evolutionary process by which human (and other) consciousness has arisen. Roger Penrose takes a different tack in his *The Emperor's New Mind*,[2] suggesting there will always be something about consciousness that is mysterious, permanently beyond our understanding, and ultimately closed to research, because, in his proposal, quantum-mechanical processes in brain cells play an essential role in our ability to exercise free choice. Indeed, there is now a team of philosophers, the Churchlands—I'm sure you'd like to meet them, with a name like that!—working in San Diego, studying neural networks in their laboratory to learn how consciousness arises naturally from physical processes. Each of these thinkers and researchers, from differing perspectives, works from the basis that there is a fundamental connection between consciousness and physical matter, a connection that is therefore amenable to scientific study but doesn't require a non-physical God to insert consciousness into matter. Sorry, but there is no deep connection between our research and your religious belief that a God is needed to give rise to consciousness."

She looked full at him, hoping he wouldn't take it personally, and hoping he

---

1   Steven Pinker, *How the Mind Works* (New York: W.W. Norton & Company, 1997).

2   Roger Penrose, *The Emperor's New Mind: Concerning Computers, Minds, and the Laws of Physics* (Oxford Landmark Science. Oxford University Press, 1989).

was aware she understood.

He was startled and disturbed to discover in her look that she understood what it felt like to have one's central beliefs dismantled.

She went on. "It appears consciousness is an activity expressed by certain complex arrangements of physical matter. Although only very specialized arrangements of physical matter exhibit consciousness, that seems to be what is happening in human brains. If this is true, it means there is an unbroken connection between physical processes and consciousness. That means those processes and consciousness are open to scientific scrutiny. The basic mechanical biological processes of matter lie at one end of that continuum and our human consciousness lies at the other end. There is no need for divine intervention in the middle."

She continued. "It could be that biological nerves are the only physical mechanisms that have the required microscopic size, the required flexibility, and the myriad inputs and outputs needed to carry the immensely complex processes that give rise to consciousness. It could be that the 'brain on a computer chip' is not possible. But that would be because silicon is too slow and too inflexible for the information processing required, and biological cells can process far faster. And it's not because there is something cold about computer chips or something mysteriously spiritual about warm neurons. It may be that only neurons have the ability to process the immense complexity required for consciousness and perhaps cumbersome silicon chips can never be sufficiently complex. But both are purely physical processes.

"And," she said, with a laugh, "I'm not saying this discovery isn't strange and deeply mysterious—after all, why should arrangements of cells, or perhaps computer chips, automatically produce a conscious person? But it looks like that's the way it is. In a funny way," she admitted, "you religious people may have a point—I doubt there'll ever be an explanation as to why physical matter produces consciousness. But maybe that's the wrong question.

"Perhaps highly complex matter just does produce consciousness, and we are so used to thinking like the ancient Greeks that matter and consciousness are two different things, that we mistakenly think something has to be explained. Perhaps complex matter giving rise to consciousness doesn't require an explanation any more than one plus one making two requires explaining. I understand religions try to explain the connection by imagining a conscious God intervening to make consciousness happen. We scientists are also full of wonder about consciousness, but no God is needed. Consciousness is simply a by-product of complex physical matter. I'm sorry if that turns religious belief on its head."

She went on. "Charles and Beverly will appreciate this," she said. "Since we know there are thousands of planets around other stars, and organic chemicals have been found to be ubiquitous in outer space, there is no fundamental reason why life and consciousness should not be arising throughout the universe. All that would be required are environments sufficiently stable, warm, and benign that chemical patterns can emerge. Such chemical patterns, if they attain sufficient complexity, may well exhibit consciousness. No external conscious creator required. Just as matter distorts space, which we experience as gravity, so matter also has the potential to become conscious. Then consciousness distorts matter when we build stuff! It's just another physical process. Wonderful and mysterious, but not requiring any external divine being to insert consciousness."

Rosalind continued. "If you want me to believe consciousness can just float around without any physical process at all, as popular Christianity believes God does or your soul does, well, I just can't follow you there. I can't prove it isn't so, but there is no evidence it ever happens. It looks as if consciousness is always a phenomenon arising from physical processes. Put the molecules together in the right patterns and consciousness happens. Interfere with those molecules in even the smallest way—such as by injury or disease in your brain—and consciousness is impaired or destroyed.

"If consciousness can operate without a physical basis, as religion claims, then when just a few molecules in your brain go awry and your consciousness is impaired, wouldn't that imply that a non-physical God had reached in to impair your consciousness? That's the implication if only God can make you conscious. I can't imagine a God doing that. The simpler explanation is that consciousness never happens apart from those underlying physical processes and the patterns they create in your brain. When you disturb the processes of the neurons, you've disturbed your neural patterns and therefore your consciousness."

All five of them were aware that it felt like four against one. But John was glad he was on his own. If he'd had some of his religious friends there, the conversation might have degenerated into an us-against-them struggle. At least this way he knew they were taking his ideas seriously.

And he was taking theirs seriously.

Which was a huge step toward learning to speak secular.

Nobody said anything for a bit. The four scientists, because they all knew what it is like to defend an unpopular theory against skeptical experts. He, because he needed time to think through whether there was anything else to say.

It had begun to feel as if no conversation was possible. Just as the non-Chichewa speakers feel when they can't figure out what *garu* means. Remember? It means 'dog.'

Learning a new language, especially a new idea-language, is daunting.

Fortunately, for whatever reason, that perhaps had nothing to do with science or faith and surely nothing to do with Rosalind sitting beside him, John kept trying.

Quantum mysticism: John's next-to-last hope

Grasping at straws is what happens when we feel we are drowning, and John had begun to feel as if his faith was being drowned in this deluge of science.

John knew it was a last-ditch effort, but it was worth trying a couple of those arguments he'd heard in religious circles. They seemed pretty convincing to him. These insights from faith might finally give him the key with which to demonstrate that faith should be an essential partner with science and that God is necessary to understand the world.

John pointed out that spirituality may be a way of explaining those strange quantum processes by which particles communicate instantaneously across the universe. Authors such as Zukov and Capra in their books *Dancing Wu Li Masters*[3] and *The Tao of Physics*[4] have suggested that there are close connections between quantum processes—the most physical of sciences—and the human experiences of spirituality, consciousness, and mysticism. That argument has been made in many religious books attempting to connect quantum processes with faith.

John explained. "You are all aware that physics has discovered connections between particles that could exist on either side of the universe and yet that seem to communicate instantaneously."

"Right," Charles broke in, "such particles are referred to as being 'entangled' and the phenomenon is called 'non-locality.'"

John thanked him. "Faith has long been familiar with this behaviour in the forms of mysticism and consciousness. People really do have experiences of communicating with others who are impossibly far away, sometimes not only

---

3   Gary Zukav, *Dancing Wu Li Masters: An Overview of the New Physics* (New York, William Morrow and Company, 1979).

4   Fritjof Capra, *The Tao of Physics: An Exploration of the Parallels between Modern Physics and Eastern Mysticism* (Boulder, CO: Shambhala Publications, 1975).

in physical distance but far away in time.

"For example, people have had awareness of other people that could not have been communicated to them by normal physical processes, or people have experiences of Jesus or Mary, bypassing normal time and space. Religion names those as 'mystical' experiences which arise from God. If that is so, then perhaps science and faith are really two sides of the same coin and science should take religion seriously as a way of experiencing that which is beyond science's examination of purely physical time and space. Quantum behaviour is open to scientific experiment, but religion provides the direct experience through mysticism."

He hoped it might be true.

Charles wondered for a moment if he should be polite and say nothing. But his respect for his colleague Rosalind and for her neighbour won out. He said he was sorry to burst this popular balloon.

"The truth is that, attractive as this analogy may seem to religious people, for scientists there is no more connection between quantum behaviour and mysticism than the school-boy proposal that since electrons circle around the centre of atoms, our planet earth may actually be a giant electron circling around the centre of some enormous atom. The truth is quantum behaviour and mysticism are utterly different and totally unrelated.

"Few scientists take such analogies between quantum behaviour and mysticism seriously. Quantum behaviour," he explained, "while bizarre to human intuition, is entirely understandable mathematically—the equations describing quantum behaviour are well known and are many times more accurate than in any other field of scientific research. Further, quantum behaviour happens only on the quantum scale—a billionth of a billionth of a centimetre, and in quantum times—a billionth of a billionth of a second—and the equations demonstrate why the behaviour is never seen on the scale of human bodies.

"The discovery that an electron on one side of the universe can be instantly connected with its partner on the other side of the universe has been misunderstood as meaning that if we moved one, then the other would move, too, or as if we could input some information into the one electron and it would instantly appear in the paired electron a universe away. Sort of an instantaneous cosmic internet. But that's not the case, even though that description is attractively easy to understand.

"It's true the two electrons can be permanently connected no matter what the distance between them, but, impossible as it seems to human perception, it's more as if they were the same electron. Not as if they *seemed* the same because they look the same, but as if they are actually the *same* electron. I hear what you say, that religious people sometimes argue that mystical experience works like that—prayer can influence someone at a distance just like those two electrons. But that's not what the two electrons are doing—they behave more as if the same one is being seen in a mirror rather than as if there are two distinct electrons that interact instantaneously over enormous distances.

"Even more strange, those pesky accurate quantum equations prove you can never know exactly what information you put into the first one—because what you put in is always random. That's central to quantum processes. So, at the other end, the distant end, you can't get a message out. Not because it's too far away and the message degrades, but because any message passing through quantum particles is always random. So, in a strange way the laws of physics aren't subverted—there's no such thing as instantaneous transmission. Not in physical reality.

"I don't think that's what religious people are talking about when they say mysticism is an experience of the same process.

"I also grew up in a religious home in which mysticism was important," Charles continued. "But in religious thought, mystical experience has never been thought of as happening on a sub-microscopic scale of billionths of billionths of a centimetre, nor being capable of mathematical analysis. Mysticism claims to describe something on a scale far larger than the tiny stage upon which quantum particles play out their lives. Humans operate in a size that precludes those mysterious behaviours by quantum particles. Sorry to disappoint you," Charles concluded, "but there's no connection between quantum behaviour in physics and mystical experiences in religion."

Besides, Rosalind wanted to add, *there is no such thing as mystical experience—it's just an imaginative illusion,* but she held herself back. She really didn't want to hurt John. He must be finding this hard enough already. Something in her admired his courage for hanging in.

"It's true," John admitted, with a sense of growing discouragement, "theologians are not really impressed by this analogy, either. Spirituality is focused on the experience of God, of truth, of ethics, of aligning oneself with the centre of all reality, of knowing oneself more deeply, and growing in maturity. Even though we can find analogies with quantum processes, spirituality is never about passing instantaneously through physical space and relating to other people, places, or times, without regard to normal space and time. Even if such 'spiritual' phenomena do happen, they are not what religion has usually called 'spiritual.' I agree with Charles about that."

Rosalind was startled at his frankness. She'd never encountered a believer who was prepared to think up arguments against belief. She found herself intrigued, impressed, and even a little attracted. *To a religious believer?* This was getting weird. *As weird as quantum behaviour*, she thought with a mental chuckle.

The power of prayer: John's last hope

John played his final card, hoping against hope he might finally find a reason for science to take faith seriously. And maybe for Rosalind to take him seriously, too. If he couldn't find some connection, would she ever take him seriously?

"How about all that research on the effects of prayer? It's been proven that people undergoing heart surgery do better if they are prayed for. That's not something science can explain, it's a result of prayer which operates outside scientific processes. But it's still real. I can't think of a better reason for science to take faith seriously."

This time it was Beverly. After a pause, "Sorry to disappoint you again," she said.

Medical research was her area. She knew about those reports. "In experiments now discredited, attempts were indeed made to demonstrate plants grow better when loved or to prove prayer influences the outcome of medical procedures in hospitals. However, in neither the case of the plants, nor of the surgical patients, have other researchers been able to reproduce the phenomenon,[5] and the ability to reproduce a phenomenon is fundamental to being certain it happened. Without verification, there is no way to be sure the original results weren't just coincidence and are never likely to happen again. The desire to demonstrate unification of the two apparently incompatible perspectives of religion and science may have been admirable, but the data were flawed.

"And of course," she pointed out, "if the effect of prayer could be proven, then science would have found a whole new area of research. Religion might not be happy with the direction such research would take. For example, if the effect of prayer is proved to be real, very important research questions will emerge. How many prayers does it take? What would be the minimum number of people praying or the minimum time they need to pray in order to have an

---

5   Harvard University. "Prayers Don't Help Heart Surgery Patients; Some Fare
     Worse When Prayed For." (ScienceDaily, 3 April 2006).

effect? Are the prayers from some religions more effective than the prayers from other religions? What about prayers by atheists? Would the effect be applicable to injuries caused by car crashes? Or to future surgeries? Does it matter how physically close the person doing the praying is to the patient? If prayer really does make people get better quicker, we will all want to know how to maximize the effect. For the sake of the patients if not for religion. If a connection could be demonstrated, insurance companies would soon be adjusting your life insurance premiums based on your friends' religious commitment.

"Would you really want to subject your religious experience to such experiments?" Beverly asked. "Because that's what will happen if experiments on the effectiveness of prayer for surgical patients turn out to be accurate."

Andy had a similar concern, about which he wanted John to be aware. When you see a colleague going down a research path that leads nowhere, you don't stand by and say nothing. He wasn't going to let that happen even to this religious believer.

With genuine concern Andy pointed out another implication. "There are even more important reasons why religion might not want such research to take place. If the effect of prayer was proven, science would look for the underlying processes and would begin to demonstrate faith and prayer can be understood as simply another natural phenomenon that can be studied within the scientific worldview. What started out as a religious hope that science can demonstrate the power of prayer and therefore the existence of God, could end up demonstrating that prayer is just one more aspect of the natural world that science can study and explain as a natural process. No God required to explain why prayer is effective! If such an effect of prayer were scientifically demonstrated, religion might well wish it had never requested the research!

"Personally," he said with a twinkle in his eye, "if those experiments about prayer influencing surgical outcomes do prove accurate, that'll open up a whole new area of research, and I can get a grant from the university and hire my grad students to do the work for me while they're getting their PhDs! Then I could set up an insurance company and give special rates for religious people!"

"Trust Andy to find a business angle," laughed Charles.

"I think," Rosalind said, "that the popularity of such putative discoveries as the power of prayer to influence plant growth, or to effect recovery from surgery, or the hope of finding mysticism based in quantum behaviours, says less about the reality of God and spirituality and more about how deeply religious people value receiving scientific affirmation of their beliefs. That just goes to show how deeply our culture accepts scientific research as a reliable form of truth. That's why religious people hope science will affirm their faith. I never hear religious people saying their faith affirms science, but wouldn't that make sense if faith and God are more fundamental than science? It looks to me, although I'm sorry to have to say it, that believers actually put their trust in science more than they put their trust in God. Why else would they think it was important that scientific research proves the existence of God or the power of prayer? Sorry," she said, and she really was, "but you can't have it both ways. You can't ask science to demonstrate God exists and then insist God isn't just another word for some natural phenomenon."

She might enjoy his company, but she wasn't going to give in to fuzzy thinking to keep the relationship going. That felt condescending and she felt really uncomfortable about that. Especially with him.

Hope dashed

For John, the disconnect between the worlds of faith and science was starting to feel really painful. He felt like a kid in the dark, not sure whether to feel embarrassed, or ashamed, or cowardly. Whatever he tried, he couldn't connect with them. He couldn't find a toe-hold by which to support his belief in God. Better to make a gracious exit than continue in this sense of being more and more alone as a religious eccentric in their world.

John thanked Rosalind for her generosity and that of her colleagues, and said how much he'd enjoyed the conversation, hiding, he hoped, the fact that he hadn't enjoyed it at all.

He walked home alone.

John felt more confused than ever. He left Andy, Beverly, Charles and Rosalind happily chatting about their research, apparently none the worse for not believing in God. For an instant some part of him envied their freedom not to have to believe anything, and to follow what they could be sure of. Too scary to look down that cliff for long, but it was enticing.

That morning, the idea of having something to talk about with his atheist neighbour had delighted him. But now after these conversations at her lab, and their social chat later, he wondered if, after all, there really was anything to talk about. Nobody in her world believed in God, and she was totally at home in that world which seemed impervious to every argument for the existence of God. Perhaps, he wondered, there is no way to have a conversation across the religion-science divide.

Perhaps he should have stayed on his side of the backyard fence after all.

He felt a twinge in his heart. It hurt to imagine no more conversations with her if he stayed on his side of the fence.

But his heart was perfectly healthy.

His potassium balance was well within normal. He was accurately conscious of the implications of the conversations. At least as far as he understood them at this point.

What if they were right, and consciousness is caused by atoms? And 'God' is just a pre-scientific way of describing that?

What then is the point of faith?

John, perhaps like us when first engaging deeply with the secular world, has come close to despair. The more he tries to learn the language of secularism the more he can't make head or tail of it and the more his faith is threatened.

But that sense of threat and disorientation is a sure sign he has recognized that another quite different language exists and he doesn't know the first thing about what it means. Which is a huge step forward in learning a foreign language.

That's when you no longer think the foreign language is a poor substitute for your own. It gives you the choice of either abandoning the learning process, or of going deeper and perhaps getting a huge payoff.

In the next chapter secular language will begin to make sense, and so start to feel like a credible, although still threatening, conversation partner with faith. Achieving fluency is closer than we think. Then, when we have become fluent, there's no knowing what delights we may discover and what experiences faith and science may have in common. Even God.

But first, we will have to immerse ourselves more deeply in the language of secularism.

Have courage. It'll be worth it!

Summary

When there are occasional reports that some scientific experiment has proved something about faith, people of faith find that affirming. The problem is such experiments have so far always turned out to be unreliable. Science doesn't have experiments that demonstrate the truths of religion. While painful for religious people to admit, accepting that science doesn't support faith in God is a necessary first step in learning the language of secularism.

When learning any foreign language, we always go through a period of being convinced it makes no sense and that we should give up. When learning a language gets that frustrating, it proves the learner is past the first hurdle of thinking that other languages are simple equivalents of their own. That's when there is a chance for real learning to begin.

Our degree of discomfort is an indication of how far we have come from the naïve idea that there is no real problem between science and faith.

There's more to learn yet, and the conviction that none of the new language makes sense won't go away for a while. But the courage of continuing to learn secular will pay off with new insight and delight and a new depth of faith.

But if we don't learn that language, we can never succeed in communicating our faith. Take courage from Archdeacon McDonald and his decision to immerse himself totally into Gwich'in culture and language. That paid off in spades, and so will our decision to learn secular. See the Introduction for more about the Archdeacon.

Chapter 5
Disbelief 101:
Stuff Just Organizes Itself—
No God Required

Even before AI your car drove you

Every morning for more than a decade, I drove from my suburban house to my downtown church using a scenic rural road as a shortcut into the city.

The start of that shortcut is a busy intersection where two main roads cross. But from that point onwards, the road going downtown winds for a couple of kilometres through a wooded park, a single lane in each direction, before emerging again into the bustle of urban traffic. Despite being only one lane in each direction, this road is a favourite shortcut for people like me going to work from the suburbs.

During morning rush hour, the traffic moves through the intersection from three directions onto this single-lane road. A steady flow of cars is always backed up waiting their turn to enter the narrower road.

However, by the time this steady stream of cars on the narrow road reaches a point two kilometres further along, where the rural road widens again into an urban artery, the steady flow of cars has ceased. Instead, the cars have become divided into little convoys. The cars now travel in groups, sometimes four cars in a row, sometimes seven or eight, but never in the regular stream with which they began driving along the single-lane stretch.

Most of the drivers take this route into town every morning and none of them decides before-hand to coordinate their speed so as to form little convoys.

So why do the drivers arrange themselves into these convoys morning after morning?

The reason is that drivers have various preferred speeds.

Many, like myself, given the opportunity, will drive over the speed limit, while some drive at the speed limit. Some very strange drivers even drive below the speed limit. The result is faster drivers pile up behind slower drivers, forming a convoy behind the slower drivers. Meanwhile any faster driver who was in front of a slow driver has pulled away, leaving the slow driver at the head of a convoy. Once the road widens out into two lanes in each direction, the convoys disperse as the faster drivers use the passing lane.

Although there is no pattern to how long each little convoy will be, they always form up. Every morning. Nobody wants the convoys. Everybody hates them. The slower drivers hate being at the head of a convoy and the faster drivers would do anything to pass the slower drivers and leave the convoy behind.

Nobody intends this pattern to emerge; everyone wishes it wouldn't happen; nobody can stop it happening.

The only way to prevent this pattern of convoys emerging every morning would be to link all the cars together in a train to ensure every car went the same speed. Then there would be no bunching up. But that would require outside intervention, and no driver wants that.

Waves happen the same way. When the wind blows over the ocean, the wind does not consist of carefully timed puffs so as to produce the regular waves we observe near the shore. What happens is, just like the cars on the road, some water droplets are blown more quickly than others and they pile up behind the slower droplets and thus produce a bump in the water—the first wave. Once a small wave has formed it catches the uncoordinated puffs of wind more effectively than the trough between the waves, and the effect is enhanced—the water in the wave pushes even harder and the wave gets a little taller. Then the random puffs of wind have more surface to blow on and the wave gets even higher. This happens inevitably even though there is no wave pattern in the wind.

Uncoordinated *random* puffs of wind result in the *regular rhythmic* wave action that we see along the shore. It seems so normal and obvious that we easily miss how extraordinary this process is—regular patterns keep emerging from uncoordinated random chaotic processes.

Patterns like waves and car convoys arise everywhere with a persistence that nothing can suppress. Whether it is ripples in sand dunes on Mars that are exactly the same as ripples on sand dunes on Earth, or the more complex ways in which ocean-going mammals like whales or seals exhibit the same body shapes as fish, patterns emerge everywhere. These emerging patterns can be simple, like waves or ripples in sand, or they can be complex patterns of patterns such as living cells, animals, or brains.

Patterns just keep emerging. Everywhere.

Why?

That brings us to the heart of the problem between faith and science. Traditional faith understands that God in some way reaches into the universe and deliberately constructs these patterns—particularly the more complex ones of life and consciousness. That's one of the messages of the creation stories in Genesis. Science has a different and contradictory explanation: patterns, including the most complex biological and mental patterns, arise from purely mechanical processes that require no forethought, no God.

Faith could ignore this contradictory explanation if it weren't for science being so successful and providing the infrastructure for our entire way of life. Whether it's talking on the phone, taking a picture, writing on a computer, driving a car, turning on the lights when it gets dark, or receiving live-saving surgery, those God-ignoring scientific assumptions lie beneath virtually everything we do in our day-to-day lives.

So, when science has no need for God, communities of faith have a problem. The everyday lives of their members are thoroughly immersed in, and made possible by, the Godless assumptions of science. No wonder so much of religion is becoming desperate and angry. By putting their trust in the products of science and technology every hour of every day, religious people are affirming the underlying scientific assumption that God is irrelevant to our everyday lives. For believers, that's a painful contradiction. As painful as kneeling in the dark on a hard wooden floor saying one's prayers in a religious school.

More attraction, more risk

John seemed to have reached a dead end. Every time he thought he had a clue about what his atheist friends were talking about, he found they kept saying, in effect, that he wasn't understanding them. He was tempted to drop the attempt, to give up on learning this new language, and simply walk away. It was just like when you try for the fifth time offering 'garage' as a proposed meaning for *garu* and the Chichewa speaker laughs and says you still haven't the slightest clue. It feels so frustrating and pointless.

Maybe it was his sense that he'd like to spend more time with Rosalind, but whatever his motivation, John successfully resisted the temptation to give up. He decided to give it one last try to learn more about this strange threatening language. John knew talking was the only way to get to know his neighbour. But talking hadn't turned out to be easy. Or pleasant. Nevertheless, he thought he'd try again. Surely it couldn't get worse.

Over the next several days John couldn't get that visit to Rosalind's work out of his mind. Disturbed as he was at the way his religious arguments had all been dismantled, he was still hoping for a way to connect his faith to the fascinating world of science. He was still sure there must be a way to demonstrate God as the necessary and ultimate creator of the universe and life and everything.

So, a few evenings later, over the back fence, John plucked up his courage and asked Rosalind if he could have another visit. He was feeling nervous. Was he being dishonest? Maybe he wasn't interested in a conversation about science and trying out some new ways of proving God. Maybe it was something else that was attracting him. But he couldn't help himself. He wanted more. But despite Occam, the safer explanation was to attribute his interest to curiosity about science, even though the simpler explanation was that he wanted to spend more time with Rosalind.

For her part, Rosalind had been a little apprehensive about inviting John to her work in case he became aggressively religious and made her colleagues uncomfortable and they began to doubt her ability to choose friends. But his respectful and thoughtful questions had impressed her. What a nice change it was to be respected by someone who was religious. And now he was asking for more. That felt really good.

Her response was more than he had bargained for. "Well," she said, "there really isn't much more to see at work. But I'm giving an introductory lecture for non-science students tomorrow evening about some of the more interesting implications of our research. Would you like to come?"

Attend her lecture? On scientific research, of all things? But the memory of how much he'd been stimulated by his conversation with Andy, Beverley and Charles, and to be honest, by her, persuaded him; even though he'd lost all the arguments. Maybe this personal invitation from her would go better. Showing less trepidation than he was feeling, he said, "I think I'd like that." But he wasn't at all certain he would.

He was confused. He liked her as a person, was fascinated by her work, and was deeply disturbed by both. On the other hand, he felt more alive than ever. But more uncomfortable than ever. He felt attracted to something that threatened to destroy his faith. What could be stranger than that?

Without John knowing it, he was having much the same reaction as Rosalind as she became aware of being impressed by John. How strange was that?

At her lecture

The next evening at her lecture, to his surprise he almost felt at home. Andy, the atheist who took his kids to church, Beverley, who couldn't find any evidence of God, and Charles, he of the two gods, waved at him across the lecture theatre. It felt like being with friends. It struck him that they were all on a journey together—all of them, including himself, were there to learn. Somehow, he was an equal colleague. How strange, to find himself so at home with atheists.

Rosalind moved to the podium.

John started off feeling pleased with himself. He was delighted to find that he was able to follow the general thread of her presentation. He knew what she meant when she spoke of a quantum particle, and at a reference to Stephen Hawking he realized that he wasn't just a brainy man in a wheelchair; that he was the person who'd invented the idea of spherical time. Suddenly it seemed exciting.

But what was really remarkable was that without noticing it, he had begun to understand her language. Not noticing he was understanding was a huge step forward. That meant he was starting to become fluent. That's what happens when you start being fluent: you don't notice when you get the meaning and you don't have to translate. It's a huge accomplishment. You start to hear what's really going on.

Self-building mosquitoes

While she was working on her lecture, Rosalind said, she had been bitten by a mosquito.

"No scientist claims there isn't design in nature. Nature is brimming with design." She went on to say that the mosquito had found her not by using its eyes, but by employing several sensors, in particular by using a heat detector in combination with a carbon dioxide detector.

"There is no question these two organs are designed to locate mammals and are designed to do so in combination. Together they are an ingenious solution to a complicated problem. Although a heat detector has a longer range, used alone it could attract a mosquito to all sorts of warm but useless things such as warm rocks or a fire. The carbon dioxide detector is great at identifying mammals, all of whom breathe out carbon dioxide. But used by itself, a carbon dioxide detector wouldn't be any use unless by accident the mosquito was already near a mammal. The slightest movement of air would blow the carbon dioxide away and the mosquito could end up literally chasing the wind. But the combination of the two detectors is a brilliant design—one is short range, one is long range, and in nature the most common thing that simultaneously produces carbon dioxide and is warm, is mammals."

Then more design comes into play. She had swatted at the mosquito and it had initiated evasive manoeuvres—a loop-the-loop series of rapid erratic flight changes that had the effect of preventing her from getting a successful aim. Sure enough, having missed the first time, she couldn't get a proper aim again. "All this evasive flight design happens without requiring the mosquito to have sufficient brain power to understand what an evasive manoeuvre is, or what a swat is, or where the swat might come from. Nonetheless, the manoeuvres are highly successful. They were very well designed. The mosquito was smarter than I," she said, to laughter, "I never did figure out its evasive manoeuvres! It won and I lost!"

Once the mosquito landed, there was more design. In its proboscis, the mosquito has a set of three tiny saws with serrated edges that operate the way an electric carving knife does, by moving back and forth along each other. When it sawed into her skin (John shuddered for an instant at the thought) it injected an anaesthetic designed to prevent her noticing what was going on. That design worked perfectly and the mosquito got a good drink. The mosquito also injected her with a blood thinner designed to make her blood easier to suck through its microscopically thin proboscis, and so on, and on. Design is everywhere. "Check the PowerPoint file on my website for more examples about the mosquito." The students busily copied down the details.

"Neither scientists nor religious believers question the ubiquity of design—everybody agrees there are astonishing levels of design in the mosquito's equipment. Neither scientists nor religious believers suggest that an insect with this complex equipment 'just happened' by some lucky chance. Nobody disputes this species of mosquito is designed to find and feast off mammals.

"What religion and science disagree about is whether such ingenious inventions as the mosquito's anaesthetic or triple-blade saw had to have been deliberately designed.

"This is no simple question. If there isn't a God, how did the mosquito come up with the exact chemical formula that anaesthetizes mammal nerves but not its own mosquito nerves? Having found such a formula, how did the mosquito design the equipment to manufacture the anaesthetic? It seems obvious that no mosquito could have thought up and then implemented such a design on its own body, with a brain smaller than a pin-head and a life-span of a couple of weeks.

"When religious people look at the wider picture and consider that this is only one type of mosquito; that other species of mosquito are designed to feed from plants, for various times of day, for differing climates, and there are billions of other types of plants and animals, many even more exquisitely designed, it would seem only an immense intelligence, far exceeding that of humans, could design such a profusion of intricate living processes.

"Nobody is suggesting that humans designed the process—these mosquito designs were in place long before there were humans. Since neither humans nor mosquitoes designed the mosquito, who did? The nearly universal conclusion, throughout all of history, is that some great pre-existing intelligence must have. This is no light-weight argument. It forms the basis for religious faith. Religion asks how this mind-boggling plethora of ingeniously designed life arose. Religion says the explanation is God created it."

John realized Rosalind understood him and his faith better than he had imagined. Knowing she was an atheist made that scary. And tingly.

"For a non-believer, like me," she said, "it is easy to dismiss the suggestion that there must be a grand designer; but we do so too quickly."

Many in the audience sat up at this. "Is she getting religious on us?"

"Ah ha," thought John, "This part I like."

She continued. "Although some animals do use primitive tools, the human ability to think ahead and plan for unique situations raised human tool-making to a distinct new level and made it one of the defining characteristics of our species. *Homo Faber* (Human the Builder) is now an official alternative to *Homo Sapiens* (Human the Wise) although that last designation now seems a bit premature....!" Chuckles.

"Every tool a human makes requires forethought and planning. Whether it is a towel-rack, an automobile, or a violin, somebody thought through the problem, visualized the solution in their head, and only then constructed the tool on the basis of what she had already imagined. Many people subsequently made gradual improvements on the original design, and users in the future, with forethought will, no doubt, find new ways to mount towel-racks," (it occurred to John that he might be able to do that for her), "drive cars, or play violins. It is impossible for humans to imagine that any complex tool could be designed without forethought because, except for rare occasions when someone produced a tool entirely by accident without intending to, the production of every tool we have ever used was preceded by a some conscious person imagining the tool and mentally designing it.

"The alternative is bizarre. Imagine someone cooking an outdoor meal beneath a rubber tree and finding that the fire melted some sand, thus making glass; smelted iron ore, making steel; all of which just fell together with the sap of the rubber tree to end up as a car complete with motor, windows, and rubber tires and a functioning engine. A mosquito, bear in mind, is far, far, more complex than any car. These things don't happen by accident. In human experience, forethought—intentional design—is essential to any organized process or product.

"It's not such a strange conclusion to assume that design using forethought is essential for anything as complex and ingenious as the mosquito's triple saw, or its mammalian anaesthetic, let alone the entire panoply of life on this planet. Design is everywhere so there must be a designer.

"A God would be the obvious answer."

Alertness in the audience. *Where was she going with this?* John wondered if he had misjudged her—*was she was a person of faith after all?* He felt confused. Not quite sure he liked this turn of argument. What might be coming? She'd laid out the religious argument so well. What if now she demolished it?

Her talk continued. "We now understand how such ingenious design can arise in living organisms without any forethought. The process is that any tiny accidental change to a new-born creature is evaluated by a sort of natural sieve that allows useful changes to pass through to the next generation, and by death or starvation prevents useless ones from being passed on.

"It's the essence of simplicity," she pointed out. John had a sinking feeling as he recalled Occam who pronounced simplicity to be the fundamental principle for deciding what's real. He felt a dagger starting to thrust itself into his body, into his faith, into his soul. He could glimpse where this was going.

Rosalind continued. "Changes that make any mechanism in an animal less useful result in greater likelihood that the animal will die, and therefore such changes don't get passed to the next generation. In contrast, even the tiniest change that enhances the animal's life is more likely to be passed on because the animal lives longer and is more likely to reproduce, and so the accidental change gets passed to its offspring which in turn pass it on to theirs. In the long run, even the smallest useful changes gradually add up over the generations to an organism that is better at surviving and reproducing. The end result is an organism that looks exactly as if it had been carefully designed for the exact context in which it lives.

"Thus, one particular mosquito that lived in the ancient past happened to have a purely accidental mutation that made its saliva slightly anaesthetic. Because of the anaesthetic, that mosquito didn't get noticed and swatted so often, so it survived and laid more eggs. When those eggs hatched, they had all inherited the same slightly anaesthetic saliva, and so more of them survived. In a few generations virtually all mosquitoes with normal saliva had died out and all living mosquitoes had this improvement. But not because an intelligent mosquito, or an intelligent designer, or God, or anyone, made it happen.

"New patterns just emerge in mosquito larvae, and if they enhance mosquitoes' lives, they continue being reproduced, and if they produce death, they don't.

"If you want to study the details, my notes indicate where you can apply game theory to the mathematical description of this process. For those unfamiliar with game theory, that's the study of how mathematics can describe the likely outcomes of various competitors such as human games or interactions of animals and their environment. The patterns of mathematics are the engine which underlies the emergence of new species, such as the mosquito that bit me.

"Design emerges naturally. That's what the plethora of unimaginably ingenious lifeforms mean. It simply means that the combination of chance with the order provided by successful individuals producing more descendants results in a creativity that's astounding. It doesn't mean there is a God behind all this. It simply means we live in a universe where innovation is simply part of the way matter, energy, and pattern interact.

"Strictly speaking there is nothing ingenious or creative about it. But it looks exactly like what ingenious humans would have done to solve the problem the creature faced. When you see the end result, it is amazing. That's one of the things that drives me to do science."

Suddenly he got it. It felt like she had hit him in his stomach with her fist.

She continued. "If you think about it, it still sounds astonishing that such a simple mindless process could produce such intricate designs. It took Darwin ten years to come to terms with it—the whole thing seemed impossible to him. He had to keep checking and re-checking because he could hardly believe it himself. And because he understood the threatening implications for religious faith, of which his wife was a faithful member.

"We take evolution for granted now, but that's just because we are so familiar with it. And you know what familiarity breeds. In this case, not contempt, but something more offensive: boredom. People think evolution is boring. That's tragic. And dangerous.

"We must never forget how astounding is the creative power of such a mind-less process. At different times and in different species this mindless process has invented, from scratch, at least eight, and by some counts forty, totally distinct and unrelated organs for seeing.[1] These are not eight stages or variations of the eyes that we have. These are eight completely different methods of seeing, unrelated to one another. Trilobites were highly successful snail-like creatures now long extinct, but some of them had immovable eyes made of solid crystal. Those eyes, like all other aspects of every animal that ever was, emerged by the unplanned process of evolution.

"Contrary to long-held opinion, this process can operate rapidly, not neces-sarily on a scale of millions of years as Darwin supposed. Species of finches off the coast of South America have been observed developing a different style of beak in only a couple of years, in response to climate change that altered the availability of the seeds for which their original beak shape had been useful.[2]

"In this example, as in all others, it is important to understand that no individual bird ever changed its beak in response to new food. It's just that baby birds, like all plants and animals and mosquito larvae, are born with

---

1   I Schwab, "The evolution of eyes: major steps" The Keeler lecture 2017: centenary of Keeler Ltd. *Eye* 32, 302–313 (2018). https://doi.org/10.1038/eye.2017.226

2   Jonathan Weiner, Alfred A. Knopf, *The Beak of the Finch: A Story of Evolution in Our Time.* (New York: 1994).

slight variations which differ from their parents. In the case of these particular finches, sooner or later a chick hatched with a beak shape that happened to be more useful for cracking open the new kind of seeds that the climate change had made bountiful. When that bird grew to be an adult, it survived the famine caused by the dying out of the old kind of seeds. Birds whose beaks were normal starved to death because they couldn't crack open the new type of seeds.

"In the meantime, the bird with the slightly changed beak had fed well and became a more prolific parent than the birds with normal beaks. Its offspring inherited the same slightly changed beak shape that previously would have been a detriment to survival, they fared better, and in a couple of generations, in the course of just a couple of years, all the finches living on that island had the new beak shape.

"But here's the kicker. *During its entire lifetime not one single bird ever changed its beak in any way whatever. It's worth repeating: no bird changed its beak.* Yet in a couple of years the entire population of those finches had new beaks that exactly fitted the new nuts.

"I know it seems impossible. Darwin discovered how. Accidental genetic changes that a particular animal is born with and which make that one individual healthier are passed on to its offspring. That's all there is to it. That's the amazing discovery that rightly made Darwin famous.

"The only difference between these birds and the ones Darwin had studied a century and a half earlier was that there happened to have been researchers on the scene who had already spent years cataloguing the exact shape and size of the birds' beaks before the climate produced a famine. So, it was easy to compare beak shapes before and after the famine. We actually saw evolution happening in the wild! Darwin would have given a lot more than his eye-teeth to have seen that!

"Sadly, the public have come to think that evolution is some kind of directed process by which individual creatures make adjustments to their bodies in order to become adapted. Nothing could be further from the truth. It's just that some individuals are born different. If they thrive because of that difference and therefore have more successful offspring, we say a new species has arisen. If they die because of the difference, they have no offspring and we never notice. We applaud the successful designs. We seldom hear about the failures.

"There is no intentionality and no forethought required for this process. It could just as well have happened that no bird ended up with an accidentally appropriate beak, in which case they all would have died out and gone extinct.

Which of course has happened to innumerable types of animals, and nobody would have thought that was odd.

"No wonder," and she worried as she said this that her guest might be insulted, "religion finds evolution disturbing. All this creative stuff happens because the universe, and maybe because pure mathematics, just are that way. But I have to say I find it amazing—there's more creativity going on than in any God I could imagine.

"What's the point of all this? Only when we recognize the power of the religious explanation—that there must be a designer behind a design—can we appreciate how more astonishing is the way it actually happens. Science proposes that, contrary to all human experience, intricately designed tools and behaviours arise in living creatures without any forethought or intelligence. It turns upside-down all our human assumptions about us being the amazing designers of tools. I'd even say it's humbling.

"Here's another amazing piece. The blueprints for beaks or anaesthetic saliva and triple saws are passed on to the next generation by DNA, which is a marvellously designed kind of blueprint and photocopier all in one. But amazingly, it contains not only the instructions for how to build those saws and anaesthetics, it also contains blueprints for how to construct more of itself including how to photocopy its own blueprint. No planning or intelligence required. It's no wonder," she concluded, "that so many religious people just can't believe that it all happens by chance. But that's just the way it is. If we ever forget what an astonishing thing we've stumbled on, we deserve their religious criticism.

"The implication to which Darwin has brought us is that design is ubiquitous: from river deltas all with the same shape, to mosquito proboscises adapted to innumerable different hosts, to the complex pumping system of the heart (John felt his own heart pumping as he watched her—*funny she should mention that*), to cicadas hatching only every seventeen years because it is a prime number and virtually impossible for a predator species to anticipate, design just won't go away. And there is no reason to think this automatic emergence of design is limited to our planet. The conclusion is: the universe can't help sprouting design."

She summed up her lecture. "I simply want to draw your attention to the fact that the work my colleagues and I do, day in and day out, is built on the foundation of something very remarkable: you might call it the spontaneous emergence of design. That's what all this really means. Sounds like a good title for a book. Thank you all very much for coming." Clapping from the audience.

By the time her talk was over, John was feeling really uncomfortable. His scientist neighbour and her secular colleagues were dealing with issues he heard a lot about in church. Mystery, awe, wonder, design, intelligence, life: all these were central aspects of his faith. How strange to discover secular scientists speaking of those exact topics, and with assurance they knew what they were talking about and God simply didn't come into it. They seemed so comfortable omitting the existence of God. The more spontaneous patterns appear in nature, the more God begins to disappear. But in everything else there was a great deal of shared experience. How could this be?

Politely he turned down the invitation to drinks and walked home. Very alone.

Getting worried

On the way home, he thought.

All his adult life he had believed in God. He'd worshipped, he'd served on church committees, he had received help in prayer and he'd been asked to hold the chalice as people drank from it—the most holy activity of their worship. But now he had this sinking feeling that he was about to lose it all. If there were no God, his entire faith was pointless. Had they been enacting a mindless ritual? Had he been that foolish? Had he been doing it because it made him feel good? Was that all it was?

What if it was true, what they were saying? What if you could remove God, and everything stayed exactly the same except it made more sense because it became simpler and understandable? What if all the wondrous living things in the universe had emerged the way these scientists said they had? The attractive part was that it was so clear and logical and explainable. And so amazing.

This kind of science didn't remove awe and wonder, it enhanced it. He could imagine the process by which the beaks in a bird species could change purely by accident and end up suiting the seeds that grew in their environment. It had never occurred to him that he would ever understand that sort of thing. It made sense. It was astounding—that without any human, or any bird, or any God, or anything at all planning it, these ingenious solutions just happened. That was staggering. Suddenly he envied them. It must be wonderful to be so free and able to investigate such wonders without worrying about who might be offended.

But he could see his whole world falling apart—if God didn't do those things, then the universe would feel so empty. He would feel empty. His faith wouldn't mean anything. Neither would all those years of being faithful to his prayers and going to church. He felt shame to be losing his faith.

He could also imagine the shame he'd feel if his atheist neighbour discovered he wanted to keep on believing in God despite his growing understanding of the facts. Even if he believed the scientists were right, he wasn't sure he would have the courage to follow through on the implications. Knowing himself to be a bit of a coward, he imagined having to pretend to his church friends for the indefinite future that he still believed. That felt really uncomfortable. He hoped passionately he could still find a way to be sure there was a God after all.

And there was something else, too. He had really enjoyed these recent conversations with his atheist neighbour. He'd been flattered to have been taken seriously and invited into her world. He'd begun to feel really alive. He had been looking forward to more such conversation. He had felt like a little boy in a sand-box. But now his eyes had been opened and he realized he was standing not in a sand-box discovering intriguing toys, but at the edge of a precipice. If he took one more step he could tumble into the abyss of atheism.

What was even more frightening was that for her this atheism was perfectly normal. It was as if she could jump off a cliff that terrified him, yet she could fly effortlessly in the air of atheism, free as a bird, loving every minute. He wasn't sure which would be worse—the thought of her pity if he refused to take the leap, or the possibility of losing his faith and so much meaning if he did.

It struck him again. If there were no God, then the universe, and our presence in it, would mean nothing. We would all be so many atoms jiggling around, eventually coming to rest in eternal darkness. Nothing remembered. Nothing of any significance beyond fleeting hope and consciousness and then its total and final extinction.

With a shock he realized he would feel exactly the same if he lost this new relationship with his neighbour. Nothing would mean anything if he went back to his religion and never saw her again. "What's going on with me?" he said, "None of this makes any sense."

But in that, he was very much mistaken.

He was about to find himself driven to make sense of it. He was being goaded without knowing it, into a pattern that would end up making a great deal of sense. It would turn out to mean everything.

Despite himself, John is well on the way to fluency. He understands what the secular language is saying. He is frighteningly able to understand that language.

In the next chapter, he will begin to fully understand the enormously important experience the secular language is attempting to communicate.

Summary

Have you found yourself helpless in the face of your car always wanting to make patterns with other cars? And then those mosquitoes! How can something with a microscopic brain come up with such complex and clever tools? Ripples in the sand, mosquitoes, cars, even human bodies all seem to have arisen entirely without any need for God.

Things just get themselves organized.

We want an explanation as to how things get themselves organized. Religions say God did it, but in the world of science there doesn't need to be any external intelligence to do it—it's just the way things are. That's the first half of understanding the language and culture of disbelief.

In the next chapter we'll see that in the language of disbelief our minds, our emotional feelings, and our ethics, are just one more example of how pattern emerges from stuff automatically getting organized. Our inner world turns out to be as committed to getting organized as the outer world is.

That drive to find organization around us is characteristic of science, which looks for reasons for things, and also of faith that celebrates the creation and re-creation of the world.

Looking for patterns in the flow or cars or of stars isn't just idle curiosity or childish playing with toys. Seeking patterns turns out to be the central pattern of human consciousness.

We are well on our way to being fluent in secular.

CHAPTER 6
Disbelief 201:
Why We Ask Why:
The Demand for Meaning

Why is there fluff?

My wife and I and our two small children are on a summer holiday trip, driving through a stand of cottonwood trees shedding their fluffy wool-like seeds.

From his car seat in the rear, one of the children speaks up.

"Daddy, why is there white stuff on the road?"

I had hardly noticed. But I was pleased he had. Better than him just sleeping through this fascinating scenery, and a welcome respite from the incessant fighting with his brother when they weren't asleep.

"That's the fluff from the cottonwood trees."

A pause.

"Why is it fluffy?"

Oh, great! He's curious. Interested in nature. Perhaps a budding scientist. A wonderful quality in a three-year-old.

"It's fluffy so it can blow wherever the wind goes."
"Why?"
"So the seeds can land in new places."
"Why?"
"So they can grow into more trees."
"Why?"
"I just told you why."
"Why?"
"Because you asked."
"Why?"
"I don't know why you asked."
"Why?"
"Because I can't see into your head to know why."
"Why?"

And so on, and on, and on. Why, after Why, after Why. Better, at least than whining.

At about three years old, children discover that the word 'Why' is a magic wand with which they can force the most strong-minded or preoccupied adult to give them full attention.

"Mummy, look at the cows."
"Uh-huh. They are eating grass."
"Why?"

Oh no! Here we go! Now it's Mom's turn to be helpless before a three-year-old armed with this formidable query. Adults are unable to extricate themselves from having to respond, no matter how bizarre the child's request for an explanation.

Using "why" to make connections and get a meaning is very pleasurable (and, yes, shortly we will ask why), and children are experts at getting pleasure. Adults readily join in the process because they also receive pleasure from finding connections. The "Why?" anticipates that there is a connection: just find it. Our desire to find a connection—any connection—is so strong that, even when the connection is demanded by a three-year old, it takes a significant act of will to refuse to engage the child's question.

Two grandkids, both on the autism spectrum, at around five years old devised a sophisticated game to enhance this pleasure of finding meanings.

Travelling on a long, boring holiday trip, out of the blue, with no context, one of them would declare "A hippopotamus doing handstands on top of a telephone pole." There'd be a moment of silence followed by hilarious laughter all around.

So, here's the puzzle. Why? Why was such foolishness funny? What's the connection between nonsensical images and the subsequent delight by young and old?

What was probably happening is the child had tricked the adults into thinking there must be a meaning, that this whimsical image must be a kind of riddle. What did it mean? What is it connected with? What's the connection between a hippopotamus and a telephone pole? We adults looked for a meaning, couldn't find it, felt the disappointment of not getting pleasure from discovering a meaning, and experienced a sense of loss that there was no meaning. That's why there was a momentary silence. But then we realized with a shock of delight that the lack of meaning was the whole point. That *was* the meaning! Meaninglessness had been magically turned into meaning.

Those kids had found a way not just to hide the meaning inside a meaningless image, but to turn meaninglessness into meaning. The double shock of discovery—that the lack of meaning was the meaning, and that the kids understood that before the adults did, doubled the adults' pleasure—they were discovering double meanings where they'd thought there were none. And the two kids loved inventing such a subtle meaning.

When I recounted this story to those grandkids some years later, they couldn't remember the incident. But it took one of them all of two seconds to come up with another. Right out of the blue. "Seventy-one fax machines lined up on a bridge." It worked. I laughed and laughed. They knew exactly how to fool me and make meaning all at once. Of course, I then asked the 'why' question. "Why seventy-one? Why not seventy-two?" "Because seventy-two is the wrong number," declared my grandchild. He's good at math. Had he known that seventy-one is a prime number and would stymie my attempt to find some pattern in the number of fax machines? It worked. There was no meaning in the number. Or any part of the image. That was the whole point. The meaning was that there was no meaning. It's a very difficult thing to do. Try thinking of a plausible image that has no meaning. It's very hard. That's because we are hard wired to find meaning everywhere even when there are none.

Puns use the same technique to provide pleasure in finding meanings. In a pun, we get two meanings, two connections, where our brains thought momentarily that there would be only one—the pleasure of finding meanings and connection is doubled, and it can be so pleasurable that we can double over in laughter.

"Why?" is a request for a connection. Why is there fluff on the road? Or, why are there exactly seventy-one fax machines? Or why are there fax machines on a bridge at all? The 'lined up' bit fools us into being sure there must be a pattern, a meaning. It took this young teen all of two seconds to set it all up. That's a very sophisticated technique and it reveals how intense our desire is to find meaning even in meaninglessness.

Why is our desire for meaning so intense?

Spiders weave meaning — their life depends upon it

To understand where our insistent need for meaning came from we can start by examining the behaviour of a relatively simple creature, the spider. Spiders are not, of course, simple, since they display a wide range of behaviours that are extraordinarily complex and ingenious. But the meanings in their lives are fairly straightforward and easy for us to visualize, and in that sense, simple. By understanding how meaning functions in the life of a creature like a spider, we can understand how the human craving for meaning became so powerful.

When an orb spider feels her web trembling, the vibrations could be caused by any number of things. Because her eyesight is poor, she must rely on the vibrations of the silk to determine what has touched her web. A fly may be caught in the web, or an insect dangerous to the spider may have been caught, or a blade of grass may be brushing against it, or the wind may be fluttering it, or a piece of cottonwood fluff may be caught in it, or a male spider may be signalling mating intentions. Each of these possible sources, and many more, are communicated to the spider by distinctive vibrations of the silk.

If she rushes about wasting energy, venom, and silk on every chance movement, she courts death from exhaustion in the long periods between meals. If she gets the meaning wrong and ignores male spiders, she risks the death of her lineage. If she gets the meaning wrong and attacks insects too big to handle, she risks being eaten herself and never producing young.

Her very life and indeed the existence of future spiders, depends on her correctly interpreting the meaning of a vibration—on making the correct connection between the type of vibration and what is causing it.

Over millions of trial-and-error responses, spiders that, by chance, happened to have a genetically determined response appropriate to various vibrations, got the meaning right, lived, mated, and gave birth to offspring that inherited their parents' genetic ability to get the meanings of web vibrations right. Spiders whose genetic makeup assigned the wrong responses to vibrations starved to death, never mated, or were themselves eaten, and so there never was a next generation of spiders that inherited genes which got the meanings of web vibrations wrong.

For spiders, making the correct connection between a vibration of their web and its cause is literally a matter of life or death. Spider offspring always descend from spider parents, both of whom interpreted vibrations correctly. None are descended from spiders which got the meanings of vibrations wrong.

All life has been genetically coded to find meanings everywhere.

Humans weave meaning—it's our oxygen

The meanings and connections we humans need to find between events are far more complex than those the spider requires, but the underlying process that gave rise to our intense need to find meaning is the same. Getting the meaning correct is as much a life-and-death issue for humans as it is for spiders.

For humans, getting the meaning right is as pleasurable, desirable, essential, and as life-giving as oxygen. Getting meanings right is associated with having enough to eat, with self-respect, with having a mate, and with having been conceived. The people who received pleasure from noticing connections and meanings got it right more often, lived well, and tended to have more healthy babies. Their babies inherited their parents' genetic code to receive pleasure from discovering meanings, and in turn they had more such children. People who didn't get pleasure from discovering meanings got fewer meanings correct, and so left fewer children. So now the entire human race seems obsessed with discovering meaning.

Including my children, asking about the meaning of fluff on the road and their children challenging us to find a deep meaning in the image of an acrobatic hippopotamus on top of a telephone pole, or in seventy-one fax machines lined up on a bridge. They inherited their fascination with meaning from their parents and from us their grandparents, going further back than we can imagine, all the way back to the most primitive forms of life. The pleasure we receive in discovering meanings encourages us to keep searching for more.

That's why jokes are funny—laughter expresses the burst of pleasure we experience when we suddenly make the connection and get the meaning.

Finding meaning keeps us alive. Is the cracking of a branch the sign of a predator about to pounce, or a sign the branch is full of ripe fruit, or a sign my lover is sneaking up to seduce me? Or her lover is sneaking up to kill me? It's essential we get the meaning right. That's why discovering meanings is our oxygen. Without that craving to discover meanings, we wouldn't remain alive.

Landscape painting may reveal one way in which discovering meaning first became important to humans. The science writer John Barrow, in his book *The Artful Universe,*[1] suggests landscape painting holds a special attraction for us because landscapes are full of meanings. A landscape painting may stimulate in us an ancient genetically programmed pleasure in finding camp-sites that are located near water, with a good lookout from which to spot dangerous animals, and with fertile land within a day's walking distance. Getting the meaning of a landscape correct was a matter of life and death for early humans, and so the desire to find such meanings has been encoded in us ever since. Through painting or viewing landscape paintings we may be enjoying the ancient and essential pleasure of finding the meanings in real landscapes.

In modern society, the ability to correctly interpret meanings remains as central to daily life as it was for hunter-gatherers. Is the wink my colleague across the office just gave me a signal he would like to team up with me as we prepare a joint proposal for the boss, or is he intending I think that is what he intends so I will relax and he can get his proposal in first and beat me to the next promotion? Getting the meaning right can still be a matter of life and death for my career. Or is his wink an invitation to explore friendship and more, or is it to seduce me into unwise trust, or is it just an innocent greeting? I need to get the meaning right. Is the threat of violence by a foreign country an indication of its real intentions, or is it just hoping to manipulate us? Like hunter-gatherers, our personal and international futures still depend on getting meanings right.

Discovering connections between the present and the future in the course of a human life, particularly our own, is a constant preoccupation. "I'm going to deliver letters when I grow up," says the little girl—she's invented a connection between who she is now and who she might be later. It's a meaning for her life. "I get a pay-cheque every two weeks driving bus for the city and I've got a home and a family," may be her satisfying meaning later on. Still later, her meaning may be, "I have weathered most of the storms, my kids are launched; what would make sense now is to teach my life experience to someone." She is

---

1   John Barrow, *The Artful Universe* (Oxford University Press, 1995).

constantly making connections and therefore finding meanings for her life. She might have asked, "Why am I here?" and now she has the answer, a meaning, and feels secure in being alive.

Our need to find meanings between apparently unconnected experiences is so strong it even functions while we sleep.

One of the likely purposes of sleep is to sort through the previous sixteen hours to find which events are worth remembering. When we find them, our brain lays down those events in some memory area. For example, the memory of driving our car today might get laid down, entirely by chance, physically sandwiched between the location of a memory about having seen an elephant in a zoo when we were a child, and a memory about being in an underground subway last week. Those adjacent memories may become activated by the insertion of a new memory next door and that stimulation raises them to consciousness. In our sleep some part of us says, "I'm experiencing driving a car, and an elephant, and a subway." Then the inevitable question. "Why?" Even in sleep our brain is looking for connections. In response to this demand for meaning, our sleeping consciousness invents a connection, a meaning, and soon we have a dream about an elephant driving a car in a subway.

That's how powerful is our need to find connections and meaning in disparate experiences, even when the meaning has to be invented.

In the morning we remember the dream and wonder about its meaning, and ask "Why? Why did I have that dream? What was its meaning?"

Its meaning was an elephant was driving a car in a subway.

If we happen to be an author of children's books, we find a further meaning. We weave that image into a best-selling children's story about elephants driving cars in subway tunnels. Children are delighted because they get pleasure in finding meanings in silly stories like this where at first they saw none.

Our need for meaning—for things to make sense—is astonishingly powerful. Remove meaning and connection, and we suffer terribly. Making a child stand in a corner for even a short time can be excruciating because their need for connection is denied. Put a person in a sensory-deprivation room without connections to their surroundings and they begin to hallucinate in order to invent meaning. Prisoners placed in solitary confinement have so much meaning removed that they can emerge significantly mentally disturbed. If someone lives in a social situation where they can find no meaning for their life, suicide will seem preferable to the pain of living without meaning.

Our need to find connections is so powerful it is even possible for that need to deform a personality. The result is a psychiatric disorder in which the sufferer has lost the ability to regulate their need to discover meanings.

Such a person pointed out to me, in complete seriousness, that there is deep significance in the fact that three leaves are sprouting on a plant in their living room, that their ceiling light fixture has three loops in its hanging cord, and that there are three buttons on his jacket. This is no coincidence to him—in a whisper he confides something very important is being communicated to him. He knows there is a meaning.

As we walk into the psychiatric emergency ward, two cigarette butts on the sidewalk seem to him to be a coded arrow directing him to a rendezvous. In the waiting room, with scarcely a glance he points out, accurately and matter-of-factly, that the serial numbers on the electric outlet next to our chairs, contain his birthdate. I feel sure he is now hallucinating so I glance at the serial number on the outlet. Sure enough, he's right. The numbers on the electric outlet really do contain his birthdate. He thinks this is nothing out of the ordinary. He finds meaning everywhere. But sadly, too much meaning.

For this sufferer, the search for meaning has gone out of control. For the rest of us, it would take enormous attention to discover such patterns, but through seeing the intensity of his aberration, we catch a glimpse into the deep desire we all harbour to find meaning and connection between objects in our world, and between us and the world.

This compelling demand to find meaning can drive us to agonizing lengths to invent meanings. A question sometimes heard by clergy from families who have lost a child is "Why?" The shocking answer families sometimes suggest is, "Did I do something to cause this?" or, "Is God punishing me for something I've done?" So intense is our need to find a meaning in the death of a child that we would rather choose the terrible possibility that somehow we caused our child's death, than have to face the even greater horror that there might be no meaning in the child's death.

That's how powerful meaning is for us.

Faith and science: both search for meaning

People have always asked "Why?" Why did the river flood, why did I get sick, why was this hunt so successful, why am I alive, why did my baby die, why does the universe exist, why is my new friend angry with me? Why, why, why, about everything. And religion provides an answer.

It is curious that science is asking exactly the same question that religion is asking: why did the river flood, why did I get sick, why was this experiment successful, why is there this variation in the genetic code, why did this medication help this person but not someone else? Why, why, why about everything.

Faith's answer to the why question is that God is the ultimate reason for everything. Science agrees with religion about the fundamental importance of the question. But the rise of science in our culture isn't just a painful blip in history that will go away as things return to normal, as communities of faith sometimes hope, nor is it the emergence of humanity from religious illusion. Science is simply the most recent form in which, for millennia, humanity has been asking, "Why?"

However, science finds many more meanings and connections for us than religion does. Proclaiming God is the cause of everything doesn't activate our pleasure centres—it's always the same explanation; we don't learn anything new about the connections around us. But science makes sense of things. It's no wonder we respond so positively to science—science activates our ancient pleasure centres that respond when we find connections between things that looked unconnected. And science does that at almost every moment in our everyday life. No wonder the fabric of our entire society is woven through and through by science.

No wonder religion is so threatened by science. Science does meaning better than religion. And, as we've seen, finding meaning is intensely pleasurable.

That's what was bothering John so much after his conversations with Rosalind's colleagues. His connections—his former religious meanings—were being removed, ironically by his new meaning of connection with Rosalind, and the deepening meaning her friendship held for him, and the meanings that her science was revealing to him. Despite the pain of losing former meanings, he was driven to keep returning to conversations with her because something in him suspected there he would encounter new and even more significant meanings and the pleasure that accompanies them. That attraction could lead him, and us, to deep joy.

But John hadn't yet found that joy. He was experiencing the agony of losing his meaning. Although he didn't yet know it, in his agony John was unknowingly sharing a deep connection with Rosalind. Rosalind was losing her meanings, too.

Both of them were losing their meanings; and both because their relationship was becoming more meaning-full.

Rosalind betrays her meaning

Rosalind had been brought up in fundamentalist religion, and had, like so many of her generation, got out of it at the first opportunity. Science attracted her early on because of the freedom and community it provided as she left her religion, but especially because of the way in which science made connections between all sorts of disparate questions that had intrigued her, questions her religion had rejected as inappropriate. That early excitement about finding meaning where it wasn't obvious, of being able to ask "Why?" about anything at all, still energized and inspired her. The possibility that she herself might make some small contribution to the discovery of new connections in the world around her gave meaning and energy and pleasure and passion to her life.

One of the ironies she delighted in was that her parents had named her Rosalind. They just liked the name. What they didn't know, and what she never told them, was when she was a teenager she discovered that Rosalind Franklin was the X-ray researcher who in 1952 produced the first images of the DNA molecule. It was she who first saw that this astonishing molecule is constructed in a spiral. It was she who gave substance to Darwin's hunch that there must be some physical mechanism by which new qualities are passed on from parents to offspring in all creatures.

But that Rosalind never got the credit. The men on the team took the credit and got the Nobel prize, and almost nobody has heard of Rosalind Franklin. Our Rosalind secretly hoped one day she might redeem her namesake's remarkable accomplishment with some significant discovery of her own, making connections between things nobody had ever seen before. That hope gave Rosalind meaning. To accomplish that would give her profound pleasure.

Discovering the accidental pattern of her name being the same as Rosalind Franklin's gave her life meaning.

But her religious family, for whom God provided all meanings, wanted nothing to do with her decision to enter science, and had disowned her.

So, she had been cautious when she found her neighbour went to church. But he had never brought up the subject of religion in their casual conversations across the back fence even though it was obvious how important his religion was to him. She had come to realize that both of them knew they couldn't talk about either of their incompatible passions. In time, she realized she could trust him about that, and began to admire his integrity. She'd never met a religious believer who treated her atheism with respect. All the religious people she knew had tried to convince her of the existence of God by using the silliest of arguments. It was hardly worth being patient.

But with him it had been different.

What a delight when he asked her about her work! Perhaps she could finally have the conversation with this religious neighbour that she had longed to have with her religious parents. Perhaps she could at last share her enthusiasm about science with a non-scientist and be understood. It would be a delight to make that connection. She had been so pleased when he'd accepted her invitation to join her at work. Even her colleagues enjoyed the persistence of his questions and how he'd made them think. He'd talked a lot at the University Club. It all seemed to be going so well.

And then he'd left abruptly after her lecture. The lecture she'd recommended and invited him to.

She felt heart-sick because she knew why.

She knew how important religious meanings were to John. She knew they had an unspoken agreement not to trespass on each other's commitments. And what had she done? She had gone and exposed him to an entire day at her work and later to an evening lecture on science in which she had pulled no punches. She had proved, using popular illustrations, in a way people in the general public like John could easily understand, why the idea of God wasn't needed any more. She had blown all his naïve arguments for God right out of the water.

No wonder he wouldn't speak to her any more—she had betrayed his trust and destroyed his central meanings.

It was a very empty feeling indeed. She was losing more than a new friend. She was losing her sense of integrity. Her whole life's meaning lay in discovering meanings and now she'd made a shambles of someone's meaning. She'd turned out to be not the discoverer of meanings but their destroyer.

In removing meaning from John's life, she had removed it from her own. She had destroyed the "Why?" on which her professional life had been built. If her science allowed her to go around and remove meanings, what kind of scientist was she? She went to sleep with an aching heart feeling more lost and confused than she had since she had first lost her own faith.

Both of them were wondering if their relationship should end. At best with polite withdrawal, or at worst with recrimination.

In the same way, faith has too often parted ways with secularism either politely, or in anger, when faith wasn't prepared to go all the way to learn this foreign language and become fluent in secular.

This is the turning point for John and Rosalind as it is for faith and science. If either has the courage to risk, then more joy and life may open up than they could ever have imagined. But if neither is prepared to take the risk of losing lesser meaning for greater meaning, the opportunity for new and deep life will have been lost.

It all depends on how they deal with that pain and fear of losing meaning.

But if John and Rosalind had remembered, and if faith and science remember, that finding patterns is the greatest pleasure humans receive and that patterns relentlessly emerge everywhere, they need not be apprehensive about what might come next.

Understanding the origin of this intense need to find meaning is to come close to the centre of the secular language in which we are all immersed in the modern world. When we have understood that central aspect of the secular language, we will have become fully fluent, and faith and science can begin to have a real conversation in deep mutual respect and mutual support.

Summary

'Things organize themselves in patterns, no God required' is the first foundational idea we encounter in learning to speak Secular.

The second is that all life seeks to discover surrounding patterns, and humans especially so. We call that searching the search for meaning. We love finding meaning. We want meaning so badly that if we can't find patterns around us, we become very uncomfortable. Finding patterns makes us feel affirmed and alive because finding pattern around us suggests the pattern that is our self is in a pattern-affirming environment. And that's a good thing!

The problem that faces religion is that science does a better job of providing meaning than does religion. While religion can invoke God as the ultimate explanation of everything, science provides more specific meanings we can use, and in secular culture people have come to believe it's simpler not to assume there is an external God planning all the patterns. Since humans crave patterns and meaning, and since science describes such patterns in detail, science has so much credibility that even religious people call upon science to affirm their beliefs.

Trust in science will turn out to be far less threatening to faith than it first seems, and will provide the foundation for the discovery of God at the very core of the secular world view.

John and Rosalind will also enter a difficult challenge personally as they plunge into unknown territory in their relationship and discover new meaning in their mutual connection.

CHAPTER 7
Disbelief 301:
Know yourself, says Socrates.
In just four steps, responds Freud.

Grumpy waiters serve up projections

I am sitting in a restaurant waiting for my meal. It's been a demanding day dealing with difficult parish issues that have no clear solution, and it's good to have a break by going out for supper. Even though the waiter has been slow coming to our table, I treat him with my usual graciousness and respect and thank him for taking my order. That hasn't been easy, since the waiter had taken his time laughing and socializing with people at a nearby table who had arrived after my wife and me. When he finally comes to my table, he is brusque and pays us minimal attention. The usual expectations of fairness and good manners are being ignored, but I make the best of a bad situation in spite of his rudeness. I generously decide even waiters can have bad days. The waiter takes my order with barely an acknowledgement that I exist.

Sure enough, the waiter seats a family with two screaming kids in the booth next to ours. Evidently the parents expect no standards of behaviour from their children. The kids shout and climb onto the divider, almost knocking into me. Only because I don't want to appear impolite do I restrain myself, but it would have been appropriate to have stood up and have given these incompetent parents public instruction about how they should take their parenting responsibilities seriously.

This restaurant does not look as if it is going to be a good experience.

Talking about taking responsibilities seriously, the waiter, as I suspected, has no idea how to do his job. He returns to ask whether I ordered milk or cream with my coffee. I nearly scream at him for not keeping the order straight—isn't that what waiters are paid to do? Keep your order straight? But, being the patient person I am, I respond with a degree of polite yet cold reserve, so he will understand his service is not up to expectation, and I remind him I'd ordered milk with my coffee. He is so rude as to hardly acknowledge my temperate rebuke.

Clearly the waiters in this restaurant are worse than incompetent. The reason for that is evident—the management has been grossly negligent by hiring incompetent waiters and by not undertaking remedial training. Clearly management is so committed to making quick profits that they allow disruptive behaviour by members of the public eating in their restaurant and hire waiters who can't do the most elementary parts of their job. One would think restaurants would have a code of behaviour so normal people could eat their meals in peace, and standards for hiring staff, so customers who pay for all this, can be well served.

The wait for our food gets longer and longer. It is becoming clear the cooks must have walked off the job and the only way to express appropriate judgement about this chaos is to walk out of the restaurant, loudly drawing attention to the pervasive incompetence of management. Most certainly, I tell myself, I will never eat here again. It would serve them right if they went bankrupt. The other customers are complete idiots to come here at all. The time for leniency is over. This time they need to learn a lesson.

Even my wife, sitting across from me has joined the incompetence—she is trying to make light conversation with me. What an insensitive and inappropriate thing to try to do amidst the utter devastation of our evening. You'd think she would at least express support for me in this unbearable experience. Since she hasn't noticed, I point out to her the obvious—the waiters and everyone in this disaster of a restaurant are not just grumpy; they are worse than grumpy, they are incompetent from management on down.

"I think it's you who's grumpy," she says.

Talk about spousal incompetence.

How did I ever end up marrying her?

Projection: false safety, agony, ecstasy

But my wife was right. The grumpiness was inside *me*. Although I was aware of the grumpiness, I didn't experience it as being inside myself. Instead, I experienced everyone else as grumpy. This phenomenon is called 'projection.'[1] Although the term 'projection' is sometimes used to describe the deliberate use of anger to intimidate another person, we will use its more neutral and earlier meaning. Projection in this sense is a common process in which one person genuinely, but mistakenly, thinks some quality in their self with which they are uncomfortable isn't present in them but is present in someone else.

When I had this experience with the waiter whom I thought was incompetent and grumpy, it was really me who was incompetent and grumpy. It had been a long day; I was tired, things hadn't gone well at church, and I was feeling as if I wanted nothing to do with looking after anyone. In fact, I felt like ignoring people and being rude to everyone I met. Those feelings were all churning inside me.

But they are feelings I don't like. I'd rather believe I'm an infinitely caring person who never gets tired or grumpy and who always accomplishes tasks competently. So, if that's the sort of person I am, as I mistakenly believed, why was I experiencing anger and rudeness? Those feelings seemed to have come out of nowhere. Just as my children were disturbed at the possibility that fluff on the road could suddenly appear from nowhere without any cause, so I was disturbed that my feelings of grumpiness could just appear from nowhere. What was the cause? My children were sure there must be a reason, a connection of some kind between the fluff on the road and something else. In exactly the same way, I was sure there must be a reason for the uncomfortable feelings of grumpiness I was experiencing. Since I was a good, kind person, the most obvious reason for my feelings was that the waiter and management and the other customers in the restaurant were rude and grumpy and incompetent. That was the meaning of my uncomfortable feelings. They were caused by the waiter. That way I could make sense of the feelings I was experiencing without questioning my image of

---

1   See glossary.

myself as a balanced, caring, unflappable, competent person.

This deliberate, although unconscious, self-deception is the central dynamic of projection. If we knew that's what we were doing, we'd have to face the fact that the uncomfortable behaviour exists inside our self. The whole point of projection is to avoid having to face the fact that those undesirable feelings are within ourselves.

But in order for this to work, I have to remain unaware that I am hiding the truth from myself.

So, when my wife pointed out that it was *me* who was impatient and grumpy, I didn't believe her, because after all I am the kind, patient person. So, her observation proved she was the incompetent one for being so mistaken about me!

This phenomenon of projection was first seriously studied and described around the time motion picture shows were invented. So, an easily-understood analogy from movie theatres was used to illustrate this psychological trick we play on ourselves. The term 'projection' suggested this mental process is like the projection of a movie onto a screen. It is as if inside each of us there is a movie projector. Just as the physical picture is mechanically projected onto a movie screen so we can see it, so we 'project' our uncomfortable feelings onto a screen where we can see them. That screen is frequently another person. When we 'project,' we see that other person embodying the feelings that are actually inside our own self.

One of the first people to study this phenomenon was the Austrian psychoanalyst Sigmund Freud. He realized that when we see the projection on another person we are seeing accurately, not inaccurately. We are accurately seeing something about our own self that for some reason we don't want to acknowledge.

Freud thought the widespread belief in God, still normative in his time, arose from the fact that in childhood all people experience feelings about their parents, both comfortable feelings and uncomfortable ones such as vulnerability and rage. Freud theorized that when we become adults, we continue to experience those feelings, but if we are uncomfortable about having some of them, instead of taking responsibility for them, we project them upon an imaginary supreme being and so we make that imaginary being the location for those feelings, whether of vulnerability or of rage. That way we don't have to take responsibility for them and become more mature.

Freud believed the role of a psychotherapist was to assist people in becoming aware of their mistaken projections. His theory was that when we come to understand what is really going on, we can then take responsibility for our own life and feelings. Instead of off-loading responsibility, as immature children might do with their parent, and as religious people do with God, we would stop projecting those feelings, take responsibility for them, change our behaviour, and enter a more mature and satisfying life.

People of faith have found Freud's argument, that God is our projection, so threatening because it makes so much sense. But as we will soon see, although Freud described the foundational human experience of projection and the way in which it explains our experience of God, he may also have unwittingly provided us with a way of encountering God far more deeply than the God he thought he had explained away.

So why all this focus on projections? Freud's point was that projections serve to inform us of something important inside ourselves. Once we have understood that it's our own feelings we have seen on whatever screen we chose to project them, we have become self-aware.

Self-awareness is the foundation of being human. It's the ability to look inside ourselves as if we were standing outside our self, watching from a distance.

As far as we know, we are the only species on earth that can fully do that. More than anything else, self-awareness is what it is to be human.

We have proudly defined ourselves as *Homo Sapiens* (the wise species) or *Homo Faber* (the tool-making species) but it may well be that what really makes us unique is the ability to look inside our own self. Socrates claimed that to "Know yourself" was the summit of human achievement. So perhaps we should call our species '*Homo Introspectus*'—the species that looks inside.

Why is looking inside important?

This ability to know our inner self is essential for engaging in significant relationships with another person, for building a secure future for humanity, and indeed even for experiencing God. In other words, looking inside is foundational to being fully human.

Freud identified four steps by which we move from the illusion of projecting to becoming fully self-aware: projection comes first, then resistance, then withdrawal, and finally integration.

Learning this grammar of the secular language requires being familiar with how that four-stage process functions. That's the final step to mastering the secular language, becoming fluent, and grasping the significance of the secular world's skepticism about God.

And it's the key to a renewed faith.

The first step in becoming self-aware is 'projection,' the phenomenon that happened when my grumpy self saw that waiter as grumpy when in fact I was the grumpy one and had projected my grumpiness onto the waiter. In this first step of self-awareness, we become aware of the quality we are projecting. We aren't mistaken about the existence of the uncomfortable quality we see; we are mistaken only about where that quality resides. This first step is like catching a fleeting glimpse of one's own face reflected in a window-pane and thinking we are seeing someone else. It was no coincidence that I chose a waiter as the screen for my projection; a harried waiter required to be gracious to everyone was exactly what I'd been feeling about myself. Clever inner projectionist!

In the early stages of professional therapy, the therapist does not overtly challenge her client's projections because projection is foundational to the client gaining self-knowledge. If a client begins to accuse their therapist of being angry, or cold, or uncaring, or incompetent, the wise therapist, if she knows herself well enough to know that she is not herself angry or cold, or incompetent, will not contradict the client. Rather, the therapist will recognize that the anger and coldness the client sees in her is actually the client's own anger and coldness and fear of being incompetent which the client is afraid to acknowledge. The therapist will encourage her client to become more aware of the anger they see in her because in so doing, the client will become increasingly clear about the content of their projection and so will be taking the first step toward becoming more accurately aware of their self and therefore able to become a more mature and fulfilled person.

That's the first step toward acquiring Socrates' self-knowledge.

Having become aware of some quality of our self through projection, the next step in becoming self-aware is to recognize that the uncomfortable quality we've seen in someone else may actually reside in our own self. Sooner or later, I will realize I have been seeing an unpleasant aspect of myself.

Of course, it is deeply disturbing to discover that the uncomfortable qualities I'm seeing in someone else are actually in myself. Even worse, when I become aware of projecting my feelings onto someone else, I discover that was mistaken—I can't even trust my observations about my self.

No wonder we are uncomfortable as we begin to see what is going on. No wonder we are reluctant to pursue the path of acknowledging the uncomfortable truth about our self.

Our reaction is to feel shame about both these insights, and to deny them.

Freud called this second step, deciding to deny the truth about our self, 'resistance.' I am determined to prove to myself and others that my projection is accurate, and insist those feelings are not in myself but really do belong to someone else. It is an ultimately vain attempt to retain the illusion about myself. I resist the truth.

There is good reason to resist this new knowledge about our self. This new knowledge, that I am the one who is grumpy, destroys the meanings I had built up about myself. And as we have seen, like all humans, I desperately don't want to lose my meaning. I may work hard, and argue hard, and even attack another person for pointing out the truth, all in order to maintain my former meanings, even if they are an illusion. It feels preferable to remain in the illusion about myself than to face the uncomfortable truth that I have undesirable qualities. This resistance to acknowledging the truth about our self is very powerful.

However, to retain any projection indefinitely will result in harm to myself and others. To continue in the projection, I will have to use more and more energy to resist becoming aware that the uncomfortable quality is within myself. In addition, I have to treat others as if they are different from how they really are, and conflict with them will escalate as they refuse to go along with my self-serving illusion about them. Projections can be maintained, but the cost is high.

With this new awareness, I am now caught between living a lie by continuing my projection, or losing my sense of meaning by accepting some uncomfortable truth about myself. It's a conundrum that seems to have no way out.

Fortunately, there is a way out, but it requires a kind of death.

Sooner or later, if we are to become truly alive, we will have to die to the illusion that enabled our projection. The projection will have to die if we are to live more fully.

That's the heart of the secular language we are learning to speak.

We are very close to being fully fluent in secular.

Freud's third step in moving toward self-awareness is 'withdrawal.' 'Withdrawal' has nothing to do with withdrawing from an addiction, or withdrawing from facing an uncomfortable truth about myself, or withdrawing from taking responsibility. Rather 'withdrawal,' as Freud meant it, suggests that we reach out and take hold of the image we had projected onto another person and withdraw, or pull, that projection back into our self where it actually already resides. Sometimes it's called 'reeling in' the projection, or 'pulling the projection back in.' It's the opposite of projecting. In withdrawal, we acknowledge that the movie we saw in someone else is actually inside us. We start looking at that picture where it actually exists: inside *our* self.

The payoff for withdrawing our projection, in spite of how painful it is to face that uncomfortable truth about our self, is that taking the projection back into our self provides us with more meaning than the original projection had provided. The original projection was powerful because it provided us with connection and meaning—the reason I felt grumpiness was because the waiter was grumpy and I was calm and mature. That made perfect sense and provided affirmative meaning for me. Withdrawing the projection is painful because it temporarily removes connection and meaning—I no longer feel mature, and the waiter may turn out to be a more balanced person than I am. That feels like death. And it *is* death: death of an illusion about my self. But withdrawal of the projection offers far greater self-knowledge, meaning, and connection than the projection had given me.

The trade-off is worth it.

It's not fun. It feels like dying to have to admit how immature I am. But then something wonderful and totally unexpected happens.

Withdrawing the projection precipitates the fourth and final step in this process of moving toward self-awareness.

The final step is 'integration.' If I'm able to affirm the truth about uncomfortable parts of myself, and realize I've got some personal growing to do, then I can laugh at myself, make fun of myself, and find myself in warm and affirming relationships with friends, my partner, and others. We can even laugh together about me. To laugh at oneself is one of the marks of maturity, because laughter is the expression of pleasure at finding deeper connection and meaning. It's the adult version of finding out why there is fluff on the road.

What felt like death miraculously becomes joy and life. Maturity, which seemed like such an impossible and terrifying goal for such an immature person as myself, and a virtual guarantee of failure if I tried to become mature, suddenly arrives in me as if from nowhere. It's a wonderful gift effortlessly received. I end up being the sort of mature person I originally but mistakenly assumed I was. Only this time it is real and solid and includes my immaturity. And I can laugh instead of being defensive.

Integrating projections isn't something that happens only once. I continue to project my grumpiness on waiters or people close to me, but after each withdrawal it takes less energy for someone to draw my attention to the fact that it's me that's grumpy. In fact, I sometimes find the projection so familiar that I can identify that its me who is grumpy all by myself! As my projections and their withdrawal and integration continue, my experience of self-awareness deepens and so does my laughter and pleasure in finding meaning in being exactly who I am—someone who sometimes is grumpy!

When I acknowledge that grumpiness is a permanent part of my character, I have integrated it. And grumpiness becomes an odd sort of friend.

I no longer need to eliminate my grumpiness in the way I wanted to eliminate that waiter. Instead, I start to have a conversation with my grumpiness. What do you want, Mr. Grumpiness? And the astonishing response is that grumpiness wants my safety. *I'm there to protect you from dangerous situations by signalling to threatening people that they'd better stay away. I do that because you are such a valuable person.* When I withdraw the projection of grumpiness on others and integrate its truth into myself, I discover I have an absolutely loyal friend, Mr. Grumpiness, who lives within me and who never sleeps and who is never distracted from the task of ensuring I am safe and never stops affirming my value. What a compliment! From the part of me that I couldn't stand! We both receive new life. Integration is complete.

It is a kind of miracle.

It happens regardless of whether I know any of this theory or not.

This integration of new self-awareness into our life is a creative and sometimes ecstatic moment, simultaneously sad and joyful. We have a word for it: 'self-knowledge.' That's what Socrates was on about. We call its acquisition 'maturity.' We experience integration as revelation—the light dawns, our eyes are opened, we feel re-born. Simultaneously, because the projection of our self is no longer getting in the way, we also see other people accurately for the first time—whether therapist, or waiter, or lover; and then we can relate to them as they really are. It is at once both a humbling and exhilarating moment and it is a significant accomplishment in becoming more deeply human.

So far, we've examined projections that arose from uncomfortable parts of our self. But projection can also be a way of dealing with attractive parts of our self that we don't want to face. For example, I may see courage in everyone around me but not in myself, because it may be safer to see myself as cowardly than to take the risk of acting as the courageous person I really am. So, strange as it may seem, I may resist withdrawing my projection of courage on other people so I don't have to see the courage in myself and don't have to act courageously. Life can feel safer that way.

When I was first in love, I experienced in my sweetheart all the things I wished were more developed in myself. No wonder she was so wonderful. She was poised, attractive, strong, courageous, sure of herself, well-organized; a competent leader in the world. She exemplified everything I would have liked to have been but thought I wasn't.

But the qualities I saw in her were the very qualities that were already in my own self, of which I was not yet aware, or of which I preferred to remain unaware. That way I didn't have to take responsibility for acting on them and being myself. No wonder I craved her qualities, fell in love with her, and longed to possess her. Unaware, I made her a screen on to which I projected qualities in myself that I didn't want to be responsible for. Because then I could assimilate those qualities I saw in her without having to undertake the hard work and risk of growing up. The downside was I couldn't take pride in who I was.

As the relationship with my lover grew, and as my lover, to my great frustration, refused to be used as a screen for my projections, I was forced to withdraw my projections from her, and I had to accept that she was significantly different from me and from what I had imagined her to be. And so was I. I began to see her accurately, open to both her strengths and limitations, and simultaneously I started to see myself more accurately and to increasingly accept my own abilities and limitations. This withdrawal of my projections was not easy, but it was the only path to a mature, enduring, and fulfilling relationship in which two real people had the chance to meet and know each other deeply.

This four-step process of projecting, resisting, withdrawing, and integrating is complex and sophisticated and is not learned quickly. Typically it takes humans the first ten years of our life to learn how to project our feelings onto other people. It's only in the second ten years of life, during our teens, that we discover the feelings we had projected onto others were really qualities of our own self. That is why teens are so self-conscious—they are finding, often to their discomfort, they are not who they thought they were. Only after we enter our third decade, as we enter our twenties, are we able to develop the skills of withdrawal and the subsequent integration which gives us maturity and adulthood. Although it may take twenty years to complete all four steps for the first time, we will continue to repeat those steps toward deeper maturity throughout our lives; each time experiencing new life and new depths of relationships and of faith, as if for the first time.

Yes, new depths of faith.

Projection: Rosalind's rocky path to meaning

On Sunday afternoon a week after John's lonely departure from her lecture, Rosalind heard John's car pull in. *He must be coming back home from church.* She glanced out the window and was startled to see him walking toward her house. Down the sidewalk to her front gate, he came. Slowly and deliberately. He let himself into her yard. As he turned to come up her path, she suddenly realized what was going on.

He is coming to tell me how it felt to have been attacked with the full force of scientific skepticism, what it was like to have his belief in God so relentlessly savaged, and to say our pleasant talks across the back fence and in the University Club are over, and he wishes he'd never gone to my lecture and he'll never speak to me again.

With growing dread, Rosalind watched John walk up her path. She could tell from the way he walked, from the fact he didn't look up as he approached her house, from the granite look on his face, that this wasn't going to be a happy visit. It was obvious he was in pain and of course, as she had already realized, she had been the cause.

As she moved to her door in response to the bell, she braced herself for her own inward attack of shame and guilt and failure, as well as for his outward attack on everything she stood for. She felt the anger rising in her. People had done this to her before—her parents had been angry at her when she had left their faith, and she still felt her own anger toward them for their rejection of all that enthralled her. *Religious people are all like that—they hold a stubborn impervious loyalty to their projection of God and they threaten emotional or even physical violence against anyone who challenges their projections.* She'd experienced that before and now it was happening again.

It all made perfect sense: that evening at the University Club when he hadn't laughed at her jokes, his decision to leave without her as soon as her lecture was over, and now his cold and deliberate walk up her path. It was perfectly clear what it all meant. In his good-natured way, he couldn't have refused her invitation to her lecture and to drinks, but clearly, he wanted no more to do with science and certainly nothing to do with someone who had betrayed his trust so callously.

No wonder he wants no more to do with me. I've pulled the rug out from under his entire world. Religious people can't take challenges. They just get defensive. Thank goodness I'm finally seeing him for who he really is.

She wondered if she should just pretend to be out. After a while he'd get the message.

She also knew she could draw on her own rage to attack any he brought. Maybe that's what made her answer the bell instead of pretending not to be home. She steeled herself for the blast of his righteous anger and for her own response in kind.

So, his first words sounded like utter gibberish.

It was as if he wasn't even speaking English.

"Look, I'm sorry if I've upset you," he said, "I hope you'll forgive me."

She was dumbfounded.

Was this some kind of cruel sarcasm?

Summary

Humans use a four-step process to satisfy our craving for meaning and connection with our inner self. We first become aware of some undesirable inner quality of our own self by seeing that quality in someone else. We call that first step 'projection.' At some point, the truth dawns on us that we might have been seeing something in our own character which we had hidden from our self. This is an uncomfortable insight, and the decision not to accept the insight is the second step, 'resistance.' The third step is to acknowledge that the quality we saw really is inside our own self—that's 'withdrawing the projection.' As our projection is withdrawn, the fourth and final step of 'integration' happens almost magically as we affirm the projection's truth and celebrate it as a valuable part of our self, and behave differently. We've become more human and have more meaning.

The four steps from projection to integration form the underlying grammar of the secular language in which faith needs to become fluent if we are to communicate within secular culture.

As we will shortly discover, this process of dying to illusion in order to gain self-knowledge applies no less to our experience of God and faith. It may be that the secular world is pointing, even if unknowingly, to the central element of the Christian faith. That irony will require the faith itself to die in order to live. But what a life that will be! John is on the verge of speaking secular completely fluently, and through that language, something is about to speak to him more deeply than he's ever heard faith speak before.

CHAPTER 8
Graduating in Disbelief:
Why we Invented God

Varieties of religious experience

For summer jobs during my studies, I worked in mines in northern Canada. It wasn't particularly dramatic, mostly I carried boxes, unloaded trucks by hand, occasionally drove semi-trailers short distances and discovered I enjoyed the workers who drifted nomad-like from mining camp to mining camp all across the north.

One day off, I decided to walk off into the bush in the Cassiar mountains along a heavy equipment trail, carved out of the wilderness by bulldozers to place drilling equipment for seeking ore from which a new mine could be developed. Nobody was around. As I left the camp, total silence closed around me so intensely it was as if I could hear it roaring. The green hills on either side of the valley where I was walking seemed like a living creature, silently breathing. I stood in awe, aware for the first time of the grandeur, the silent power, the omnipresence of a reality that included me but that had been a living presence carpeting the hills all around me in that exact valley for who knows how many millions of years before humans arrived. Too bad Wordsworth grew up in the cultivated English countryside and only had fields of daffodils near Tintern Abbey to expose him to an experience which he named "...a sense sublime / Of something far more deeply interfused...."[1] If he'd lived in the powerful wilderness of northern British Columbia he'd have been stunned into silence by something really overpowering. It was a sense of being immersed in an all-surrounding presence. Disturbing, frightening, electrifying, ecstatic, joyful and disquietingly intimate all at once.

I was ordained within sight of that valley, in a tiny church in the mining town of Cassiar where I was employed for several summers.

The night before my ordination John Frame, the bishop of Yukon, whom I had asked to ordain me, took me aside to go through the next day's ordination service. He wasn't concerned about the mechanics of the liturgy. What he wanted was to ensure my scripted responses would be genuine and carefully considered when he put the formal required questions to me next morning in the service. The various questions, about whether I believed the scriptures and the creeds, were straightforward. I agreed with them in general and knew I wasn't supposed to get into specifics about the varieties of interpretation of faith and scripture.

But then he came to the question about my calling. He read it to me from the official book he would use the next day.

"Do you believe you are truly called by God to this office and ministry?"[2]

There was silence while I considered it.

"Do I believe I have been called by God?"

I had to be honest. I had absolutely no idea.

So that's what I told the bishop. I'd tried to set up a community among the workers in their bunkhouses where I also lived, but after long gruelling shifts of intensely heavy labour, there wasn't much time or energy left. But if the church would arrange for me to be paid, then I'd have the time and energy to really work at helping people understand the revolutionary God who loves us so much. Ordination was the way to get approved and paid, so that's why I had

1   William Wordsworth, "Lines Composed a Few Miles above Tintern Abbey, On Revisiting the Banks of the Wye during a Tour. July 13, 1798"
2   *The Book of Common Prayer and Administration of the Sacraments [...] According to the Use of The Anglican Church of Canada.* (Anglican Book Centre, 1962). p. 640. Title abbreviated.

asked him to ordain me. But did God want me to do this? I'd never had a word whispered in my ear, I'd never had a red telephone on which God called me up. I'd had no revelatory experience. So, "No," I told the bishop, I had no idea whether God was calling me.

After a pause, the bishop asked me if I thought I was doing this for ulterior motives. I thought not—the congregations in the north paid less than anywhere else in Canada, and they were mostly so small there could be no reason to do this other than because I wanted to share what I knew about God. The bishop seemed satisfied.

Next morning in the service, in a loud voice, the bishop asked each question required by the ordination ritual. Finally, he came to the problematic one. In full voice, he asked, "Do you truly believe you are called by God to this office and ministry?" Then he leaned forward, and whispered so only I could hear, "As you and I have discussed it." And so, this pastoral bishop, a deeply committed conservative believer, made it possible for me to answer in the affirmative, and for him to proceed with the ordination. He had given me space to question the official projections upon God, and to affirm what I thought was the deep truth that lay behind those projections. The service proceeded and I was ordained without a hitch.

Five hundred miles north of that valley was the first church in which the bishop placed me. It stood on the bank of the Stewart River, a large tributary of the Yukon River. It might have held fifty people, packed full. On the east wall of St. Mary with St. Mark, Mayo, above the altar, is a traditional Victorian stained-glass window of Jesus holding a lamb in his arms. There were, of course, no lambs within a thousand miles, and the First Nations people had never seen one outside stained-glass windows. When I spent time alone in that church following my ordination, I realized I had as little understanding of priesthood as the First Nations had of lambs.

What made it worse was that the stained-glass Jesus had large liquid black eyes that bore into my soul and knew that I knew nothing whatsoever about being a priest. Whenever I went into that church, and wherever I moved within the church, those eyes never left me. It was both disturbing and comforting. The projection of Jesus gazing at me and seeing into my soul was powerful and expressed the truth that I was, as I am still, intimately present to some deep presence of reality. Even though I knew, and still know, virtually nothing about it.

In that same community, some years after my ordination, a First Nations elder told me he had been out hunting as a young man before white people arrived and he had seen in the bush a caribou carrying a cross on its head. He looked me straight in the eye and explained that he and his people had known all about Jesus long before I and my people had arrived. I knew immediately this was his way of claiming dignity and equality with white people and their superior missionary proclamations. I also knew this wasn't just a made-up story. He was telling me a truth. But he was sophisticated enough to tell it to me in a form I could understand. This elder knew that there are a variety of projections through which the deep truth of faith can be understood. He cut right through all the sociological explanations and simply asked me to participate in his culture's projection. He was asking me, a recent settler, to take the vast experience of First Nations seriously.

The variety of these religious experiences was a variety of projections.

In that silent valley where I walked on a day off from my summer job, I projected conscious presence upon the vast forest. In the ordination, I withdrew my projection upon God and affirmed I knew nothing about God and whether God had called me. Maybe that was the call. To learn that I knew nothing about God. In that first church, I projected awareness upon the stained-glass window, and received comfort and challenge in return. In his simple log house, that elder taught me how to integrate his culture's projections and receive new life and truth. And how to integrate my own culture's projections.

Becoming skilful with projections is central to becoming fully human.

Having understood the central drive of individual humans to find meaning, we are ready to hear the central message of this grammar of secular language.

We are close to secular fluency!

Projection: from pain to joy

As Rosalind opened the door, she steeled herself for the blast of John's righteous anger at her having undermined his faith, and for her own raging response in defence.

So, his first words were utter gibberish.

It was as if he wasn't even speaking English.

"Hi. Look, I'm sorry if I've upset you," he said, "I hope you'll forgive me."

She was dumbfounded. Was this some kind of cruel sarcasm?

The gibberish continued. His words continued meaningless.

"I really haven't thanked you properly for having me to your lecture. I've never had a conversation about religion and science with a scientist and her colleagues, and I've never been to a science lecture before and I've spent all week thinking about it. It was fascinating and wonderful! What I really want to say is that you took a big risk inviting someone like me into your world, and I really appreciate it. I want to thank you for that. Sorry not to have talked with you after your lecture, but I needed time to think."

He stuck out his hand. It was lucky he did, because shaking it gave her something mindless to do while she got her breath back and picked up the ruins of what she thought had been going on. For a split second she regretted his complete absence of anger and recrimination. At least she would have known how to respond to that effectively.

She had no idea how to respond.

But with his next words it only got worse.

"I really appreciate your inviting me into your world, and.... well, I wondered if you would like to explain to me more of what you were talking about."

He couldn't mean that.

She was still projecting her rage onto him.

Rosalind stood at her door dumbfounded. She had destroyed her neighbour's world and shredded the most important meanings in his life with her onslaught of science, and here he was asking to come in and spend more time with her. She'd love for him to come in, more than anything. She'd come to respect and care for him, but nothing was making any sense. She still wasn't getting the meaning. He couldn't be meaning this. *Why is he saying this? What's going on?*

"Ah!" she said. But it was really just her first breath since she'd opened the door. "Come on in and I'll get you some coffee." Then a brilliant thought—get the focus back on him. She took a big chance. "Tell me what you thought about my lecture and our conversation at the University Club."

So, he did.

She busied herself with the coffee, thinking how bizarre this whole thing had become. *I'm making coffee for this religious guy in my own house and a moment ago I was ready to kill him?* She wondered if she knew herself at all.

"You wonder what I thought about your lecture. Well, I can tell you now. I was upset. When I visited your work and talked to your colleagues, the topics were somewhat technical, so while I knew there were some pretty strong challenges to faith in those conversations, I didn't really take it all in. But when we went out for drinks, every argument I could muster to support faith was demolished by you and your friends. It got worse when you explained it in your lecture with such clear examples. I realized you had thought deeply about this and that you and your colleagues were dismantling my entire experience of God.

"But then I thought to myself, you aren't doing this for malicious purposes— it was clear you weren't deliberately attacking religion just for the fun of it—you were exploring the implications of the truths you've discovered and being loyal to the facts. And strangely, I felt respected by your refusal to coddle me. If truth dismantles my God, then my God must have been too small. My tradition has always equated God with truth. So somehow the God who is truth cannot be in opposition to what's true. No matter what it is that's true. Somehow, there has to be a connection between faith and science. The logic you are all following, disproving God, has to mean something. Either that, or science is somehow profoundly wrong about everything, but that doesn't make sense either.

"I don't get it. Which is why I want to talk more about this with you."

She saw how deeply he was struggling so she stayed quiet.

After a silence, he took a big risk.

He asked her what she thought the point of religion is.

"You're the one who specializes in making connections and finding meanings, so what do you think about religious faith? So far, I've been putting out my arguments, and you and your colleagues have been making mincemeat out of them, but I want to know what you think."

Was that what he felt like in her presence? Mincemeat? She must be more terrible than she'd imagined.

She also realized what a compliment it was that he would trust her that much. Trust the person who'd dismantled everything that made meaning for him? How could he do that?

"You really want to know what I think about religion and its meaning?"

"Yes."

That was all; just, "Yes."

Something in her leapt at such courage.

So, Rosalind plunged right in. She told John what she thought is the meaning of religion.

Why cultures project and what that has to do with God

"Religion isn't just a mistake about whether God exists; the belief about God has a purpose. There is good reason for religion, but its purpose has now been accomplished. Our culture is moving on. As it should."

Rosalind laid out her thoughts.

"Here's what I think the purpose of religion is and where God came from.

"Projection is the process by which we humans satisfy our craving for meaning and connection within our own self. Projection and its withdrawal are essential for humans to know ourselves and to know others. Without projection we would never see our own qualities and without withdrawal and integration we'd never embrace them as our own. That ability to have self-knowledge is fundamental to forming significant relationships and being able to plan cooperatively which is essential for the survival of humanity. But becoming self-aware is a very complex process.

"So, it makes sense that cultures haven't left us to fumble our way on our own to navigate this process of projection, leaving each individual to rediscover the process from scratch. Instead, cultures encourage and guide their members in the skills of projection and integration.

That way, their members become self-aware more quickly. Cultures that didn't encourage the process of projection, withdrawal, and integration would be at a disadvantage compared to those that did. They would easily be overtaken by people who had more developed self-awareness and the consequent abilities to organize and cooperate. So, one of the fundamental roles of any culture is to support the journey to self-awareness. Cultures do this by guiding the process of projection.

"In time of war, for example, it becomes particularly clear how a culture guides the projections of its citizens. During the Second World War, our culture encouraged us to project our anger, heartlessness, and deceit onto our enemies. Movies made in Allied countries during the Second World War uniformly portray German and Japanese soldiers as implacably cruel, menacing, and untrustworthy, as if our enemies were inhuman monsters. The Axis countries did exactly the same in projections about us. Yet the truth is, it would have been easy for people in Allied countries, by simply talking to their enemies, to determine German and Japanese soldiers were as deeply caring, sacrificial, and as warmly human as Allied soldiers. Yet no Allied movie during the war ever showed a German or Japanese soldier risking his life to save a comrade. No wartime movie ever dared show a German or Japanese family grieving the death of their son or daughter from Allied bombing, in spite of the fact such behaviour among our enemies was commonplace. Our culture made an absolute demand that we project evil upon our enemies. Speaking well of Japanese or Germans during the war, or even being descended from those countries, could precipitate severe consequences. Our culture required that we all participate in those projections. And almost everyone did.

"Our culture has now begun to withdraw those projections so it is obvious to us, long after the war, that we deliberately portrayed our enemies as savagely cruel, by projecting onto our enemies the very qualities we most despised in ourselves. We used that technique to mobilize our own cruelty in order to kill our enemies. That was a deeply evil process.

"We were guilty of exactly the inhuman qualities of which we accused our enemies. Those inhuman qualities we saw in our enemies were so believable precisely because they were our own. We were aware of cruelty but could not face the fact that the cruelty was inside us; so, we defended ourselves from that truth by projecting our cruelty upon our enemies and simultaneously gave ourselves permission to enact that cruelty upon them. You can see," Rosalind concluded, "how powerful cultural projection can be."

"That's still true," John responded. "Contemporary movies, and media reporting, about international politics portray the family lives of our leaders in detail and show our leaders struggling with complex moral issues, taking risks to be generous and caring, and engaged in sensitive relationships with their own families, but never show foreign leaders exhibiting such behaviour. Foreign leaders are presented as devious, untrustworthy, and always wanting to take advantage; exactly the qualities in ourselves and our culture we don't want to acknowledge."

Rosalind agreed. "You're right."

She continued. "Not only do cultures manage our projections, they also manage the way in which we withdraw our projections. The former Allied countries now embrace immigrants from, and encourage cultural exchanges with, our former enemies. We now condemn the kind of prejudice which was commonplace during the war—we forbid insulting epithets that we widely used and encouraged at that time. We apologize for the internment of Japanese Canadians and the cruel treatment of Germans who remained in Canada after the war. We are proud of our apologies to First Nations who suffered under our projections upon them of our own brokenness, although our support of their recovery from our culture's abuse is still minimal. Not many decades ago such apologies would have been unthinkable. These changes indicate that our culture is beginning to withdraw some of its former projections.

"Integration of those projections is the final step to cultural maturity. However, full integration of that self-knowledge is only just beginning. As one might expect when dealing with those projections, resistance remains strong against acknowledging our projections and that resistance is expressed through intolerant political movements and glacially slow acceptance of the need for restitution.

"There is a modern temptation, and yes I get the irony!" Rosalind said smiling, "That we retain the illusion we are all newly generous and inclusive people. But withdrawal and integration require we acknowledge with humility that these changes aren't the result of enlightened opinions arrived at by newly generous individuals. The truth is our culture is managing the process. It is our culture, not a general moral improvement by each individual, that has moved us even this small step towards integration and full responsibility for our past actions."

"All that is fascinating," John replied. "But I don't see what it has to do with religion. That's what you said you were going to tell me about. I think you got sidetracked into finding connections and meanings in sociology and politics and psychology!"

He took a chance. "Typical scientist!" he teased.

"You hope! Nope. I'm getting to the really interesting part. I wanted to be clear about what's going on when cultures manage our projections because projections are central to the emergence of human consciousness.

"And religion is the foundation to our becoming self aware and conscious and fully human."

"You think religion is that important?"

"Yes."

"So what happened?" John wondered.

"The gods gave birth to us."

John was startled. "I thought you were a determined atheist. What happened to all that rejection of religion? Suddenly you've got religion?"

"Yes, but probably not in the way you think." She smiled wryly.

Pre-animist projection

"Here's how I think religion's central role in the development of human consciousness may have emerged. The first step of these cultural projections probably took place in the very early history of the human species although, as is so often the case in the development of life, the very earliest stages are forever hidden from us. Cultures developing this first stage of human self-awareness have long since been superseded by subsequent stages and so no longer exist as extant cultures, as far as we know. Nevertheless, it is possible to undertake informed speculation about the first stage of cultural projections about self-awareness. We can make a reasonable supposition, based upon patterns of cultural and personal development for which we do have historical experience.

"Here's an imaginative reconstruction of a possible 'pre-animist' culture'."[3]

> *My mate had chosen a campsite with a good view. There were no lions as far as we could see, and after listening in silence for a long time, we were pretty sure there were none hiding nearby. If there were, they weren't talking among themselves. Thoughtful trees gave us shade. We could hear a river not far away chattering to us so we would know where it lived. This campsite was a safe place to sleep. During the night the moon took care of us by shining particularly brightly so it would be easier for us to see if a lion approached. We slept well. In the morning my mate went in search of food and I took my daughter by the hand and we set off to ask the river for water.*
>
> *Half-way to the river my daughter suddenly fell to the ground crying and bleeding. After I checked to see she was not seriously injured, I turned to see who had done this terrible thing. There, crouching in the middle of the path, was a stone who had deliberately reached up and attacked my daughter. I was very angry with it. I told the stone in no uncertain terms how shameful it was to take advantage of a little girl. Soon my daughter stopped crying and came back to stand next to me, drawing herself up to her full small height to show the stone that she, too, was displeased with it. The stone kept very still, cowering in front of us, even when I stamped my foot near it. But I knew it was afraid. Just to be sure,*

---

3   See glossary for "'pre-animist' culture.

I told it off again and turned my back to shame it and to let the lesson sink in. I hoped this insolent stone would be sufficiently disgraced that it would never forget the lesson.

In silence my daughter and I continued on our way to the river who was generous to us with her water.

Every day, as long as we stayed at that campsite, I took my daughter along the same path to the river. But although that cruel stone continued to make its campsite on the path, it had learned its lesson well and not once did it ever again dare to attack my daughter.

I am so glad I was present when that stone first bullied my daughter—she was too small then, all by herself, to demand the stone respect her. I'm old now, but I'm proud because now that babies have come out of her, too, I've seen her protect her babies by disciplining cruel stones and insisting they obey her. And they always do. I'm so proud of her, a smart, strong woman who knows how to discipline irresponsible stones.[4]

"Seen from the perspective of our culture," Rosalind explained, "it is a peculiar world in which adults successfully reprimand stones as if they were cruel little conscious beings, and where stones listen and obey. But if we retreat into our modern psychological perspective and explain the happy ending by pointing out that the mother was unconsciously but effectively drawing the little girl's attention to the location of the hazardous stone, we miss the point.

"The story asks us to enter into a time when adults experienced every object in the world as conscious, even stones on a path. The point is not that this ancient family is naïvely imagining stones are conscious, but that their culture is taking the unprecedented step of enabling its members to become aware of the fact of consciousness. People did that by projecting their own consciousness upon external objects. So, everything seems conscious to them.

"This hypothetical culture had taken an amazing step toward human self-awareness. It does not matter at this stage that they are mistaken about the location of consciousness. The entire outer world provided the screen upon which those early humans could project their consciousness. Since they

---

4   This proposal is elaborated from a suggestion of the cosmologist Edward Harrison in his book *Masks of the Universe*, Edward Harrison, *Masks of the Universe: Changing Ideas on the Nature of the Cosmos* (Cambridge University Press, 2003), p. 15 ff.

projected consciousness everywhere. In their experience, consciousness was the primary reality of all existence. This was the first and foundational step to humanity becoming self-aware, to becoming truly human.

"What was the very first occasion on which some human noticed there was such a thing as consciousness, even if she saw it in a stone? What incident prompted that stupendous discovery? We will never know. But by the time we meet this hypothetical family, the awareness of consciousness has spread to the entire culture. Everyone who is born into this culture is aware of consciousness. Every single event, from being tripped by a stone, to being warmed by the sun, or being enlightened by the moon, or drinking from a stream, is experienced as a conscious decision on the part of the objects with which humans interact.

"Our wry saying 'The deliberate obstinacy of inanimate objects' still retains for us a hint of this ancient worldview. Indeed, to us, a world in which stones deliberately trip people seems mad. Yet such a world was the essential corner-stone for our own."

"Curious," said John. "Consciousness everywhere. Reminds me of the way in which your colleagues were speculating that consciousness could be emerging everywhere in the universe."

"I doubt that ancient culture had some special insight about that," Rosalind replied, "but it is a suggestive parallel. Sort of like the discovery of fractal geom-etry—where similar patterns emerge at every dimension, such as branching leaves being similar to the branching of the tree itself. Who knows? Maybe there is some deep connection.

"Anyway, we still experience this kind of pre-animist projection. And we love it! Why do people go to movies? Nobody really believes the movie theatre actually holds intergalactic spaceships, rampaging monsters, or glamorous lovers. But we delight in being encouraged to project our awareness of certain feelings—that actually lie within our selves—onto a white wall in a large dark room. Lest we underestimate the power of projection, we should remember that our projected feelings upon a white wall are so intense that people actually weep or laugh or cringe or fall in love with what is only a projection, forgetting for an hour or two that all they are doing is sitting in a dark room watching a wall. We think, for an hour or two, that the wall is alive and conscious. The projection is very effective: we don't think, 'It's fun projecting my feelings on a white wall.' Instead, we immerse ourselves in the experience as if it were completely real and are very disappointed if that experience of the wall being alive doesn't happen. We all love going back to the pre-animist world in which even a wall is brimming with consciousness.

"Maybe we enjoy movies so much because being aware of consciousness provides us with additional connections to our inner self, and as we've seen, humans crave connections and love finding them. Enjoying the sense of consciousness in a wall increases that pleasure."

"But," John asked, "why would an entire culture encourage such projections?"

"That's basic Evolution 101," said Rosalind. "As individual members of a society became aware of consciousness, they would accrue significant advantages from this new awareness. One advantage would be the ability to be aware of other people's self-awareness and therefore to have an increased ability to predict other people's behaviour. Such people could take leadership roles and over time the whole population of such a culture would have developed that sophisticated social skill. Since to be human is to be self-aware, and to be self-aware is advantageous for planning and survival, cultures that encourage their members to become conscious of being conscious are more likely to thrive. When it became a cultural norm, it became real for everyone in that culture. Just as real as did the projected experience of unmitigated cruelty by our enemies became real for us in wartime."

Withdrawal of pre-animist projection

Rosalind continued. "Here's how the withdrawal of that projection might have happened for pre-animists.

"As soon as the projection became a cultural norm and the people of that culture had become aware of the fact of consciousness, their self-awareness could become more complete by withdrawing the projection and integrating its insight into their lives. Only then can the members of the culture take ownership of their own consciousness as a quality of themselves, and become even more effective in their relationships.

"There is a significant advantage to members of a pre-animist culture when someone discovers that stones are not conscious beings. Knowing stones are not conscious saves a great deal of time and energy a person would otherwise have to expend in holding conversations with stones, and it increases that person's power when they realize stones have predictable and unalterable qualities that allow them to be used as tools or building materials or weapons. At some point, when sufficient numbers of people in a pre-animist society withdrew their projection of consciousness upon every object, it became a cultural norm to accept that stones are not tiny conscious living beings. Instead, they are simply inanimate objects. That would have been a revolutionary discovery.

"But most importantly, as the projection of consciousness upon inanimate objects was withdrawn, the people of that culture would become aware of their own consciousness, and they could begin to integrate it into their lives and become even more effective in their relationships.

"This withdrawal of projections would not have been easy, just as it was not easy for our society to own the fact that the cruelty we saw in our former enemies was the projection of that quality in ourselves. At first, discovering stones are not conscious would have been experienced as a painful contradiction at the centre of their world. Anyone brave enough to point this out would have been shouted down as an atheist and a thousand convincing examples would have been given in an attempt to keep the old worldview intact. Sound familiar?"

"Yes," said John. He was thinking of his own desperate attempt to present arguments proving the existence of God.

"After all," continued Rosalind, "it remained true that children were still injured by stones—there was no question the child cried, and you could see the wound, exactly the sort of wound a cruel stone might deliberately inflict. The resistance to withdrawing the experience of universal consciousness would have been powerful. But over time, and in spite of determined resistance, the projection of universal consciousness would gradually have been withdrawn as the evidence mounted that stones were just stones and not small conscious beings.

"While the projections of consciousness upon physical objects were being withdrawn, people of that culture would have felt consciousness itself was dying. The world that had been suffused with consciousness was turning into an inanimate world where everything was just dead. It would have felt utterly meaningless and increasingly frightening and would have led to a crisis of credibility for the former culture."

"That's how many religious people feel about a world without God," said John.

"Exactly," responded Rosalind.

Animist projection

"Go on," John requested.

"When pre-animist societies withdrew their projection of consciousness upon every object in the world, their members would have become aware of an aspect of human consciousness which was new to them. They would discover that each person has their own unique personality—their individual way of expressing their consciousness. This discovery means that each person would have to relate in a variety of different ways to other peoples' varieties of personalities. Being able to relate differently and effectively to each diverse person is a skill that makes teamwork possible and that would be a substantial benefit to the community.

"You won't be surprised that in order for each person to become aware of their own style of consciousness, they would first have to project the variety of consciousnesses onto a screen. The resulting culture is the animist worldview of which we have ample experience.[5]

"In the animist worldview, consciousness no longer exists everywhere, but is associated only with particular objects or living creatures that have some special significance to the culture. Each of these objects has its own unique style of consciousness. This individual unique consciousness is what we now call a 'spirit' and thus we call the culture an 'animist,' or 'spirit' culture.

"Here's how it might have felt to have lived in such a culture."

It had been a long winter with deep snow, and I was glad now I had made myself unpopular with the young men, insisting they hunt moose longer into the winter than they had wanted to. Each moose had easily outrun the hunters at first, but since the young men were on snowshoes and could walk on top of the snow and out-manoeuvre the moose, forcing it to wade through deep snow drifts, the hunters could gradually exhaust the moose. This could take days.

When the hunters were as near to exhaustion as the moose, the spirit of each moose had generously laid down in the snow so the hunters could walk right up to it, kneel down on the snow next to its great head, and ask it the ultimate question. Would it willingly give up its life for the village? The moose would look directly at the hunters with its great liquid eyes and make some small movement. If the movement indicated "Yes," the hunters gave it their gratitude and received its life. Which would become their own and save the village from starvation. But if the movement indicated "No," the hunters respected that decision and risked

5   See glossary

their lives, and those of everyone in the village, made the moose comfortable so it could regain its strength and then moved off to allow the moose to recover, and began looking for the tracks of another moose.

This winter many moose had said "Yes" and the village had thanked them all. We had come through the winter well, and with luck we would have much to eat through the spring and summer. There had been great feasting and joy and praise for the young hunters.

But now in the spring it was clear something was very wrong. Earlier in the day the children had come running to say that the river was undermining its banks, and now the women reported it was flooding into some of their houses. I ran down to the river to see for myself, and indeed the blocks of spring ice had ceased to move. The river spirit had decided to bunch himself up in front of our village. As I watched, the water was rising fast up the bank. If nothing was done we would lose everything—stored food, our fire, our shelters, perhaps even the trees would be torn up by the river spirit attacking us with his enormous blocks of ice.

Spirits can be frightening. I wouldn't know how to talk to this one, and this spirit would never listen to me anyway. I'm too small a person. Our only hope was our ancient elder. Thank goodness he hadn't died last winter, or there would be nobody to talk to the river spirit for us. Because he was deaf I had to shout to explain what was wrong, and I led him by the hand to where he could see the river. There he stood, at first in silence, shaking, but soon moaning louder and louder in a language we had all heard him use before, but that none of us knew. The river spirit must have been wrestling with him because the shaking got so bad we had to hold him up. The river spirit was shouting back at him with great cracking noises threatening death to our village. One of the young men was so frightened he fell in a faint beside the old man. But still the river spirit kept rising and threatening to destroy us.

When he could speak between gasps, the old man told us what was wrong. The river spirit had seen how well we had supplied ourselves with food from the moose we had killed last winter. The river spirit himself was hungry, and if we did not share willingly he would punish us for our pride and selfishness in having looked after ourselves while we cared nothing for him. He would take everything from us. The river spirit was demanding we share our food.

Dried meat and fish, skins, blankets, berries, even necklaces and pendants we threw into the river. If the river spirit thought we were full of pride and selfishness, we would do anything to prove him wrong.

Yet the waters still rose. Did the river spirit need even more from us?

And then, with an enormous crash, the river spirit split the ice apart and with a sigh of satisfaction lowered himself silently back down the banks, taking with him all the gifts we had showered upon him. Within minutes the river regained its usual level and the blocks of ice floated silently away.

The old man died later that year. The young man who fainted was never the same again; he shakes at every loud noise and speaks the old man's mumbling language. We are sure he can talk to the spirits.

Every spring now we are careful not to give the river spirit the impression we are proud or selfish and so we throw food and blankets into the river every year. And never again has the river spirit threatened our village.

We are so lucky to have a young man who can speak to spirits. We look after him very carefully. There's no knowing when we may need him to speak to the spirits for us.

"In the culture of an animist worldview, projections of consciousness are still encouraged, but in animism it is not just the bare fact of consciousness that is being brought to awareness, it is the behaviour of individual consciousnesses that is the focus of the cultural projection.

"In animist culture two important developments have taken place. Firstly, not all physical objects receive projections. The objects upon which projections are made tend to be living or moving, since movement suggests life and therefore consciousness. Small stones strewed along a path, or little streams, are not experienced as having consciousness. But large rivers or overhanging boulders, or significant animals are. These centres of consciousness are not experienced as being identical with the physical objects with which they are associated, as they were in the pre-animist culture, but individual consciousnesses, projected in the form of spirits, are intimately related to individual significant objects.

"The second development that characterizes animism is that the spirits— the various centres of consciousness—have personal motivations, individual personalities, and a life-story of their own. The spirit of a river has the character of sudden flood, the spirit of a large rock has the character of unpredictable and overwhelming force or alternatively, of refuge and safety, and the spirit of the raven has the character of a trickster. The association of particular types of consciousness with the habits of particular animals or objects is likely the way in which humanity became consciously aware of the variety of characters and personalities present in the human community.

"In such a worldview, spirits can be approached for favours, or can even be considered equals, as when the spirit of an animal is thanked for allowing itself to be hunted and for giving its life for the human community. Intimate knowledge of the detailed character of each spirit is essential for human survival.

"Experiencing this diversity in the spirits was the first step toward awareness of the diversity of human character. Thus, the characters of various spirits range from being kindly to malevolent, from being saviours from starvation to being impassive, from being upholders of morality to being tricksters and deceivers. This is exactly the range of human motivation these more complex societies were learning to manage among their own members.

"Not only individuals but groups also have personalities. To function well, a tribal society needs to know how to manage both. Entire clans could identify their own personalities with a projection upon totems and with the spirit of that totem: with Bear, Eagle, Killer Whale, Wolf, or Raven, to name but a few.

"In the animist experience, spirits require us to negotiate our priorities with theirs if we are to be in productive relationship with the wider world. We must ask the spirit of a moose for permission to kill it, or ask the spirit of the clouds to give us rain, or ask the spirit of the earth to make us fertile. In animist culture we can no longer assume food, rain, and fertility will always be showered automatically on us as was the case in pre-animist cultures where humans were surrounded by a diffuse all-embracing consciousness. Instead, in animist culture we engage with respect in teamwork and negotiation with the spirits to achieve our needs. An animist culture teaches its members how to disengage from their own immediate needs and how to engage with the needs and desires of the spirits.

"Modern westerners delight in temporarily entering the animist world of spirits. Mature adults receive a sense of healing, peacefulness, and belonging, in the presence of the grandeur and mystery of nature. And although it is metaphoric, it's not much of an exaggeration for an adult to say that the trees spoke to him after having received a renewed sense of peace or wonder while walking in a forest. Spirits are still important to us. Members of our culture wonder if cold scientific analysis and destruction of spirits has destroyed imagination and wonder in the modern world."

"Why would an animist culture arise at all?" John asked. "Why not become directly aware of the variety of human personality? Why make it all so much more complicated with a whole additional world of spirits?"

Rosalind explained, "Perhaps the full experience of individualized consciousness would have implied cultural chaos if every person in your community suddenly had their own independent motivation and just acted upon it. How could teamwork function if suddenly everyone had different goals? The society would self-destruct. The projection of negotiating with spirits enabled people to gradually understand the unpredictable personalities and how to deal with interpersonal issues among the members of your own community.

"But, as rewarding as full integration ultimately is, there would have been resistance to integrating the former pre-animist projection. A pre-animist culture would be astonished and terrified at the temerity with which animists picked up stones and broke them to form tools. At every moment, the pre-animists would expect the stones to hit back with deadly aim for being treated with such contempt.

"Animists, on the other hand, encountering a pre-animist culture, would laugh at such childish attitudes. It is possible the animists would discover they could use the pre-animists' fears to enslave them by telling them, for example, that if they didn't obey as slaves, the animists could instruct a group of stones to inflict terrible wounds on the pre-animists. The animists, too, might use the pre-animists as a screen onto which to project their own secret fear of having violated nature when their culture removed consciousness from physical objects.

"Terrified that their world was being destroyed, as indeed it was, the pre-animists might well have fought back with violence. This would only confirm the worst fears of the animists that the spirits were out of control, and so the tension between the two cultures could escalate with tragic consequences. All such transitions between projections have the potential for misunderstanding, suspicion and danger."

"That feels," said John, "not unlike the war that is going on between the cultures of faith and science in our day. Each feels itself to be in a life-and-death struggle for survival. It can feel violent."

"That's right," replied Rosalind. "Violence isn't new to faith. Resistance is a potent force. When a culture resists integrating new knowledge that's the equivalent of how an individual resists the implications of discovering their own projection."

"Just as I did," Rosalind said self-consciously, "when I thought you had come to tell me you'd never talk to me again!"

"You thought that?" John suddenly realized for Rosalind to admit to discomfort about having projected such feelings upon him, she must care deeply. He was glad she continued perhaps too quickly and he didn't need to respond.

Withdrawal of animist projection

"In time," Rosalind was explaining, "as the human population grew and cities emerged, it would have become crucially important to understand how entire cities and even groups of cities interact. People would have begun to notice that certain types of behaviour, especially in the large-scale human world, could no longer be understood as the actions of spirits.

"Sometimes, even though my city or my warriors are obviously better prepared for battle than those we attacked, we were defeated. Why? Sometimes the person I have fallen in love with rejects me, even though I have provided every possible inducement. He may even couple with someone utterly inferior to me. How could such a thing be? Why would that happen?

The issues of which the classical world was becoming aware—outward large-scale interactions between cities and entire cultures, and the inward large-scale histories of the human heart—could no longer be adequately explained by spirits associated with individual objects or animals. The canvas upon which the dynamics of this much wider political and interpersonal world were being played out was just too big for the spirits of the animist world.

"The spirits of trees and animals that had inhabited the world of animist cultures would then have seemed simply silly in the face of forces that could influence the course of international history, decide the outcome of entire cities in battle, or direct the mysterious course of one's life and relationships.

"It would have been disturbing to discover," Rosalind continued, "that one had responsibility to pilot one's entire life, or even guide the interactions of multiple cities and cultures."

Olympic god projection

"Enacting continent-wide responsibilities would be far easier if one had a vantage point from which to survey the entire sweep of political history. To exercise power on such a grand scale, the spirits had to be re-located somewhere from which the entire world could be seen and supervised. Such abilities and responsibilities were so much more powerful than those of spirits that they had to be carried by a new projection and be given a more prestigious name. The ancient world called them 'gods' and they lived on Mount Olympus from which vantage point they could supervise the entire world.

"Unlike the animist spirits, the Greek polytheistic gods lived lives of full social interaction among themselves, and could influence the personal motivations of members of ancient society as well as direct the course of international events.

"Let me paint you another scene," Rosalind continued.

> *Five thousand of us had been pressed into labour to repair the Tiber's banks. Caesar was building on to the Capital again and the last thing he wanted was another flood. Neither did any of us, and we willingly worked under the direction of Caesar's skilled engineers.*
>
> *Even so, we were worried.*
>
> *What worried us wasn't the possibility of being whipped to discourage lazy workers. What we worried about was enemy ships sailing up the Tiber. At least Caesar had a use for us, but the attackers would slaughter us the first chance they got. Everyone knows they are utterly merciless.*
>
> *As I made my way back from the Tiber to my parents' home one sundown, I saw Messalina talking with Tullius. It made me mad because I'd known her first, and all I was waiting for was a slack time to build my own hut so I could take her as my partner. But now Tullius had come along, all smiles and good looks and persuasive words—I knew he spent as little time as possible fortifying the Tiber—and there she was gaily laughing with him. To be disloyal to Caesar and get Messalina by that*

disloyalty was absolutely unfair. I wouldn't be a bit surprised if he took her to bed that very night. But I wanted her so badly, and I knew her first.

I would have offered to fight Tullius, if I thought I'd have a chance, but with his cunning, he'd find a way to cheat and then I'd lose not only Messalina, but my self-respect, and maybe even my life. I'm not nearly as brave as he is, although I'd never tell anyone that.

It's when a person is up against it like that, that you realize how much you need the help of the gods. I also realized my sacrifices to them had lately been perfunctory.

When I got home I delayed my meal and went straight to the shrine in the corner. I decided it was Mars and Venus whose help I needed most. True, Zeus could arrange anything, but he was far too busy and distant to care about me. Our household gods, although fully committed to me, were too weak for something as important as this. No, risky though it was to go above one's station and appeal directly to Mars and Venus, I was prepared to take that risk. The stakes were high.

If I could get the attention of Mars, and if enough of us prayed to him, he might be persuaded to take part in fighting off the invaders. Venus could easily implant desire for me in Messalina's heart. And of course, if Mars and Venus were spending this night together, then that would double my chances of being heard. Of course, they might be so preoccupied with their own desires that they wouldn't hear me at all, but that was a risk I had to take.

So, I prayed my heart out. I did my best to remember the official prayers I'd overheard in the Capital, to address them both with the deepest respect. I recounted their great exploits to assure them of my unfailing attention and admiration. And then I poured out my heart, imploring Mars to keep us safe from invaders and imploring Venus that Messalina be mine. In the end I had to leave it in their hands.

Before I ate, I placed a little of my best food in front of their small statues. Even as a child I had known the statues didn't eat. But the point was we cared about the gods, and if we cared about them they were more likely to care about us. So, I left more food than usual, and added some of the best fat, and poured some wine over it. Mars and Venus could have no doubt of the genuineness of my love for them. With adoration as devout as mine, they couldn't just ignore me.

That was a year ago.

The invaders never did arrive. We heard they had been sunk in a storm. Thanks be to Mars! He must have spoken to Poseidon on our behalf. And Messalina has had a son. With me. Thanks to Venus!

Tullius? I never heard what happened to him. He just sort of faded away one day and I never saw him again.

There's no question Mars and Venus heard my plea. I will be eternally grateful for the rest of my life, and I will show my gratitude by teaching respect for the gods to my son, and he in turn to his sons.

And now the emperor Augustus wants us all to sacrifice to his adoptive father Julius, who became a god when he died, so Julius will favour Augustus' expedition into Spain. I'll make the sacrifices with all my heart. Besides, I might need emperor Augustus' divine help myself one day when he becomes a god. He'll remember me if I've been loyal to him.

"Speaking of libations to the gods, how's yours? Coffee. Not gods." *I sure hope he has a sense of humour.*

"I could do with some."

Was that a joke about gods, or is he just being polite? His coffee was a bit low, so she got him some. *I've been tearing down his gods, now I'm filling up his coffee. He said he'd like more, but which? Coffee or gods? Something very symbolic about me standing here pouring warmth into his cup. How did all this come about?* She tried to make eye contact, but was he deliberately staring into his cup?

"Thanks."

Either he was gently teasing her, or he had missed the whole thing. She wondered if she'd ever know. After a pause she continued.

"Of course the ancient Greek gods were projections. They were the projections of an entire culture and they served a specific and essential need. Human culture had expanded its control far beyond local clans and villages. Political decisions on a civic and continental scale touched everybody's lives. Humanity projected responsibility for this newfound global political reach onto gods as a way of becoming aware of their ability to exercise large-scale control over the world, over human society, and over human relationships. Humanity was discovering we could manage history and culture and our own life-stories. Becoming aware of such power would have been daunting at first, which is why we needed to project it to become aware of it."

Withdrawal of the Olympic god projection

"I'm catching on," John broke in, "It would be no surprise if those gods in their turn had to be withdrawn as human society integrated this new power. You said we still enjoy the animist spirits. Perhaps we still enjoy the gods?"

"Exactly." Rosalind responded. Pleased he'd grasped the implication.

"Even though there is universal acknowledgement that those gods were projections, we continue to experience them in our world. Freud and Jung, studying our interior psychological worlds, identified ways in which the gods are now even more significant for us than they were in the ancient world.

"The truth is the aggressive Mars, the seductive Venus, and the powerful but distant Zeus all live in me and in you and in our international politics. The sooner we recognize the implications for human behaviour, the more we will be able to act responsibly.

"Nobody would think it odd if someone announced they had fallen in love by saying, 'Cupid's done his thing to me!' or named a submarine *Poseidon*. It's not just that we don't believe in the pantheon of gods any more, it's rather that we now know they are real, and exist as important parts of our selves, and are now even more significant than when classical Mediterranean cultures thought they were divine beings of sometimes questionable morality living on a mountain. These gods have finally come into their own—they reveal the abilities and motivations in our own lives and culture for which they were originally projected. Having died as projections they now live lives of even deeper significance within us and within the international relationships of our world. They continue to enable us to be increasingly self-aware."

But John was becoming aware of a disturbing implication. "So," he asked after a pause, and with some trepidation, "what happens when the projection of gods is withdrawn?"

The gods die giving birth to God

Rosalind suspected he'd figured out where this was going.

"As humanity became aware of our increasingly powerful techniques of control of, and ability to take responsibility for, our world and our social institutions, humanity began to realize we have power that is potentially global. Whether the size of that globe was the known world such as the ancient Mediterranean and Europe, or the entire planet, it was a new and disturbing experience to conceive of humans having global responsibility and perhaps even cosmic reach. In face of that human ability, the pantheon of Olympic gods would have seemed increasingly puny and irrelevant. So the gods of the classical world simply faded away.

A more adequate understanding of human consciousness was required by which we could take responsibility for our newly discovered global and possible even cosmic responsibilities. Humanity could begin to be aware of those new potentials by projecting humanity's cosmic power upon a single cosmic external source of wisdom, God.

"I wonder if that's the God you experience?" asked Rosalind.

"Yes," John replied.

"Can you tell me what that experience is like?"

John thought for a moment and then told her how he experienced God. This is how he described his experience of the one supreme God.

> *"The world around me, my own self, and the presence of others are sources of wonder. Wherever I look, I am met by awe. That I should be at all, is more than I could ever have asked, and I am moved to give thanks to the One who has created all this. That mysterious God is forever beyond my ability to grasp, and all I can do is to offer my thanks and praise in return.*
>
> *"Placing myself in the presence of almighty God, I ask for the things I need. Food, love, a future. Safety in dangerous times. I say to God every day, 'Deliver us from evil.' I know I may not receive that for which I ask, but that is not because God does not care, but because God has something more important in store. What I really need and want is to put my roots ever more deeply into God's eternal reality so my own maturity and wisdom will be in some small way like God's. I know this request will demand more than I can give, but I know that by being taken up into*

God's life, I may receive that depth of life for which I was made. Whatever disasters befall us, and there are many looming in our time, I trust that in the end God is in charge.

"I pray, too, for others. At a simple level I ask for healing for their pain, both physical and relational. But at a deeper level I know such prayer is not magic, and what I ask is that my life and theirs be aligned with that of God. In my prayer, the caring of the ultimately loving God finds expression in me, and that is all that any of us could ask.

"There are events in my world that seem permanently beyond anyone's control. Will humanity ever stop devising more powerful ways to kill one another? Will we ever accept our responsibility for everyone, and will we ever love our enemies? If we don't, we are doomed. While we all know that, we seem powerless to enact it.

"The only route ahead is for God to take action and put the world to right. I long for that more than I can say, and I will do what I can to be part of God's action to make that happen.

"I know it sounds strange, but when I hold the cup for the congregation to drink God's life, I have this sense that I'm taking part in God's action to make ultimate goodness happen and put the world right. I can't explain it, but it feels so real. So real, it's almost scary.

"Outside my window is a river flowing day in and day out, year in and year out. It makes me realize that there is a river of deep goodness flowing through the centre of this city and because of God's goodness, international relations can be healed and all can receive whatever is needed for dignified life. I need to drink from that river and, in my own lifestyle, guard it. In the meantime, I learn to trust ever more deeply, if very slowly, that the world, indeed the cosmos, is in God's infinitely powerful and loving hands and that in the end, because of God's ever-flowing love and goodness, all is well.

"When my earthly time is completed, I long to be taken up into God's eternal life. What that may be like, what form it may take, how to describe that process, are matters about which I know nothing. Whatever eternal life is, I doubt it will be like a continuation of earthly socializing. But based on the little we know of

how God has created this universe, it will as far exceed all our
expectations as do the gifts we have already received in this life."

"That's how you experience God?" asked Rosalind.

John thought a bit, and answered with care. "Yes. That's the best way I can put it."

"Well, it's the most real way of thinking about God I've ever heard," Rosalind responded.

"What I think is happening is this," said Rosalind. "The character of this God you speak of exactly reflects contemporary human experience. This one God models for us how a mature person lives, how a mature society operates, and how a mature humanity is called to live in global or potentially cosmic community. The mature person, society, or human race, is not subject to whims, driven by passions, terrified of danger, or subservient to others as were the Olympic gods. So, too, with the one God. The one God is utterly God's self. There is no pressure from other gods, no imperfections that would lead to chaotic behaviour, no rivals to fear, no superiors to assuage. This one God models exactly the sort of mature person each of us longs to become, and the kind of culture our global human race must embody if humanity is to flourish into the future.

"Knowing that one God is to know yourself."

John broke in, "This is precisely the God that Judaism, Christianity and Islam commend as our path to human wholeness." And to himself, "*Perhaps this is the argument that I couldn't think of the other day. All the other versions of spirits and gods were immature and inadequate. God is the final realization, the final image, the fulfilment of all that went before. We've found the true nature of God. I like where she is going.*"

But part of him wasn't entirely confident. Something wasn't quite right.

"Exactly," said Rosalind. "If humanity, with our potentially cosmic responsibilities, needs to become profoundly mature, then the projected image of a single utterly integrated God who is pure love and calls us to be pure love is what we need so we can become aware of our potential human love and our potential ability to build an all-inclusive community. Imagine having to deal with issues of planetary economic, social, military and perhaps cosmic policy with only the Olympic gods to guide us! No wonder they died."

She summarized her understanding of religion. "The transition from the classical polytheism of the Olympic gods to modern monotheism is, for us, simply the most recent and familiar of these transitions. In each of the former transitions, a culture integrated their projection and by doing so deepened their members' experience of what it is to be human and self-aware. Although strongly resisted each time, each transition involved the death of universal consciousness or of spirits or of gods. Each withdrawal was the process by which human culture could receive the gifts presented by each projection, integrate them, and thereby deepen human self-awareness. That's the process by which humans become human—we become more deeply self-aware, and therefore more responsible and more human, every time our culture encourages us to take responsibility for what our spirits or gods used to embody."

She hoped he would understand the implication. She'd rather he got it himself than have to explain it to him.

He did get it. All too well. He could see exactly where she was heading.

She was saying the one true God is a projection and would also have to be withdrawn if we are to integrate that maturity into our humanity.

He was right. That was exactly where she was heading.

Why even the God projection must die

"I'm sorry," she said, "but this latest projection of the one true God in its turn must also die. And indeed, it is dying. It was important that God die, indeed, essential for humanity that God die, but the time has come for religion to admit its role is over. You've got the choice of remaining in the illusion that your projection of God really is an actual conscious being living out there, or of integrating that projection and enacting the immensely life-affirming awareness of human love and fully inclusive society.

"I think thoughtful believers today are caught between two options. On the one hand believers can accept the secular interpretation of God's origin as a projection of humanity's deepest abilities, and thereby embrace atheism. Or believers can deny the knowledge being unveiled by science, and retain religious faith in a divine being. But by refusing to withdraw their projection of God, believers refuse to integrate humanity's responsibility to enact what the God projection is presenting to us about ourselves. But withdrawing the projection of God is exhilarating because it offers even deeper meaning—it connects us to so much and makes so much sense.

"For believers it's a pretty daunting choice. I get that.

"I understand why withdrawing the projections is so terrifying for faith.

It removes all the meaning that had been provided to humanity by belief in a projected God. It's no wonder withdrawing the God projection is met with strong resistance, in the same way as were the withdrawals of the former religious projections. That's why my parents rejected me when I left their faith—they'd rather continue in their loyalty to their projection than take me seriously. In a funny way, I understand them better now than I ever have."

John wasn't at all sure he felt understood.

Learning this secular language was turning out to be a disaster for his faith.

But not for the first time, he was very much mistaken. Instead of disaster, he was on the verge of experiencing a profound and far more powerful God than he'd ever imagined. He had become fully fluent in secular and was about to receive from secular culture a deeper faith than he'd ever known.

This death of God was about to become a life-changing event.

As his faith had always claimed.

Summary

The actual history of humanity's growth into consciousness probably didn't progress as simply and logically as Rosalind's proposal of religious projections and withdrawals might imply, but her approach can provide us with a useful perspective by which to understand how our culture has come to be so deeply skeptical about the existence of God.

In hypothetical pre-animist societies, people would have thought all physical things are conscious. In animist cultures, the centres of consciousness called 'spirits' are related to larger animals and significant physical elements of a landscape and the spirits express their character through the behaviour of those creatures and significant objects. Classical cultures around the Mediterranean basin didn't think that animals had individual spirits, but they experienced gods who lived on a mountain and whose aid could be solicited to help people or entire cities and countries. Modern western culture doesn't believe there ever were such gods. We understand they were projections by classical culture of their new-found global power. Our own culture has until recently experienced there being one God who doesn't live in any special location but is everywhere simultaneously and who embodies maturity and love on a cosmic scale.

The implication is obvious—western culture's experience of a single God has also been a projection allowing us to see the full mature life being offered to humanity and enabling us to integrate that maturity into our global relationships.

Religious people of our culture aren't disturbed that those former religious experiences were projections. But it is very disturbing to contemplate the possibility that belief in the one cosmic God may also be a projection. There is enormous and very understandable resistance in the faith community to Rosalind's proposal.

However, perhaps it's no coincidence that Christianity is centred on a God who dies so that all humanity may rise to deeper life. Christianity may have been the breakthrough in which humanity first became aware of the implications for us if we integrate the projection of the one cosmic God. So, counter-intuitively, facing the possibility that the one God is also a projection to be withdrawn and integrated, may be a path to deeper faith and new hope, and may be fundamental to the meaning of Christianity.

John has become completely fluent in secular.

He's at the point of being able to speak fluently about God within secular society.

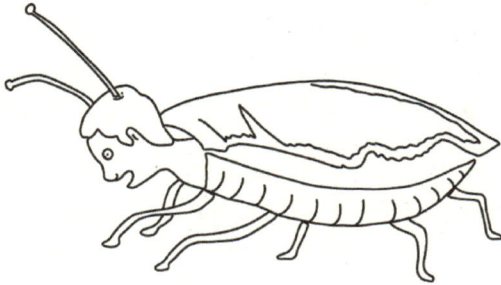

CHAPTER 9
Part 1 Concludes: What we've learned in speaking Secular

Faith's worst fear: irrelevance. A dead God in a secular culture

For secular people, who have moved further along the process of recognizing and withdrawing the projection of God than have people of faith, the churches' hope of reviving faith in a literal being called God strikes them not so much as wrong, but as silly, and certainly not as profound or life-changing. That is what causes our society to be so skeptical about God, not selfishness, or laziness, or some malevolent hatred of faith, or being forced to go to church as a child. Although the concept of God may still function at a personal level for some people of faith by bringing a sense of comfort to their private feelings—"I just know God in my heart," as a believing respondent said to me in my research— God no longer functions that way for our culture.

Our culture fails to find God to be a source of meaning or comfort on the large scale because 'God' no longer connects us to anything more significant than our private feelings. Nor does 'God' provide much comfort even on the small scale of feelings because that requires believing in something like an imaginary friend floating around somewhere in the sky. Or inside my heart.

But as we've seen, cultures desperately need to discover meaning on the large scale because cultures are not local clubs. Connecting with personal feelings is too small to satisfy our culture's need for large-scale meaning. Universal consciousness, spirits, gods, or God used to provide that large-scale meaning. But when those projections are withdrawn, a crisis of meaning emerges for the entire culture because the implication is that there is no surrounding under-lying deep pattern caring for us. That means there is no meaning. And, as we have seen, humanity craves meaning.

The depth of this religious crisis is reflected in that fact that even religious leaders have no expectation that God will act on a global scale to change the course of history. No religious leaders seriously expect God to intervene and suck the excess carbon dioxide out of the atmosphere to save the planet from climate collapse, nor to snatch nuclear missiles out of the air before they can explode, nor to nudge away an earth-threatening asteroid.

But if not, then what use is God? God is powerless and therefore pointless on the global scale, the scale essential for humanity to have a future. A supreme being who is limited to acting only inside our heart and who cannot act to rescue the human race isn't much of a God. Such an impotent God is no God at all. Which is what our secular culture is saying to communities of faith and is what communities of faith hear as looming disaster. Already too many congregations have retreated into becoming clubs of friendly people with a serving of religion on the side.

This growing, if unconscious, sense even among religious believers, that God will not act may explain the strange resistance to the threat of climate collapse in an especially religious country like the USA. To take climate disaster seriously and call for humanity to act would be to admit that God is powerless to address the future of humanity. To accept the reality of a looming climate collapse would bring to consciousness the fact that God is a projection. Better, some forms of religion believe, to deny climate collapse than to face the possibility of an impotent God. It's a last-ditch attempt to avoid the implication that there is no one out there to rescue us. It's classic resistance to integrating a projection.

That's a horrifying prospect, because it removes all meaning. What's the point of even having existed if the cosmos doesn't care?

This all-pervading sense of cultural meaninglessness was first given voice by existentialist writers. They described what it was like to live in a world in which meaning could be found only by courageously facing the absence of meaning. In one short story, written a hundred years ago, an ordinary man wakes up to find he is a cockroach.[1] That story wasn't intended as a sci-fi thriller like the movie "The Fly", but as an accurate description of what it is like when you wake up into modern awareness and find yourself in a totally meaningless universe. No God, no purpose, no meaning, just a puny accident in one corner of an immense uncaring cosmos. Those existentialist writers were saying that on a cosmic scale, with no God behind everything, which is what we now widely experience in western society, we might as well be cockroaches. That's the implication of our society withdrawing the projection of God.

That's what meaninglessness feels like.

No wonder churches resist this disappearance of God tooth and nail.

But the existentialist writers were insisting, in face of intense resistance from their society and condemnation by faith communities, that our secular culture must take seriously the death of our former, and now inadequate, projection of God. Only through the death of that projection, the existentialists claimed, could we become truly human. They proposed that the courage to disbelieve in God and to insist on the reality of meaninglessness requires the ultimate courage and that's what makes us fully human.

What if they were right? What if that is what secularism is about? What if secularism is recognizing the projection of God as a projection, and inviting us to withdraw it so we can receive its gift of life? What if secularism is exactly what God needs us to experience? *What if the journey into the darkness of unbelief is the only way for our culture to be faithful followers of Jesus who did exactly that?* What if not to do so would be to betray Jesus?

However, as we've seen, humans can't live without meaning, so secular culture and religious faith both invent meanings to satisfy that need.

Our busyness culture offers endless entertainment as if that were the purpose of life—spend every moment being entertained[2] or create a bucket list and tour

---

1   Kafka, *The Metamorphosis* (1915).

2   A recent 45 minute flight from Calgary to Edmonton was preceded by an apologetic announcement that the entertainment system would be unavailable during the flight. Not to be entertained for 45 minutes was clearly a significant failure on the part of the airline for which an official apology was necessary.

every exotic place in the world and you'll have achieved the pinnacle of human
fulfilment. If you're on the internet you'll receive several invitations every day
to travel the world. For many people, that is the only point of being alive. You
work hard, then if you're lucky when you're old you have fun for a while as the
reward for your hard work. Then you're gone. That's what our culture considers
a good life. Is that sufficient meaning for a life? A bumper sticker put it well:
"The one who dies with the most toys wins." Doesn't sound much like Socrates'
admonition to know yourself as the way to be fulfilled. And as we've seen,
knowing our selves is the path to being human.

Faith communities resist the meaninglessness of an absent God by pres-
suring people to "believe"; without "belief" some religious traditions say, we
are threatened with superficial relationships, with a pervasive sense of boredom,
with more meaninglessness, or with eternal damnation. Belief, it is claimed, will
give you friends, make you happy, ensure your financial success, and of course,
give you eternal life after death instead of eternal punishment. Churches use
all kinds of such pressure to *attract* members! But better that than face the fact
that God is no more. Only by restoring belief in a literally existing God, and
threatening people with consequences of not doing so, many churches think,
can we restore order in our chaotic world.

That reaction sounds familiar, doesn't it? The world is ending, we'd better
go back the way things were. It's what was said at every previous withdrawal
of projections—pre-animists said it when the animist spirits emerged, animists
said it when the Greek gods replaced their tribal spirits, the ancient Greek
religions said it as Judaism's and Christianity's monotheistic God took their
place. And modern religion is saying it as the projection of the one God is
being withdrawn.

Yet each time the spirits or gods died, something new and wonderful
emerged as the former projection's death became a gift to be integrated and
the source of new life and awareness. That's what's always happened when gods
died. As so often in the past, from such deaths has arisen an even deeper experience of God and of humanity's gifts.

That ancient pattern would imply that a new and wonderful experience for
faith and God may be emerging in our time. It's that experience of powerful
new knowledge of ourselves and of God that faith communities will now be
able to offer. And as a by-product, faith communities will receive vibrant new
meaning and purpose and energy. Exploring that new meaning, purpose, and
energy is the focus of the second half of this book.

There is good news in face of this meaninglessness. It's absurd. But good. Very good.

God's tomb: faith's womb

Absurdly, the Christian faith has at its centre a God who deliberately dies in meaninglessness. "Eloi, Eloi….." "My God, my God, why have you forsaken me?" Jesus said as he entered the darkness of death by excruciating torture. Christianity has the killing of God and therefore the killing of meaning as the path to meaning and deeper life. Modern secularism is presenting faith with a renewed experience of God's absence and the loss of meaning. But those were the central experiences of the one who is understood to be the very image of God and who deliberately journeyed toward execution by torture. Those events became the driving force behind the birth of Christianity.

It is hard for people of faith to take seriously that God must die, not just long ago, but again in our time. Just as hard as it was for the original disciples. But those early Christians were subsequently led, as they put it, by the Spirit of Jesus from disaster into a whole new way of life that turned their world not upside-down as Rome had done, but right-side up. They were not filled with grief at the passing of their projection of God in the form of Jesus' death, but were filled with a joy and energy that transformed them.

For the early Christians, this made perfect sense and gave them meaning. They could easily interpret Christ's as the fulfilment of ritual sacrifices. That made total sense in their cultural context in which priests and animal sacrifices to God were the forms in which they had experienced ultimate meaning. Christ's death connected everything. It turned their world right side up. The Roman empire might kill you with their horrific engines of torture, but God had astonishingly turned Christ's death into the very ritual that connected everyone with God! They described this amazing rediscovery recovery of meaning as 'resurrection.' They experienced seeing it happen in Jesus. They commended this revolutionary discovery to everyone they met. It made sense of the violence and oppression wreaked upon them by the irresistible power of the Roman empire. But God had turned that horror into new life and joy. No wonder they travelled around the world proclaiming this great news.

What's happening now is that we, living in a secular age, have a new opportunity to experience that ecstatic joy; it isn't limited to those Christians who lived in the ancient world. Now is the most exciting time ever to be a Christian.

We may be walking the path with Jesus towards death and into deep new meaning in a way that has never been walked before. Animal sacrifices aren't symbols that make sense to us, but secular society and science are filled with symbols that make possible a more powerful and significant experience of Jesus' resurrection than has been known since the time of Christ.

Why the church must die

It's a path forward that always leads through death, and in our day that implies a particularly difficult challenge for the modern church.

Christians have always assumed that our success in world evangelism was due to our faithful proclamation of the Christian faith in death and resurrection. That success was a sign of how good and faithful and God-like we Christians were.

What makes that path particularly difficult in relation to modern secularism is that modern Christians have inherited more than fifteen hundred years of missionary 'successes' that maybe weren't. The attitude that we Christians know our faith is superior lies behind so many failures in relating to unfamiliar cultures. That's a disastrous way to approach a culture because it expresses superiority and control and rather than loving respect. That may be a major cause of the church's failure in commending the faith to a secular society. We don't respect the culture to which we are commending the gospel.

Further, it's possible that our missionary success in past centuries may have been as much due to the technology, grounded in western science, which we brought to those cultures as to what we said to them about God, or even how loving we were. Or weren't. The very fact that we travelled to them and not they to us meant we had the technology to get there and therefore our technology was more impressive, at least superficially, than that of the people to whom we travelled. That's one reason no missionaries from spirit cultures travelled to Europe to convert Europeans to animism. What we thought was the success of our superior faith may turn out to have been the success of our technology.

But in our secular age, faith has no impressive technology to bolster our claims. To regain our power and influence faith has tried to claim we have a 'spiritual technology.' We claim that prayer can influence surgical outcomes or that happy families, good mental health, self-confidence, or worldly or spiritual success will flow from being a person of faith. But the difficult truth is that the Gospel will have to stand on its own terms: just a naked cross, the ultimate symbol of meaninglessness. Perhaps for the first time since Christianity and the Roman empire colluded to gain power, people of faith can present a fully visible and naked gospel, Christ crucified, and not a gospel clothed with alluring technological or religious pay-offs for potential converts.

That would be humility for Christianity. But that death of the illusion of superiority could become the empty tomb leading to a whole new depth of faith.

There is precedent. We aren't the first to tread that path.

The resurrection of mission

The earliest missionaries, such as Paul of Tarsus, brought no technology whatever to their proclamation. They just spoke of the disaster of Jesus' execution and the experience of his resurrection. At their best, subsequent missionaries didn't rely on technology either. One of their greatest claims for credibility is that they took the cultures they met seriously, and learned the languages they encountered. And found God already there. Archdeacon McDonald is just one example. That approach was an embodiment of sacrificial love. The best missionaries gave up the illusion that they knew everything and humbled themselves to become babbling babes, learning from scratch how to speak. They could do that because they were convinced they would find God already present within the unfamiliar culture. After all, how could there be a place in the universe where God could be absent? Not even in the crucifixion, the place of the absence of God.

And not even in secularism.

Just as the best missionaries in the past didn't insist people learn English before they were taken seriously, so our modern mission calling is to enter into the world of secularism and within that worldview to find for ourselves how God and Christ are already present and being experienced. People don't have to learn to speak Religion first.

That approach, called 'inculturation,' was developed in the 1960s by David Bosch, a South African theologian.[3] That's the way forward because it assumes a posture of humility and respect, a loving posture, towards every culture, even the culture of secularism.

We've learned some of the vocabulary of secularism such as the quest for meaning, and some of the grammar such as the process by which humanity

---

3   David Jacobus Bosch, *Transforming Mission: Paradigm Shifts in Theology of Mission*, (Maryknoll, N.Y: Orbis Books, 1991).

becomes human through projection, withdrawal, and integration of religious projections. We've seen how science has uncovered the way in which creative patterns arise throughout the cosmos—which could be a secular way of experiencing creation. We've experienced science describing what lies behind the human quest for meaning—which could be a secular way experiencing love. We've seen science unveil how human consciousness has arisen through experiences of God as a projection repeatedly dying and being integrated —which could be a secular way of experiencing Christ. Finally, we've understood how science, particularly in the work of Freud, describes the universal experience of maturity arising through repeatedly withdrawing and integrating projections and thereby living more fully—that could be a secular experience of Spirit.

We've been taking secularism seriously, finding it a frustrating challenge and yet beginning to love it. And because we've become fluent, we will shortly find God present within our secular world in a very different way than we've ever known before.

Welcome to secular fluency!

Speaking of God in secularism

Being fluent makes it possible for faith to speak about God and Christ *from within* secular culture.

How might we do that?

In English, faith uses the simple word 'God' but its very brevity can unconsciously mislead. In Chichewa, the language of Malawi, the word used for 'Almighty God' is far more expressive than our tiny word 'God.' Their expression is "Mulungu wamphavu zonse" Wonderfully evocative in its sound, its literal meaning is 'Spiritual power over all things.'

Like that East African phrase, expressions of God within secular culture won't sound the same as 'God' does in our familiar religious culture. Nor will secular phrases mean exactly the same, but secular expressions may be as evocative and effective in the secular West as "MLUNG-gu wham-pam-vu-ZON-say" is within an African culture.

How appropriate if we found that God was already present in secularism before we arrived! How affirming that would be to discover God and Christ is everywhere and in every person and culture and religion without exception. After all, our traditional description of faith states that God is imaged in the Christ who was physically embodied in the ancient culture of the eastern

Mediterranean. Why should that process be any different just because we live in modern secular culture? Could God and Christ not be embodied here in secularism just as well?

What an irony, that secular society is providing faith with the gift necessary to recover its central identity—the identity of self-offering love. That gift is the necessary knife of humility—that the faith has no superior technology to bring with its proclamation. With that sharp knife we will be able to sacrifice our assumptions of power and superiority and discard the allure of seducing, controlling, and oppressing.

What an irony that secularism has become the foundation for a resurrection of faith! Or, to put it in religious language, what an ingenious God!

Summary

For perhaps the first time in history, faith finds itself within a culture in which the foundation of faith, the existence of God, is no longer credible for growing numbers of people. So far, faith has experienced this crisis as disaster.

But once people of faith get over the challenge of speaking the unfamiliar language of Secular and abandon our need to be seen as superior, and when we have become fully fluent in speaking secular, we will discover God already present in secular society. Then a whole new energy and joy are ready to open up for us. Much must die in order that so much life can burst upon us and our secular culture.

Learning to speak effectively of God and Christ within secular will be a delight! Both for us and for those who hear.

Walking that path to delight is the next part of our journey.

PART TWO

God in Secular— Alive and Well, and Hiding Out in Plain Sight

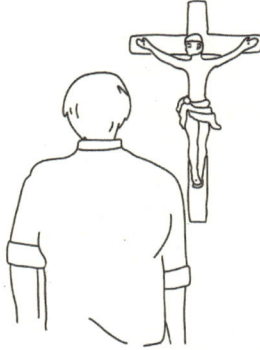

Why have you abandoned me?

CHAPTER 10

Your God Died in Seminary and Surgery. Congratulations![1]

God dies in seminary

My father was a priest. In the ancient world a priest was the person who was in charge of a sacrifice. It was the priest who actually killed the animal in the religious ceremony. So, it is no wonder that when that priest's teenage son was given the gift of Occam's razor in high school, the son knew deep down that one day he would have to use it as a straight razor to kill God. That's how he got to be a priest. Sort of makes sense.

---

1   Robert W. Funk, Luke 6:20-21, *The Five Gospels: What Did Jesus Really Say? The Search for the Authentic Words of Jesus,* (HarperOne, 1996). p. 289 The Sermon on the Plain, Luke 6:20-21. Jesus congratulates people who are in grief: "Congratulations, you who weep now! You will laugh!" The traditional translation has Jesus saying, "Blessed are those who mourn....", but this version gets at the meaning behind the words, the implication being that those in grief are on the path to deep acceptance, peace, and joy but those who deny their grief deny themselves new life.

Here's how it happened.

A decade after Doc Cac and the dormitory, and after three fulfilling years teaching high school science in East Africa, I returned to Canada to study theology. I didn't enter my studies to be ordained, as did most of my fellow students, but I went to find out if there really is a God. Because if there is a God and God loves us as much as Christianity says God does—enough to die for us—then that would be the most important thing in the world for people to know.

My reasoning went like this: if everyone knew they were loved enough to die for, then humanity's insecurity and selfishness would be healed because nobody would have anything to worry about. People would be more mature and fulfilled and they could take the risk of loving each other because, under God's all-surrounding love, there wouldn't really be a risk. The world would be a happier place. I couldn't think of a better way to spend my life. That made sense. That had meaning. That answered so many of my own "Why?" questions about what the point of this planet is, and the point of my life, and provided so many connections between human fulfilment and human tragedy and meaning for my own life. It made great sense.

But it all depended on whether or not there really is a God.

I'd studied Greek and Roman history in my first degree and I knew that gods were taken for granted in the ancient world. That world, in which the gods on Mount Olympus played such significant roles, has given us so much—art, philosophy, government, engineering, administration, mathematics (later taken to new depths by Islam), and more; so, the concept of the ancient Olympic gods didn't seem preposterous. It worked for their culture. Maybe a single supreme God could be just as real and credible in ours. For many people, including my own father, God was still real and credible.

So, upon my return from Africa, I enrolled in Trinity College, University of Toronto, which had the reputation of studying the best thinkers, and I anticipated learning how to be sure there is a God. What a relief it would be to understand the errors in all those powerful secular and scientific arguments that seemed to prove there is no God.

But the studies failed me.

I soon discovered you couldn't prove God from the scriptures—we studied the cultural, sociological, historical, literary, and manuscript origins of the Bible, but there was no way to demonstrate a divine source. All of it could have been of human origin. We studied the best thinkers but I soon discovered they could only think up systems by which to affirm the existence of God if you already believed in God. At least one of the great Christian thinkers, Anselm, a monk, abbot, philosopher, and theologian who was Archbishop of Canterbury from 1093 to 1109, admitted this, stating that belief comes first, and then understanding. That didn't seem a very secure basis on which to build the rest of my life.

Even Jesus, the central figure of Christianity, faded away behind layers of interpretation by early Christians. While there is no doubt that a person called Jesus had actually lived and died by crucifixion—there are non-Christian references to him by contemporary Roman historians—nevertheless everything else that is foundational to building a religion about him could have been the product of human ingenuity.

I began to suspect that all this belief in God and Christ was really just a house of cards. If you started with the premise that there is a God, and Jesus reveals God, then you could build whatever belief system you wish, but if the premise of God's existence was doubtful so was everything else. Naturally, religious believers would emphasize the arguments that pointed to the existence of God or to the historical accuracy of stories about Jesus, but to build one's life on the basis of a personal preference like that seemed dishonest.

I needed more certainty; a more reliable foundation, and it wasn't forthcoming. If the theological college with the best reputation in the country for disciplined thought couldn't come up with a better demonstration of the reality of God, then there was no such demonstration. If they couldn't prove God, nobody could.

Then it got worse.

I had figured a way out of my problem. If I couldn't believe in God, at least I might be able to be a loving pastor, and by loving the people in my future congregations I could make up for the fact that I didn't believe. Maybe loving other people could be my inarticulate way of believing in God, the next best thing to actual belief. I had a sense this could work—God is love, so if I'm a loving person, then I'm spreading God. Made sense. Sort of.

So, I took a course in how to be a caring pastor. But when a roleplay was presented in class for me to practice counselling a student who was playing the role of someone in crisis, I had no idea what to say. I was unable to respond. I simply froze. The roleplay ground to a halt.

The conclusion was obvious. I could probably get away with fooling people that I believed in God. But there was no way I could fool people into thinking

I loved them when obviously I couldn't.

I walked back to my residence room that day aware that not only had I failed in learning how to believe in God, I had now failed in the one ability that might make up for that—the ability to effectively love anyone. I was a total failure at both the theory and the practice of being a priest.

This was more shaming than being discovered praying on the dormitory floor. It wasn't just that I would have to give up hope of telling people about the loving God I once believed in. It was worse than that. My parents were highly respected leaders in my church tradition, people of deep faith and profound caring, and I shared the widespread respect for them. If their son left the best theological college in the country because he couldn't believe in God and was unable to care for parishioners, that would cause quite a stir.

But there was no way I could continue with my degree. If I did, I would end up spending my life proclaiming a lie. I simply couldn't live a lie for the rest of my life, even if I humiliated my parents and myself, and even if it left me with no idea of what to do for the rest of my life. I'd loved teaching in Africa, but I wasn't an African. My home, my people and my future were here in the secular west. I had no idea what I would do. But one thing was clear. I didn't believe in God. I couldn't be a priest.

I began to plan my exit from seminary.

The prospect was excruciating. I had grown up in a happy family; I had a priest for a father who was renowned for his depth of gentle yet deep spirituality and practical love; I was enrolled in the most capable academic college in the country, and I had just completed three wonderful and adventurous years teaching in East Africa. My life had been working out just fine.

And now everything was falling apart.

As I sat in my residence room summoning up the courage to leave, my mind went back to the time when I was a little boy and had to attend those incredibly boring church services. The most boring of all was the dreaded three-hour service on Good Friday afternoon, marking the three hours of Jesus' crucifixion, when my mother took me to church and I had to remain silent for the full three hours of interminably dreary prayers led by my father.

But boring as it was, there was one moment in the Good Friday service that I always found fascinating. When my father, the priest, read the story of Jesus being crucified there was a place where Jesus' words were quoted in the original language. As a small child it intrigued me that my dad could say those strange words with such fluency. It was something he could just do. I never forgot the words. *Eloi, Eloi, lema sabachthani?* Helpfully, the Bible immediately supplied the translation: "My God, my God, why have you forsaken me?" What a strange sound in the original. What a strange thing to say, even in English.

I was intrigued every year by the oddity of it.

Sitting alone in my residence room, experiencing despair at the complete failure of everything that had made sense of my life, and facing the end of everything I'd hoped for, those words from my childhood memories of Good Friday came back to me.

"Eloi, Eloi….. My God, my God, why have you forsaken me?"

I was thunderstruck.

It was happening to me.

It dawned on me that even if I could know nothing else about Jesus, I knew for certain he had said that. It might not be possible to ever know anything else about him, indeed he might be of no importance at all, but I knew he had suffered in the same way I was suffering. He had exactly described my experience. After living such a good life, growing up with loving parents, in a deeply mature religious faith, God had abandoned him. Just like me.

I understood him. He understood me.

How bizarre. My total failure as a believer and as a pastor had connected me with the central figure of the faith I didn't believe in and with the religion I was planning to leave, and with the love I couldn't enact.

How weird. Everything that had ever meant anything to me—my childhood attempt to find God in my puppy, my adolescent courage at being loyal to God on the dormitory floor, my adult desire to learn how to prove that God exists, all those hoped-for meanings had been destroyed when God died. Then, in the very act of God dying, and my own hopes and meanings being crushed, meaning came flooding back.

I was connected as never before to the one who had come to mean nothing. His despair, his meaninglessness, his atheism—on the cross there was no God for Jesus—had given me meaning. I found myself connected and renewed in meaning by my very decision to abandon faith. Jesus' loss of his meaning on the cross had just become my meaning.

How could such a thing be? This made no sense.

But in that, I was very much mistaken. It made perfect sense. I just didn't get it yet.

A faith that takes failure seriously has a certain credibility. Such a faith is worth taking seriously because it is so counter-intuitive. If you wanted to make up a successful religion, you'd make it full of fun and happiness and joy, and you'd include hard work and challenge and sacrifice—that would be the formula for a successful religion. And an utterly superficial religion.

But a religion whose founder cries out in agony at being abandoned by God deserves to be taken seriously. Because that is such an incongruous foundation for a religion. It would be like inventing a new product and then advertising it by quoting someone who said it didn't work. Surely, after two thousand years, someone would have noticed that the founder of Christianity said, in the end, God wasn't there.

Like the self-evident truth of Occam's razor, this total failure by the person the whole religion is built on, rings self-evidently true. Nobody would invent such a story—it disproves the entire project.

Another way of imaging God

In her kitchen, Rosalind had been describing the central role that the idea of God plays in the emergence of human self-awareness. She'd described how the various spiritual experiences, from the universal sense of surrounding consciousness, through spirits, gods, and finally God, have been ways in which humanity has emerged with our quintessential character of being self-aware. Each projection fulfilled its purpose when it was withdrawn and its deep truth integrated into human character. The final stage in the process, Rosalind had explained, was happening in our time—the projection of God is being withdrawn in our culture so that the character previously projected onto God could become integrated as our character.

They sat in silence.

Rosalind, wondering if her explanation of how God was just another projection enabling humanity to know ourselves would be the end of her relationship with John.

John, wondering if it was the end of his faith. And perhaps of his relationship with Rosalind. So much of what she had just laid out made sense. It made sense that the Olympic gods had been projections of new cultural and political abilities—of course they were, whether the ancient Greeks knew that or not. So why not our one monotheistic God? His heart sank at the thought.

But how could he blame her? He'd asked for her thoughts about religion. She'd said what she thought. In doing so she'd honoured him. That was a tiny consolation. Maybe he wouldn't lose her, even if he lost his faith.

Clearly, it was up to him to keep the connection going. He didn't want to lose his connection with her. Or with God.

He had an idea.

"So, I'm wondering," John interjected into the silence, "might there be a different way of thinking about God? One that really connects us? I mean," he added a little too quickly, "connects us to the cosmos. And gives us meaning."

"Seems like a funny question," she laughed. "How do you mean, think about God differently? What's to think about? Either God exists and you and religion are right, or God doesn't, and, I'm sorry to have to say it, but science is right and religion, no matter how socially productive and well-meaning, is built on an illusion."

"I'm not so sure," he said, "that either God exists or God doesn't. I think there might be another way of understanding God."

She looked puzzled. "What do you mean, another way of under-standing God?"

"The foundational experience in all religion is the concept of God. Right?"

"Right. Which is why I don't believe in religion."

I really like how clear she is. It's so refreshing. Sitting in her kitchen and she just telling the truth. Something very special about that. How often are people that honest? I should feel disconnected, but I feel more connected. How weird is that?

"As you explained," John replied, "in classical Greece the central spiritual experience of their world was that a group of divine beings lived on Mount Olympus. From that lofty position those gods intervened in international events and provided explanation and meaning for whatever happened on the international or interpersonal stages. In the modern world, we no longer believe there ever was a community of divine beings actually living on a mountain in Greece. But we understand the pivotal role which that concept played in the classical world, and the way in which the pantheon of gods expressed, and still expresses, fundamental human experiences and meaning. So, you argue, the same applies to the modern concept of God."

Rosalind broke in. She couldn't stop herself. "Don't you think," she said, "that your idea of a single monotheistic God is really not much different from the gods of ancient Greece? Surely the only difference is that for you there is only one God instead of many. But in all other ways your one God includes all the best qualities, albeit in improved form, that the Greek gods once had. The Greek gods lived on Mount Olympus and your God lives in heaven, or perhaps everywhere. But if your God is just a new improved one-god version of the multiple gods on Mount Olympus, that seems all the more reason to abandon hope of rehabilitating the idea of God!"

She felt herself back in the position of betrayal by removing a meaning that was so important to him. She was still taking away his meaning. But she wasn't going to abandon the truth just to make him feel good. That wouldn't feel good. But she didn't feel good doing it.

His response startled her.

He smiled.

"You got it! That's my point. Religious faith must rethink what we mean by God. I believe exactly what you said—if our one God is no more than an updated version of a group of ancient Greek gods, then there's no point to religious faith. If that's all God is about, then God has no meaning and connects us to nothing except perhaps a private emotional need for reassurance. Such a God doesn't impinge on the wider world. Which is what you and your colleagues keep telling me. Difficult as it may be for people of faith, we have entered a time when our concept of God will need to be significantly reinterpreted. Otherwise, the one God will simply disappear as a credible concept in our culture just as the ancient Greek gods already have."

She was tempted to say, *that's what I've thought for a long time.* But she saw how much it would hurt him and kept her thoughts to herself.

He seemed to read her mind.

"I bet that's what you've always thought!"

"I wasn't going to say so in so many words, but…." She smiled.

"We agree for once!"

They were both delighted. But neither was sure where this was going to lead.

There was a slightly uncomfortable pause. They both wondered what that meant. That there might be more meaning was attractive. And disturbing. For both of them.

He moved on.

"In the past, spirits or gods or God enabled humanity to connect to and find meaning in our world—to the local forest in the case of spirits, to the Mediterranean basin in the case of the Olympic gods, and to the entire cosmos in the case of the one God. Why do things happen? Answer: Because spirits or gods or God makes them happen. What's the point of humanity and what should our priorities be in light of the growing powers we have? Answer: To follow the will of the gods or God. The images of spirits or gods or God made sense—it connected us with everything else we knew and with the future.

Those connections gave us meaning.

"But with the advent of our culture's cosmic awareness—that our planet is a microscopic part of a galaxy that is itself microscopic in relation to the cosmos—the concept of God as a supreme cosmic being doesn't connect us to that cosmic context. The idea of God as a being no longer provides meaning on the largest scale. That's why in our culture the final refuge for God has become the human heart. That's the only scale on which the popular idea of God can function. The private heart of the believer is the last hiding-place for a god-sized God. God, even as the supreme being, is simply lost in the vastness of the universe.

"When churches talk about God, secular culture hears us giving the name 'God' to something that's ridiculously small, something that is just one more insignificant item in an enormous universe. Just a product of our tiny imagination."

"Yes," Rosalind said. "Exactly."

"The problem for faith," John continued, "is that the idea of God as a supreme being has come to sound ridiculous. It makes God look rather like an enormously big, imaginary human, which is why the idea of God as a supreme being has so little credibility in our time. That kind of God just isn't real. God can no longer be imagined simply as a very big, intelligent, conscious being. No matter how loving.

"Even to think of God as a very, very, *very*, VERY big SUPREME BEING is to diminish God by making God too small! As descriptions of God, superlatives become diminutives. The concept of God as an intelligent being, no matter how big or powerful or spiritual, is no longer credible in secular culture. God as a conscious intelligence is too small to be taken seriously.

"Such an idea of God just seems silly. People crave meaning and pattern and connection, so they rightly reject this concept of God because it doesn't provide meaning or connection to anything. It's too small to connect with all the other things we know."

Rosalind was all ears. "That's exactly what I remember my colleague Andy saying. He said to me, just the other day, 'I can find awe in nature. No problem. But there's no awe in the idea of God. The idea of God is just silly. But nature: there's plenty of awe there. That's why I'm a scientist and not a believer. The idea of God is just silly in relation to the immensity of the universe. But where that leaves religion is going to be a big problem for churchgoers.'"[2]

---

2 Verbatim quote from a respondent in the author's research.

Re-imagining God: bigger than existence

John agreed. "But," he suggested, "I think there is an alternative to completely abandoning the idea of God. I've got this cute nephew. He asks the most profound questions. Latest example: 'Who made God?' Can you believe it? At five years old?"

"Hey," she said, "We might make a good atheist out of him!"

"You hope! Childish as the question may seem," John went on, "it points to a very serious problem with the concept of God. If God is a being who exists in the universe, even the supreme being, then God must be subject to all the usual characteristics of things that exist in the universe. Everything in the universe must have come from somewhere, including a supreme being called God, and everything in the universe must be limited because the universe is limited.

"The usual religious response to the child's question is that it is the wrong question. We say to the child, 'God isn't like that. God made everything. God doesn't come from somewhere. God isn't made.'

"But the child really does have the right question. What my nephew is really saying is that whatever God is, God must be fundamentally different from everything else in the universe. If God is something in the universe, and everything in the universe came from somewhere, then God must have come from somewhere. God must have been made by something. That something would be the real God. So a supreme being existing in the universe wouldn't be God.

"What we don't recognize when a child asks that question, is that the child is searching for connections—for meaning—for what is behind everything. That would be the ultimate connection. But if God came from somewhere, or if something made God, then that something is the real God and not the God who was made and who exists in the universe. So, my nephew is asking, 'tell me about the real God.'

"We can get as this in a different way," John went on. "If God created everything that exists, then God cannot be one of the things that exists. In traditional religious belief, the universe and everything in it was created by God. What we forget is that God created not only everything that exists, but created existence itself. This means that whatever God is, God is not a being, or a person, or an intelligence, or a supreme being, or a centre of consciousness, or a force, or a spiritual reality that exists somewhere in the universe. If we were able to find something like that existing somewhere, whatever that being was—even if it were the supreme being no matter how intelligent or powerful or spiritual—it would remain simply one of the things that exists in the universe. It would simply be another thing—even if it were the supreme thing—but it wouldn't be God because it wouldn't have created existence. Whatever created existence, that's the real God."

"But to have created existence, it must have been outside existence when it created existence."

Re-imagining God: to be God, God must not exist

John continued. "The concept of God that religion now needs will have to be bigger than anything that exists. Because anything that exists will be too small to be God and too small to make connections between us and the cosmos and therefore provide us with meaning, and answer the ultimate question, 'Why?' Whatever we call 'God' will have to be bigger than existence if it is to have meaning for us."

Rosalind thought about this. "Are you saying that the universe is everything that exists, and so if God exists, God must live in the universe, and if God lives in the universe, then God would stop existing if the universe stopped existing? Which wouldn't be very God-like?"

"Exactly," he said.

"So now you're saying that to keep God being God, God has to be outside the universe, and therefore, outside existence. And anything that is outside existence doesn't exist."

"Right, again," John said. "We'll make you into a theologian yet!"

"This is a very peculiar idea of God," she laughed. "A God that is more real the less God exists!"

"You got it!" he said. "Which explains another religious puzzle my nephew came up with."

"The young atheist! I'm starting to like him!"

"Well, yes. So do I. A lot. What he asked was, 'If God is everywhere, why can't I see God?' Now, religious adults are all familiar with the idea that God is invisible, and that no one has ever seen God. But his question is more important than that. What his question helps us understand is that God's invisibility is not a special physical quality characteristic of divine beings, but that God is invisible in all senses of the word.

"The fact that no one has seen God doesn't mean God is physically invisible, sort of like a ghost, or as if God were transparent, like air. To say we can't see God means that God is invisible not just to our eyes, but to our understanding and to our imagination. God's invisibility means that God cannot be *imaged*—not because God is too big or humans are too small—but because to image God would be to imagine that God exists. We cannot imagine something that doesn't, and couldn't, exist. If we imagine that God exists, then by definition, what we are imagining is something that isn't God.

"This is why Judaism and Islam forbid images of God and why Judaism forbids even pronouncing the name of God. Judaism recognizes that looking at any image of God or speaking the name of God would encourage us to think we could imagine God, and in doing so, we would be led to think God is not significantly different—except for just being bigger—than everything else in the universe. We might even imagine God is like an infinitely big, loving, creative human, and therefore, except for a difference in scale, no different from us. That wouldn't be God at all—it would just be a projection of ourselves. It would be us pretending we are God. It is essential that God be invisible, precisely so we can be prevented from imagining God is something that exists. Which, by definition, wouldn't be God.

"Christianity is at a disadvantage here, which is why Christians find it so difficult to think of God as not existing. Because of Christianity's emphasis on the physical incarnation in Jesus, Christianity did something that at the time was blasphemous—Christianity allowed images of God. This has had the unfortunate consequence of encouraging Christians to think that God exists—because images of God are common in this faith.

"Everything in the universe—us, stars, forces, the universe itself, the chairs we are sitting on, your kitchen, this coffee cup, you and me—are all existing. I am, you are, this chair is. We could say they go around is-ing.

"What I'm trying to get at, what I think the word 'God' should point to, is that God doesn't 'is.' God is not an 'is-er.' See what I mean? There just aren't words for it. And if there were, we'd be suspicious that we were only talking about another thing that would be the product of our imagination, or a projection, but not the source of existence. I guess there just aren't concepts for it, but at least we can say for certain what God doesn't do. God doesn't 'is.' Maybe God is the source of is-ness, maybe God is the foundation of is-ness, maybe God is the essence of is-ness, maybe God invented is-ing, but God doesn't 'is.'"

Rosalind was smiling. "Sounds like an ad for a new soft drink—all that f-*izz*-ing!"

"I like that—it makes it clear we're talking about something beyond our ability to talk about. So, what do you think? Would you buy this divine soft drink? Would you buy this idea of a God who doesn't 'is'?"

"If this were the Pepsi test," she replied, "I'd say the f-*izz* feels tingly."

Tingly? That's exactly how he'd been feeling around her.

She continued. "Something feels a bit familiar about this. When I first talked with Charles about his work, he told me about these weird quantum particles and how they can be described by the Schrödinger equation,[3] and I thought, Hey! I'll study the math enough to understand that equation, and then I'll get it. But no. It turns out that Charles can explain to you how to solve the Schrödinger equation that describes how a quantum particle moves, but what he'll tell you is, that although we can see how the equation is working—and the equation describes the particle's movement with perfect accuracy—we haven't any way to visualize how the quantum particle is moving. Yes, it moves, and the equation tells us everything about how it moves, but not in a way anyone can understand or imagine."

"Not sure I get that," John said.

"OK. Imagine this: what is four apples plus a minus-one apple? The answer is obvious: three apples. But there is no way to describe the minus-one apple. Is it a sort of anti-apple, a vacuum-apple, a non-apple, a negative apple? You know the math works perfectly, but you can't picture a minus-one apple. Your God that won't 'is' reminds me of that. You want to talk about God, but you want to insist there is no way to visualize God. Which makes sense because you and I both know there's no such thing as God. Because God doesn't exist! And *you* said it! Gotcha!"

"Exactly!" John beamed. "It means faith, and going to church, wouldn't be about making a supreme being pleased with you by getting your worship or your behaviour correct. The purpose of going to church would be to become more and more exposed to, and aware of, and influenced by … the thing that doesn't exist but which lies beneath existence, both cosmic and personal. It's like….. It's like…. I don't know what it would be like. It would be about becoming more and more aware of, and closely connected to, and enjoying …"

His thoughts wandered for a moment…..*closely connected to and enjoying….* *her.* He pulled his attention back.

"…. Closely connected to whatever that is, that is closer to us than we are to ourselves. Because it is the foundation of existence. And we exist."

That certainly made him feel connected. That meant something. *Getting more and more connected with something closer than ourselves. Keep your mind on*

---

3   See glossary.

God. But that was getting harder to do the more he shared his ideas.

"If you're right, it'll work perfectly," she said. "But nobody will be able to imagine it."

She knows what I'm talking about! She's with me! Amazing!

She went on. "If I've understood you right, you're saying that in the faith community, the naïve idea that God is a great big, intelligent, spiritual being must be replaced by something much greater than any being. Religion has to be about what is ultimately real, not about an imaginary, supreme being. Right?"

"Right. For what it's worth, since I can't get the right word, I'd call it what you just said, 'ultimate reality.'[4] I guess we could call it, 'the character of reality,' or 'what's ultimately real,' or 'the ultimate source,' or 'how things actually are.' But 'ultimate reality' seems like as good a term as any. And you suggested it, so that's OK with me. OK?"

"Sure. It does give a different sense than 'God.' Bigger. I could take 'ultimate reality' seriously. 'God' just doesn't do it for me."

He wondered if he'd ever learn what did.

She was silent for a moment.

"I've got a problem with this. If ultimate reality is what this is all about, then why not just talk about ultimate reality and abandon the word 'God?' That would be a lot simpler. Just have done with the idea of God. Ultimate reality just is, and that's the end of it. You and I can certainly agree on that, but I don't see that it makes any difference. You would just have the obvious: reality. You wouldn't have any kind of religion. Sorry to say it, but I can't see that it would make any difference. There is no God. There is ultimate reality. So what? It still wouldn't mean anything. Nobody would care."

She wouldn't care.

He hoped she didn't notice how devastating that would be.

It dawned on him how right she was. *If ultimate reality doesn't care, then we wouldn't have any significant connection with anything beyond ourselves, any more than we would have a significant connection with a stone. She's right. It wouldn't mean anything. So what if there's ultimate reality? Who would care? Nobody. We'd be back in an ultimately cold, dark, meaningless universe. That didn't seem like much fun.*

Maybe ultimate reality wasn't such a good idea after all. But the only alternative would be to revert to the naïve idea of a supreme being. And he knew that had lost all credibility. Even for him. He knew we have withdrawn that

---

4   See glossary.

projection. He found himself between the rock of a meaningless universe and the hard place of a meaningless God.

His resistance was growing to the withdrawal of this final projection.

It was Rosalind who had brought him to this uncomfortable place. A few minutes ago, he was delighted to be with her. Now he was disconnected from the universe, from God, and now from her.

He'd had such high hopes. And now she'd helped him discover his bright idea didn't mean anything. Perhaps sitting here with her didn't either. He could feel his anger rising, as if he'd been betrayed. But he stayed polite.

"Time to go," he lied. A great way to get out of this discomfort.

"The source of all reality can keep me is-ing, but it takes the real stuff to keep me awake. I guess that coffee was just decaf. Just as well, I'd have bored you a lot longer."

"I really appreciate you came over."

"Thanks."

"So, you don't like my decaf. You feel like it, I got fizzy caffeinated pop. Might make up for your non-izzy God."

"I'd kinda like that."

But he didn't think he would.

"Free tomorrow?"

He hesitated. Why did she want to keep meeting him? Had she guessed that he had virtually become the atheist she is? Then he gave in to the urge to connect. The hope for meaning was just too strong. He was even prepared to give up God to find meaning. If only with her.

"Three OK?"

"Sure."

But he wasn't.

That night he lay in bed wondering. *I'm not a kid anymore, so what's going on? There was a connection, but exactly what? He focused on his feelings. It's sort of like being with a friend, but not exactly. It's comfortable, but, no, not comfortable at all. She's destroying my faith. I feel more fragile than since I was a teenager. Does it mean anything? I hate being silly. I wish I knew what it was. It's like….. It's like…..* And he fell asleep unable to say exactly what it was like to be with her. Just like his non-existent ultimate reality God.

He didn't know how to relate to either of them. And he wished he did. He really wanted to connect.

God dies in surgery but the operation was a success

I've been thirty-six years a priest, and my lover of thirty-five years and I have been sitting on the sofa in silence after a very long conversation.

Early tomorrow morning she is due at the hospital for a major operation on her heart that may give her new energy and mobility. Or, as the cardiac surgeon has responsibly explained, the surgery could result in a mild stroke, a severe stroke, or a coma. A small percentage of patients, he told us, die. He could not guarantee that wouldn't happen to her. A tiny piece of plaque could be knocked loose, could be swept up in her blood stream, and block some essential blood supply to a muscle, a nerve, or her brain.

The dearest person in my life might become permanently disabled, be unable to speak, or could become a vegetable. Or could be dead.

Tomorrow morning.

We have talked through the worst-case scenarios. We have thought through what we wish for each other if the worst should happen. We don't even know which outcome would be the worst. Now there is nothing more to do but go to bed.

Being a sensible lady, that's what she does.

But I stay up. I sit in an armchair in the dark and wish there was a God who could be relied upon to fix this. With all my heart I want to pray. But I dare not. Because the surgery is so delicate, I want no part in messing with it. Because I feel silly asking for some divine intervention in a highly technical surgery—I know that's unrealistic. Ask God to keep pieces of plaque from sloughing off the insides of her arteries? Ask God to ensure the heart-lung machine doesn't break down? Ask God to prevent dangerous clotting just this one time? Ask God to make the surgeon concentrate?

Something in me rebels at that. To ask that would be to ask a lie—I know the world doesn't work like that. There is no supreme intervenor who will abandon my lover unless I pray really fervently for her. That's just silly. That's actually blasphemous. That would be to fool myself into thinking God is just a bigger self-centred me who needs pleading in order to respond. That would be to accept that God is just a projection of myself. That would be the lie. That would be the blasphemy. I sit in my armchair in the dark and fight the temptation to believe there is a God out there who will intervene to keep my lover safe if I pray hard enough.

Feeling like a traitor to the faith that I commend to others, feeling like a hypocrite for being a priest who doesn't believe when my lover's chips are down, still I refuse the projection. With integrity I can do no other.

I feel like a fraud. A priest who is determined to fight the temptation to believe in God.

But equally, I'm determined I will not submit to the temptation of despair—that there is simply blackness and our agony of suspense the night before the surgery is of absolutely no significance and doesn't matter. I refuse to believe this all means nothing.

What can I say to the God I am supposed to believe in, but don't?

One must always tell the truth.

Who said that?

Did the darkness whisper that to me?

I *can* tell the truth.

I say the truth over and over to the darkness, that more than anything in the world I want her to be well. I'm startled to realize I'd happily give my life for her. That's the truth.

But I am really scared. Because there is no God to help. That's also the truth.

I've said my two truths: that I would do anything to keep her safe. Anything. And that I refuse to pretend that my projection of God is real.

Then I suddenly realize that the darkness already knows my two truths, and now we both know that the other knows. In my saying my truths and asking for nothing, not belief, not reassurance, we have touched, that mystery and I. Somehow the dark mystery and I are friends in our common experience of being utterly abandoned by God. Otherwise, the dark mystery wouldn't be dark.

I revealed two difficult truths to the darkness. That I love her more than anything. And that I refuse to believe in a God who is just a projection of me. And the darkness gave me two truths in return. That I love her far more than I thought I did. And that I am deeply known by the darkness and understood and loved in my helplessness. And so is she.

The mystery healed me through my refusal to believe in it.

The darkness of unbelief gave me love and peace and acceptance.

Something whispered again, "It's time to go to bed." Maybe it was my imagination. Maybe it was me accurately hearing a third truth, that sleep would now be possible knowing how deeply I was understood.

Having told the truth in the dark, and having heard the truth in return, there's nothing more to be done. I slip quietly into bed and lie beside my lover who is already asleep. Who may be gone forever by this time tomorrow.

That darkness, that absence, became the deepest and most comforting reality I know. Crying into the darkness, "I want her safe!" made me aware of a depth of love I had thought was not possible for me, a depth of love that could happily be the death of me if I could put myself on the table in her place. Somehow, I knew the darkness heard and knew I knew. In that way the darkness healed me by revealing in myself a love deeper than I could have imagined. And the darkness loves her, too, just as much as do I. Maybe the darkness was loving her through me. Maybe that's where the deep love came from.

I slept well.

So, what happened that night?

Did the dark mystery actually whisper to me? Did it really give me all I needed? Was it just projection on my part, but somehow a projection which worked? Or maybe a projection that was true? After all, I did go to sleep with a sense of quiet calm, in the face of knowing my lover might be dead the next day and knowing I'd told the truth in refusing to project my needs onto an imaginary God.

My experience was that the darkness spoke. I know perfectly well there was no physical voice I could have recorded—I was under no illusion there was an audible or even a psychic voice speaking to me. I know it is a projection when I say the darkness spoke, but that is a far more accurate description of what happened than saying nothing happened, or that I just had an insight. Giving up the naïve belief in a simple God who would fix things if I asked fervently enough, enabled me, through a conscious projection onto the darkness, to experience something far more significant.

What was happening, although I didn't become aware of it until years later, was what we have seen happening throughout human history. Each time a cultural projection is withdrawn, the god of that projection dies. Yet each time something else then emerges that is even more powerful than that which died. Which is exactly what one might expect, looking back on the long history of this process.

I was transfixed by pain and fear that night before the surgery. I struggled hard to retain my projection of God, but when I let it go, I was surrounded by love and peace. One projection of God had died in order that its love and strength could be fully given to me.

God died so I could be really alive. What a God!

Summary

A great many people in our time find the idea of a literal God simply not credible. Yet God is fundamental to religious belief.

But if God is real, there has to be another way of experiencing God in a culture where science provides the universal idea-language. John and Rosalind develop a way of thinking about God that is actually a very old idea.

Religion has always said God created everything. But we didn't usually notice that "everything" includes not just things, but existence itself. God created existence, not just the things that exist. That means God is outside existence, and therefore doesn't exist. It's the only way for a real God to be real.

That solves the problem posed by science about not needing God to explain the universe, or how life arose, or anything, and why science doesn't find any research results that suggest there is a God.

The reason science doesn't find evidence of God is not because science is limited to studying physically observable phenomena and God is a non-physical invisible being, although that's an argument widely used by religions to respond to science being silent about God. The real reason science doesn't discover God is that science operates within existence and so studies things that exist. But as we've seen, God is outside existence. In a certain sense God doesn't exist—which is exactly what science and our secular culture are saying to religion.

If faith keeps insisting God does exist, we reinforce the secular perception that we are naïvely commending belief in a tiny god.

John and Rosalind need to find a way to avoid having to imply that God exists, so they use the phrase 'ultimate reality.' They could have said, 'That from which existence arises' or any number of other terms to get at the same idea.

In the next chapter we'll see how this source of existence, ultimate reality, might be more than just a clever theoretical idea but is intimately involved with us and exhibits the characteristics of love. Without which nobody would care about ultimate reality.

But if ultimate reality is as profoundly personal as the old idea of an existing God was, then we may have stumbled on something really important.

Being fluent in secular has its benefits.

CHAPTER 11

Ultimate Reality:
Source and Care

A blind 90-year-old lady saves me from freezing to death

My first parish in the Yukon had four churches, one hundred and twenty miles apart. One winter evening, with the temperature dropping below minus fifty and no traffic on the road, driving home from the village where I had been visiting was too dangerous. To go off the road or to have a mechanical break-down could end up with me freezing to death before another vehicle passed. So, I was billeted for the night with a blind ninety-year-old First Nations lady who could only hobble slowly with the help of a cane. I knew her well since I picked her up for church every week, and she taught me words in the Gwich'in language. When I said the words back to her, she'd look blank for a moment and then burst into side-splitting laughter. I never did find out what I'd said, but I used my few words as often as possible. They were quite an ice-breaker.

It seemed odd to me that the village would choose to billet me on such a night with the frailest person in the village. But knowing their culture just a little, I knew that when things don't make sense to me, they turn out to make sense. A bit like learning a new language. Maybe they wanted to honour the elder with hosting me, the young reverend. It never occurred to me that they might have wanted to honour, and educate, the new priest by hosting him with a revered elder.

Persis Kendy lived alone, her cabin just four log walls with no interior rooms, two beds, a barrel stove for heat and a pile of wood. I snuggled into the five-star sleeping bag I always travelled with and slept well until the early hours when I woke in total darkness to discover that the fire in the wood stove had burned out and the temperature inside the cabin was well below freezing and rapidly getting much colder. I knew by now it would be colder than minus sixty outside and it wouldn't be long before it got close to that inside. I lay there wondering what to do. My hostess' English being pretty non-existent, there had been no instructions about matches or how to handle late night emergencies. There was no electricity, my blind hostess having no need of electric light.

As I lay there wondering how to be a hero and rescue us both from death by freezing, I heard her moving. Soon it was clear that in the pitch dark she was gathering firewood, carrying it to the barrel stove, lighting it and getting back to bed as if it were all perfectly normal. Which it was for her. Darkness and light to her were both alike.

In my youthful strength I would have gotten up, blundered my way around, moved things and caused her to stumble and lose her way or worse in her own cabin. But in my helplessness the elderly blind woman who had lived there since before white people arrived, had saved me.

As if this were nothing out of the ordinary. It was a lesson about the necessity for trust and respect of an ancient culture I would never forget.

In the morning she re-lit the stove and made bannock and sweet tea for our breakfast and we ate together. She still living in pitch blackness. As far as she was concerned nothing of note had happened during the night.

As far as I was concerned, I was surrounded and startled and humbled by an intimacy which had seemed so absent and ineffective and turned out to have known exactly what it was doing. And of which in my darkness I'd had no inkling.

Can ultimate reality be intimate?

John had suggested a way of thinking about God not as a conscious spiritual being, but as something much more significant—as that which underlies existence, that which gives rise to existence, that which is the source of existence. Rosalind had come up with a way of naming it—ultimate reality.

But the problem that Rosalind had pointed out, and that had become all too clear to John, was that although it was a credible way of thinking about what we mean by 'God' without using a projection, nobody is likely to relate to ultimate reality on a personal level. John was worried that this new idea of God might be the end of his faith because there wouldn't be any meaningful relationship with such a theoretical concept as 'ultimate reality' and therefore no point to religion. If God has to die as a projection, then obviously religion would too. Religion was always about relating to the spirits, the gods, or God. But 'ultimate reality' seemed like an empty nothing. Just out there, not in any way personal. Maybe the scientists were right and it came down to there being no relationship of any significance with whatever ultimate reality is.

John had gone to sleep that night and his mind did its best to find connections and meanings between the disparate memories being laid down during sleep. Without his knowing it, his unconscious mind felt its way toward a solution for the meaninglessness of this way of thinking about God. He dreamed of a God made of atoms, of falling into a black hole and being crushed to death, and then, waking up scared and relieved and floating in safety on a cloud of intimate care.

The dream made no sense. But it intrigued him. What did it mean?

Next afternoon, as arranged, John and Rosalind sat in her backyard.

Fizzy pop. Non-is-ing God.

John not at all sure this was a good idea. But unable to resist.

Rosalind began. "I've been thinking about our idea of ultimate reality. Actually, it was my idea, wasn't it? As I said yesterday, if God is replaced by ultimate reality, that would seem to be the end of religion. I can't imagine anyone worshipping ultimate reality or praying to ultimate reality or believing ultimate reality cares the way religious people want their imaginary God to care. I think you are doing more than just substituting a more credible concept, 'ultimate reality', for the illusion of 'God,' which we both know is a projected imaginary being. You are actually removing the religious point of God. I applaud you in this, but nobody is going to participate in a religion based on ultimate reality any more than they'd take part in a religion based on arithmetic, despite the fact that arithmetic is true. I like your idea about ultimate reality being beyond existence, but as far as I can see, substituting 'ultimate reality' for 'God' is going to be the death of religion. Which is where we started and still makes complete sense to me. Just wanted to make sure you got the implication."

"That's what I thought yesterday," John said. "Now I'm not so sure.

"I had a dream."

"'Think you're Martin Luther King?" she joked.

"At least he thought God was present even in the implacable racial injustice of his time when lots of people with power counted on their being no God, at least no God of justice who actually cares. But his dream changed the world. I'm no Martin Luther King, but I'm wondering if ultimate reality may care about us. I think that's what my dream was saying."

"So, tell me about this dream." She couldn't keep the skepticism out of her voice.

Atoms and intimacy

He did. "Think about it. More than in any other age, science has shown what an intimate relationship we have with the cosmos. For example, as your colleague Charles told me, all the hydrogen atoms in the universe were formed shortly after the big bang. Those atoms now form the basic constituents of every part of our bodies.

"But here's the thing. They are the very same atoms. Each of the hydrogen atoms in our bodies is fourteen billion years old and each one was formed moments after the big bang. They never wear out and no new ones have ever been made. Our bodies are constructed from the original hydrogen atoms formed at the creation of the universe. Most of your body is fourteen billion years old. That's impressive."

John paused. "Can't get away with that, can I? I assure you, you don't look a day over twenty-one."

"That some kind of religious test? To see if I'm so gullible I'll believe anything?"

They were both smiling.

But she was pleased he cared. That meant a lot. Funny how she could feel connected to him when this whole religion thing was so weird. But at least he was trying to take her world seriously.

John continued. "As Charles explained to me, all the other kinds of atoms in our bodies, mostly oxygen, carbon, and nitrogen, weren't formed at the big bang. These other atoms didn't exist until billions of years later. These more complicated atoms have their own interesting but completely different origin. Every one of these carbon, oxygen, and nitrogen atoms was made from some of the original hydrogen atoms. Here's how Charles told me that happened. Over time, those original hydrogen atoms clumped together forming enormous balls. When those balls, that we call the first generation of stars, became too large, they collapsed under their own weight in enormous explosions called supernovas. Some collapsed so violently that some of their hydrogen atoms were actually forced inside each other. The hydrogen atoms that were forced inside each other became new and more complicated atoms such as oxygen or carbon or nitrogen. So, every one of the non-hydrogen atoms that our bodies are made of—mostly carbon, oxygen, and nitrogen—were formed out of the original hydrogen atoms. And each of them is billions of years old.

"Our bodies are literally made of nothing but fourteen-billion-year-old atoms from the big bang mixed with the almost-as-old crushed remains from some of the original hydrogen atoms. That's what we are made of. Nobody who learns about this process remains unmoved.

"So, what does this discovery mean? It is no exaggeration to say that our being made of fourteen-billion-year-old atoms shows that our relationship with the cosmos is more intimate than we can possibly imagine. It's as if the cosmos was pregnant with us for fourteen billion years and we now live and move and have our being in an intimacy in which we are bathed by everything we need, from photons, to food, to.... to friendship."

Was that too risky? Were they friends? He rather thought so, in spite of her atheism. But how do you know? How close do you have to be to know that?

"If I learned anything from your colleagues and your lecture," John continued, "it's that none of those processes was invented by us. We are the upshot of processes that were in place from the beginning of existence. Those processes made us. And still keep us alive. And ultimate reality is what lies behind existence. That feels intimate to me."

"Intimate?" Rosalind said. "That's a curious way of thinking about it. I don't feel at all intimate with ultimate reality. It just is. I'm not sure it makes much sense to call it intimate."

"I understand," John replied. "But I think in this case, feelings may be optional. I think there is a kind of intimacy that is simply factual. For example, I suppose very few people think of insects as being intimate with us, but, as you know better than I, more than half of our human genes are present in both spiders and spinach. And yes, I know spiders aren't insects, but you know what I mean! It's the extraordinary degree of connection we have with other creatures that makes us intimate with all living things, even with plants. Of course, when we apply the term intimacy to another human, we imply all sorts of conscious awareness and complex interactions and emotional feelings. But in a purely physical sense we are intimate with all things and therefore with what lies behind everything—ultimate reality."

"You're talking about deep connection. Much as I'd usually be hesitant to help a religious person build their argument, I've got an idea for you."

"Can't wait," John replied, with a smile. Maybe she was going to make a theologian out of him.

"I think there's a deeper way in which we are related to everything. But I don't know if it'll help religion."

Patterns and intimacy

Rosalind continued. "As my colleagues have experienced in their own special-ties, we are in a deep relationship of awesome and mysterious power reaching back into the very roots of mathematics. Over and over again, we are the product of mathematical processes. We have our origin in the mathematics that determined the characteristics of the early sub-atomic processes out of which the first hydrogen atoms emerged and as you pointed out, our bodies are still composed of them. It was complex mathematics that determined the intricate processes by which those simple hydrogen atoms could be squashed by collapsing stars into more complex atoms like carbon which can build bodies. Humans arose through evolution which is driven by the mathematical process of multiplication of successful variations and the subtraction of unsuccessful ones. Finally, our consciousness arises from the unimaginably complex mathematical interactions of billions of connections in our brain embodied in patterns of neurons made out of those very same atoms from the early universe."

Rosalind continued. "The whole point of science is to identify patterns. Astronomers look at the sky and see there are stars, but they find the stars aren't just random: they are grouped in galaxies and the stars all come in certain types according to their size and history. The same is true of the galaxies—they aren't just random; they also come in groups, and each comes in a certain shape according to its size and history. The same when biologists look at microscopic cells—cells aren't random, they have predictable patterns.

Everywhere we look there are patterns.

"Patterns are just the way mathematics organizes things.

"When patterns arise—whether water waves or sand ripples or patterns in evolution or the patterns in our brains—all these patterns happen within the basic patterns and processes of mathematics. Fast cars bunch up behind slow cars. There's nothing mysterious; it's just basic arithmetic. Scale that up, (yes, a long way up!) and we have consciousness and human self-awareness. In the end, everything arises from mathematics and the study of mathematics is simply the study of the basic template which emerges into the patterns we see everywhere. We are one of those patterns that simply emerged."

"I think I see where you are going," said John. "Patterns keep arising everywhere. We humans are just one of those patterns, albeit the most complex, but sufficiently complex for us to be self-aware. The obvious question then is, 'What's the origin of mathematics?'

John continued. "Traditional religions, including mine, use the image of a conscious creator being—God—who made the patterns that mathematics reveals. In the Jewish scriptures, it was God who created pattern out of chaos—using the same pattern each day for six days. Even though we understand that story to be poetical, it did deal with a fundamental question: 'Why is there order and pattern everywhere?' Answer: 'God made the order. God made mathematics. God made patterns.' But if the projection of is being withdrawn, then religion has to ask what is the origin of these patterns we see in mathematics and in ourselves if it isn't God?

"Yesterday when we talked in your kitchen, you and I agreed that the idea of a non-physical spiritual being arbitrarily creating stuff just doesn't make sense to increasing numbers of people in our culture. So we tried to describe what's beneath existence that gives rise to existence. You called it 'ultimate reality' for lack of a better term. It is ultimate reality—whatever that is—which is the source of existence and of patterns."

"So you're saying that ultimate reality created mathematics?" asked Rosalind.

"I'm not sure I'd put it like that. Perhaps another way of thinking of it is that there has to be some pattern in existence or else there would be only chaos and existence would collapse. So maybe the only way existence can exist is to be grounded in some logical pattern and we call that mathematics.

But curiously, mathematics isn't entirely logical, which leaves room for creativity, otherwise I suppose all existence would be like being stuck in concrete—no room for change or development. Mathematics contains curious contradictions such as there being no pattern of when prime numbers appear and yet in some sense each prime number gives rise to a whole new series of numbers. And even stranger, logical contradictions have been found to be fundamental to mathematics.[1] So I suppose, yes, you could say that ultimate reality is the source of the logic and pattern and of the creativity that we experience within existence.

"But what's significant to humans is that mathematics is the substrate, the blueprint, or the template in which we can see pure pattern. That pure pattern is intimately related to us because it is our template. Whether it is the applications of the mathematics of levers that determines how we move our arms or fingers, or whether our neurons communicate through the mathematics of tiny electrical charges, it's mathematics that enables us to move and think. Most of the time, we take that for granted as if it didn't really matter, but science has shown that we exist and are alive and conscious only within the underlying matrix of mathematics. Those processes which allow us to exist are closer to us than our breath, than our heartbeat, even than our own neurons. In that way, ultimate reality is so intimate it's closer to ourselves than we are. I would call that intimate, whether or not we experience that intimacy as a feeling."

Rosalind responded. "Certainly, what keeps me fascinated and energized to do my research is the awe and wonder and attraction to knowing more about the patterns we discover around us. It seems an unusual concept of intimacy, but on the scale you are talking about, I can see it could make sense."

John agreed. "I think it's true to say that when we consider how ultimate reality has given rise to existence and to the unimaginable patterns that have become us, awe is a profound response. I think awe is the discovery of intimacy. I think that's what motivates your work as a scientist. And if you'll forgive me for pointing it out, awe is the central component of worship. Its all about intimacy."

Here he was in her garden, and they were talking about intimacy as if it were the most natural and important thing in the world. And she felt right at home.

Intimate with a believer? It was the very last thing she'd ever imagined would happen to her.

That's about as intimate as it could get, John was thinking. *Just as when we unexpectedly find ourselves close to someone who really understands and cares.*

---

1   Kurt Gödel, 1906-1978, one of the pre-eminent mathematicians in history, proved in 1931 that a mathematical system can be either complete or logical, but not both at once. All mathematics is either illogical or incomplete.

Summary

Religion isn't about discussing a theoretical idea of God, such as John and Rosalind's idea of ultimate reality. It's about actually experiencing God. But how can we experience a God that doesn't exist? Ultimate reality is a good solution for thinking about God without having to use the illusion of a divine being floating in the sky. But how can we relate to ultimate reality?

    Even though we can know next to nothing about ultimate reality, we know one thing. That one thing is all we need to know and all we can know: ultimate reality keeps making patterns. And mathematics is the form in which we experience the fundamental patterns from which actual physical patterns emerge. That's the reason stuff keeps organizing itself and that we exist. We are one of those patterns that has emerged from ultimate reality. We are all made of emerging patterns.

    That means the reality beneath existence that gives rise to patterns is closer to us than our breathing, than our thinking, even closer than our own self. We live and move and have our being within those emerging patterns, which is how it's possible to experience ultimate reality even though it is outside existence.

    In one sense, we are made out of ultimate reality, because we and the entire cosmos emerges from ultimate reality.

    Which is about as intimate as it can get.

    That's how intimacy with ultimate reality is a real experience. But does ultimate reality experience intimacy with us? Could it enjoy us? Could it care for us? If so, we'd have the basis for a full relationship. As long as we didn't turn ultimate reality back into a projection of ourselves. We'll see in the next chapter if that's possible.

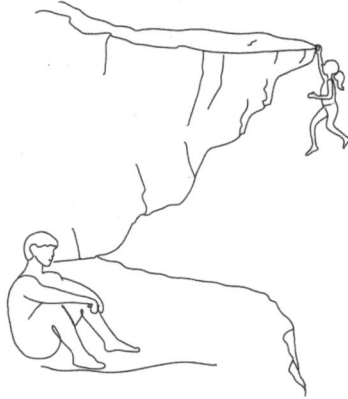

CHAPTER 12

Ultimate Reality: Intimate, caring, and funny

Giggling teenage girls crash a naked men's retreat

I'd been ordained for about thirty years, my sons were entering manhood, and it seemed a good time to find out what it is to be a man in my mature years. So off I went to a men's retreat in Oregon. The retreat was designed by Richard Rohr,[1] whose insight was that physical strength and aggression are necessary qualities for men to acknowledge and integrate if they are not to be abusers but guardians for those they love.

But whereas aboriginal cultures have effective ways of integrating that strength into creative channels when boys first enter manhood, western culture provides no such guidance. The dreadful alternative, now normative in our culture, is that without cultural direction, many young men express their

---

1   Richard Rohr is a Franciscan priest who has written books on spirituality such as *Falling Upwards* and *Everything Belongs* and who writes daily meditations and is one of the most popular speakers and writers on spirituality and mysticism.

strength through violence. No wonder our culture worships violence as the ultimate solution for all problems.

'Primitive' societies would be horrified at such violence. Ours thinks it's normal.

The men's gathering was to enable us who hadn't had the benefit of an indigenous upbringing to integrate our fragility and fear which leads so easily to the violent abuse of masculine power. Facing our fragility and embracing our strength was to be accomplished through a series of rituals modelled on those that most human cultures have always used.

The approach Father Rohr had designed was that we would undergo visceral experiences of power, symbolic violence, and physical fragility, all carefully supervised, many requiring substantial bravery. We discovered what it was to feel vulnerable and to accept that as a kind of strength, to be proud of our masculine power, to integrate it and be able to use it to support and guard and uphold community.

We met daily in a remote wilderness location in Oregon, surrounded by desert-like hoodoos, hills, and coulées.

The climax of our integration came at the end of the week when each of us was to claim a remote private place completely alone in the wilderness, strip naked, and remain in our chosen place for a full day, regardless of what might happen, awaiting a revelation about who we really were. I was wondering about my future as a priest and considering to what other role in life I might be called. This retreat seemed the perfect combination of credible theory and personal challenge. I looked forward to their synthesis during the final day-long wilderness retreat revealing the path ahead for my life.

So, on the final day of the retreat each of us selected some isolated place in the desert hillocks, and prepared to spend the entire day naked alone in silence. From my vantage point I could see one or two others in the far distance.

I sat down to wait.

As the hours passed nothing happened. I wasn't surprised or concerned. I didn't expect to be struck by a revelation right away. But a growing sense of centredness or clarity would have been nice. I'd driven a thousand miles, spent a fair bit of money, and energetically engaged in a full week of preparation for this final revelation. If I trusted the process, which had been revelatory up to this point, then I would reap the benefits and return home with the clarity I sought for myself and my future.

Still nothing happened. No insights, no revelation, no message about my future.

But after four hours of silence, I began to hear voices.

A couple of giggly teenage girls were climbing down a sheer crag a quarter of a mile away from me. At first, I couldn't see them, but gradually two small dots came into view and I realized they'd got themselves into some dangerous rock scrambling. I could see them hanging onto ledges, working their way down the cliff, alternating between giggles and terrified screams. I'd done a fair bit of dicey rock-scrabbling on days off during my mining jobs in the north and knew how dangerous that could be.

I abandoned my vain attempts at silent meditation and began developing a plan for how to get medical help if the worst happened. My closest colleague meditator was too far away to shout to, so I figured out a way that I could signal to him to communicate that there was an emergency, trusting the message would be relayed from meditator to meditator and ultimately to the conference centre from which an ambulance could be summoned. We'd all made solemn vows to remain in our spot for the full day no matter what happened—that was the test of our determination to receive our vision. If one of the girls fell and was injured, there was no question in my mind that I'd break my vow; but until that happened, I was bound to remain where I was.

It took the girls several hours to work their way down to the ridge on which I sat, and I worried the entire time about their safety. Finally, they were off the crag and I could stop worrying.

But then I was faced with a new dilemma. The most obvious path for them would be to continue down the dry stream beds that would take them within viewing distance of myself and the other naked men in meditation. As they got within shouting distance of me, I put on trousers, stood up and called to them that there was a silent meditation here and it would be good to take an alternate route to the valley below. They understood, and soon were out of earshot down another coulée.

By this time, it was late afternoon and with evening coming on all of us were to return to the retreat centre. I tried one last time, without success, to enter a deep inner silence in which to receive the revelation for which I had travelled so far and worked so hard.

But again, nothing. Time had run out. My vision quest was over. I had received no vision.

I returned, took part in ritual bathing, and accepted that my vision quest had been a failure. It reinforced what I had always suspected about myself, that I was really a spiritual fraud and maybe this whole religious thing was an illusion after all and I should find some other role in life. Clearly I was a failure at spirituality, the core of my supposed calling.

When I got back home, I told the story to my colleagues, but cast it as an amusing incident to cover my grief that I'd received nothing from the climax of the week's retreat—the silent day alone in the wilderness had been useless. I used humour to cover my anger and resentment at the girls' intrusion into my sacred time and the waste they had caused by their pointless interruption of my one opportunity to explore integrated masculinity and receive direction about my future life. Two silly girls scrambling irresponsibly down a sheer rock face had snatched away everything I'd gone for. I did my best not to reveal the anger I was feeling.

For a priest, whose central job is to commend spiritual growth to others, to find oneself angry, upset, and frustrated and to have failed at what should have been a profound experience of God's call is to have failed in my life's calling. I'd lost my meaning. It was a vulnerable, fragile, and humiliating discovery.

Perhaps I should never have been ordained.

Long after, it dawned on me what had really happened.

I had received exactly the revelation and vision I had requested.

I had summoned God to an appointment at a day and place convenient for me, at which God was to turn up on time and provide me with spiritual insight. Like a customer in a restaurant, I had placed my order with the divine waiter, and the waiter's job was to serve me. But the waiter was grumpy and incompetent and couldn't even arrange for silence during my vision quest. I had every reason to be upset and angry.

But it was I who was incompetent. I who was projection. The waiter was more than competent. God did indeed turn up precisely on time, exactly as requested, but in the form of two giggling teenage girls who revealed to me in no uncertain terms that I was a bit of a joke to think I could order God around and request spiritual insight when it suited me.

The course had worked exactly as planned. When I became aware of my own fragility and silliness in imagining I could summon God to turn up when I wanted, and how easily I loosed my anger at my weakness and failure, it all fell into place. What other way to disabuse me of the idea that growth in spirituality was something I should do? The very word implies it's up to Spirit. Otherwise, we should call it human-uality.

And those girls? I thought they were the ones who were fragile. But that was only me projecting my own experience of being a fragile spiritual leader, unsure of his footing in a secular age, onto them so I didn't have to take responsibility for my fragility and my anger.

Ever since, whenever I get the idea I should develop my spirituality and become a deep person profoundly aware of God's call, I hear God, ultimate reality, double-giggling at me in the form of two silly teenagers.

I've learned to giggle back.

Think I'm called to be a deeply spiritual person?

The cosmos thinks that's hilarious.

And it expects me to join in the laughter.

And when I do, I know how deeply I'm cared for. Which was the whole point of integrating my male rage and strength into mature masculinity. The course had done its work well. I'd grown and, despite myself, had received a vision of exactly who I am. And how cleverly and gently ultimate reality cares and reveals to me the truth about myself.

Which is exactly what I'd asked for.

Ultimate reality got my order straight. And served me a full helping of mutual laughter. My calling turned out to be joining with ultimate reality in mutual joyful delight and laughter. At myself. And at other creatures. Dung beetles which gather their prize and navigate home by moonlight. Dogs who nearly knock themselves over with tail wagging because it's all of ten seconds since they last saw a dog. A priest who imagines he can summon God to make him holy. It's all utterly hilarious. I couldn't have had a better call to a better future as a priest.

Thank you, divine patient waiter.

Fragility: our solid foundation

John and Rosalind were continuing their conversation in her back yard about whether it is possible to be intimate with ultimate reality.

John struggled with himself. Here she was, affirming the importance of intimacy as if it were the most normal topic in the world. Was she ignoring the second level of meaning about their own intimacy that pressed so strongly on him? Or did she just not notice? Or maybe she just didn't feel anything for him.

Rosalind had just said, "What keeps me fascinated and energized to do my research is the awe and wonder and attraction to knowing more about the patterns we discover around us. It seems an unusual concept of intimacy, but on the scale you are talking about, I can see it could make sense."

"Well, it's nice to know it makes sense to someone....." John was about to say "....I care about," but hardly missing a beat, changed it to "....I respect." That seemed quite intimate enough. For now.

"But there's something I don't yet get," Rosalind continued. "I get, one hundred percent, that through mathematics and atoms and patterns we are intimate with everything from insects to iguanas. And stones. But I wonder if we shouldn't use a different word? 'Intimacy' carries the implication of something much deeper and more fragile and mutual."

John tensed. And hoped he'd covered that up.

"Because," she went on, "it could confuse people. I can see it would be congruent with religion's assumptions about a loving God, but we'd agreed that was a projection and we weren't going to treat ultimate reality as if it were a supreme person. I know I'm made of mathematics and am in relationship with every part of the cosmos through that fact, but I don't think mathematics can be described as being in mutual relationship with me, or being aware of me, or of being intimate or caring in any way we normally use that word. How about just saying ultimate reality is our source and we are in awe of that. But intimacy? I don't think so."

John felt fragile as he said, "True, one of the things about intimacy is that it's supposed to be mutual. So I'm wondering about intimacy. Don't you think intimacy always involves being vulnerable? You don't really get to know someone until you're prepared to share something of your own fragility. That's to make yourself vulnerable and to try out what it's like to trust the other person. So, to have a relationship with ultimate reality it seems to me there'd need to be vulnerability and fragility on our side. And maybe for ultimate reality as well."

"Being vulnerable seems like a good reason to avoid a relationship," Rosalind responded. "I doubt anyone is going to be attracted to that." But what she didn't go on to say was how strongly she was attracted to this deeper sense of intimacy.

"True," said John, "but the alternative would be to live in denial, claiming I'm not vulnerable and fragile. But I've heard you and your colleagues say your professional commitment to what's true is so important that you accept as necessary the fragility of finding out that your favourite hypothesis has been proved wrong. Fragility goes hand in hand with commitment to what's true. Even just being a self-aware species is in itself to be fragile because to know one's self is to know one's limitations. It seems to me fragility is a pretty central experience for humanity, not something to be avoided.

"The patterns we call consciousness arise naturally the way waves of water or waves of cars do. However, the patterns in the physical matter of our brains, which we experience as our consciousness, are extremely fragile not just because they are in the form of jelly but also because those patterns, which are my real self, depend upon many, many layers of other fragile patterns. Our consciousness depends on our heart beating, on the provision of nutrients to our neurons, on a specialized process for removing waste products from our brain, on innumerable hormones and regulatory chemicals, on the plasticity of the neural connections and their being stimulated at the right time during infancy, on a benign environment with predictable patterns of temperature and pressure, and on and on. If any one of these, or a hundred thousand other underlying patterns over which we have no control, goes wrong, our consciousness is impaired or destroyed. That's to be fragile. It's an inevitable part of being a self-aware human. To be self-aware is to know our fragility.

"No doubt that's why we've developed thick skulls—wrap-around helmets made of bone—to keep our fragile, self-aware neural patterns as safe as possible."

"You understand evolution better than I thought!" Rosalind laughed. "You must have attended one of my lectures!"

John felt fragile. Being understood. And cared for by her.

Scanning outside for patterns

John continued. "We agree, I think, that fragility is fundamental to life and especially for humanity. Fragility is scary, yet without it we'd just be inanimate rocks.

"Our brains and our consciousness being as fragile as they are, we have to be constantly on the lookout for threats to our fragile consciousness. If we didn't scan for threats, whether in the physical environment or in our social environment, we'd soon be eaten by some predator or taken advantage of by some ruthless colleague. We also have to check what's going on inside us if we are to form solid relationships with other persons, other consciousnesses. If we didn't check inside, we'd likely offend so many people that we would have no companions willing to engage in relationship.

"Because threats to our fragility can arise in a virtually infinite array of possible forms, we need a quick and dirty way to scan for threats. The easiest way to do that is to determine whether there are many or few patterns around us. If we find there are few, that would suggest that our surroundings may not be supportive of patterns, or might even be chaotic and threatening. If that's the case, our life and fragile consciousness may be in danger. That's why it is so excruciating for a person to be locked in solitary confinement, or for a child to be made to stand in a corner, or for a parent to experience the meaningless death of their child.

Such situations usually imply that we are in a context where patterns are not upheld and so our own fragile pattern of consciousness rightly becomes anxious and threatened. Equally, if our own interior patterns puzzle us and lead to unpredictable outer behaviour, we may lose friendships and supportive relationships. No wonder we call such a context threatening or malign, and name it evil.

"But we feel safe when we find predictable patterns in our outer physical, social, and inner environments. If we find ourselves surrounded by predictable patterns both inside and outside, that implies our environment is supportive of patterns and therefore is likely to be supportive of our fragile consciousness. In such an environment, I am reassured the pattern that is me is likely to continue. We call such a physical, social, or inner environment affirming or even caring.

"I think that's why we go to murder mystery movies—we can't see the murderer approaching and our inability to grasp the pattern of what's going on is deeply disturbing. We are so desperate to find meaning that we'll pay actors to take the meaning away for an hour or two in a movie and then give it back at the end in the form of the deep pleasure of finding the hidden clues, the patterns we missed. Then it all makes sense and we are reassured and safe. Alfred Hitchcock made a lot of money when he figured out that people would pay to have their meanings taken away in order to experience the delight of getting them back!

"Any conscious beings that didn't scan their physical environment for support or threats would soon die of starvation or be eaten. Those that didn't scan for threats from other consciousnesses could be taken advantage of, and those that didn't scan their own thoughts and motivations couldn't interact in trustworthy ways with other people. But those who scanned those three environments—physical, social and internal—prospered and reproduced. So, we are the descendants of creatures that successfully observed their three environments—physical, social and inner —and adjusted their behaviour accordingly. Those are every one of our ancestors.

"For a child, this human need to search constantly for patterns and be reassured that patterns are all around, lies behind questions like, 'Why is there fluff on the road?' It's disturbing even for a child to imagine there is no pattern to the fluff; that random fluff can just happen— that would be chaos. For a disturbed adult I heard about, it is the need to find a connection between the apparently randomly numbered electrical outlets in a hospital ward and his own birthdate. That way each of us knows we are safe—we have identified patterns around us and therefore we know we are in an environment that supports patterns. That's reassuring. And it feels caring.

"When cultures encouraged projections of God, this desire to find pattern and meaning was expressed in stories of order emerging from chaos. The ancient Jews identified pattern in their carefully constructed description of the six days of creation in which pattern overcame chaos. They did the same thing in their carefully constructed history, composed in a time of profound chaos, in which a faithful God provided the underlying pattern for everything, good and bad, that happened to them regardless of how little they cared about God."

Rosalind picked up his train of thought. "The same is true in our culture of science—the whole point of science is to discover connections and patterns between every process we can observe. Einstein found a pattern that connected gravity to geometry and so provided an explanation about how objects move everywhere in the entire universe. A similar search is underway for a Theory of Everything that would be an over-arching pattern that could incorporate all local patterns and so provide cosmic connections. We don't ignore every new scientific discovery as an anomaly; instead, every anomaly triggers a search for the pleasure of discovering previously unknown patterns which underlie the new information. Science is motivated by the fact that the more patterns and connections we find around us, the surer our consciousness is that we are likely to continue to exist; and thus the more affirmed and confident we feel. It's a wonderful feeling to be upheld by our environment.

"When I was a post-doc, I made a discovery about an essential protein-forming process going on in a virus. We'd been trying to find the connection for six months and I stumbled on it. I think I scared everyone with the yell I let out when I saw the connection! Finding that pattern in the chaos of data was one of the most wonderful experiences I've ever had."[2]

"Exactly!"

Then he thought about it. "Scientists yell? Really?"

---

2   As related to the author by a respondent during the author's research.

"Oh yes! We live for those moments!"

"That's wonderful! So, your whole professional life is built around the assumption that you are going to find patterns everywhere you look. No wonder you were so happy and so fulfilled!"

John realized for a moment he had entered her world and experienced her joy.

It felt almost frighteningly intimate. He was startled at how much he cared. He hesitated for a moment before continuing. He was aware of the implications and of his own fragility. And hers.

"Being fragile is terrifying, and yet essential for any significant relationship.

"I can tell you, I was doing a lot of scanning when we were at the University Club, and later, at your lecture. A lot of the time, it sure didn't feel as if the other consciousnesses were supportive. True, they were committed to finding patterns, and that kept me from despair and from feeling completely alienated. I also experienced a kind of affirmation in their relentless pursuit of patterns because it was so obviously not personal and not designed to critique me and my faith. It was clear that you and your colleagues were open to alternative ideas, although not prepared to give in to the hopeful but groundless proofs I kept raising in my attempt to demonstrate the existence of God. Strange as it seems, that felt like caring. But it was scary. And I felt very fragile."

"Yes," she said, "I had a sense of that."

She had? He felt very supported. By the pattern of her consciousness being aware of, and caring about his pattern of consciousness.

There was a pause. Both of them wondered what this meant. Some kind of deep connection had just happened. Something meant something. They had experienced a deepening of pattern between them through their mutual fragility. Each of them was aware that their inner self was responding to the other, and wondered if the same was true for the other, and neither were ready yet to be so fragile as to ask.

Scanning inside: déjà vu, and self-awareness

But the awareness of her own fragility and of scanning inside herself triggered something in Rosalind.

"Although I suspect it doesn't support your religious beliefs, you might be interested that science has identified the area of the brain that is associated with the ability to scan one's inner self and to become self-aware. The area lies behind our foreheads, in the pre-frontal cortex. Our pre-frontal cortex is associated with being conscious of what we are about to do or say in the next one or two seconds, and what we imagine will be the response of the person with whom we are interacting. We are observing our own self and simultaneously we are imagining the self-aware consciousness of the other person with whom we are in conversation. All in a couple of seconds or less. That's a remarkable juggling act. This is why human foreheads are so large compared to those of other animals. It takes highly complex patterns among the neurons in our brains to produce such an extraordinary phenomenon as observing one's own observing.

"If we were to find a species that reflected on their lives and thought about what sort of individual each of them was, we would be astonished. We would treat such an animal as if it were a human in a non-human body, just because it was self-aware. We may even have observed the nascent emergence of that ability in some non-human species. Some primates and some cetaceans and some birds (and even, it seems, some fish!)[3] show glimmerings of being self-aware by being able to identify themselves in a mirror, although none, as far as we can tell are fully self-aware, engaging in private self-reflection, observing their inner feelings, discussing them with other orcas, or birds, or fish and consciously adjusting their behaviour on that basis.

"We are increasingly impressed with various new forms of intelligence we are now encountering, such as that of octopuses whose intelligence is distributed within its eight arms. However if a degree of self-awareness comparable to ours is present in other creatures, we've not yet become aware of it. Which of course doesn't mean it isn't there, just that at this point in our knowledge we've found no evidence in other creatures of self-awareness at the depth we have inherited it.

"As far as we are aware, fully self-aware creativity, social responsibility, imagination, and ethics are unique to humans because we have such a highly developed ability to observe our inner self as if from someone else's perspective and know we are observing our self.

"But," Rosalind continued, "here's something curious. Orcas don't use their pre-frontal cortex for self-awareness—their brains have developed a different area for that function and it is a region that doesn't exist in humans.

"You may have noticed I'm not a religious person." Rosalind smiled. "But I

---

3   M. Kohda, *et al.* "Cleaner fish recognize self in a mirror via self-face recognition like humans," *Proceedings of the National Academy of Sciences*. Published online February 6, 2023. doi: 10.1073/pnas.2208420120.

must say I have a sense of awe and mystery about that. Creatures with enough brain function to be even slightly self-aware presumably form more creative bonds, build lasting communities, cooperate better and reproduce more. So there's evolutionary pressure to become self-aware. However, regardless of what pre-existing brain structures are available, patterns enabling self-awareness find a way to emerge, all through ordinary evolutionary processes. That's remarkable. If that's happening throughout the universe, that says something about the universe, even if I don't know what."

She continued. "We may even be able, in real time, to observe the mechanisms which enable our own self-awareness."

"You can look into your own brain and observe yourself observing?" asked John, skeptically.

"That's right. We've all had the strange déjà vu experience of being startled that sometime in the past we've already had the exact conversation we are now having, even though we know the conversation can't have actually happened in the past. But the sensation of this exact conversation having happened in the past is undeniable. This strange experience never lasts more than a couple of seconds but it may be a window into understanding how our brains can be aware of our own self.

"Here's how déjà vu probably works. Our brains are constantly forming memories about everything that is currently happening to us. We can easily remember what just happened to us a few minutes ago. That seems obvious. But when someone has short-term memory loss and cannot remember things from a few minutes ago but can easily remember things from decades ago, it's clear there are two different memory processes going on—one for the past few minutes, and one for things that happened long ago. In the déjà vu experience, what is likely happening is that memory from the last few seconds is accidentally being accessed by the part of our brain that normally receives memories from the distant past. The result is an illusion that what is happening right now also happened in the past. It's a curious and rather fun little glitch in our mental processing.

"In case you're wondering," laughed Rosalind, "my memory inputs are functioning just fine—I've had no déjà vu experience that long ago you and I have already had this conversation about déjà vu! But I'm not saying I wouldn't enjoy it twice! But so far, I've no doubt that right now is the real thing!"

"Feels real to me," John responded, wondering on how many levels she might take that.

"The glitch we call déjà vu," Rosalind continued, "may solve a conundrum about self-awareness. The conundrum is that if I'm observing my self, who is the self that is doing the observing? And who is the self that's being observed? Do we have two 'selfs'—one self deciding what to do, and a second self observing the deciding self? That seems very odd. But déjà vu provides us with a possible explanation. In déjà vu we experience one event—the current conversation—as two events: one happening now and another that happened in the past.

"In self-aware consciousness, we may be experiencing a parallel phenomenon—we decide to do or say something and then a moment later we become aware of that decision. It could be that we experience those two processes as separate, and so we experience our inner self as if it were two—one self deciding to say something and a second self observing the first self. But what's really happening is that we are experiencing a normal delay between deciding to do something and being aware of our decision to do it."

"You mean," asked John, "that our self being aware of our self might be just a different version of the memory glitch that causes our experience of déjà vu?"

"It could be, I don't know, but I have to say that my sense of humour would be tickled if it were! Imagine if our research observing our human self-awareness—our unique ability to observe ourself observing—arises from us getting our observing processes confused! That tickles my funny-bone!

"What's significant," she continued, "is that this double awareness happens all the time and just feels normal, whereas the memory glitch happens rarely and therefore we notice it's a glitch. Perhaps what may have started out as a glitch—the illusion of one inner self observing a second inner self—turned out to be a highly useful illusion which enables us to be aware of our self. Being self-aware would have carried enormous advantages for humans who could do that, and their success ensured the glitch was carried on in their descendants. That's how humanity was created. After all, that's how all evolutionary development happens."

Scanning inside: an fMRI[4] technician knows what you're going to decide before you do

Rosalind continued. "While it's fun to imagine that self-awareness might be a variation of the déjà vu glitch, we do have some solid experimental evidence of the mechanism that expresses self-awareness. If we place someone in a functional MRI scanner and ask her to decide, whenever she wishes, to move either her right hand or her left hand, we can observe the activity of her neurons as she decides which hand to move. That seems obvious, but the strange discovery is that the neurons which indicate which hand she decides to move are activated as much as a couple of seconds *before* she decides which hand to move. If we watch the neurons through the scanner, the operator knows which hand the person is going to decide to move before the person herself decides. It seems the neurons have made up their minds *before* the person did, sometimes several seconds earlier.[5] Sometimes even ten seconds earlier. This is very strange."

"That's an understatement!" said John. "What's going on?"

"One interpretation of this phenomenon is that we aren't as free in making decisions as we think we are. That interpretation implies that we don't actually have freedom to decide which hand to move, that's just an illusion. The actual decision is never in our conscious control, but we mistakenly imagine a conscious self is deciding things.

"But a more intriguing explanation is that the process of observing our self takes time, and it takes a few moments to observe the decision we made. What may be happening is when we make the decision to move one of our hands, the fMRI machine correctly reports the neural activity associated with that decision at the moment we made the decision. But it may then take a period of time for the part of the brain that observes decisions to receive that information and present the information so we become aware that we made the decision. The person in the scanner reports she made the decision to move her hand only when she becomes aware of having already made the decision. The time lag between making the decision and being aware of having made it explains how the operator of the machine knows what the subject is going to do before she does."

---

4   An fMRI (functional MRI) is a specialized MRI machine which takes videos, usually of the brain, over a period of time. MRI machines take 3-dimensional still photographs.

5   Nat Neurosci, 2008 May;11(5):543-5. doi: 10.1038/nn.2112. Epub 2008 Apr 13. *Unconscious determinants of free decisions in the human brain* Chun Siong Soon 1, Marcel Brass, Hans-Jochen Heinze, John-Dylan Haynes.

"That's fascinating," John said. "But far from not helping my religious proposals, it seems to me what you've said supports my suggestion that ultimate reality is caring. After all, these layers and complexities of emerging patterns that enable our own consciousness to be aware of our self would give us the sense our ultimate environment is highly supportive of patterns. If we are supported that deeply by processes that happen and aren't caused by us, I think we can call that an experience of being cared for."

"Sorry." And they both knew she wasn't. "Isn't it a bit of a stretch to say ultimate reality cares? These are just natural processes, remarkable as they seem to us. No caring God or caring ultimate reality required."

She was surprised how much energy it took to resist her desire *not* to explain to him what was really going on. She didn't want to threaten the chance of more time in conversation, but neither did she want to destroy the connections and meanings she had worked so hard to achieve. *It must mean*, she thought, *that I value his reactions. Maybe I do care about him.*

But John didn't seem concerned.

"You're completely right, as far as you go. But," he said, "the best is yet to come."

She looked up sharply. *Now what did he have in mind?*

Intimacy was one thing. But being cared for was another. Rosalind had a sense John cared for her, and that was scary. But ultimate reality? Could ultimate reality care? She wasn't sure she wanted to raise that question, partly because she was sure it couldn't, and partly because by raising the question she might end up pulling the rug out from under his faith, and she never wanted to do that again.

Being surrounded by the ever-present sense of being upheld and surrounded and enabled by processes beyond anyone's comprehension was both delightful and scary.

Scanning the ultimate environment: intimacy is caring

But could ultimate reality care? She hunched that John hoped it did, but she knew it was just a mindless process and if they weren't going to start a new projection, then she knew she'd have to challenge his desire that ultimate reality can care. She hoped she had the courage to honour him and not avoid telling the truth.

John was continuing his proposal about how ultimate reality could care.

"As you've told me, scientific study delights you. You revel in the discovery of more patterns of which you hadn't previously been aware. You yell when you've discovered something wonderful. I think you could rightly name that as a direct experience of being cared for—we are always delighted when we feel cared for. It could have been, I suppose, that everything science discovered was boring and not connected to anything. But that's not the cosmos in which we live. The more science learns, the more we are intrigued, fascinated, and delighted by the unending discovery of new interactions of patterns.

"Don't you think that proves you scientists are especially cared for by ultimate reality? Ultimate reality gives scientists so much pleasure! My turn to say, 'Gotcha!'" John said, with a twinkle in his eye. "But I'm serious, too."

Rosalind felt cared for. "OK. Just for now, I'll agree I've been had!"

They'd both just been had. By each other.

The silence, as they digested that truth, was painful, fizzy, and tingly.

It was like the pleasure of having a really skilled partner to play against in scrabble or squash. Every once in a while, your competitor shows you a pattern you'd never have seen yourself. And that doubles the pleasure.

"So," John went on, "if a centre of consciousness perceives the physical world and the social context to be supportive of patterns, wouldn't our consciousness describe that context as being pleasurable and affirming? Or even caring? And if our consciousness discovers that inside us is a pattern of self-observation that has always been on the lookout for our welfare, even if we had never noticed it, won't we say that inner process of self-aware consciousness is affirming and caring? And on the largest scale, since the patterns that affirm us in the physical world, as well as in the social world and even the patterns of self-awareness within our self all arise from ultimate reality, why wouldn't we say the same thing about ultimate reality? That ultimate reality can accurately be experienced as caring?"

"Are you trying to say," Rosalind responded, "that all of us experience ultimate reality as being, in some way at least, supportive of us, otherwise we wouldn't have happened at all?"

Sort of," John replied. "I don't mean to suggest ultimate reality thought of us before we evolved, or did anything intentionally, or is conscious in itself. That would be to revert to imagining ultimate reality as just another projection of ourselves, and we'd be back at the idea of God as a supreme being tinkering with the universe. I entirely agree with your rejection of that interpretation.

"What I mean is that one of the qualities of ultimate reality is it provides the substrate for consciousness to emerge. We have evolved in the context of an enormously complex environment, any aspect of which could easily have prevented us from ever happening. But we did happen. We are, in fact, supported by the pattern-creating quality of ultimate reality. In that sense, we can't help experiencing ourselves as having arisen from, and being supported at every moment by, a deeply caring ultimate reality.

"Since it's the emergence of the patterns through the process we call evolution that has given us the ability to be intimate with our own inner self, we could indeed say our self-aware consciousness, our self-intimacy, arises from ultimate reality. After all, we didn't sit down to invent self-awareness; it just emerged in our brains the way it does in orcas and other social creatures. Since ultimate reality has given us intimacy, with our self and with others, I think it could be scientifically accurate to say ultimate reality is indeed intimate with us. There are even physics researchers exploring a version of this possibility."[6]

"That means ultimate reality is closer than our heartbeat, closer than our neurons, more alert to our protection than we even know. I don't see how we can experience that in any other way than as profoundly caring. I don't mean ultimate reality cares in any way that is like human caring, but the experience of human caring is the closest we can get to describing what it's like from our end of our relationship with ultimate reality.

Rosalind paused as she considered this. "It makes a lot of sense, but I think there is a problem you've overlooked. I think you are cherry-picking the facts. We can't cherry-pick facts."

The "we" felt very connected to him. As if he were being invited again into her world. That felt very caring indeed. But what did her "but" mean?

Rosalind explained. "It now looks as if the universe will expand forever. When something expands it gets colder. That's how fridges and air conditioning works—the machine allows a gas to expand rapidly, it gets cold, and that's where the cool comes from. The exact same thing happens on the scale of the universe. If the current cosmic expansion continues indefinitely eventually

---

6   Constructor theory, developed by David Deutsch and Chiara Marletto of the University of Oxford has been described as "...a kind of bedrock of reality from which all the laws of physics emerge." While Deutsch and Marletto are not concerned with the personal relationship we have with ultimate reality as considered in this book, their study of the "bedrock of reality" (which we are calling 'ultimate reality') suggests that the idea of a foundational process behind all physical reality is a credible concept being taken seriously within the physics community. The Physics arXiv Blog, quant-ph > arXiv:1405.5563, May 28, 2014.

everything will evaporate into cold featureless darkness. Even protons, the most long-lived components of atoms, will eventually evaporate into pure energy, but in an ever-expanding universe, even all that energy will not keep the temperature above absolute zero. Nothing will be left to make patterns out of. In the end, the universe will destroy all patterns, and that would mean the universe is not supportive of us and our consciousness, and so is not meaningful or caring as you are suggesting. The universe will ultimately destroy us. That's not an experience of caring.

"I don't mean to be a pessimist, but I wonder if you aren't just projecting again? Ultimate reality doesn't care. Then your hope of building a religion on the idea of a supportive and caring ultimate reality will simply be wishful thinking. Better to admit it."

She paused. "I'd rather face uncomfortable facts than live in an illusion. "

"Honestly." And she was. "I'm sorry, because it was a great idea."

"Sorry." But he wasn't. "I think it's you who's projecting! The universe isn't the same thing as ultimate reality. When the universe ends in ultimate blackness and infinite cold, ultimate reality will not cease. The universe may end, because the universe exists, whereas, as we decided, ultimate reality is beyond existence. When the universe ends, mathematics doesn't cease to be. Mathematics is eternal—its logic is still real even if there were no objects in existence to count. Ultimate reality would still remain the potential source of endless patterns.

"Contrary to what you suggest, I think we can put our trust in ultimate reality and experience it as caring, in the sense that it eternally supports the emergence of patterns into existence and therefore, supports the emergence of consciousness, and us. That would still be true even if, in the end, no things exist from which patterns can be made. As Charles pointed out to me, there may be an unending number of universes, all arising from ultimate reality, so maybe ultimate reality cares so much it can't help creating more universes."

"All right," she said. "I can see you might think about ultimate reality as if it were caring and giving rise to existence. And I do have to admit that just going on existing is a nice feeling."

Yes, sometimes it's very good, isn't it! Like now, existing with you, he thought.

"So," Rosalind said, "I can see how we could think about ultimate reality being intimate and caring. It's sort of attractive but has an odd scary sense about it. I'm not totally comfortable thinking that I'm surrounded by ultimate reality that's so entwined with me. On the other hand, if that sort of caring is true, it does provide a solid argument for a more responsible and respectful attitude toward the rest of life and toward our common environment that keeps us all alive."

Science needs intimacy

"I think," John said, "it might be important for scientists to speak more explicitly about this intimacy that you and your colleagues enjoy so much and that we've identified in ultimate reality. There is a currently popular attitude toward science that dismisses science as a childish 'gee-whiz' geeky fascination with obscure mechanical processes. That attitude may have arisen, because science seems to have no place for values, or experiences of beauty, or personal significance, or commitment, or passion, or intimacy, or justice. For a lot of people, that's a poor sort of world if that's what science is pointing us to. Understandably, quite a few people are doubtful about the value of science if it doesn't relate to what's most important to them and to their deep humanity—various kinds of intimacy."

"I get that," Rosalind responded, "but science has to insist that personal feelings have no place in determining truth, otherwise we'd just have chaos. Anyone could manipulate information to suit their own preferences. Science is dedicated to the search for what's real, not for what we'd like to be real. I don't see how we could take feelings and personal preferences into account as we do our research."

"Yet you scientists, as you say, are motivated by your feelings. You wouldn't be doing science if it bored you. I'm not saying personal feelings or preferences should be the basis of scientific conclusions. But I think science may have overreacted to the way religion resisted science dismantling some cherished beliefs and insisted on the primacy of personal conviction over objective truth.

"There's a very practical implication if science were to declare we cannot avoid being intimate with the universe, and therefore humanity must acknowledge and honour that fundamental relationship. That would undercut the assumption of our culture that the world is a dead machine that exists for the sole purpose of turning out whatever kind of widgets humans have been led to desire. Unless science upholds the fact that we are in intimate relationship with the planet, there isn't any reason not to consume the entire planet for our own purposes. Down that route lies environmental disaster. Which could happen if science is perceived only as a hobby for people who like that kind of thing, the adult equivalent of playing with toy trains, or only as a machine for producing more stuff."

Faith in Doubt

"Touché!" Rosalind responded. "That's exactly how we in science think of you religious types—fine if you like that sort of thing, but dangerous as a misleading prejudice. Just like you just described science."

John was startled. Was she joking about her life's passion? If so, there was a commitment to truth in her that impressed him.

John continued. "It could be, if you'll pardon me, that religion may have something important to contribute to science. We have lots of experience describing and expressing awe and intimacy on the cosmic scale. But the objective truth—that we are in intimate relationship with all life, and through cosmic processes with the cosmos—ought to be front and centre. If the implications of that discovery are ignored, we place ourselves and our planet in real danger. Don't you think the religious experience of trust in ultimate intimacy could provide resources for science to affirm the intimacy of that relationship?"

Rosalind hadn't thought of that before. It was an attractive approach to something that had always given her energy. She did indeed feel fulfilled, and almost intimate, every time she stumbled upon a new connection or found a new pattern through her research. Maybe that's why she enjoyed being with this believer—she had a chance to share her passion for the connections she felt. And then he pointed to more connections. That was a kind of intimacy. Just like a new research discovery.

"I've always thought of intimacy as optional," Rosalind said. "Something that might be really nice, but not central to who we are. But you're suggesting intimacy is essential for the survival of the human race, in that if we don't appreciate our intimacy with the rest of life, we will just use it up and destroy ourselves in the process. That's a powerful argument for intimacy not being the icing on the cake but for being the solid food of life. Thanks, I appreciate your insight." She wondered if science should take this seriously.

Both of them couldn't help wondering how this might apply to them. Neither was prepared to raise the question. It was too disturbing. The more intimate they became and the more they cared for each other, the more fragile they felt. Just like all human consciousness.

Was ultimate reality laughing at them...in a caring way, of course?

Summary

In the previous chapter, we saw how ultimate reality is intimately entwined with our very existence—it's what we are made of. It is more intimate with us than our bodies, than our personhood, than our very self.

Because our patterns are fragile, we continually scan our physical, social, and inner environments to see if our environment is likely to support patterns and therefore support us.

Because we are made of patterns and are surrounded at every moment and in every dimension by pattern—in the outer physical world, in the world of relationships and in our inner world of self-awareness—and because we know how fragile we are, the more patterns we find around and within us, the more secure we are and the more we feel cared for, just as happens in a human relationship. We can't help being aware of being intimate with ultimate reality and being surrounded by its caring.

What ultimate reality is in itself, nobody knows, but from our perspective as patterns within the cosmos, scientific research implies ultimate reality can indeed be accurately experienced as caring.

And that makes all the difference when we withdraw that projection and discover the same is true of us.

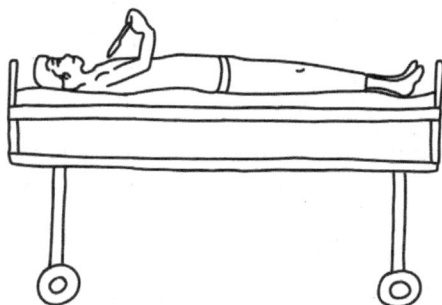

CHAPTER 13
Ultimate Reality: Dying to Love

The joy of surgery

It's the morning of my sweetheart's surgery.

This is something neither of us had ever imagined happening. It happens to other people and we express care and sympathy. But now it is happening to us and it will change our lives forever. But it's not our lives I'm worried about.

I can hardly bear the thought of them cutting her up, disfiguring her body. Even if it's the only way to protect her from the cancer.

Without warning, an urge arises in me. I want to pick up the phone, call the surgeon, and ask him to do the surgery on me so he won't have to do it on her. I'm struggling not to dial the phone in case he thinks I've gone out of my mind; but the urge remains. *I'll come into the hospital right now, Dr. Jones. Do the surgery on my chest.*

As a priest, I've been with people before and after surgery countless times. I've seen how hard it is. But I have this urge to phone the surgeon. *Please do it on me.*

Once might not be enough. I'll volunteer to do it twice. Twice, waking up nauseated but glad it's over, and twice, as the pain in my chest and vomiting get worse the next few days; as they wake me up to check for fever every few hours night and day; twice, as it seems as if I will never heal over the weeks ahead. Twice, as stitches have to come out; twice, as one learns how to live with a scar and lack of flexibility. Not twice. Ten times. Fifty times. *Please, Dr. Jones, do it on me. I'll come in right now so you don't have to do it on her.*

Where did that come from?

Not from me.

Mostly, I'd been pretty self-centred in our relationship.

I tell this story at the risk of being misunderstood. The story isn't about my being so loving that I wanted to take her disfiguring surgery on myself. It's precisely because I'm not that loving that I describe what happened.

That urge to phone the surgeon and take the surgery away from my sweetheart came unbidden, without forethought, without my having thought through to any conclusion as to whether it was a good idea; without my wanting or even deciding to do it. It was as if it came from beyond me and it persisted despite my determination not to look like a fool and actually make the phone call. I had no idea I'd want to do such a thing. I'd always thought I didn't love her that much.

Go under the knife fifty, a hundred times, for her? It would have been a joy.

Where did this urge come from? I'm not masochistic, nor do I have a saviour complex—the urge wasn't some kind of aberration or magical thinking. It was, however, profoundly loving. I don't claim that as a quality for myself—if that had been the case, I would have sat down already and thought it through. The way one might think of donating a kidney to somebody one cared for. My strange urge was so that the surgery be done on me and not done on her at all.

This sudden urge came from outside my normal decision-making—everything in my normal decision-making resisted it. I can only say it expressed the deepest 'me'— a quality I had no idea was in myself and that I experienced as coming from beyond me. In one sense, this urge that came from 'beyond' was indeed a projection, but at the same time it revealed something that was deeply real. Just as all projections are intended to do. My little, immature, self-centred love had been replaced by a love of which I could be proud. Even though it wasn't mine.

Where did such deep desire to love come from?

My desire to have her surgery done on me despite its pointlessness arises from our deep human commitment to patterns. To be deeply committed to patterns implies that, paradoxically, one is prepared to have one's own patterns disrupted—even to risk death as the ultimate disruption—to enable someone else's patterns to be upheld. That is real commitment to patterns. That is real love.

That has an extraordinary implication. Contradictory as it seems, the deepest possible pattern a human can have is the readiness to give up one's own pattern to uphold someone else's. It's about dying so someone else can live. That's the deepest pattern we can ever enact.

That's who we really are. We are comprised of patterns. So, it should be no surprise that our most real self could be so committed to upholding patterns that we would give up our own for somebody else's.

The only reason this surprises us is that we had mistakenly thought we weren't that committed to patterns! Perhaps we thought we were made of something fragile and impermanent! But the fact is, we are made of ultimate reality, the reality that is the most real and permanent thing there is. So perhaps it's entirely normal to give up our pattern to value someone else's.

If you and I are capable of dying for someone, what does that say about the nature of the ultimate reality that is the source of the patterns from which we emerge?

Ultimate reality: dying to love

Rosalind was looking thoughtful about John's suggestion that living within ultimate reality means we experience ultimate reality as caring for us.

"OK. Are you saying that from the point of view of consciousness, the affirmation we feel in discovering we are surrounded by patterns that uphold our brain patterns in self-aware consciousness is something that, in any other context, we would call caring? Is that what you are getting at?"

"You get what I mean!" he said, hoping his centre of consciousness would receive support and affirmation from hers.

It was worth the risk. He plunged on.

"I have an idea."

"Oh, no! Help! There's more!" Rosalind said in mock horror.

"Yup. It's about love. Think you can handle that?"

"Like water off a duck's back. If you're going to try to connect love and ultimate reality, I'll need a tall one."

She refilled their glasses. With the caffeinated fi-*izz*-y stuff.

"OK. I'm all ears. But watch yourself about this love stuff—I'll begin to think you've got something in mind."

"OK." he said, "I've been warned!"

But he did indeed have something in mind.

"I want to propose to you...." *whoops! pre-frontal cortex almost missed that one,* he thought, ".... suggest to you that science, in discovering this automatic emergence of patterns, has discovered that ultimate reality loves us."

Her immediate reaction was to guffaw. But her self observing her self thought better of it. But not quite soon enough. She stifled the laugh, but not having caught it in time, had to pretend she'd coughed and then sat back and listened. When he'd come to her house so solemnly up the steps and she'd opened the door to his rage, she was sure he was talking gibberish. But it turned out to mean a lot. So, if only for a moment, she was prepared to listen to this rubbish. Who knows? It might turn out to mean something. Besides, she was feeling strangely connected, perhaps even a little intimate and caring, and she didn't want to endanger that feeling again. Must mean she cared.

For a brief moment, she had a sense of how much she would hurt if she had hurt him by her guffaw. It was a kind of love that she'd covered up her guffaw with a cough. Not romantic, but true.

Thank goodness she'd successfully fooled him—he hadn't noticed she was covering up.

John was already sharing his idea. "You and your colleagues have demon-strated to me that ultimate reality is intimate with us—that we are made of the particles that emerged into existence from ultimate reality. And ultimate reality continues to uphold mathematics and patterns that, without our help, have emerged in the form of our self-aware consciousness. We can't help experience that as caring."

"I know that's what you'd like to think," Rosalind responded. "You'd like to think ultimate reality is ultimately reliable; that even in the extreme case when the universe ceases to contain any objects at all, ultimate reality is still there lurking in the background to provide at least the potential of pattern that could become life and could become conscious. That would be comforting; I can understand that." She hoped she sounded supportive.

"I hunch there's more going on," John responded.

Did he know what had been going on? Suddenly she felt very known. Too known. And relieved he didn't know what was going on. She hoped. She looked at him carefully. No sign he'd noticed she'd just laughed at him. She let out a silent breath of relief.

John continued. "You and I agree that because of the fragility of our consciousness we are driven to ask incessantly about the stability of the environment in which we live. So now, think about the worst-case scenario.

"What would it mean if ultimate reality abandoned us? We'd simply cease to be. Ultimate reality is our ultimate environment. The worst possible scenario is that ultimate reality might stop upholding existence and patterns. If that happened, what would that mean? For us, it would mean we'd simply cease to be."

"Yes, I get that. Makes sense."

"But here's the more.

"What would that mean for ultimate reality?"

Rosalind was startled. That was a question she'd not anticipated. Where was this going?

John continued. "To give rise to patterns that are an expression of its deepest self, and then to permanently destroy all pattern by withdrawing the emergence of pattern would mean ultimate reality would be in contradiction with itself.

"Why?

"Because ultimate reality is the source of patterns and yet would destroy patterns. That would mean ultimate reality would be destroying itself, since its central character is to create patterns. So, if ultimate reality were to abandon patterns, ultimate reality would be in a self-contradiction that would be the end of itself as the ultimate source of pattern. It wouldn't be ultimate. It also wouldn't be reality because destruction of patterns would be the final reality, and that's the opposite of what ultimate reality is.

"Imagine the implication for us if, in some strange way, it were normal for ultimate reality to destroy patterns. Since we arise from ultimate reality, and we can't help embodying its character, destroying patterns would be the deepest pattern of being human. So, if ultimate reality ultimately destroys patterns, then so will we. It would mean our central character as humans is to destroy everything, from personal relationships to the cosmos. If destruction of patterns is our deepest nature, we would enact that ultimate violence not as a sad truth, but as glorious destiny.

"That means humanity would be most deeply filled with joy the more we destroy everything.

"But that cannot be. Not because we would be appalled at finding violence is our central character (we wouldn't be appalled because that would be who we were and being ultimately violent would fulfil us), but because to destroy everything would include the destruction of joy and fulfilment. And the destruction of ourselves. Either way, we cannot have joy and fulfilment by destroying joy and fulfilment. And destroying ourselves.

"If ultimate reality were to abandon patterns, that would create a contradiction in itself and in humanity and in the cosmos. How then could such a contradiction be ultimate? It cannot. It would be the destruction of patterns and of ultimate reality itself.

"If ultimate reality would destroy itself if it abandoned the patterns it had brought into existence, then the only other option is that ultimate reality will make the support of patterns its absolute priority. The astonishing implication is that ultimate reality must be so committed to bringing patterns into existence that it would sacrifice the pattern that is itself in order to preserve the patterns that are us. Not through a sense of duty, but as its highest expression of what ultimate reality, the source of patterns, is. That is its pattern.

"If it's not to contradict its own nature, ultimate reality must be prepared, if necessary, to destroy itself in order to uphold our patterns. That must be its ultimate nature. Otherwise, it wouldn't be ultimate and the ultimate source of pattern."

Rosalind was silent for a bit. "Are you saying what lies behind everything, ultimate reality, would value us more than itself? That's mind-boggling."

"The way I see it," said John, "there's no way around it. If ultimate reality is ultimate, and its ultimate character is to give rise to patterns, then its greatest loyalty to itself would be to abandon itself in order to remain loyal to the patterns to which it had given existence."

Rosalind thought this was the most bizarre idea she'd ever heard.

But then a recent experience struck her.

She had recently babysat her niece. It had been a revelation to her that she could be so moved by this tiny child. It was as if this little mite of a being held her whole heart, her whole life, in her little hand grasping Rosalind's finger. Would she give up her life for that child? She shuddered at the thought, felt guilty that maybe she wouldn't and then found herself suffused with a joy of total fulfilment. Of course, she would! To give up her life so that little girl could live would make more sense than anything she'd ever done. Was John saying that's the quality lying behind the entire universe? What if it were? Rosalind didn't notice, but a gentleness came over her face and she felt more relaxed than she had for a long time.

John noticed, but said nothing. But he knew she knew. Not knew about. Knew. Directly.

What John didn't realize was they were together having the same experience of joy in another's fulfilment.

But John wasn't finished yet.

He feared he was about to tread on raw nerves by stating the utterly obvious. With his heart in his mouth, he said it anyway. How could he not?

"We experience ultimate reality as not just being supportive and caring, but as actively risking the sacrifice of itself to uphold the patterns that have become us. It seems to me, then, the only possible human response is to call that quality love."

After a moment, "So…I suppose we respond in love?" It was a statement that included the sense of falling off a cliff. It felt like the riskiest thing she'd ever said. She hoped he'd think she was teasing. And hoped he wouldn't.

"Yes," John replied. "Such as when you give up something for a person to affirm them."

"I think it happens all the time."

Rosalind felt she'd been punched in the stomach. Had he noticed my near-guffaw after all? Had he guessed? Is he protecting me by pretending not to have noticed? Is he describing what I did in stifling my laugh, as loving? In which case, if he was raising it this gently, then he must care enough to be sure he isn't embarrassing me. That is really caring. Perhaps even loving. If so, it was as bizarre as his idea that ultimate reality might destroy itself to be faithful and loving to us. And makes wonderful sense.

This felt too intimate, so she moved on to a safer response.

"You actually want me to love ultimate reality? Are you kidding?" She wasn't entirely sure whether she was kidding. Or not.

"Yes and no! Yes, I'm kidding by putting that so bluntly. But no, I'm not kidding because, if ultimate reality loves us in the sense of giving itself up for us, then we cannot help loving back. That's what always happens when you find yourself loved."

"There you go again. You want me to love ultimate reality."

She wanted him to hear that as a joke. But she found it more disturbing and at the same time more fascinating and attractive than she was prepared to say. Somewhere deep, it tingled. Again.

Curious, that the image of a razor in the hand of Occam turns out to be the image of a knife in the hand of a priest killing a sacrifice, which turns out to be the image of me asking the surgeon to turn the knife on me, which turns out to be ultimate reality ready to turn the knife on itself so we can do the same for one another by using our self-aware consciousness to love that other. At any cost.

No wonder Rosalind was feeling so vulnerable. Suddenly, she felt as if she were standing at the edge of a cliff about to fall off, not into a black hole, but into an overwhelming light. If this were true, it would turn her whole life, and everything else, upside-down. Something in her wanted desperately to step away from that precipice. It was that attractive.

And she was feeling more fragile than she had for a long time.

It had been a long conversation.

Time to conclude before she became even more vulnerable.

"It's been great, but I've got a seminar to prepare for tomorrow and I really should get to work on that."

As she walked him out of her garden his hand wanted to touch hers, but he decided not to. But his hand did anyway. Accidentally, of course. Just brushed hers. Neither commented on it. Both of them highly aware. Both denying to themselves that it meant anything, or that there was any connection or meaning in that touch even though connection and affirmation and care and meaning and, perhaps even loving touch is what they both longed for more than anything.

They were standing at her gate. Their hands hadn't really touched, had they, so there wouldn't be any ulterior motive if he invited her to his home. It wouldn't exactly be a date, but it could be a step to making more connections. Of all kinds.

"My turn to have you over to my place."

She'd wondered what his place was like. You could learn a lot about a person by seeing their home. So far, so good with him, but an inside view would be better.

They agreed to meet the following week.

At his house.

Summary

We have seen ultimate reality is intimate with us because it gives rise to patterns that emerge as us. Because we are surrounded on every side and in every moment by that pattern-emerging process, we therefore experience ultimate reality as not only intimate, but also caring for us by upholding the patterns which are our self.

But a strange implication follows from that. If the fundamental character of ultimate reality is to give rise to patterns, then ultimate reality must be committed to those patterns because they are an expression of itself.

How far would ultimate reality go to be committed to the patterns to which it has given rise? If ultimate reality really is ultimate, then there is no limit to how far it would go. It would even abandon its own self to remain committed to the patterns to which it had given rise. Otherwise it would abandon its own character.

It would die for us in order to be what it is.

That is what it is to be loved.

And because we emerge from ultimate reality, that's what we are made of.

Nothing could be more wonderful and astonishing than that. And that explains how from time to time we do amazingly loving acts we never thought ourselves capable of.

PART THREE

Faith in Secular—
Practical Implications

When all the projections upon divine beings have been withdrawn, we are left with no divine beings in which to believe. Human self-awareness probably began with a sense of all-surrounding consciousness which gave way to the sense of individual spirits which in turn gave way to the community of gods which were themselves superseded by the one cosmic God, and when that God projection is withdrawn, as it is in our time, we have none. We've gone from infinite surrounding consciousnesses to none.

The entire point of faith has been dissolved into nothing by the "acids of modernity." For communities of faith, this is an unmitigated disaster, the death of all they'd held dear.

So, now what does faith do?

That was the precise experience of the first Christians. For them, the acids of Roman violence had crushed their hopes for a world of fulfilment and joy foretold by their prophets and enacted by Jesus, and the Romans would shortly crush their ancient Jewish faith embodied in their temple to the God of justice. Anyone would have said it was the end of hope and the start of eternal despair.

And yet, to the astonishment of the early Christians, it wasn't. The details of how that transformation got started may be forever lost to us, but the end result is obvious—those despairing followers travelled around the world proclaiming with joy that a cosmic victory had been won, and that the fulfilment they had hoped for was at hand, and that the world was on the brink of completion.

All because God, in the form of Jesus, had been destroyed by human violence.

In the remainder of this book, we will explore how the early Christians' experience of cosmic joy and victory could become ours within our secular loss of the one supreme God.

The key to our modern experience of the resurrection is that the first Christians didn't experience Christ's resurrection as doing away with Judaism or even with the Greek religion of the "Unknown god" as St. Paul, formerly known as Saul of Tarsus, reported it. On the contrary, they experienced an enhancement of their former deep religious experiences.

With the demise of our religious projections, we can also anticipate not a dissolution of faith, but a deepening of the projections' meanings for us. None of those projections were ever inadequate but failed attempts to know the ultimate meaning of creation; rather each was profoundly true. Each projection willingly laid down its life for us, as did moose for First Nations hunters, in order that each projection could feed us with itself.

Each projection was a profound gift to humanity, and each gift remains with us and can become even more significant in the future. Religion's purpose in a secular world, as we will see in more detail shortly, will be to lead us into unpacking the depths of each projection's gift.

Having withdrawn belief in a literal supreme divine being hovering over the planet, we can then more deeply experience the glory and wonder surrounding us on all sides.

Having known each projection more deeply and knowing that each died that we may live more fully, religion's role will be to enable us to respond to the call of each of those former projections as we encounter them.

Although for the sake of clarity, we have described them sequentially, it's not a developmental process from lesser to greater, but an opportunity to be loved into fullness through a variety of projections in each of which we experience our source and lover, ultimate reality more and more deeply.

In the next three chapters, comprising Part 3, we will explore how such a freedom to move among the projections can enable John and ourselves to deepen our ability to enter intimate relationships with growing depth and joy. We will also see how with Rosalind we can expand our awareness to embrace fulfilment for the planet and for every culture and faith. Contrary to our usual assumptions about Christ and the past, resurrection is now approaching us from our future.

CHAPTER 14

Your Romance Died. Congratulations![1]

Mile-high love: plane tickets, ecstasy, and a crash

I am with a group of young couples gathered in one of their homes to talk about the upcoming baptism of their children, and for other couples, their upcoming wedding. To focus the conversation in the direction I have in mind, I explain how enlivening it is when one partner makes a significant sacrifice for the other. I ask if they have had any such experiences.

After a pause, one couple describe a difficult conversation they have recently had.

They had each booked time off from work for a winter holiday trip, but

---

[1] Robert W. Funk, *The Five Gospels: What Did Jesus Really Say? The Search for the Authentic Words of Jesus*, (HarperOne, 1996). p. 289. The Sermon on the Plain, Luke 6:20-21. Jesus congratulates people who are in grief: "Congratulations, you who weep now! You will laugh!" See footnote 1 in chapter 10 for the implications of this curious pronouncement.

haven't been able to agree on a destination. The deadline for booking tickets is rapidly approaching.

The problem is he wants to go skiing and she wants to go to Hawaii.

They each know what the other wants and they each know what they themselves want, and they've gotten nowhere with making a decision about where to go. She just wants to relax in the sun. He's been an avid skier and is looking forward to a great time on the slopes.

She's explained how tired she is and how much she just wants to be quiet. He counters with the fact that he hasn't been able to go skiing for two years now and it's his turn to go.

Recognizing that they're getting into an impasse that is feeling more and more uncomfortable, the past week or so the conversation has gone like this. "It's OK," he says, "I'm fine with going to Hawaii. We can ski next year." To which she dutifully responds, "No really, dear, let's go skiing. I know how much it means to you. I'm OK with skiing." "That's really sweet of you, honey, but honestly, I think we should go to Hawaii." And so it goes. They both know it's a sham. They get no further with these superficial expressions of care than when they were each arguing for what they wanted.

They realize they'll never go anywhere on their holiday if they don't make their bookings soon. So, they set Saturday morning after breakfast as the final decision date. He has errands to do the night before, so Saturday morning works perfectly.

Saturday morning comes, they finish breakfast, and she says, "I've really thought about it, and I've decided we really should go skiing. Honestly, it'll be great. You know I like skiing, too. I'm fine with that. I'd enjoy it. I really would." But she's not enjoying the conversation and she wonders if this is the first crack of things falling apart for them.

"No," he says, "I still think we should go to Hawaii. I know you need the break." "Thanks, Sweetie," she says, "but I really mean it. I've made up my mind. I really want to go skiing with you. Honest. I'm not fooling, I'd like to do that." She really means it, but isn't sure she means it.

He reaches into his pocket and pulls out an envelope and hands it to her. On the outside of the envelope he had written, "Should you wish it, I humbly request the pleasure of your company on a trip to…." She opens the envelope with some trepidation. Inside, there is a single sheet of paper with the word 'Hawaii.' "Turn it over," he said. On the back he had written, "I checked with the hotel and the airline last night, there's still space. They're holding a room for us if you want it. Love from: Your Lover." She looked up at him, and he was all smiles. "You still want it; we're off to Hawaii!" And they were.

It was exactly the sort of story I'd been hoping for. My point was that when we make that sort of generous sacrifice for someone, what seemed as if it would be a sacrifice turns into a delight. A kind of relationship-resurrection happens.

So, I asked what happened next, expecting she might have given him a hug. They looked sheepishly at each other and she blushed. It didn't take much to imagine they had celebrated the resurrection of their love with more than a hug. There were chuckles and affirmation all around from the other couples there.

All of us felt embraced by the way in which love had leapt up among us. It felt so good, so positive, so much along the lines of the experience of death and resurrection in a relationship I had hoped for in this seminar, but much more dramatic and moving than I'd anticipated. This was the experience of the God of love I'd wanted them to feel.

The class was a great success.

Why love projections are necessary and must necessarily die

The ecstatic joy of that couple following the offer of the holiday trip to Hawaii was their experience of being immersed in ultimate reality's deep surrounding love. For some time after, they would have thought they'd had the ultimate experience of love. But like all projections, their mutual projection on each other—that their partner was the embodiment of all-surrounding pre-animist love—would have to die in order for their love to grow.

I wonder what we'd find if we went back and visited that couple five, ten, or twenty years later. It's not likely they'd still be basking in the warm glow of that moment of long-ago generosity and renewed romance. Much more likely, they would have been through some tough times, and the Saturday morning surprise offer of the trip to Hawaii would have become a nostalgic memory. It could even be, sadly, that we might find them divorced. Not because there was anything wrong with that delightful gift early in their marriage, nor because they hadn't repeated it enough, but because breakdown would inevitably happen if they had never moved into deeper love territory beyond that first enthralling experience of being surrounded by romantically projected, pre-animist, all-surrounding love.

Alternatively, we might find them even more deeply in love, and if that were the case it wouldn't be because they were simply repeating that original romantic experience, but because they would have moved through the loss of that early joy, would have experienced distance and loss of love, and would then have regained their joy more deeply by dying to their projections upon each other and to their illusions about themselves. Strange as it sounds, the delight of giving and receiving that dramatic act of generosity would have had to die in order for new and deeper love to emerge.

Projections aren't errors or mistakes.

Projections are essential to love and to any significant relationship.

Projections are essential to any significant relationship, especially at the beginning, because at the start of a relationship there is a sort of Catch-22 that can be resolved only by a projection upon the other person.

The Catch-22 about becoming close to someone is we can't know the person well enough to know if we would want to be close to them until *after* we have become close to them. You wouldn't woo someone unless you thought you would want to live with them, but you can't know the person well enough to know if you would want to live with them until after the wooing has been successful! You can't know someone at depth until after you know them at depth. So how can we know someone enough to make a profound commitment to them when we can't know them until *after* we've made that commitment? It would seem to be an insurmountable obstacle to the formation of any significant relationship.

The way to solve this dilemma lies in projections. We relate to someone using our pre-animist projection on them (that the other is an infinitely wonderful person) as a substitute for the as yet unknowable real person. The projection forms the necessary bridge between the meagre knowledge we have at the beginning of a relationship and the deeper knowledge that will become available only after the relationship has moved into commitment and the projection has been set aside. Only then can the real person be known and loved.

The young couple struggling to plan their holiday was enthralled that Saturday morning by the startling discovery of how deeply they loved each other. But they would discover such all-surrounding love could take them only part way on their journey. In a year or two he'd tire of making such sacrifices and she'd tire of being passionately responsive. Their projection of the other as the perfect lover would be withdrawn. And they would wonder where their love had gone.

That would feel like the death of their joy and perhaps the end of their marriage.

But the whole point of projections is to die; so they can become part of us, and something even more fulfilling can emerge.

Just as it is with knowing God. All-surrounding consciousness, individual spirits, global gods and even the one cosmic God are all projections by which we can know and integrate that which is beyond all knowing. But none are mistakes or inadequate images. All are essential as each draws us into deeper maturity and deeper life and deeper relationships.

John's pre-animist projection of romantic love

As John lay in bed the night after their long talk about ultimate reality and how it loves us, he was thinking about how wonderful it was be to be with Rosalind. Then he imagined taking her into his arms.

To keep her safe. To help her know her own beauty. To hold her.

Oh, yes, to hold her.

It started to feel sexual.

She was attractive. He knew he'd been checking her out when she wasn't looking. But he felt such desire for her was not inappropriate—it would be a wonderful way to celebrate the deep connection he had found with her. They *were* deeply connected—they had been enjoying each other more and more, having these stimulating conversations; taking her to bed would be a marvellous way to celebrate and affirm and deepen their growing friendship. He'd love to be with her like that. What a joy it would be to sleep together! With someone so strange and so special.

Falling asleep in someone's arms is immensely desirable because it happened to all of us as infants when we experienced our mother as the whole cosmos holding us in safety. We may not have been able, at that stage of infancy, to distinguish between our self and our mother and the cosmos—we may have had a global undifferentiated sense in which the cosmos and mother and the self were all one. We may not even remember that experience. But to fall asleep, even as an adult, in complete trust of another is a way of emotionally experiencing being surrounded and upheld by ultimate reality. No wonder John longed for that. Intimacy with Rosalind could embody that pre-animist experience of cosmic fulfilment.

The experience of the cosmos surrounding us with care, and of our being utterly at home in the cosmos, is not wishful thinking, nor is it an escape into infantile projection, nor is it a silly remnant from humanity's pre-animist childhood when every stone was conscious. Rather, that projection of all-surrounding love is a highly sophisticated ability to be directly aware that our very existence is upheld at every moment by caring ultimate reality. The truth is, we exist only because we are surrounded by love in the form of ultimate reality. Pre-animist cultures experienced that fact directly.

As do lovers, in intimate embrace.

No wonder we all long for such intimacy.

John's projection of pre-animist romantic love must die

Next morning, John poured himself a coffee and recalled those night fantasies and wondered whether they meant anything.

It seemed ridiculous. Was he really having sexual fantasies about the atheist scientist next door? Was he losing his integrity? Was he regressing into a self-absorbed teenager?

He had a sinking feeling the answer to all three would be 'Yes.'

So, he tested it out—just like Rosalind would test a new discovery in her work as a scientist. He deliberately recalled the feelings he'd had last night and tried them out on himself in the light of day. It dawned on him that he was making use of Rosalind's suggestion about the déjà vu glitch enabling self-awareness, to be aware of himself! He laughed. There was indeed a delightful intimacy.

By examining his projection on Rosalind, he was giving up the power of the fantasy of emotional union, attractive as it was. By examining his own feelings, he was separating himself from his feelings and so becoming aware of them as projections. The act of becoming aware of the projection removed its hold over him and freed him from being controlled by it, and so allowed him to incorporate its significance into himself as he allowed the projection to die. His pre-animist glimpse of emotionally fulfilling union with her was being laid aside in favour of a difficult truth.

They weren't lovers.

That hurt. Of course it did, because the projection was dying and that meant losing hope of profound connection, meaning, and fulfilment with Rosalind.

Time to put the fantasy away and accept reality. Whatever else he felt, he knew he wanted to relate to her as a real person. The projected fantasy had shown him how much he wanted intimacy, but now he realized he wanted the real thing, he wanted at least to relate to who she was, not to some imaginary image in his own head.

He wanted the reality, not a projection. He actually wanted the projection to die.

And without his expecting it, the miracle happened. Right there.

He had integrated into himself the truths the projection had shown him.

The projection had shown him he was capable of, and longing for, as deep a connection as possible with Rosalind.

To his astonishment he felt fulfilled that he hadn't slept with her.

That was the gift the projection of physical intimacy had given him the moment he had integrated the projection and allowed it to die and give him new life.

He was surprised to find his desire for her fulfilment had become more important than his desire for emotional ecstasy with her. He discovered himself hoping she had completed her preparation for the lecture and found himself glad they hadn't spent more time together the day before, and even glad they hadn't spent the night together, if that was what it took for her to be well prepared to confidently deliver an insightful lecture.

He was longing for *her* fulfilment.

By dying, the projection had completed its purpose, had come to live fully inside him, and had connected him to his ability to love much more deeply than he had thought he could. By letting go of the projection he'd got its truth back even more powerfully.

He chuckled at the irony.

John's spirit projection of teamwork

As John relinquished his fantasy of finding ecstasy with Rosalind in his arms, he found himself thinking about how satisfying it would be to give up his own priorities, his own time, even emotional ecstasy, as a way of loving her. Perhaps he could find some way to support her in her work. He would love to be a loyal team member with her.

He was beginning to enter into the awareness that another deeper kind of union with her could be possible: not the ecstatic union of bodies, but the union of wills as they became a team together. He found himself very attracted to that possibility. He had even discovered in himself an interest in science.

This could work perfectly.

What would it be like to team up with her? In any good team, whether a flock of birds wheeling as one, or a hockey team making a triumphant play, or a symphony orchestra performing a great piece with precision and passion, the quality of a team's action depends on each member constantly being aware of what each of the other members is doing. John would need to be aware of her at a far deeper level than through his fantasy of emotional union. His attention would have to be out there, away from himself, focused on Rosalind, the real person. By paying attention to her, he would find himself in a new kind of deeply satisfying connection as a team member supporting her.

What might she need? Perhaps he could provide something that would serve her and fulfil him at the same time. He could offer to provide some administrative support she might need and in return he'd be recognized as a partner in her public role. As her behind-the-scenes assistant he would feel important—he would receive, through teaming with her, the public recognition he craved. That could work really well, and he'd be doing something for her, not just for himself.

Yes, that would work.

Members of an animist culture learn how to team up with spirits in order to have their needs fulfilled. That's how John was now imagining relating to Rosalind. She'd get a live-in assistant and he'd get a whole new exciting life. That would be real teamwork.

John was starting to experience the animist style of projection in which relationships are about teaming up with the surrounding spirits. He was entering the spirit style of projection imagining the two of them as team members each with their own gifts and limitations. That felt great. That would be so mature and satisfying. He'd get to know her much more deeply, just as shamans come to know spirits.

John's spirit projection of teamwork must die

As he thought further about how good it would be to support her research and enable her preparation for lectures, he realized that to get serious about doing that would involve some difficult adjustments on his part. To really be in a team with her, he would have to make some painful decisions about his own beliefs and priorities. He would have to team up with an atheist. And take her seriously.

But it was utterly silly. They hadn't exchanged a word since their conversation yesterday when they'd had such very different views about God and faith, and yet here he was imagining himself as a team member with her. It was almost a betrayal of her to allow himself to imagine he could support her research about which he still felt ambivalent and knew next to nothing. If not a betrayal of her, then certainly it would be a betrayal of himself to dwell on what was so evidently just his own imagination. Besides, she might have no interest whatsoever in being in a team with him.

His spirit projection upon her was dying and its truth was ready to be integrated into his life. That truth was that he was capable of really knowing someone. Someone very different from himself.

Only then could a new projection emerge, a projection of a much deeper and far more significant relationship with Rosalind.

In real life, integrating one projection and moving to the next is more complex than this quick overview may suggest. We've touched on the highlights of how the first two projection styles, pre-animist and animist, can each provide us with new depths of self-awareness and relationship. Next, we'll touch on the highlights of the next two styles of projection—that of gods and God—and their withdrawal, and see how they enable further depth and self-awareness.

Summary

Humanity is constantly receiving what a projection offers when it is withdrawn and is integrated. We've seen how that process works on the scale of entire cultures, as for example, when the experience of local spirits replaces the experience of universal consciousness.

This process also happens to us within our own most intimate relationships.

When we fall in love, we project upon another person all our own hopes and needs and qualities that we weren't ready to acknowledge as our own. But if our relationship with the one we love is to grow past infatuation, then the projection we have upon them will have to die in order for us to integrate who we really are. Only then do we know who we are and who the other really is. John had allowed his projections of all-embracing ecstasy and of teamwork to die. He is now ready to receive even deeper knowledge of himself and Rosalind.

CHAPTER 15

Your Marriage Died.
Congratulations![1]

*The newly-ordained priest begins his
ministry by betraying his wife*

One of the reasons I became a priest was because I was a particularly loving person. I was also especially aware of God's love and was glad I could demonstrate that love in my own life. It was an honour to be called to such a ministry so people could experience God's love as they observed me.

Naturally, I would also become an especially loving spouse. That would be natural for a person like me.

After a year's engagement, my fiancée and I were married and I became a

---

1   Robert W. Funk, *The Five Gospels: What Did Jesus Really Say? The Search for the Authentic Words of Jesus*, (HarperOne, 1996). p. 289. The Sermon on the Plain, Luke 6:20-21. Jesus congratulates people who are in grief: "Congratulations, you who weep now! You will laugh!" See footnote 1 in chapter 10 for the implications of this curious pronouncement.

deeply loving husband.

The problem was that my wife, while basically a good person, turned out not to be as nice as she had been when we were courting. That didn't seem entirely fair to me, but, being a loving person, I hoped my example would soon rub off on her and we'd become a wonderfully loving couple. I patiently waited for her to grow up.

But things got worse. My wife became increasingly insensitive, even to the point of saying I wasn't always as loving to her as I knew I was.

I understood entirely—she wasn't as sensitive as I was. So, I could understand how she could miss the subtle and loving cues a really sensitive and respectful spouse like myself would use to communicate my love to her. It was disappointing to find myself misunderstood by the person I had married and disappointing, too, that she would turn out to be insensitive in her demands on me. Nevertheless, I soldiered on, trusting one day she would discover what a special relationship she was in.

A couple of years into our marriage, she pointed out to me yet again, some particular way in which she claimed I had just acted in an un-loving manner toward her.

I was dumbfounded. She was right. I had been insensitive.

Not that I let her know. Because clearly it was a rare inadvertent oversight on my part.

But when, soon after, she pointed out yet again an example of that uncomfortable truth, I knew she was right. I was doing it a lot. It dawned on me that I wasn't a loving husband after all.

With that, my world fell apart. I wasn't a loving husband. Or a loving priest.

I wasn't honouring her as the prime person in my life.

It was the end of my marriage.

I would be the cause of us divorcing. The ultimate shame for a priest.

There couldn't be a greater disaster for me as a priest. How could I possibly be a priest, embodying God's love, if I couldn't even do that in my own marriage? I should have quit seminary after all.

And immediately, the miracle happened.

For the first time I saw her as she really was and I saw myself as I really was. It was painful beyond description to give up my life-long illusion that I was a wonderful person, and to give up my projection on her that she would be my mirror-image and express love in the same way I thought I did.

But it was also delightful to find myself living with a woman I'd never known.

She seemed to like it, too.

After several years of marriage, for the first time I met this fascinating woman to whom I was already married. For the first time I began to learn how to be her lover.

It was like learning another language. She needed to be cared about in ways I didn't need, so I began to pay attention to her—what really made her happy? In some ways it was too easy; I just had to give up assuming what made me happy would make her happy. Sometimes it felt like cheating—what made her happy would be something so easy it seemed it shouldn't count, but I'd get a response out of all proportion to some small thing I'd done for her. It was as if a whole new dimension, a whole new universe, had opened up, the way it did the very first time I went on a date with a woman. But this time it wasn't just a date. It was the whole of my life.

Other times it was harder to love. Sometimes what made sense to her just didn't make sense to me. But when I could simply accept she had a right to be exactly who she was, and to be completely different from me, that's when the miracle happened and heaven broke through. The deaths of my projections on her became the foundation for deepening life and love for us both.

She might tell a similar story from her point of view, but that's her story to tell.

For both of us, the death of strongly held projections was the journey into deeper and more satisfying love for each other. In spite of our committed resistance to withdrawing projections, when we allow them to die and then integrate their truths into our life, heaven really does break through. Even after half a century.

You'd almost think it was a pattern.

John's god projection of life-long happiness lives and dies

After breakfast, John undertook another thought experiment about his relationship with Rosalind.

As he withdrew the spirit-animist projection of their being perfect team partners he was able to integrate the truth about himself which the spirit projection had presented to him. He found in himself the ability to imagine what someone else needed and that he himself, with his particular needs and skills was someone worth teaming with. Those were new insights about himself and he was warmed and encouraged to find there was more depth in himself than he'd thought. He was proud to discover he was capable of a commitment deeper than the fleeting commitment of his earlier two fantasies.

By withdrawing the spirit projection of teaming with Rosalind, and taking the resulting learning about himself seriously, he could receive the gift of a yet deeper projection. This projection appeared in the form of the Olympic gods. He was feeling a call to entwine his entire life with Rosalind, just as those ancient gods called the Greeks to responsibility for their entire world.

What would it feel like not just to collaborate on an academic project, but to engage with Rosalind for the rest of their lives?

He felt riveted in place. It took his breath away.

Rather than relating to her by just supporting her work, the relationship he was now drawn to would include every facet of both their lives. They would be thoroughly entwined with one another.

To permanently give up his independence? To throw his lot in with someone who stood for so much that made him uncomfortable? With this particular neighbour? With this atheist? No part of him would be exempt from such a commitment. This would be much more than teamwork. This was profound commitment. It was scary, but it would be the most mature and fulfilling commitment he'd ever undertaken.

Nothing would be the same if he were to live with an atheist scientist—a great deal would have to change in his own life. He began to look inward to determine whether he really wanted to commit himself at such depth.

Was this just another passing fantasy like those about emotional ecstasy or social success through associating with her public profile?

But no, he wanted to spend his life with her because that would give him a sense of connection and purpose and meaning that would fulfil every aspect of who he was. Through the fog of fear, he knew with certainty if she would accept him, he would live with her and give her the rest of his life.

Together they would form a global commitment encircling the two continents of their lives. Nothing in them would be unconnected. Everything would be meaningful and fulfilled and deeply happy. This is what he had been made for. This would be his ultimate joy. Being suffused with meaning is what humans long for. How wonderful it was that this experience was about to be given to him! No wonder he gave himself so fully to this Olympic god projection that offered him total meaning on the global scale of their two lives.

But as soon as John began to imagine the two of them spending the rest of their lives together, he realized that, too, was a projection.

Not just because they were only recently friends, if indeed they even were, but also because it was a fantasy to imagine a life-long commitment to her. In the words of a popular TV sitcom, they would commit to live together, "As long as we both shall love."[2] His projection was that the purpose of their life partnership was to be happy and fulfilled.

What could be wrong with that?

It was an attractive vision. But he knew that it's when life gets unhappy, when things go wrong, when you fail yourself and your partner, that you really get to know yourself and the other person. Did he really want to know himself and Rosalind that deeply?

Terrifying as it was, the answer was 'Yes!'

Their relationship would have to be about more than committing to life-long happiness and fulfilment. Their relationship would have to be about something deeper than that if they were really to know each other.

He knew people who had made such commitments but he never understood how they did it and couldn't imagine himself ever engaging in that depth of commitment including what wasn't happy. But as he withdrew the unrealistic Olympic god-like projection of life-long love and happiness with Rosalind, and integrated its truth, he discovered for the first time that he was capable of an unlimited life commitment. The truth was, to his astonishment, that he was capable of profound love. The god-style of projection had died and in doing so revealed to John that more depth of love than he had imagined possible was already within himself.

John's God projection of unconditional love lives and dies

It wasn't enough for John to want romance, nor was it enough to want to be in a team with Rosalind, nor was it even enough to want to have life-long happiness for them both.

But, if his desire for life-long mutual happiness with her wasn't enough, what was?

As his global Olympic god projection died, it dawned on John what he really wanted was to make an unconditional and absolute commitment to her.

This wouldn't be a commitment to their mutual happiness; it would be a commitment to everything and anything that could ever happen in their future. Happy or not. Fulfilling or not.

---

2   Rhoda. CBS Sitcom, October 28, 1974.

The Olympic projection had seemed global, but it lacked a way of addressing the inevitable sorrow, pain, and brokenness that happens in real relationships. It wasn't really global. To include those difficult aspects of life, John needed a deeper commitment than that of life-long happiness that the Olympic god projection promised.

He needed a cosmic projection in which all experiences possible in the universe of life, including sadness, pain, deep hurt, and even guilt would be included in his relationship with Rosalind. He was entering the projection of the single cosmic self-sacrificing God who embraces everything, including guilt, pain and even death. And turns them all into joy.

To make the commitment absolute, their relationship would no longer be about enjoying each other. It wouldn't just be about their happiness. It wouldn't even be that she would be his priority.

The relationship itself would become his priority.

To be committed absolutely to a relationship was even more frightening than to be committed absolutely to a person. There might be lots one didn't know about another person, but you could at least negotiate with a person. But with a relationship? To be committed to a relationship? That would be very risky. Perhaps foolish. Very likely impossible.

That would be to commit to marriage. To an indelible relationship. There's no negotiating with such a relationship, just as there is no negotiating with God. God simply is. God isn't a god you can team up with when it suits you. God is ultimate reality, not some aspect of the world that might adjust itself for our convenience in the way the gods could, the way "As long as we both shall love" could. John was imagining a relationship with Rosalind through a projection of the cosmic God with whom one cannot negotiate. No experience could be negotiated out of such a relationship. That would be the absolute commitment he would have to make in order to move their relationship into the depth for which he longed.

But just as he had begun to recognize in his conversations with Rosalind that there wasn't much credibility left in the idea of a literal God watching over us, so also, he realized there wasn't much credibility left in his making an absolute God-like commitment to a relationship. He knew himself too well and he'd already experienced some of Rosalind's shortcomings. It wasn't likely either of them would be able to make and keep a life-long commitment to include any and all circumstances that might arise for the rest of their lives. He could say the words of an absolute commitment, to live together "as long as we both shall live," and so could she, but he knew that would be a hopeful sham. Neither of them might be able to enact such a commitment to the unknown.

John was becoming aware that the goal of an infinitely committed marriage was another projection, and it wasn't enough. He wasn't enough. They weren't enough. The truth was they were incapable of carrying out such a commitment.

His God projection of absolute commitment to each other was dying.

He wanted something even deeper than that. But what could be deeper than that? There were no other projections once the God projection of unlimited love had died.

That didn't make any sense.

But it did.

Managing love projections—love's gift to us

The reason each projection of personal love has to be withdrawn and die is that when we embrace a projection, we allow the spirits or gods or God to summon us from outside. We are no longer the lover. We are asking the universal love, or spirit, or the god, or God, to be the lover. We anticipate God upholding our marriage if we make a vow in God's name. And if the relationship ends, well, that's the fault of God, or Cupid, or my unrealistically hoping for too much. I should have settled for less. It's my fault. And hers. We hoped for too much.

In order to own our deepest ability to love and enact it, we must allow all the projections to die so we become the lover which each projection had revealed to us about our self. Only then can we act upon the love which the projection revealed *had already been part of us.* It's up to us, not Cupid, not the gods, not God, and not good luck to ensure we become lovers open to the ultimate depth of connection and meaning.

By dying and rising through each projection and by allowing even the final projection of cosmic commitment to die, we take on the character of ultimate reality. We are then enabled to love more than we could have asked or imagined. Because the self-offering character of ultimate reality is the basis of who we are.

Receiving this deepening fulfilment depends upon us managing our projections. If the projections manage us and we try to live with the projection of our self or the other as the perfect Adonis, the perfect super-model, or the perfectly-adjusted personality, there will be no ecstasy. When the process is naïve and our projections manage us, we say, "That person over there—wow! If only I'd met her years ago, before I married my spouse, then I'd have true fulfilment." We've all known that experience. It comes from outside us, not from our real self. We are tempted to enact that projected fantasy, to remain in that projection of the other as the imaginary perfect partner, and if we accept that projection as real, our real relationship starts to fall apart. The projection was intended to show us something about our self, not about the person who has become the screen on which we see the projection.

But if we manage the projection, then we can, with full awareness, allow the projection to present to us a glimpse of our own self when we experience the ultimate glory in the other very ordinary person with whom we live. When that projection of the other as the perfect partner is withdrawn and integrated, I and the other will both accept that neither of us is a bronzed Adonis nor a glamorous super-model, but just an ordinary person with ordinary looks and ordinary personhood with ordinary limitations. And yet still be infused with glory.

The withdrawal of all our projections enables moments, across the supper table or in intimate embrace, when the wonder of the other very ordinary person takes our breath away. As that glory is integrated into our own self, when we withdraw and integrate the projections, we experience a union of two remarkable people far beyond our former imagining.

In such moments, we lose ourselves in the mystery of the other, letting go of our awareness of the rest of the world, allowing ourselves to be transported into an ecstatic union in which we find our very ordinary self profoundly fulfilled by that other very ordinary self.

Through managing our projection, every person is able to encounter the holy—ultimate reality—through their very ordinary partner. Managed projection enables us to experience a deeper truth: "I'm going to allow myself to slip into that glorious sense of being loved by an infinitely wonderful person right now." And then one allows one's very ordinary partner to do just that. And then our own self becomes infinitely wonderful.

That is to re-enter the original pre-animist projection, but this time as a conscious decision. In that way, the projection reveals more about myself and my partner than the first time when the projection was unconscious.

It works the same with the other projections.

When the pre-animist projection has revealed its truth to us as glory, we can then enter into a deeper commitment to serve the other in teamwork through spirit projection. Through the god projection we are able to commit even more of all that life offers in pain as well as in joy. Finally when the last projection dies, and we cannot enact that perfect love we promised, we find within ourselves a depth emerging from ultimate reality that we had never guessed was there.

That process takes a lifetime

What better use of a lifetime?

After the death of the love projections

If John were serious about the deepest possible relationship with Rosalind, a relationship of commitment without limits, there could be only one way to make that possible.

All his projections would have to end.

Even his fantasy about marrying her, that he had glimpsed through the cosmic God-like projection of commitment without limit, would have to die.

He would have to allow her, even invite her, to extinguish his fantasy of the ultimate commitment in marriage. He needed Rosalind to challenge his resistance to the necessary deaths of all his projections. He would have to offer his projections to her so they would both be aware of them as projections. She could then accept or reject what they represented.

And he would do the same for her.

What if she accepted his proposal? If she accepted him, the projections would be over and they would be arranging a permanent partnership, not an imaginary relationship. What if she rejected him? If she rejected him, that, too, would be the end of his projections about their relationship. Either way, all his projections upon her would be withdrawn, die, and be integrated.

The projection of sexual union had given him an awareness of the glory that was in Rosalind and in himself. The spirit-like projection of a relationship characterized by teamwork had taught him he could care for someone besides himself. The projection of a god-like, life-long relationship had taught him that he was capable of long-term commitment. From the God-like projection of a permanent marriage he had learned that commitment wasn't about himself. In embracing and then releasing each projection, he could own the depths in his own self and he could give her the power and the freedom to exercise her self-hood.

Even if that power and freedom led her to reject his self.

Allowing that to happen would be the pinnacle of who he was.

He would have to die to become himself in order to relate to her, as she was, from who he was.

If he offered her his life without projections, he would be putting his entire future into her hands. He would be left naked, with no defences, fragile and vulnerable to that over which he had no control. He would simply be himself, presenting his naked self to her. He could be close to her only by removing all the projections with which he had clothed himself and her until now. Only then, could he speak to who she actually is from the person he actually is. His naked self proposing to her naked self.

This was what it was to love. He would bring nothing—no illusions, no projections, no gifts, no requests. All belonged to her, and in the ensuing silence all he could do would be to wait.

He had never been so frightened in his life.

This didn't feel like fun.

It wasn't.

But he was more alive than he'd ever been.

Because he was enacting what ultimate reality is all about.

Dying to enter the very deepest intimacy.

Summary

In recent Western experience, entering into marriage has become the symbol of making the ultimate commitment to our lover.

But that symbol is widely dying in our society. Many people in deep commitments do not experience getting married as the way to express the deepest possible commitment to each other. Like the death of God as a credible idea, it may be that the image of marriage may also have to die if we are to enter the most life-giving form of relationship offered to us by ultimate reality.

We must die to the illusion that by marrying we can enter an automatic process by which psychological forces will propel us into deep fulfilment as if they were Olympic-god-like processes guiding our limited experience of the other person. That is a useful illusion and projection at the start of a relationship, but it has to be given up if we are to live deeply in relationship and truly know the other.

The final stage in this process toward self-aware consciousness is to deliberately give up all projections about our self and the other, and to offer to the other our naked self, clothed with no projections at all.

Then we can enter a deep relationship in which each person sees and knows the other as they are and not as they were imagined to be through a projection.

It can seem strange that we must give up all projections about love and live within the unvarnished truth about our self and the other in order to attain the deepest possible intimacy with that person.

But it makes sense when we realize that we arise from ultimate reality that is itself prepared to give up its own central identity to remain in relationship with us. So, it is not surprising that to be deeply united with someone will require the same process of the death of our projections and the ensuing resurrection of our deepest human self.

CHAPTER 16

Your World Died.
Congratulations!¹

Candles as subversive technology

My church youth group decided to go on a pilgrimage to Iona, a barren island off the west coast of Scotland, where Celtic Christianity, a creation-centred interpretation of the faith, had been brought in the late 500s.

The Abbey, a great stone church built in medieval times, began to be a popular centre for pilgrimage in the 1950s and continues so today. Many people speak of it as a "thin place."

In traditional Celtic imagery the eternal world is only three feet away—close enough to reach out and touch with an outstretched arm—but in a thin place

---

1   Robert W. Funk, *The Five Gospels: What Did Jesus Really Say? The Search for the Authentic Words of Jesus*, (HarperOne, 1996). p. 289. The Sermon on the Plain, Luke 6:20-21. Jesus congratulates people who are in grief: "Congratulations, you who weep now! You will laugh!" See footnote 1 in chapter 10 for the implications of this curious pronouncement.

the eternal world is even closer. In such a place we can more easily be in contact with the spiritual world. Iona is said to be such a place.

A wonderful image, I thought, and no doubt lucrative for the tourist industry upon which most of the tiny population of the island depends.

I was skeptical about the value of such a trip. I was quite sure ultimate reality doesn't come closer to us in specific geographical locations. What then would be left for the spiritual experience of most of us who could never afford to travel to another continent? Couldn't we who stay at home experience ultimate reality (or 'God' if you prefer that image) as well as globe-trotters? Does anyone seriously think ultimate reality pokes through on a barren island in Scotland more than on barren islands on the Pacific coast of Canada, or in cities, or in places of deep poverty? But the youth group was inspired and was determined to go, and I said nothing about my reservations. So, of course I went.

After all, they would need a chaplain, wouldn't they?

One night early in our visit to Iona, I found myself seated in the Abbey, the great stone church, as the electric lights were turned off and the only illumination in that immense building came from flickering candles. We were to sit in silence for an hour. No guided meditations, no scripture readings, no singing, no quiet music, just silence.

I knew the routine. I'd used it back home. The lights are dimmed for effect, the silence becomes an all-embracing presence, and on that night at Iona the dense silence of our usually chattering youth along with many others from around the world induced a sense of awe and expectation.

I knew exactly what the kids and I were supposed to feel and I knew, much as I loved the kids, that this was a way of trying to convince us all, by playing on our feelings, that God was especially present here. I'd grown up on another rocky west coast on another sea beside another continent, and the winds and the raw presence of nature were familiar to me from childhood. I knew I wasn't going to experience God any differently than we all could have back home. And saved the air fare. But I was loyal to the kids and stayed there for them.

Sitting in the dark, I was looking at the candles and thinking of how curious it is that churches still continue to use candles when we have all the necessary technology to dim the electric lights to the same level. We even light candles in broad daylight.

Of course, it's for effect.

I noticed, too, how nobody was doing anything. Just being in silence. A lot of people doing nothing. I hoped some of the kids might be having deep experiences of God, or perhaps deep insights about themselves; but for me, and for others, I suspected, we were doing nothing. Just being loyal to those for whom this was important.

It was a lot of nothing. No electricity. No music. No talk. No planning. No sharing. No experience of God. Nothing.

We were doing silence, wasting time, thumbing our noses at modern technology.

We were doing everything the rest of our society never does.

It occurred to me to wonder what would happen if a government minister dropped in. To sit in the dark without accomplishing anything would undermine everything governments stand for. I wondered if the British or Scottish governments really understood what was going on—that we were claiming an alternate priority to the frenetic lifestyle commended by everyone who wants our economy to grow, our standard of living to go up, our GDP to increase. Not to mention the side effect of larger profits for those with lots of money already.

If this practice of doing nothing began to spread and lots of people started doing nothing, sitting in silence in near darkness, I suspect the government would not be pleased. Leaders of government, business, and industry would find this non-activity seditious if the public began to take it seriously. In fact, it dawned on me that if the government really understood what we were doing they would come and shut us down.

Sitting in the near-dark of a cold medieval stone church doing nothing had become an immensely powerful and subversive political act.

We had effectively challenged the assumptions about endless growth and implacable accumulation that drive the entire world. And are driving us all to death.

I don't know if it was a thin place, but something came bursting through those three-foot thick stone walls as if they were tissue paper. Whatever it was changed me.

The world we assume is normal must die.

That's power. And to accomplish that, the only technology we need are candles and silence.

Killing the mother-projection on our planet

Rosalind went to bed the night of her long talk with John about intimacy and love and ultimate reality and how ultimate reality is prepared to die for love of us, or it wouldn't be ultimate.

She wasn't sure what she thought about these concepts of ultimate reality, but there was something attractive about them. It felt really good to be so close to something that loved that much. She remembered how John had teased her about scientists being especially close to ultimate reality because they received so much joy in discovering the patterns that emerge from ultimate reality. She liked that.

But she'd also heard the challenge he'd raised about science allowing itself to be treated as if its purpose was to enable profit-making manufacturing and national death-machine accumulation instead of proclaiming the intimacy and love that undergirds existence and the joy which drives scientists.

The problem of science being misused not for purposes of awe but for awful purposes had been bothering her for some time. She was uplifted by her discoveries of new connections in the world she researched, but she was aware that government and business funding, both of which have a huge influence on what gets researched, were moving her professional world into the priorities of economic and military production and away from the ecstatic discovery of new connections and deeper meanings.

For example, she knew some species of dung beetle navigate at night by polarized moonlight so they can get home in the dark with their booty. They even take account of the fact that the moon is moving while they are on their journey. Her heart jumped at the thought of how ingenious that is, and how rewarding it would be to trace the evolutionary steps by which such an ability evolved. But her heart sank at how offensive, and perhaps even blasphemous it would be to turn that glorious and extraordinary ability into manufacturing something such as improved night-vision goggles for fighter aircraft so we could be more effective at killing our enemies. Something in her shuddered. Science would have conscripted that marvellously improbable insect to teach us how better to kill one another.

How could this have happened?

It occurred to her that perhaps the pre-animist projection she had described to John, as a way of understanding how ideas of God emerged, might be alive and well within our modern culture. The pre-animist projection is that every single physical thing is conscious. If our culture is projecting that upon the planet, we will experience the planet as an infinitely fecund mother longing to shower upon us the fulfilment of our every whim. Within that projection, every aspect of our planet, including dung beetles, would exist solely to satisfy our wildest self-absorbed desires. And science would have become the technique by which to wrest whatever we want from the planet.

Isn't that what the planet is for? To meet our every whim? That's what the pre-animist projection tells us when we refuse to withdraw it and integrate its truth. Sounds like what is going on in our culture, Rosalind thought.

Ever since she had left home, Rosalind had been dismissive of her family's fundamentalist religion, but now it dawned on her why so many people would be attracted to it. Perhaps that style of faith affirms the pre-animist sense of a world madly in love with us, using the projected image of God who is able to do anything we ask. That would feel nice, if true.

But the downside would be that when we don't get everything we want, we blame science, or the planet, but not our projection. No wonder her family had disowned her when she gave her life to science.

Her family's religion experienced science as turning our adoring maternal planet into a dead machine with no place left for God and consequently no security left for humanity. That style of religion, she realized, would take as its responsibility the duty to stand for meaning and love by publicly resisting science because it was proclaiming the image of a vast and uncaring cosmos. Rosalind could understand why conservative religion is motivated by the desire to retain the illusion of planetary and cosmic love for us even at the cost of denying truths uncovered by science.

But she knew how destructive it is when a person or culture resists and refuses to withdraw a projection and integrate its truth. The important truth revealed by the projection of a fecund planet infinitely in love with humanity is that there is indeed enormous generosity around us, located within humanity as well as within the natural world. The purpose of the pre-animist projection on the planet is to reveal to us our human ability for deep giving to one another as well as the virtually infinite generosity of the cosmos which emerges us. But of course, that generosity can only be enacted when we withdraw the projection of an infinitely doting planet and integrate the projection's truth as a fundamental aspect of ourselves.

Rosalind remembered how angry she had been with John when she was projecting her own anger and rage onto him and experienced him as attacking her. So it seemed to her that since our culture refuses to withdraw the projection of infinite fecundity upon our planet, and since the planet cannot fulfil our every desire, we will experience that as a failure by the planet to care for us. We then have a right to be enraged, and that in turn permits us to rape the planet to fulfil our desires. Which is exactly what she saw happening all around her. And, most terribly, being enabled by science.

Rosalind also recognized that our culture is responding to the constant failure of technology to get us everything we want, with demands for more technology. But she realized the only path to a fulfilling life for humanity is not more technology, but for the culture to withdraw the pre-animist projection and integrate the projection's gift of revealing to us the depth of human generosity. And then enact it. If we were to integrate that knowledge about our humanity it would trigger acts of deep care for the planet and all its life. We would then be carrying out exactly what the pre-animist projection is for, and would receive in turn new security and joy. Technology would then receive its meaning—to enable generosity.

But Rosalind saw signs of resistance everywhere. Political leaders encourage the projection of a world that owes us anything we want—because that gives them the power and the right to force the planet to bend to our will and thereby enhance the leaders' power. They give lip-service to caring for the planet by creating tiny zoos of trees or creatures for humans to gaze at and be entertained by. If our economic and social policies leave many people and creatures in dire poverty or even death, that's the fault of the miserly planet, not of our leadership or our refusal to withdraw our projection on a planet that it owes us everything.

Our resistance to withdrawing that projection gets its power from our pervading sense of scarcity. That sense of scarcity is the outcome of our refusal to integrate the pre-animist projection upon the planet of all-surrounding generosity and abundance. Therefore we are unable to identify such generosity as our own character, and we have to fill our emptiness with getting more stuff.

That's why nothing, not species at risk, nor ancient forests, nor the future of humanity must ever get in the way of economic growth. Unending "growth" has become a necessity and a human birthright in a cosmos that exists to serve us. Our leaders can then re-affirm our culture's priority of extracting even more from the planet thereby giving more power to the leaders and more wealth to the wealthy and more poverty to the poor. "Growth" has become an insatiable political and economic priority that can only end in beggaring us all.

Rosalind knew that if we do not change direction, our planetary future is bleak. Science is making that very clear. Rosalind began to feel rage about what's happening to us and the planet. And to her as a scientist.

She glimpsed the path forward for scientists like her. She was experiencing a call to give leadership in challenging our culture's assumptions about the planet's infinite fecundity and unlimited commitment to humanity, and simultaneously our bottomless scarcity. Science would have to stand up to the culture and insist we can't have everything we want and that we already have resources within us of joy and generosity beyond our imagining.

That wouldn't be popular. Giving leadership like that would take courage. Rosalind wasn't sure she had that kind of courage to stand against our society's leaders. But at least things had begun to make sense.

Something felt very right about that and she slept well.

Killing the science spirits

In the morning, Rosalind wondered what would happen if our culture did indeed withdraw its projection upon the planet as an infinite mother-lover committed to fulfilling our every whim. She knew the infantile image of humanity suckling at a cosmic world breast would need to be replaced by something adult.

What projection could replace it?

When she had begun her career, like all young researchers she had imagined she would soon stumble upon some significant discovery all on her own. But it rapidly became clear that wasn't remotely possible. She was conscious of being upheld by the legacy of those who had begun research in her area centuries ago and now in collaboration with multitudes of current investigators all working with instruments and techniques implemented by an army of technicians and engineers who made her experiments possible. She knew if she'd tried to work alone, she'd destroy any chance of making any significant discovery. Science worked by teamwork.

Teamwork was not just the way to go, it was the only way to go.

She remembered explaining to John how animist cultures had first become aware of their ability to work as teams through the projection of spirits with whom humanity could practice teamwork and cooperation. Animist cultures experience themselves in intimate relation with their planetary relatives of all species and in teamwork with their environment. The mutuality of those relationships is central to their understanding of reality.

Rosalind was struck by the possibility that our culture, and indeed her profession, is already functioning within a projection of spirits. Our culture doesn't call them 'spirits' but calls them 'the laws of nature.'

These modern 'spirits' are the constants of physics, the intricacies of electronics, the understandable processes that lie behind engineering, chemistry, medicine, economics, sociology and psychology. Our culture is fascinated by the engineering accomplishments of exploring other planets, by the medical technology in repairing hearts, by electronic communication and computation, and even at such a mundane level as the science of sanitation that enables large cities to be livable. Each of these accomplishments depends upon our culture teaming up with the underlying forces of our world. For our modern culture, those forces are our spirits, with whom we are in teamwork and upon whom our day to day life depends.

Indeed, teamwork with the science spirits has become the defining character of our culture. We are proud, above all, that we do not live in the stone age, or in the Middle Ages, or even in the nineteenth century when, we think, people knew almost nothing. For our culture, those earlier times are the very definition of ignorance and superstition and hopelessness because people back then knew nothing about how to negotiate with the spirits of the physical world. Only we, living in the age of the full flowering of science, can be fully alive because we have learned how to negotiate with the spirit-forces of nature and thereby improve our lives.

Over her morning coffee, Rosalind realized she was, in effect, a modern shaman whose role in society is to be in touch with and mediate these science spirits to the rest of our culture. The shamans who mediate our relationships with those mysterious spirit-like laws of nature and who can speak their language, receive great respect and we cannot imagine life without them. She became aware of the pride she felt in her ability to understand and team with the spirits.

Rosalind was startled to realize how important that social role was to her. She liked being such a shaman. Which meant she was becoming conscious of her animist projection. That meant she was poised to integrate its truth— that humanity has the ability to team up with other cultures and countries, as well as with nature, not using our teamwork with the science spirits for our own advantage, but for everyone's fulfilment. That's the deep truth our spirit projection exists to show us about ourselves—we are in a team with all life and with all humans. In fact, there's no other way for humanity to live and survive. Teamwork, not only with the laws of nature but also with all life, is not only the way to go to reach human fulfilment, it's the only way to go. Science is right about that.

But to fully receive and integrate the truth that humanity can successfully team with the planet, with life, and with other cultures and nations, our projection that the laws of nature exist to serve us will have to die. The laws of nature just are, they don't exist to fulfil humanity's every desire. The challenge for Rosalind would be to communicate that truth. If those laws aren't spirits, but just the way nature is, then she would have to die to the highly respected role of shaman of the modern spirits.

Noticing how strongly she resisted withdrawing that projection made Rosalind aware that not only she, but also our entire culture resists becoming conscious of our spirit projection of teamwork with the planet. Giving up the spirit projection would mean giving up the belief that the laws of nature are there so we can get what we want. The hard truth is the planet and the cosmos isn't about us. That would be a hard truth to incorporate. But essential to life.

Rosalind wondered if John might be right. Could the purpose of science spirits be to make us aware that teamwork with nature is not for building bigger bombs or bigger refrigerators with built-in televisions? But to establish deeper relationships with all life and all cultures? Could humanity withdraw that projection and claim our ability to team up to everyone's benefit?

There are some signs, Rosalind realized, that our culture is beginning to feel uneasy about the projection of science spirits. Worries about science going wrong are common in our culture—from Faust who sold his soul to the devil and got nothing back but impotent knowledge, to Frankenstein who had no soul, to nuclear war which could end humanity's soul, and perhaps already has in that we retain and continue to update our ability to kill virtually everyone on the planet many times over. Such worries are indications that our culture is aware of the need to withdraw the projection upon science spirits as the way for us to get whatever we want. At some level we all know that if the projection is not withdrawn it will destroy us. As all projections do when we refuse to integrate their truths.

Rosalind was aware that withdrawal has already begun. The spirits, the underlying forces of nature studied by science, are already seen to be just too small to provide a path for the deep relationships and commitment humanity now needs. Perhaps that's part of what lies behind the widespread skepticism about science. Perhaps it's not just the result of ignorance, but an expression of dissatisfaction with the spirit projection upon science as the technique by which to satisfy our every desire. We all know deep down that the hope for some new technology to solve everything is simply child-like magical thinking. The projection of science spirits is being withdrawn.

Killing the history-gods

In the classical world of ancient Greece, spirit projections had been withdrawn so the projection of gods could present to us humanity's ability to manage large-scale political and economic challenges and manage our personal life stories. Rosalind wondered if something parallel may emerge in our time.

Could the equivalent of a god projection present to us a fulfilled future for humanity now that we exercise truly global power? Such a projection could enable us to envision a future in which there will be no end of creativity in the arts, in the nurturing of languages, in commitment to justice for all, in upholding huge variations among cultures, in supporting scientific exploration of evolution and cosmology, and even in affirmation of the various forms of religion. Imagine a planet where the task of humanity is to cultivate new Einsteins, Bachs, Gandhis, Dag Hammarskjolds, and Mother Teresas;[2] to cultivate ancient languages and cultures and species, and to develop social systems where justice and fulfilment for all is the norm. That's the potential of humanity that a god-style global projection could reveal and that humanity could subsequently integrate and enact. From the global perspective of an Olympic god, we could see what real human being is. A god projection could be the path to making the planet and all its inhabitants a place of joy into the far future.

As a young person Rosalind had delighted in such a vision presented from a cosmic perspective in science fiction writing, and through movies such as Star Trek and its successors. Those stories presented science as enabling global human, and even alien, community to come true on a cosmic scale. Science would enable humanity to move into an ever more inclusive history. Science wasn't just about production of goods or armaments, but about the construction of a cosmos of fulfilment and cooperation of which humanity could be proud. It was a wonderful vision, and along with her experience of awe, propelled her into her life's work. It was a god projection of global justice and fulfilment.

If science fiction was the form in which Rosalind experienced the global god-science projection as a young person, she was aware that an adult version of the global god projection has emerged centred, more realistically, upon our planet.

---

2   On 4 September 2016, she was canonized by the Catholic Church as Saint Teresa of Calcutta.

This more sophisticated god projection appears in the form of powerful historical processes which will inevitably draw humanity into a glorious future.

The god projection of an underlying historical force appears in several forms: free enterprise, the Marxist dissolution of the state, democracy, the long arc of history bending toward justice, my nation as god, or even as in Rosalind's world of science, the expectation that more technology can bring us utopia. Each of these gods has assured us they are the path to the permanent international generosity that is required for humanity to have a safe and fulfilling future. For many people, those projections of inevitable progress are the only hope that humanity even has a future. But they haven't fulfilled their promises.

The god 'Free Enterprise' promised unfettered creation of wealth which would benefit everyone and dispel poverty, but we are increasingly aware it is destroying us, from within and without, by creating a vast disparity of wealth and by the extreme poverty that free enterprise enables and requires. As always, there is intense resistance to withdrawing the projection of this god. Only unwavering worship of this god, it is said, can save the world.

The god 'Marxism' promised that the natural process of class struggle, allowed to run its course, would bring humanity into a new age of equality and dignity, but we know how hollow that promise became. As hollow as the god 'Free Enterprise'.

The long arc of history bending toward justice, is another hopeful form in which this god projection appears. However when we look at history, and particularly that of the West, and the priorities of military expansion and international economic exploitation now embraced by so many nations, this god appears to be dying, if not already dead. There is no evidence history is bending toward justice, much as we wish it were so.

The god 'Democracy' promised that the motivations of individuals voting for their own narrow self-interest would somehow translate into wise and generous global policies. But that god, too, seems to be leading us toward ever greater inter-nation and inter-nature conflict and is a disaster for planetary ecology.

Communications technology has enabled a god projection upon the nation as if the nation were a god. It is a kind of worship—the nation deserves our absolute loyalty. Just like a god. And just like a god, the nation's leader can magically appear in your living room and look you in the eye and tell you they are your saviour. But without a Zeus to enforce peace and order on each of these nation-gods, each vies for ultimate power over all the others, and together they are sacrificing humanity to their desperate attempts to achieve dominance.

The final form the history-god projection takes is that of technology. Technology is extremely important. It saved my life and that of my family several times. But technology isn't a god, automatically generating a fulfilled future for humanity. Unlimited adherence to the god technology always requires more technology when the limits or unanticipated consequences of a former technology produces problems we can't solve. We throw more technology at the problem and are surprised when that technology demands yet more to solve the problems it produced. When we attempt to address the problems caused by carbon-burning technologies by proposing carbon-capture technologies we are surprised to discover carbon-capture on an industrial scale will require far more energy input than we have. Our loyalty to this god will destroy us unless we withdraw its projection as a saviour god.

The growing doubts about the historical god-forces inevitably drawing us into a great future, are evidence that the historical god projection is also being withdrawn. If we integrate the truth of those projections—that we have the means and ability to construct such a future, we could enact it, but as long as our culture insists on placing its hopes upon mythical historical forces to save us and refuses to withdraw that projection, we cannot integrate the truth about ourselves that those history gods show us. Global and cosmic community will be forever beyond our grasp so long as we delegate responsibility for that hope to the history-gods and don't take action to embody that hope. If we retain that projection, those gods will destroy us.

Rosalind births the God projection

Rosalind realized an even more comprehensive projection is needed to provide a vision of how humanity can guide ourselves into a safe and just future.

A new projection would need to present the planet and all life upon it as if it were our spouse. Our relationship to the planet would need to be our ultimate and permanent commitment, a commitment like that of life-long marriage. Because, of course, as science has explained, that is the actual relationship we already have with the planet. We are wedded to this planet forever. Visions of humanity migrating to other star systems are simply fantasy and allow us to continue the projection of a technology god ready to save us, and thereby avoid our responsibility for the health of this planet. Our marriage to this planet, to all its lifeforms and to the rest of humanity is indissoluble.

The only issue in question is whether we will honour that marriage.

The only possible projection that could carry such an image of absolute commitment would seem to be that of a single cosmic call from the future to which all humanity could give loyalty.

Give loyalty to a disembodied call from the future?

This was exactly the image of the monotheistic God Rosalind had spent her entire adult life dismantling. And now was she feeling attracted to it? Was she actually imagining God could save humanity?

She didn't know whether to burst into humiliating giggles or to weep.

Could she tell John? Would she tell John? Would he collapse on the floor in laughter? She knew he wouldn't say "Told you so," unless he knew she knew full well it was a tease. But, "Gotcha?" Now, that was very possible.

But if it was a projection, you didn't have to actually believe in it, did you? But it wouldn't be a projection if you consciously decided to believe in it. So, bringing her research experience to bear, and despite her prejudice against this image, she decided to test it out, although hoping it would fail, just as one would test any hypothesis. It was a very courageous experiment.

Her hypothesis was, Could the projection of a single monotheistic God be what humanity needs for its future? Could God save us after all?

What would such a projection of God look like?

The moment Rosalind began to imagine it, she began to fall in love with that projection. The projection of a single infinitely loving cosmic God could provide the necessary image for humanity to enact a wonderful history lasting into the far future. Only such a projection could reveal what it means to be committed to a relationship to all humanity and to this planet not for a hundred years, or a thousand, but for millions upon millions of years—to be exact, for the five thousand sets of a million years each which are in store for this planet. For all practical purposes, for the infinite future.

Such a commitment wouldn't be about humanity and how we can survive and be happy as the pre-animist and animist projections had suggested. Or passively wait for fulfilment to happen as the historical god processes promised. Instead, a God projection could enable commitment to a truly cosmic vision that would include loyalty to the cosmos as we experience it on this planet. Marriage to the planet and the future requires a cosmic God to bless it and call us.

It might just work, Rosalind thought. Perhaps presenting the image of a beneficent cosmic God to the global community is the only path to humanity's future.

Are you serious?! she said to herself. What would that mean for her professional life?

Yet another of her worlds, her adamant atheism, had begun to die.

Killing the God projection and what happened next

But, attractive as this projection would be, Rosalind knew it would, in its turn, have to be withdrawn and die in order to be integrated and enacted, just as had all the former projections.

She knew the death of the God projection is inevitable. Sooner or later the forces of nature will overwhelm us and no projected God will intervene to save us. Another asteroid could collide with earth at any time, causing unimaginable disaster, and the very real possibility of human annihilation. The eruption of a supervolcano, driven by the implacable nuclear reactions at the centre of our planet could devastate all life.[3] Biology may rise up and destroy us, whether by our having engineered resistance to antibiotics, or through the natural emergence of a new and virulent virus—in either case we will always remain vulnerable to the possibility of world-wide plague. Horrific destruction from one of our technologies is a possibility lurking close by, whether by nuclear war, or by climate collapse, or by the incremental side-effects of the numerous chemical manipulations we have invented, or perhaps by artificial intelligence. If by good luck humanity escapes all these dangers, our sun will eventually swell so large it will incinerate the earth. And no God will intervene, no matter how attractive that projection. The God projection of absolute commitment to the earth and its people carries the seeds of its own death.

How strange, she thought, that science is now in the role of priest, wielding the dagger by which God must die.

Where does that leave humanity, without any cosmic God to love and protect us and ensure our future, Rosalind wondered. Maybe the existentialists were right and we are just freak cockroaches.

Rosalind was facing into the final darkness. She was accepting that, despite all that science has learned, despite any advance she might contribute to human knowledge, humanity can never have an assurance of ultimate safety. We will

---

3   Partial radiogenic heat model for Earth revealed by geoneutrino measurements. The KamLAND Collaboration, NATURE GEOSCIENCE, VOL 4, SEPTEMBER 2011

always live with death by our side.

As long as we retain the God projection unintegrated, our response to having to live permanently with death hanging over us will be defiance, rage at God, denial, or despair. Because God has abandoned us. "Eloi, Eloi…My God, my God, why have you forsaken me?" God deliberately stands by while we drown in meaninglessness. No wonder we desperately seek distraction in violence or addictions or denial of many kinds. The God projection must be withdrawn and integrated or it will destroy us.

Maybe, Rosalind wondered, that's why so much religion is angry and believes in an angry God.

Accepting the fact of humanity's death, the cosmos' death, and our own death, means that we are forced into knowing that it's not all about us. For a moment that was a terrifying but also immensely liberating.

Instead of it being all about us, it's all about ultimate reality and how we embody its love. We do that by upholding its patterns shown in persons and in the planet. We embody ultimate reality when we embrace its dying and rising as we die to the ultimate God projection and embrace the life-giving joy that even though we live constantly under the threat of death we are always united with ultimate reality. Knowing that all could end at any moment, we use every atom of existentialist courage, not to face into darkness but to face into joy, preparing for, and counting on, full human flowering as the embodiment of ultimate reality. Knowing it could all end in a moment but standing in full stature for self-offering love, we would embody ultimate reality's commitment to life and so be filled with life ourselves.

Rosalind saw that would leave us simply naked in front of reality with no projections about ourselves or the cosmos to hide behind. We would know and be known fully. And, of course, the God-science projection had to die to make that possible.

Her God projection hypothesis, as she had secretly hoped, had indeed died. But in doing so, it had been integrated into her vision for the future. Because of that death Rosalind was able to place her trust in the deep pattern-providing process of ultimate reality. She had participated in the full sequence of projections and their integration and so had received each of their gifts. The truth of how deeply she is loved and how valuable she is came surging into her awareness through her withdrawing and integrating the God projection.

She realized that by receiving those gifts, given through the death of God, we laugh at the darkness, we affirm and embody the life and joy arising from ultimate reality, and we will remain fully alive to the end of our time.

Rosalind felt a moment of joy rise within her. That knowledge was the most liberating and life-giving knowledge she could ever have.

And it didn't end there.

She could now allow her life's passion to re-enter the cycle of projections from the beginning and to experience them even more deeply. Just as John had learned how to re-enter the cycle of personal projections upon Rosalind, and to live more deeply through them.

Knowing she was absolutely dependent upon ultimate reality, Rosalind could immerse herself in the almost sensual joy of working within a cosmos suffused by consciousness and generosity in giving us existence. She could then delight in her role as a shaman leading teamwork with the physical world to uphold all life in a creative relationship with the planet and the forces of nature. She could even grasp with firmer conviction the possibility of a world of long historical fulfilment. Moving from that projection she could embrace the cosmic-God projection that while the cosmos is not about us, nevertheless we are utterly at home here forever.

And then re-experience that ever-deepening cycle yet again at new depth.

It all became clear to Rosalind. Our work as a culture will not be to imagine the planet as an infinite store of products, nor as an object with which we need to negotiate, nor as the place where humanity can live happily into infinity. Nor will we need to place our trust in some imaginary God to provide us with absolute safety. All those projections must be allowed to die so we can enter unlimited relationship with the actual world in which we find ourselves, and its source, ultimate reality. Rather, Rosalind realized, when the projection of God is withdrawn, the planet itself becomes for us the projection of ultimate reality.

The planet becomes, as the theologian Sallie McFague has said, "The Body of God."[4] Since the God projection is dying, and all Rosalind's projections on science are dying, we can anticipate new experiences of fulfilling life to very soon emerge.

The world turns out to be in love with us after all. The question is whether we are in love with the world.

---

4   Sallie McFague, *The Body of God: An ecological theology* (Augsburg Fortress Publishing, 1993).

Summary

John had put to death all his projections about Rosalind and those deaths had revealed depths about himself he'd never believed possible. So many illusions about himself and her had died, and those deaths and integrations made him more alive than ever.

Unknown to him, Rosalind had also been struggling. She'd been deeply disturbed at John's insight that all was not well in the world of science because it was enabling the rape of the earth. Science seems to be increasingly prostituted as a tool for entertainment and selfishness and death, the very last things she had thought science was about, and to which she had committed her life. How could this have happened?

It looks to Rosalind as if the same process by which cultures have projected experiences of spirits, gods, and God is now happening in our relationship with the planet which had been her life's love and study.

If we insist on continuing to live within any of those projections, we will see other cultures, or the biosphere, or the universe, simply as a projection of ourselves, and we will futilely attempt to subvert that other—whether person or planet or culture—to our will, and we will destroy ourselves in the process. As we see in current world politics, this is a very present hopeless and self-destructive path. We need urgently to withdraw such projections so that we can integrate their gift of self-aware power.

The death of the last projection of an external divine being called God leaves us in naked intimacy with ultimate reality. But when we allow those projections to die we will be greeted with self-offering love in return. And we will find ourselves fulfilled beyond all imagining.

Like John, Rosalind had also put to death her illusions about the nature of her life's work. And she, too, had come to a new disturbing yet enlivening awareness of a fulfilling future which would challenge her beyond any call she'd known before.

PART FOUR

Religion in Secular Space—
Dying to Be Alive

Religion is widely understood in secular society, and sometimes even among its own members, as a hobby for people who like religion, or as a social club featuring religious music. If you've ever asked church attendees what is the most important part of going to church, you'll find they very often say that connecting with their friends at church is their prime attraction to faith. They seldom speak of God or Christ, the central meanings of Christianity.

Building social contacts is very important, especially in a society as fractured as ours. That's certainly a good thing. And it reflects the fundamental and intimate relationship we have with all the cosmos. But religion never saw itself as a social club. Religion was always about God, not about socializing.

So, what's the point of religion now, when the projection of God is being withdrawn? If all that's left is for a religious community to be a social club dressed up in religious clothing then let's say so and stop speaking as if religion matters.

But that would be to miss the newly emerging role of religion in a secular society.

What if religion were not about encouraging people to believe in a divine supreme being, but about enabling people to experience what that projection offers when it is withdrawn? What if religion were not about threatening people with damnation if they didn't believe in Jesus, but about enabling people to move through their various deaths into ever deeper life?

What if that were true of the Christian faith itself?

"Congratulations, you who weep now! You will laugh!"[1] If Christians are mourning the loss of the God projection in our society, 'Congratulations,' says Jesus, 'you'll be filled with laughter!'

Indeed, we will.

We are about to see how.

1   Robert W. Funk, *The Five Gospels: What Did Jesus Really Say? The Search for the Authentic Words of Jesus*, (HarperOne, 1996). p. 289. The Sermon on the Plain, Luke 6:20-21. Jesus congratulates people who are in grief: "Congratulations, you who weep now! You will laugh!" See footnote 1 in chapter 10 for the implications of this curious pronouncement.

CHAPTER 17

Your Religion Died.
Congratulations![1]

The Sunday when Wolf and Eagle came to church

I don't know why I was asked to preach there. Perhaps it was because my father had taken their culture seriously.

The Nisga'a have lived along the Nass River in northern British Columbia "from time immemorial," as they describe their relationship with the land. Archaeologists trace their presence back for at least fifteen thousand years before whites arrived from Europe. As their bishop, my father had been the first to ask his clergy to live with the Nisga'a in their villages and to integrate with the Nisga'a culture. Maybe that's because he'd twice already lived with the

---

[1]   Robert W. Funk, *The Five Gospels: What Did Jesus Really Say? The Search for the Authentic Words of Jesus*, (HarperOne, 1996). p. 289. The Sermon on the Plain, Luke 6:20-21. Jesus congratulates people who are in grief: "Congratulations, you who weep now! You will laugh!" See footnote 1 in chapter 10 for the implications of this curious pronouncement.

poverty-stricken: with the Tl'kemtsin people of Lytton in British Columbia's interior, and before that, when he was first ordained, among the oppressed and exploited coal miners in England's notorious Wigan district in Lancashire. He understood the importance of being close to people for whom most of society cared nothing.

Family loyalty is immensely important in the Nisga'a culture, so I expect that's why I found myself preaching from the same pulpit from which my father had preached years before.

It was an ordination. A young Nisga'a man was about to make vows and be ordained an Anglican priest. The previous night, the villagers had held a huge feast with drumming and dancing in full regalia. The pounding of enormous drums in the shape of huge packing-cases as tall as a person made our insides shake. Mysterious dancers emerged and disappeared from various doors in the school gym.

It wasn't hard to imagine what the experience would have been like before Europeans arrived. In a clearing in the forest, at night, emerging through the smoke into the flickering fire-light, accompanied by the same enormous pounding drums—each made from a single cedar plank bent to shape—mysterious creatures would appear, encircle the awe-struck human community, and return again to the unending primeval forests spreading to the ocean on the west and the mountains on the east.

Villagers might have had a sense that the towering, two-legged bear figure emerging unexpectedly from the darkness was at once the tall elder who was a spouse's father but simultaneously Bear, whose deep reality had chosen to reveal itself to me, a child, a mother, a young man, or an experienced leader. With my insides buffeted by the pounding drums, my emotions at full alert, my feelings close to terror, I would have been astonished and graced and raised to ecstatic heights of joy to be visited by that which held ultimate power and significance for our life. If I myself were of the Bear clan, this visit would be the ultimate affirmation of my identity. My entire cosmos, the forest, the rivers, the mountains of my world had graciously chosen to reveal to me and all in my village a glimpse of their overwhelming power and significance, and had come to visit and bless us, their relatives. To be in near terror and joy at their approach was to know exactly what I should know if I were to be a true descendant of the people who had understood this world so well that they had thrived here for over fifteen thousand years without any help from outsiders.

Without that awe of the forest and its living creatures, and without knowing they and we are close relatives, I'd die of ignorance and arrogance.

The young man being ordained in that church was being ordained into that wisdom.

So, of course spirits would be present to initiate him into that relationship with the ultimate reality in which he and his people have lived from time immemorial and whom he would serve as a priest.

After I had preached, I sat in my assigned chair, my view somewhat obscured behind a pillar, watching as the ordination ceremony unfolded. On either side of the young man stood two elders in full regalia, one, Wolf, the other, Eagle. They were silent throughout, but their proclamation was deafening, in part because I was behind that pillar. Every few moments one of those figures made a small involuntary movement, exactly as a live wolf would, exactly as a live eagle would, because being their relatives, we humans make involuntary movements as we stand alert just as our relatives the creatures do. Because my view was partly obscured behind the pillar I was repeatedly caught off guard as one or other of the figures made one of these small movements. Every time this occurred I was momentarily alarmed to see an enormous Wolf and an enormous Eagle taking ownership of their place within the cosmos, guarding and enfolding and empowering and naming the young man, and all of us, within their encircling presence.

We could not forget for a moment that the vast forest home of these creatures lay mere yards from the church door, where the forest carpets mountain ranges as wide as the heavens, where rivers run as long as time, where the rain, the fish, the wolves, the bears, the eagles, the ravens and the killer whales and their human cousins, have lived together as a single fruitful family from time immemorial.

It was into that unity of all living things that the young man was being ordained. There could have been no ordination if Wolf and Eagle had not come to church to bless his ordination.

It mattered not a whit that we were in a wooden building modelled on nineteenth-century British ideas of cathedrals, or that so much of the ceremony had its roots in the Mediterranean culture of classical Rome and the European high Middle Ages and British imperial culture and religion. Those creatures who had shared life with the people for fifteen millennia were as accepting of my recent European roots as they had been of all visitors from long before anyone could remember.

Something about that culture works. Not once in fifteen thousand years, despite all that has happened—tsunamis, floods, erupting volcanoes—have the animals or the people gone extinct. We of European descent think we have a long history going back to the ancient Egyptians. But our entire western history is merely one quarter of Nisga'a history. For them, our ancient roots in Egyptian civilization mark our culture as a recent newcomer. The integration of their cosmos with their culture, through thought, feelings, ceremony, story, and governance got something right.

Do we really anticipate that our current western civilization will still be flourishing fifteen thousand years from now? Sounds like a joke. We know it cannot. Our treatment of the cosmos as something that we can manipulate, something we can use up, something that is dead and with which we have no intimate relationship, is an insoluble self-defeating contradiction threatening our society's survival and indeed the survival of the world.

To see the world as dead is to see ourselves as dead.

Our projection that the cosmos exists to serve us, must die and be integrated into awareness that we are relatives of every living creature; only then can long term stability of full life be ours. We can learn how to do that from indigenous peoples like the Nisga'a, who have been practising this integration with the earth and its life for millennia.

Those shocks of recognition as Eagle and Wolf visited us continue to reverberate in me. That the forest sent two creatures to embody their cosmos and to generously enclose that young man and myself in their life and power endures in me as a life-altering experience. Although Wolf and Eagle never once looked my way, I knew they encircled me as surely as if they had transported me physically into the vastness and mystery of their eternal forests.

Along with the young Nisga'a man, I was ordained by those spirits in their weaving of ancient First Nations intimacy with nineteenth-century western ceremony and with twentieth-century science that had enabled some of us to travel from around the province to this ordination.

Into what was I ordained by those ancient creatures? I didn't lose my trust in science or my fascination with the intricacies of creation scientific research reveals, nor my appreciation of my life having been saved more than once by medical research. Instead, Eagle and Wolf ordained science into a meaning and a significance and a life-giving quality that our secular culture has been unable to provide.

Eagle and Wolf didn't accomplish that gift of new life by presenting new research data, nor did they resist scientific knowledge, nor did they suggest they have a superior culture to that of the scientific secular west. They did it by connecting humanity to the cosmos through embracing powerful life-affirming projections. Although science has revealed our intimacy with all creation, western science has yet to embody and present the implications of that intimacy. Eagle and Wolf provided a way for science and for the secular West to participate in the life-giving power of the intimate relationships we have with all life.

What was clear in that ceremony is that the cosmos, the creatures, indeed all of creation, are our relatives and we owe them honour and loyalty. That's not a poetic image or a philosophical idea or a recommendation for new priorities. Wolf and Eagle embodied the *fact* of those relationships in their physical presence. That we would treat the creatures or the planet as a product to be consumed is unthinkable. That's why Eagle and Wolf chose to be central to an Anglican ordination. To have done otherwise would have been a contradiction of their nature in which all life, including human, are relatives. They couldn't not enact that.

Everyone present at the ordination, except myself, knew who was wearing the wolf regalia and the wolf mask and who was wearing the eagle regalia and the eagle mask. Everyone present knew they weren't dressing up or pretending. This was not a colourful play or a cultural display or a religious ceremony or a symbolic seminar. That's how western culture interprets such an event. Everyone present knew that Wolf and Eagle, our relatives from deep time, had come to encircle and honour what we were doing and encircle and honour the young man who was being committed to religious leadership. The Nisga'a know how to embody that projection and receive its gift of fully integrated planetary life by allowing the projection to express its full power and thereby be open to its meaning.

No doubt that's the secret of their culture's longevity. It could be ours, too.

For the Nisga'a that's all perfectly obvious. They long to share the obvious with us so we too could have the same fullness of life they've lived from time immemorial. Aboriginal people around the world are ready to do the same.

They'd love to teach us how to use projections to experience the intimacy and love with which we are surrounded at every moment. It would make an enormous difference if our culture could do that.

Managing projections, believing in God

It was a week after John and Rosalind's conversation about ultimate reality loving to die. John had invited Rosalind to his house and she had accepted.

When Rosalind entered his house, she was startled.

His house wasn't nearly as religious as she expected. In fact, not religious at all. *Odd,* she thought.

"How come you're so religious, but your house looks normal?"

He took it as a compliment. Perhaps even an affectionate one.

Watch out for projections, he reminded himself.

"Well, I never thought I had to surround myself with religious stuff. Somehow that would feel as if I depended upon a whole lot of support to believe. My faith, I guess, is about what's ultimately real, not about making myself feel religious all the time."

"I don't feel like making myself religious all the time either! Makes sense to me!" she laughed. "I'm with you there!"

She was? Well.

He'd baked muffins for her and had some special coffee blend. Neither had anything to do with religion. But they might have had a lot to do with his wanting to be more connected to her.

They settled down at his kitchen table.

Rosalind picked up the conversation where they had left off. The way friends do.

"I get what you mean about our having emerged from ultimate reality for all these fourteen billion years, and I get the sense ultimate reality is the totally reliable source of patterns—that way consciousnesses like us experience ourselves to be in a secure and loving environment. I can see how we then experience ultimate reality as caring and loving and even being ready to sacrifice itself for us. It's a remarkable idea. If it were true, it would be really important.

"But it looks to me as if what we've done in identifying God as a projection to be withdrawn is to dismantle religion. Without God there's really nothing left for religion to be about."

"Yes," John said. "When that projected image of God dies, it does look as if the whole point of religion is over. And I agree with you, as far as that goes. But I think in dying, religion may find itself with an even deeper purpose and new meaning and energy."

"I'm all ears. First you want me to believe in a God that is more God the less God exists, and then you want me to love ultimate reality, and now you want me to take religion seriously when it's dead. You religious people really do believe miracles still happen. I can't wait!"

They both knew it was a declaration of affection.

Something in her had died. And something very good had come to life.

She could tease. Herself. And John. About religion and disbelief.

John continued. "Managing religious projections is very important. When a culture's final religious projection is withdrawn, as it has been in ours, the culture loses not only its projection but the meaning the projection provided. We've seen how devastating it is for a person not to have meaning, but it's even more so when an entire culture loses its meaning. In the absence of meaning, our insatiable need for meaning becomes a desperate search for substitute meanings, whether in consumer addiction, or military violence, or zombie-like sleep walking through life, or in endless entertainment to distract us from noticing that meaning is missing. A culture without meaning is deeply vulnerable and urgently needs to rediscover life-giving meaning if it's not to self-destruct. Managing that process will be of critical importance to the future of humanity. Otherwise our frantic search for substitute meanings will kill us all.

"In our secular society, the role of religion will be to encourage and support people to re-enter the former projections and to receive from them new depths of meaning beyond what we had previously received.

"What if," John continued, "instead of religion fighting to uphold a projection of God in the face of secular skepticism, the point of religion were to guide our culture's withdrawal and integration of each of those projections? Religion's role would then be to preside at the death of each projection so the deeper self-awareness the projection had carried could be integrated and embodied by our culture. Rather than defending its projection against all comers, religion will encourage the various projections and then facilitate their withdrawal and integration. Which was the whole point of religious projections in the first place."

"Religion should encourage withdrawing projections of God? Wouldn't that be a sort of self-contradictory religion?" Rosalind teased. "Like your self-contradictory, non-existent ultimate reality?"

"*Touché!*"

He *was* touched. It hurt and healed both at once.

He continued. "The key is to recognize that although secular culture rightly rejects the projection of God as a literal divine being, our culture is resisting the integration of that projection. If religion were to integrate the truth that was previously carried by that projection, then our culture could embody the characteristics of ultimate reality and become more pattern-affirming ourselves. That would enable humanity to become more creative, whether in parenting or in painting; more intimate, whether in wooing or in world order; more awe-inspiring, whether in courage or in accomplishment; more trusting, whether in relationship or research; and more ready to gift our own selves to other persons and nations. That's a delight that would fill us with purpose for the virtually infinite future. We'd get our meaning back, and our joy.

"That's why religion is right to refuse to be relegated to the role of religious entertainment or to become simply a religious version of a social work agency, or to be drawn into the struggle for political or cultural power. If religion abandons its role of assisting people to regain meaning in our secular context, then religion has lost its purpose and its own meaning and has become pointless and joyless. Fundamentalism got that right."

"Now you're defending fundamentalism!"

Rosalind respected her colleagues who could graciously acknowledge the truth in a competing scientific theory. Selfish people don't defend their enemies. This was someone to whom she could entrust herself.

John responded, "I have no disagreement with fundamentalism that the purpose of religion is to enable fuller and more complete life. That's the gift the projection of God was intended to give us through our withdrawing and integrating it. The same process is true for the other projections of universal consciousness or spirits or gods, whether they are expressed culturally or are experienced privately in people's lives. Fundamentalism is afraid that if religion acknowledges the existence of projections such as of God, then there'll be nothing left.

"But strangely the death of God is the whole point of Christianity, so I think Christianity now has the role of managing the process of taking each projection completely seriously, in order to fully integrate its gifts. We do that by allowing the projection to die and then live within us. That's its purpose; for humanity to live fully."

"That's a pretty tall order," Rosalind replied. "That's a whole different role from what most religion is now focused on. Most religions think their job is to persuade the secular world that God exists. They do that by trying to prove they are more loving, or more threatening, or more mature than secular people, or they know more about science than science does. But if religion is about encouraging cultures to find meaning in ultimate reality without being committed to any one projection, religion will need to undergo an enormous change. I'm not at all sure that's possible for religious people. Present company excepted."

"Exception noted!" John smiled.

"You're right. It's going to be an enormous change, particularly for leaders of religion. In the past, religious leaders and members needed to believe they were actually encountering God or gods, and not projections. Religious leaders would commit themselves to upholding, and themselves to personally embodying, a projection that was the point of contact between humanity and God. To challenge that assumption seems at first to undermine the whole religious experience. You're right about that.

"But when religions were unaware that their Gods were projections, each religion had to insist that its particular projection was utterly real and all others were at best blasphemous and at worst outright evil. That's because each religion understood itself as the divinely-instituted channel by which humanity could be in contact with the spirits, the gods, or God of that religion. To maintain credibility, religion had to discourage people from noticing that it was enabling projections. Otherwise, people wouldn't have taken the projections seriously and wouldn't have been able to integrate and receive their life-giving power.

"For example, in your hypothetical pre-animist culture everyone has direct contact with the all-surrounding consciousness. In such a culture there is no experience they would have called religious—there was nowhere that consciousness was absent—reality and consciousness were the same thing. Everyone had direct contact with the projection of universal consciousness. In contrast, the shaman in animist cultures has the gift of speaking with individual spirits who live throughout the culture's natural environment and who embody essential life-giving respect for all living creatures. In Olympic religion, highly specialized priests or priestesses with esoteric knowledge of animal entrails, or ability to enter a trance state, have direct contact with the gods and can convey the gods' responses to questions about personal or global issues and so provide power to interact with a larger world.

"In a monotheistic religion such as Christianity, the priests, the pastors, the sacraments, ecstatic emotion, or the Bible itself, are the divinely-appointed points of contact through which humans are able to directly encounter the one supreme God and integrate God's life into our personal, cultural, and political priorities. The faithful shaman, priest, or pastor, understands themselves as having been selected as the enabler and embodiment of this divine-human contact. To feel so chosen is a humbling and often deeply sacrificial experience. But it's essential that the content of the projection be taken seriously if it is to reveal who we really are so we can become that."

"You are a very religious person. Have you ever felt like that?" Rosalind asked.

"Yes, when I've been given a role in a church service, I've felt that. I hold the cup from which the congregation each drink a sip of wine as a way of being intimate with ultimate reality. For me it is always a bit scary, knowing I know and simultaneously don't know what is being communicated through me, and yet I am a channel by which people experience intimacy with ultimate reality. I've wondered what it must be like for the clergy who do it all the time. I suppose you could get used to it, but I think the good ones never do."

"But what about other religions? Won't your idea of religion encouraging projections and their withdrawal end up in conflict with religions which may not take kindly to the proposal that their God is a human projection? And wouldn't that be a violation of the affirmation of other cultures and religions this new role for religion was supposed to enable?"

"It's true," John responded, "in our multi-cultural world, many Christians think of Christianity as one religion among others, just our local version. That assumption arises from secular culture's belief that religious experience isn't supposed to be taken seriously. In light of Christianity's history of disparaging other faiths that's an important corrective and to many well-meaning Christians that can be a loving, accepting and generous approach to other faiths. It's a good start.

"However it's significant that Christianity originally understood itself as 'The Way,' and not as a new religion. Early Christians understood their experience to be a perspective by which to understand life, 'the way' of living a full life, but not as a new religion attempting to replace others. Paul, the earliest Christian whom we know in some detail, affirmed the truth of other religions such as that dedicated to the "Unknown God" when he preached in Athens. And in the earliest Christian writings there are repeated references to Christians continuing to worship as usual in synagogues and in the Jewish temple—they took for granted that they were Jews and would continue so. For them Christ provided 'a way' for participating even more deeply in Judaism, not for replacing it and certainly not for starting a new religion.

"Further, there's no suggestion in the early texts written about Jesus after his life, that he had any intention of starting a new religion. In fact his constant insistence that he not be presented as the messiah, and his refusal to settle down and stay in one place in which he might have become the founder of a new religion, may not have arisen from self-deprecating humility, but from an adamant and deliberate decision not to found a new faith. That gives us a new perspective on what Christianity's purpose may originally have been, and suggests what it could be now.

"If it's true that Christianity's purpose wasn't to be a new religion, it need not be in competition with any faith now. The purpose of Christianity would not be to prove it is a better religion than any other, but to encourage everyone's experience of ultimate reality through the process of participating in religious projections and, though integration, receiving their truths. Whatever their religion. Such a form of Christianity could affirm and uphold every religion's projection and integration of ultimate reality through any of their projections—even including the religion of traditional Christianity which insists God must be experienced only as an existing divine being!

"But now that the projection of God is being withdrawn in our culture, instead of becoming irrelevant, religion has a whole a new purpose—to support people through the process by which religious projections are made, withdrawn, and integrated. In that way we can avoid the immaturity and self-destruction that ensues when a culture or a religion—yes, even Christianity—resists integrating the truth carried by its projections. Projections aren't mistakes that have to be corrected, they are the essential waypoints on the path toward fuller self-awareness and the embodiment of our meaning.

"And of course, that's been religion's purpose all along even when the projections were understood literally."

"I've got a problem with that," Rosalind responded. "You said this new function for religion is to affirm the projections of other faiths and enable their projections to be withdrawn and integrated. But not all projections are good just because they're projections. Otherwise you'd be commending the projection of ancient Roman emperors being divine so they could claim their violence was blessed by God. Modern world leaders claim God blesses their absolute power as the path to full life for humanity. You can't be saying that. Blessing all projections could become just another way of avoiding responsibility for a destructive projection. Or of claiming religious superiority—my faith's projection is better than your faith's, so, I'm in touch with God and you're not because you use an inferior projection. How are you going to handle that problem? How do you distinguish a good projection from a destructive one?"

I really like your clarity. He could love this woman.

"You're right," John responded. There has to be a touchstone by which to assess which projections are appropriately affirmed by religion.

"Since ultimate reality is the source of patterns, the projections we use for it must always affirm patterns, especially the patterns of other consciousnesses which are the most complex patterns we know of and particularly those who are the most vulnerable. Any projection that didn't encourage giving up our security for another's safety would not be a projection of ultimate reality. But if a projection supports consciousnesses and therefore would be experienced as loving, and if it were so supportive it could put aside its own patterns to uphold someone else's, even by giving up its own life as a religion, then it would be consistent with ultimate reality, the source of all patterns. Any projection that didn't affirm the most vulnerable in society, thereby affirming their consciousness, or didn't offer it's own life in order to love effectively, wouldn't be a projection of ultimate reality.

"That's how religion in its new role can decide which projections of ultimate reality to affirm and which to discard.

"So, what do you think?"

"I think it's getting worse and worse! First a God that can't exist, and now a religion that refuses to be a religion and makes that its whole purpose!"

"But," Rosalind smiled, "I have good news for you. This could demonstrate the existence of God because it'll indeed be a miracle if you think anyone of faith is going to be enthusiastic about this proposal!"

"On the contrary. Scientists have already led the way. Should be easy for you. You place your trust in Schrödinger's equation describing with exquisite accuracy how quantum particles move and then you say no scientist understands it. I guess you're right, miracles still do happen! But to atheist scientists! Gotcha!"

"OK," Rosalind laughed. "Again, I've been had! But that doesn't let you off the hook!

"I've got a question for you.

"How can we relate personally to ultimate reality? We agreed last week that ultimate reality must be intimate and caring and even loving, but if it's permanently beyond our comprehension, and doesn't exist, how can we relate to it at all? Isn't that the purpose of religion? Surely you can't have a religion that has no sense of personal relationship with anything? Are you sure you haven't turned your faith into a theory about ultimate reality and have abandoned any sense of personal connection?"

"I think there's a way we can still be in deep connection," John responded. "Experiencing ultimate reality as loving is the *only* way we can relate to it. That holds true even if we can't know it directly. Religious thinkers have come to the same conclusion about the traditional idea of God—in traditional religious thought, even though we experience God as loving, we have no idea what that's like from God's perspective. Since traditional faith says we can't have an accurate first hand experience of God (we'd have to be God to have that), we need a variety of projections to deepen our experience of God's love for us. The same for ultimate reality."

John continued, "This new role for religion doesn't require us to leave projections behind and settle for an idea such as 'ultimate reality.' You're right, nobody is going to experience loyalty or inspiration or even relationship through such a theoretical concept. We've seen why projections are essential in the initial stages of getting to know a person, even though it's necessary to eventually withdraw the projection; the same is true in getting to know ultimate reality. The projection of an all-surrounding consciousness, or spirits, or gods, or a divine being, God, is what makes the initial relationship possible. That's why it's essential that religion uphold and manage the projections.

"The trick is to take the projection totally seriously but not to be so tied to it that we cannot withdraw and integrate each projection and receive its life.

"This isn't a new idea for Christianity. In traditional Roman Catholic and other sacramental traditions, meditation upon, or worship of the consecrated bread and wine accomplish the same purpose. Worshippers know the bread and wine are bread and wine, but simultaneously experience them as embodying God. That projection carries immense truth because the bread and wine are feeding us physically—which is to be loved—and so through our projection allow us to directly experience ultimate reality's love for us. But that projection also has to be withdrawn to avoid magical and even destructive implications of the holy bread and wine. In Reformed Christianity the Bible served a similar function—believers still knew it was a book, but simultaneously they experienced it as a revelation from God. But that projection also has to be withdrawn lest the Bible be used as a weapon. Aboriginal cultures do that projecting all the time and think nothing of it—they take projections of the spirit world completely seriously and thereby are able to incorporate the gifts of those projections into their cultures and personal lives. And yet, to use western terminology, they know they are projections. That's worked for them from time immemorial. It could work for us, too."

Jesus: the projection of projections

John had come to a crossroads. He knew he'd have to take a huge risk, the risk
of losing Rosalind, if he was going to tell her what he really thought. His respect
for her was so deep he had to take the risk. If their relationship was to deepen.

"Now here's something I hunch you may not have seen coming."

She looked a little startled.

"Religion's new role will require a projection by which we can become aware
of and relate to the underlying process of dying and rising by which all these
projections of God or gods or spirits can be integrated into our self."

"You're wanting a projection of a process? Really?" she joked. "Yup, I didn't
see that coming!"

John didn't laugh.

"Up to now the withdrawals of projections just happened naturally as new
knowledge or cultural needs required. That's what's happened to the projection
of God in our secular society. But now that religion must pro-actively manage
the projections, we need a way by which to relate to that process of projecting
and withdrawing itself if we are to manage it well."

"OK," she said, hesitantly, "I can see it would help to have an image of how
projections must be embraced and withdrawn so we can integrate their power.
What do you have in mind?"

"Jesus."

He paused.

She said nothing.

Her tone had changed.

"You're right. I didn't see that coming.

"I had really begun to think you weren't religious after all and you'd have some
way out of this religious stuff." She looked full at him. Betrayal and anger just
beneath the surface. He knew she was serious. And he knew she felt betrayed.

*She'd come all this way with him, listened carefully, allowed him into her life,
had worked hard to take his religious beliefs seriously, and now that she was in
his house he was going to betray her? And get religious on her after all? She should
have guessed.*

Her trust almost gone.

But something about his silence kept her from giving in to her deep anger.

He could see the struggle, and he waited. Until she could focus. Until she
could withdraw her projection on him as a betrayer.

That was a deeply loving pause.

"Think of it like this," John said when he sensed the time was right.

"We've been talking about how each of the various projections of ultimate reality have enabled humanity to integrate and own the qualities the projection presented to us. Even though those qualities were already inside us. We just needed to see where those qualities really lay and give up the desire to avoid taking responsibility for them. That's the service the projection provided. Each time, the death of the projection made possible the integration of those qualities giving rise to a new depth of self-awareness, and therefore deeper maturity and fullness of life.

He paused.

She waited.

John continued, "That underlying process is absolutely essential, both for us as persons in our relationships with one another as well as for our life on this planet, as well as for relating personally to the emergence of the physical universe and life itself.

"What's really important isn't the details of each projection. What's important is participating in the projections, withdrawing them, letting them die, and then integrating the truths they each embodied. If we didn't let the projections die, each projection would become a straight-jacket, a way of hiding who we are from ourselves, a way of avoiding the creative and potentially risky acts of love that reflect ultimate reality.

"In order to relate to that underlying universal process which has given rise to us, we need an image, which would itself be a projection. Only then can we support and manage this deep underlying process."

She couldn't quite disguise her disdain.

"So, you want Jesus to be that image."

"I'd put it the other way around. I'm not wanting Jesus to be the screen onto whom we project that underlying process in order to prove something about Jesus. What I think happened is that at the time of Jesus people were, perhaps unconsciously, looking for a projection by which to relate to that underlying process of death and resurrection. Through their long history of being repeatedly conquered and yet surviving, the ancient Jews already had an awareness of an underlying implacable love that valued them in spite of their not valuing it in return. Some of them saw that underlying implacable love enacted by a peasant who got executed for insisting on sacrificial love in opposition to violence. That image enabled them to relate to ultimate reality's unreasonable loyalty to them.

"The people who knew Jesus personally were amazed that he took ulti-mate reality that seriously and lived, and died, embodying ultimate reality's self-offering love. He made a costly choice to embody that pattern-serving life as the only alternative to the pattern-destroying death wielded by the Roman empire. People who knew him experienced him as totally present to ultimate reality. That's why they named him 'Son of God' because 'God' was the most credible projection at the time, and so with that title he became the projection for their experience of self-offering ultimate reality.

Giving him that title also critiqued the Roman emperor of violence who'd already named himself 'Son of God,' hoping to enforce obedience through his culture's violence. By giving Jesus the same title as the emperor they used him as a projection for what we are calling 'ultimate reality' and simultaneously denied that role to the Roman emperor of violence.

"Of course they didn't use the term 'ultimate reality' that you thought up, but I think that's what was going on. They did use terms such as 'form of God,'[2] 'fullness of God,'[3] and 'permanent mystery'[4] to hint that there was more significance to him than the literal projection of a 'Son of God.'

"The problem we've got ourselves into about Jesus is we have kept the projec-tion going too long. We've done what he explicitly refused to do. He insisted he had to die—that his projection had to die. But we insist he remain alive as a projection in which he's become exactly what he refused to become—an Olympic god. Perhaps the reason we keep him alive is to keep him at arm's length so we don't have to take him seriously.

"When we don't let him die, Jesus becomes an Olympic god because as a god he floats above the real world and embodies an invulnerable distant Olympic perspective which is why we have to pray hard to get his attention. It's easy for him to love because nothing hurts him. Which means he doesn't really love. He's become either an impossible saccharine image of sweetness and light and passivity and disconnection, or the image of threat and punish-ment and violence. Especially when he dies for us and we kick him in the teeth by sinning more. There's no forgiveness for that and we anticipate his rage will break out at his second coming when he'll balance the books and

---

2   Philippians 2:6
3   Colossians 1:19
4   Colossians 1:26, interpretive translation.

settle accounts with a final act of cosmic violence."[5]

Rosalind was taken aback. She wasn't sure if he was serious or sarcastic. He certainly gave words to her own rejection of the Christian faith.

John paused, knowing Rosalind agreed and scorned that controlling and violent Jesus. He waited for a moment.

"But that's not real," John said. "It's all our projection. And, as you may have noticed, projections have to die.

"And here's the thing. Any projection of that underlying process, by which projections are birthed, withdrawn, die, and are integrated into our own life, must itself participate in that process. A projection of the process of death and resurrection that didn't die wouldn't be a projection of that foundational process. That's why the projection of Jesus works—his death is central to who he is. He's a projected image that doesn't just stand for an idea, but embodies it in physical historical reality. He did die, deliberately. That was the point. All the violence connected with his death was there to prove that he really did die. As he insisted he must.

"And of course he has to rise, too. We experience that when we've integrated the projection into our lives—that's the experience of resurrection. We begin to live the mature life of love that was within us all the time.

"The secular misunderstanding of Jesus as a nice person who got executed long ago, or as a vengeful religious dictator, has arisen because Christianity refuses to let him die. So, strangely, secularism is keeping faith with Jesus. It's Christianity's refusal to take him seriously by refusing to let him die that turns him into a passive dreamer or an abusive divine dictator.

"He was right, after all. He only saves us when he dies."

Rosalind was silent. It sounded so much like the oppressive faith she'd grown up in, and yet it sounded so very different.

"Your house isn't very religious, but all this talk about Jesus dying for us sure seems religious."

He knew it was a question, and might even be a plea for a way out of her conundrum. He suddenly realized she didn't want their connection to end either.

"Here's a way to understand that contradiction. Calling the underlying process the Christ-process would make it clear we aren't trying to relate to the

5   Pat Robertson, "God is tolerant and loving, but we can't keep sticking our finger in his eye forever." BBC News, http://news.bbc.co.uk/2/hi/americas/4427144.stm, November 11, 2005.

projection of Jesus as an imaginary friend from the distant past, or as a great teacher, or as a sort of Olympic god who can be persuaded to take an interest in us, or as a lovely presence that surrounds us in the way the pre-animists experienced. Instead, the Christ-process is a way we can speak of how all projections of ultimate reality have to be made and subsequently withdrawn and die so we can receive their life. That could be both religious and not religious at the same time."

Rosalind asked, "If you're telling me I'll never understand it, you're either teasing me or you're on to something. Just like Schrödinger's cat[6] which is alive and dead at the same time, so your Christ-process projection has to be both alive and dead. How about calling your idea 'the Schrödinger Cat' process?"

John smiled. "That could work since dying and rising happen together. But some of us non-scientist types might think we'd need to learn higher mathematics. Could you take pity on us and just call it the 'Christ-process'? Would you still talk to me?"

She just smiled. No commitment. But no denial, either.

"To participate in that process and image it, we need to project it on a screen, and that screen can be Jesus. His deep trust in the underlying self-offering of ultimate reality and his extraordinary commitment to justice at ultimate cost to himself makes him the perfect screen for a projection that is consistent with the process he presents to us.

"For Christianity to be consistent with this projection, Christianity itself will have to die to claiming special authority. Only then will the Christian faith be transparent to the Christ-process that makes sense of how the cosmos works on both the largest and on the most intimate scales. Since ultimate reality is prepared to die so we can live, so must the faith die, but then live, and so must the projection upon Jesus through which we can relate to that deep process."

Rosalind was smiling. "Well, I don't know whether to laugh or cry, or cry from laughing! First you have a God who can't exist, and then a religion that is determined to self-destruct, and now you have a 'Schrödinger Cat' Jesus—both alive and dead at the same time, and Jesus—he's a projection of the Christ-process! The Schrödinger equation has nothing on you!"

Rosalind paused.

---

6   See glossary. Erwin Schrödinger illustrated the strange behaviour of quantum particles by imagining a cat which would be simultaneously alive and dead depending on a particular quantum particle which would be both present and absent at the same time.

"I hope you're not insulted. I just mean if someone was looking for images, this multi-meaning Jesus could illustrate what you are saying. So would the Christ-process. So would the Schrödinger Cat Jesus. They all have multiple meanings."

"Guess what?" John said, trying to keep a straight face. "We've made a theologian out of you after all."

"And you think that's a compliment?"

And they both laughed.

He was pleased she cared.

He felt more alive than he had ever been.

Something very good had happened.

In spite of Jesus.

Summary

Humanity has become self-aware, and therefore human, through projecting aspects of ourselves, withdrawing those projections and then integrating them into our life. The Nisga'a have been doing that for millennia, and continue to take their projections seriously. By using that process from time immemorial they have embodied the power of projections to enable full life for their culture.

The underlying process of projections being embraced and then being integrated is the central dynamic of full human life. When the projection of God is withdrawn, religion's new role will be to support awareness of, and participation in that process by which the various projections are integrated into our lives. We might name that process the 'Christ process' and Jesus can be the screen upon which we project that fundamental process of death and resurrection.

And of course, the projection has to embody that which it is presenting to us, which is why Jesus must die. As he insisted he must. And then rise in the form of our own deepened life of self-offering love when we've integrated his self-offering and embodied his resurrection.

CHAPTER 18
Re-imaging God:
Managing Multiple Projections

Bishop: What do you believe?
Elderly illiterate First Nations lady: What do you believe?

In my tradition, bishops decide who they will ordain. So, having almost finished my degree and found a way to believe in God and Jesus, my next step was to find a bishop who would ordain me.

Any bishop.

I only knew one.

So, that's the one I asked.

John Frame, the Bishop of the Yukon, took me out to supper in Toronto where I was studying.

Before he made his decision about whether to ordain me, he wanted to know what I believed.

I was delighted to be asked.

I told him the Christian faith made perfect sense. I drew upon my studies of

Paul Tillich, a German theologian who taught in the U.S. after fleeing persecu-
tion by the Nazi government. I explained to the bishop how God could be
understood as ultimate reality, Jesus could be understood as the New Being—
through Jesus we live renewed in ultimate reality—and how God is much more
real when God doesn't exist, but is existence itself or the source of existence or
the power of being.

Because we exist, we face three limitations of all things that exist. These
limits are, first, physical—the limits of our physical bodies. We are always
potentially vulnerable and all of us will die and we know it. But we are afraid of
dying and so avoid enacting deep love which always involves risk and sacrifice.
Second, there are limits to our knowledge—we can never know with certainty
what our deepest motivations are or what will be all the outcomes of any moral
decision we take and so we can never be sure we are making fully loving moral
decisions. So we are all guilty of immoral acts and attempt to cover this up
from ourselves by imagining we are perfect, but are full of self-focused concern.
Third, there is no way to know if our life has, or will have, any significance—in
the vastness of the universe we may mean absolutely nothing. And so we despair
and experience deep abandonment and brokenness which we attempt to ease
by accumulating power or belongings. In each case we are deeply vulnerable—
physically and morally and being subject to meaninglessness.

I went on to say that Tillich's solution to the challenge of our profound
brokenness is that ultimate reality has acted to include us in the limitless reality
of God and has done so through the historical event of the Christ, who is
the New Being, entering into the real world of existence and integrating and
therefore healing our three types of brokenness. In Christ those three vulner-
abilities, seen impinging on him at his crucifixion (physically, morally, and
being without meaning), are overcome in his resurrection, in which, while still
in the three-fold limitations of existence, he is united with ultimate reality or
'the ground of being,' as Tillich calls it. The point is, we are able to be incorporated into Christ's New Being, enacted in our baptism, and to be taken up into
ultimate reality. That would be unlimited joy and fulfilment.[1]

I was a bit breathless at that point, but had told my future bishop what I
really believed, what had excited me and had finally made sense of Christianity.
That's what had converted me. That's what I now wanted people to know. That
would give people hope and purpose and make a huge difference to the world.

---

1   Paul Tillich, *Systematic Theology: Three Volumes in One* (University of Chicago
     Press, 1967), passim.

I'd written a major paper on the subject and those studies had restored me to faith.

My explanation was followed by a long silence.

I feared the bishop would ask me to take a year off and travel and come back and think again. But I'd done my travel in East Africa and in the Middle East, and done my thinking, and discovered how it all made sense. I just wanted to get started with telling people this great news.

My heart sank as his silence continued.

Finally he spoke.

"Do you think you could say that in a way that people could understand?"

I thought that was exactly what I had just done, but with a humility I didn't feel, I said I thought I could try.

That summer he ordained me.

A week after my ordination he sent me to a tiny First Nations village in the Yukon, on the banks of the silent but powerful Pelly River.

It was my first congregation.

The day I first set foot in the village, one of the ancient grandmothers with no western schooling came up to me, hobbling on her cane, bent over, her head wrapped in a bandana.

No pleasantries.

"Why didn't they baptize that baby?"

I hadn't the slightest idea what she was talking about.

"What baby?"

"Linda's. Dead when it got born."

An answer was required. She wanted to know why the previous priest had refused to baptize the corpse of the still-born baby who would have been her great-granddaughter.

In a flash, I sketched in my head the outline of an essay, drawing upon all the latest theologians, describing the nature of human life as the form in which ultimate reality, or the ground of being, expresses itself through us, and the encounter with the triadic limitations of existence, one of which is the limitation of death, and the way in which this lady's experience of death might well be a profound encounter with the death of God, and how, at the end of time, all will be made new in Christ who is the New Being.

The ground of being, ultimate reality, would graciously gift me, the elderly lady, the still-born baby, and indeed the entire universe with New Being. That was the point of Christianity. It all made perfect sense to me. That's why I had been ordained—to explain this to people so they would be filled with confidence and hope, even in the face of a tragedy like this.

The elderly lady with the gloriously wrinkled face was, astonishingly, putting her entire trust in me. She wanted to know why her still-born great-grandchild hadn't been baptized. And she wanted the answer now.

And if I told her my answer, after the first three words she'd know I was as useless as I suspected I was.

Then the miracle happened.

I had to kill God. Which is how you get to be a real priest. Remember? Priests are the ones who do the sacrifice? I had to kill ultimate reality.

So, in a flash, I whipped out Occam's razor and did the deed.

The simplest explanation is most likely to be true.

So, I told her why the priest before me hadn't baptized the dead baby.

"He didn't baptize your still-born great-grandbaby because when her soul gets to heaven Jesus will baptize her there."

I counted on her thinking baptism by Jesus would be much more holy than baptism by me. That way I could avoid having to baptize a corpse.

She nodded thoughtfully, was satisfied, said not a word, turned on her cane, and hobbled back to her one-room log house.

Thank God for Occam and his razor. The simplest explanation, for her, was the true one—Jesus *was* baptizing her great-grandbaby in heaven. Without Occam to cut out my extraneous learning, my pastoral care would have been a disaster.

That old lady with no western schooling completed my education. She gave me the greatest gift I could imagine as a young priest. She helped me see that the nice old man in the sky was literally true after all. Every bit as true as the idea of ultimate reality that satisfied my need for clarity about God. For her sake, I had to kill God. Not the projected God whom I had already killed the day I failed the counselling roleplay, but the sophisticated ultimate reality God that made it possible for me to believe and be ordained. The issue wasn't what I believed, but what the truth was for this elder.

There are, apparently, no limits to which God will not go to die for me and for the elderly lady without any western education.

Was the New Being incorporating her still-born great-granddaughter into ultimate reality through transcending the existential limitation of death? Or was Jesus baptizing her still-born great-granddaughter in heaven? Maybe it was the same thing.

That discovery was my baptism by a grieving elderly First Nations lady into a more mature faith. I never forgot her lesson and used it frequently in pastoral care. Thank you, Ella.

But it may also be that Ella was saying something I couldn't hear as a young priest. Perhaps her silent departure was making it clear that I cared nothing for what she and her ancient culture needed and to which she had a right as the babe's grandmother. Maybe she needed her grandbaby's body to be blessed. But I knew my Christ was better than her inadequate understanding. One more white man telling her what was best.

Perhaps she was also walking in the footsteps of another woman who once challenged Jesus for calling her a dog by saying, "Yet dogs eat the crumbs that fall from their master's table."[2] Was Ella telling me I had just called her a dog? But doing so without humiliating me on my first day in her village? If so, I thank you, Ella, for your kindness and for having the courage to tell the truth to authority anyway. If that's what really happened, I want to honour your truth telling by re-telling it as best I can so many years later. I know that you and your stillborn great granddaughter are in heaven with Jesus and that you'll welcome me home with undeserved generosity when I join you there.

Trusting projections: plumbing their depths

John and Rosalind had been speaking about how religion's role in secular society will be to enable people to engage with ultimate reality by participating in the birth and death of projections about ultimate reality. John had named that underlying process the 'Christ-process.'

But Rosalind had a concern.

"I don't see how you are going to get people to take belief in God seriously when you're encouraging people to explore a variety of projections of God rather than to just believe in God. Aren't people going to say, 'If it's all projections, then why should I believe anything at all?' I'd worry that any religion that does that is doomed to self-destruct."

"That's a really important question," John replied. "If we have only one projection of ultimate reality, 'God,' then we are back to imagining God is an object existing in the universe and then God becomes just a larger projection of myself.

"The way to keep that from happening is to know that people experience

---

2   Matthew 15: 26-28

ultimate reality in very different ways depending on their circumstances. So, even though all of us are embraced in, and emerge from, and are loved by ultimate reality, our experience of it varies greatly from one situation to another and from one person to another and from one time in life to another.

"Trying to shoe-horn everyone into the single projection of 'God' may be one of the reasons faith is losing credibility in our culture. People just know that no matter what religions say, there can't be just one description of whatever it is that the word 'God' is pointing to."

He went on. "It's not about picking a convenient projection. Since everyone is equally related to ultimate reality, regardless of their education, or culture, or faith, or atheism...," he popped that in as a tease and a truth, "...we must learn to speak about ultimate reality in ways that it is experienced by each person in their particular circumstances. We must be able to use the image of 'God' or 'ultimate reality' in a wide variety of projections—almost like multiple languages—in order to be faithful to people's wide variety of life experiences. Using different projections with different people is not over-simplification, nor some kind of communication technique, nor condescension. Managing the many possible projections upon ultimate reality is to be faithful to the infinitely deep reality to which all the various projections point. That is religion's role in a secular society.

"Because ultimate reality relates to us in so many ways, we need to become adept at moving from one projection to another. To do that requires each religious leader to have undergone each of the projections and their withdrawal. Only in that way can we team up with whomever we are in conversation with and join them in their projection and affirm it.

"God must become multi-valent."

"A multi-valent God?! You've got to be kidding! Multi-valence is the way in which some atoms take on different qualities in different chemical contexts. Not exactly like Charles' quantum particles that can be anywhere they like— but pretty flexible. You've been hanging around us scientist types far too long!"

"Oh, I don't know about that," he said. And kept his face carefully neutral.

She looked up quickly. What was that expression on his face? But she could see only his eyes over his coffee cup. She couldn't read his eyes. Yet. And she got the implication of her own 'yet.' She'd really like to. *Better he not know that. Get back to the topic.*

"A multi-valent God! Now I've heard everything!"

"Maybe not. Just wait! But you're right, nobody is really going to relate lovingly to 'ultimate reality.' Nor should they."

"Right! Exactly my point!" Rosalind said. "So, how is your multi-valent God going to help people relate to ultimate reality?"

"Imagine how differently ultimate reality is experienced by an elderly lady with no western education I heard about whose granddaughter had just had a still-birth. For her, ultimate reality is a kindly spirit who will care for the baby forever in heaven. For a young lawyer who has just entered upon marriage with someone more wonderful than she could have ever wished for—for her, ultimate reality has emerged through her lover as a joy beyond imagining—no wonder she calls him her soul-mate. For a professor who has had the wisdom not to accept an appointment as the department chair—ultimate reality has taken him down a difficult path toward maturity in which he has deepened his strength by dying to the seduction of power. For a teen bringing embarrassment to his family and moving through it into responsible adulthood—ultimate reality has been for him both threat and rescue. For a family experiencing divorce, ultimate reality may feel like judgement—hopelessness, anger, failure, and loss, but when those truths are faced, ultimate reality becomes the astonishing discovery that it is possible to move beyond the past into a future that had so recently seemed utterly impossible.

"So, for example, some people in some circumstances will find a pre-animist diffuse, all-pervasive consciousness to be an effective way to image ultimate reality, but for others or for the same person at another time, ultimate reality might be better projected as an approachable spirit, or a local god, and for still others, the traditional 'God.' There may even be some people who might find the idea of ultimate reality to be an effective image."

He looked at her meaningfully. She just smiled.

John went on. "Probably the most common experience that people of our culture have of ultimate reality is the pre-animist projection of a diffuse all-pervasive consciousness—it is a feeling of being surrounded on every side by an embracing and affirming power. This often happens to people outside religious contexts. On a mountain top, 'I just feel God all around me,' or 'I have a spiritual experience when I'm alone in silence on a lake,' or 'I feel God in my heart,' or 'I felt the trees speak to me' are some of the ways people experience ultimate reality through the pre-animist projection. Religion should not dismiss these experiences as simplistic or naïve. Such projections are entirely accurate because the creativity and intimacy of ultimate reality does surround us at every moment, just as science describes. Such projections are wonderful ways of experiencing ultimate reality. Religion should encourage them, not disparage them as if they are inferior to the projection of a divine being living in heaven.

"Religions have always encouraged that kind of projection, although they have usually limited it to a religious context. Within Christianity, a Bible allowed to fall open at random will present to some people, in the first verse they see, a specific message from God about how to manage their day. God must really care about me to do that and to be present even in randomly selected words on a random page. Or the image of Jesus' face may appear on a rain-soaked wall, showing us that Jesus' loving presence surrounds us in every place, even in the stained walls of an old house. Or a vision of the Virgin Mary reaching out her arms in embrace can be experienced if one travels to a special holy site. Or Jesus' body and blood can be experienced as physically present in the bread and wine of Holy Communion bringing his omnipresent cosmic love inside ourselves.

"That's what's happening when I hold the cup for people to drink from on Sunday mornings."

"You really experience that?" Rosalind asked.

"Yes." The simplicity of his answer moved her.

After a pause, he continued.

"Some religious traditions encourage an intense emotional projection of being surrounded by care through the practice of religious ecstasy and speaking in tongues. Liturgical churches, and especially the Orthodox and other mystical traditions, specialize in encouraging experiences of deep unity with ultimate reality in the context of mystical worship or meditation. Even astrology provides its followers with a sense that we are surrounded by a predictable and understandable universe that constantly gives us clues, based upon our birth-date, for how to live wisely every day. These are all appropriate ways in which various religions and even secularism present us with a variety of projections of ultimate reality as a surrounding presence.

"This pre-animist sense of being surrounded by cosmic love is a wonderful feeling. For many people that is the whole point of religion—to provide us with that all-embracing experience of safety and comfort. There is nothing wrong with that.

"But as we have seen in the history of religious projection, the purpose of a projection is to be withdrawn so its truth can be integrated into our life so we can live more fully.

"The truth is Bibles don't magically fall open to a page with a message specifically tailored to our immediate need. The truth is, speaking in tongues doesn't guarantee any special ability to love, nor do the ceremonies of ordination or marriage; and horoscopes don't predict daily events in anyone's life. Giving up each of those projections, both personal and religious, difficult as that is to do, enables us to assimilate their truths and become more deeply who we are.

"So, someone with a religious background experiencing a dilemma might open a Bible at a random page and read the first verse they see. If the verse speaks to them and increases their clarity about their dilemma, they've allowed an insight to come to consciousness. They will have seen something about themselves in the projection, withdrawn the projection, and then will have assimilated its truth and made it their own. Which was the whole point of the projection in the first place. But then they will need to put the Bible down and take action, on their own responsibility, for the insight their Bible revealed to them.

"In the same way, if the random verse turns out to be meaningless, then the same thing happens—the Bible is put away and the person takes responsibility in some other way for the decision they have to make. Even if that were to look at another random verse.

"But refusing to withdraw the projection would ensure failure. To continue to use the Bible or some other pre-animist projection to avoid taking responsibility would be to abandon one's own strength and remain childishly dependent upon reading chance verses or basking in nice feelings without ever integrating those strengths, and learning they exist already in our own self and ensuring others have them, too. It would be highly irresponsible and self-destructive to use the projection as an escape from our true self. The same thing is true of speaking in tongues or of going through a marriage ceremony blessed by God or of being ordained. Each is a projection that enables us to know something deeper about our self, and each must be withdrawn in order that we integrate and take responsibility for what the projection showed us about our self. Only then can we enact it and become the person we already are."

"Makes sense to me," Rosalind said. "I hate to say it, but a lot of religion seems to me to be people wanting to have a nice time—they enjoy religious music, or they feel better that they are loved, but in the end it's just about themselves. Sometimes it seems to me church is sort of like watching a religious Hallmark movie—the point is that everyone comes out feeling good. But nothing ever changes."

She was startled by John's response.

A big smile.

"You are so right!" He felt like hugging her. "Yes! You said my house wasn't very religious—that's why. It's so easy to make projections of ultimate reality into decorations. Or entertainment. Or absolute truths. Then we'd lose the gift that ultimate reality is designed to give us—that we become more and more loving just like ultimate reality."

"So, you are saying the less religious you are, the more you are like ultimate reality? In other words, the less religious you are the more religious you are? And since God doesn't exist, nor does ultimate reality, religion therefore makes no sense. That makes complete sense to me!"

He laughed. It was a moment of intimacy. Just like what they had been talking about ever since that day in her garden.

"OK," Rosalind said. "Enough about being surrounded by cosmic love. Let me guess. That projection of all-surrounding love has to die? So, what's next in religion's role? I'll bet you are on to animist spirits next."

"How'd you guess? It's your fault, you thought this up!"

"The next aspect of religion's new role in managing projections will be to assist people to see, withdraw, and integrate spirit projections. Children are taught by religious parents that God is a very nice person who is close by them and loves them all the time. That's God in the image of my personal friend—in the role of a protective spirit hovering over me. It's a highly appropriate way to express to a child the deeply supportive relationship that ultimate reality has with all of us. It's healthy for children to have the sense of security such an image provides. There is nothing wrong with encouraging the animist sense of a benevolent spirit close to us since that's how a child can best experience the supportive presence of ultimate reality."

Rosalind remembered being taught about God like that, as a small child before all the adult religion came and ruined everything. It was a happy memory.

John continued. "The fact that this image of God, or ultimate reality, as a spirit hovering nearby is a very simple idea does not in any way make it an inappropriate projection. After all, science has demonstrated it to be true. Using a more sophisticated description of 'ultimate reality' would be highly inappropriate with children because that would not convey to them the closeness of ultimate reality. Nor would describing our intimate relationship with the first atoms from the big bang. No adult need feel they are condescending to children if they speak of ultimate reality as a nice person. The 'nice Jesus as your personal friend' is an accurate and powerful way of enabling children, and sometimes adults, to experience the intimate presence of ultimate reality as if it were a spirit hovering close by."

Rosalind had recently baby-sat her young niece and the little girl was upset because her parents were away overnight. She'd found herself longing to tell the lie that God was close and would look after her, but she'd disciplined herself not to tell those stories because they weren't true, and she had simply comforted the child in her arms. But it would be wonderful if those stories were true in another sense and she could tell her niece the stories without losing her own integrity.

Could this story of a caring God be true and not true both at once? What if that were an appropriate way to help her niece experience the reliability and loving support of the cosmos? After all, that's what her research was all about—the predictably reliable patterns she had found everywhere. Something felt simultaneously scary and right about that.

"But," John was continuing, "surprise, surprise! That projection, too, must be withdrawn. It's unfortunate when religion allows the spirit projection to continue into adulthood without managing it. That's probably another reason our culture is so skeptical about religious faith—most religion has been reluctant to encourage people to withdraw the projection of God as a kindly spirit.

"No wonder our culture thinks faith is for little children, and no wonder there are so many cute stories and cartoons about funny things children say in prayers. Never about adults in prayer. When the huge numbers of Sunday School children in the fifties and sixties never came back to church, it may have been in part because they were never exposed to any image of ultimate reality beyond a child's conception. The upshot was an entire generation of Sunday School kids who thought religion was for kids. They grew out of a child-centred spirit projection of ultimate reality, but were never exposed to a more inclusive projection which might have had credibility in secular culture.

"When religion refuses to withdraw that spirit projection of 'Jesus as my personal saviour' it can become a self-centred way of imagining ultimate reality—as if Jesus were a spirit I can persuade to look out for my personal advantage, without any sense of my own self-offering love for others being the character to which the spirit image was calling me. No wonder our culture doesn't take that spirit projection seriously. If churches don't find ways to move beyond that spirit projection as the only way of experiencing ultimate reality there's not much hope of credibility for faith in the secular world.

"The spirit projection must die as an image of ultimate reality in order for us to integrate its truth—that I have the ability to team up with people of less power and influence than I. Otherwise, if I don't withdraw that projection, I might imagine Jesus is offering a contract—if I believe in him, then he'll protect me, and that would be just another form of self-centredness. It wouldn't be anything like the deep love we know and want for ourselves. Not at all like ultimate reality. It's essential that religion allow that projection to die."

This was a revelation for Rosalind. She'd been made to chant "Jesus is my saviour," at church camps she'd been sent to as a teen, and she'd come away hating Jesus. She'd never quite figured out why, besides a sense that Jesus violated her integrity by forcing her to say things that weren't true. But now it dawned on her there was more. Something in her also suspected Jesus was becoming a sort of spiritual attack dog to keep people inside that projection. *What an enormous relief to find a religious person saying that image had to go.*

John noticed she was looking serious. But she didn't volunteer what it was about. So he didn't ask. His need to know died so he could love her better. Just as she was.

So, he continued to explore religion's new role of managing projections.

"The projections of gods, in the way that projection was used by the ancient Greeks can also be an accurate way to experience ultimate reality. People pray, 'Loving God, let there be peace and justice in the violent places of the world.' In that prayer we are using the symbol 'God' as if we were speaking to an Olympic god who could be persuaded by our plea to carry out our wishes on a global scale.

"This projection accurately presents the fact that there are real patterns arising from ultimate reality that can be embodied as healthy personal, cultural and international relationships. Through such a prayer, we are saying it is our desire for an increase in such patterns and therefore an increase in loving service rather than of domination, or exploitation, or colonization. And such patterns must become the norm for the international human family. That would be to uphold the priority that all consciousness is to remain safe. Such a prayer would be consistent with our source even if it appears to us in the form of invoking a classical Greek god to oversee our planet."

John continued "Of course, to honour the process, religion is also respon-sible to ensure we withdraw that god projection. Not to do so will have tragic consequences—we will rely on God, (as an Olympic god) to bring peace and care for the poor, and therefore absolve us of the need to act, and so we will be enabled to continue in exploitative cultural, international, and economic relationships. Retaining the god projection enables us to avoid enacting justice.

"We see that happening all too often when countries invoke God to bless their national priorities. They are really asking an ancient Greek god to intervene for their own benefit, regardless of the effects on other countries, and so avoid national responsibility of care for other cultures and countries.

"Without withdrawing that god projection, church prayers easily become prayers that everything will be well so that we don't feel guilty or need to take the initiative for doing something about the injustice or making changes in our lifestyles so justice can happen. After all, we asked God to act, and if God didn't act it's not our fault. That's evil. It's a deliberate misuse of the god projection for our own personal comfort. That's what happens if we don't withdraw the projection. We start to die as full humans.

"Only when we withdraw the projection of asking a god to act on our behalf are we enabled to integrate the quality of that projected god into ourselves, and take our rightful responsibility for global issues. That's the point of ultimate reality—to bring us to the full maturity of becoming people who value people—the patterns that have arisen from ultimate reality—even above our own pattern, which is our own self. Integrating that god projection is to discover it is already inside us. That makes justice, the enacting of love on the global scale, the deepest quality of our humanity."

Rosalind was thoughtful. "No wonder my stomach turns every time I hear a politician invoke God's blessing on their country, and by extension, on that leader. If I were religious, I think I'd call that blasphemy. It's so obviously someone dressing up their own self-interest as if they were God and then telling everyone else to trust they speak for God. Isn't that what the Roman emperors did? Even if I don't believe in God, I find that use of the image highly offensive."

She paused.

"Sorry, I didn't mean to get religious on you. Consider it an experimental glitch."

"Sure," John replied. But he knew it wasn't a glitch. *She a glitch? I don't think so. She's more centred and makes more sense than anyone I've known.*

John picked up his train of thought. "Finally, we are left with religion's responsibility for managing the cosmic God projection. To become aware of our own deep, inner security we first must project it upon a cosmic God. We rightly use that projection for cosmic assurance—that nothing in all of history, nothing in our past and nothing in the deep future in all of the cosmos, can ever separate us from the cosmic love which is ultimate reality. How could it? That's what the cosmos is made of!

"However, even though the projection of a cosmic God ruling in love over the universe is an accurate image of ultimate reality, pain, abuse, tragedy, disappointment, and death still happen to every one of us. When tragedy strikes, as it does for all of us, we need to withdraw our projection of the cosmic God of universal protection. Refusing to withdraw that projection of God will leave us in the position of angrily blaming God, or moving into desperation, or despair, or denial, or violence when God fails to act to set everything right in the global sphere of our personal or planetary life.

"I know it sounds hard," John said, "but unless we allow that projection of a supreme being to die, in order that we can assimilate its truth and discover that deep calm assurance inside ourselves, we will not grow into the maturity of being able to face inevitable tragedy and death without being crushed by them.

"However when we withdraw the projection of an infinite God, we can then integrate the fact that, beneath whatever darkness may come to us, we remain forever anchored in the deep goodness of ultimate reality. Then it becomes our responsibility to act on that deep security by claiming our freedom from fear.

"Of course all of us will be emotionally shaken and at times in deep grief. It's not that those feelings can be avoided or removed by withdrawing the projection of a cosmic God, quite the opposite. It's the deep assurance of safety in the end that allows us to plumb the depths of grief. Which is to be deeply alive.

Managing projections: dancing nimbly

"So," Rosalind said, "I get how people use different projections to experience ultimate reality. That makes sense to me. But I'm not sure I trust that. It can't be simply a matter of arbitrarily preferring one projection over another."

"Here's how that could work in practice," John suggested.

"Imagine two friends are talking. One is a traditional believer who takes the projection of God as a supreme being literally. The other does not. The traditional believer says, 'While I was driving past Mrs. Jeffrey's house yesterday, God spoke to me and told me I had to stop and visit her. When I went in, she had just heard her niece had been in an accident. Isn't it wonderful how God speaks to us!'

"Her non-believing friend no longer believes there is a supreme being called 'God' who directs people to go into specific houses. But she doesn't imagine the other person had an auditory hallucination while driving her car, nor that she is an immature religious literalist.

"If this friend is comfortable with the multi-valent use of the symbol 'God', she may say to herself, 'I know exactly what she means. It is important for me, as well, to be open to those intuitive promptings that arise in me. I, too, have been thankful to find myself in just the right place at just the right time without my having arranged it. Those moments are wonderful gifts for which I too give thanks.'

"However, she lovingly puts aside her preferred projection and moves nimbly to one that will support her friend, so she says, 'I'm so glad God spoke to you. I've heard God's call too, and it's amazing what can happen when we listen.' Although she no longer believes in a divine supreme being, she can say these words with complete integrity. If she had instead started a discussion about the nature of ultimate reality, or a debate about the existence of God, or the need to withdraw and integrate projections, she would have completely ignored what her friend was experiencing. To adopt her friend's projection is to be consistent with ultimate reality. That's to be a mature religious person, to give up one's preferred understanding in order to assure someone they are surrounded by love. That's to love.

"Giving up one projection and moving consciously to another, is the process that most deeply connects us to ultimate reality. That's because ultimate reality itself creatively gives rise to patterns (which ultimately become us) and simultaneously, ultimate reality has to be prepared to love so deeply as to die to keep us safe. So, to be faithful to ultimate reality we must always be ready to withdraw our preferred projection in order to care for someone. That way we can never say my projection is right and yours is wrong. All projections, even my own, have to die. We have to be nimble with projections. That's the way to love. That's what religion is now called to do in a secular world.

"Imagine, for example, someone's niece has just been killed in a car accident. In that context we must never use the image of God as a local spirit using the animist style of projection. If we did that, we would end up saying something like, 'I am sorry your niece was hit by a car—it seems God wasn't watching over her.' That would be the implication of imagining God as a local spirit that had been distracted by some other concern or doesn't care about the niece. It would be abusive because it would present a false image of the profound relationship ultimate reality has with the niece and with her grieving aunt. To use the projection of an unpredictable local spirit in such a context would be cruel. Such a symbol for 'God' would contradict what that symbol stands for. It would, in religious language, be blasphemy.

"Religion must become responsible for ensuring people of faith know that in such circumstances we must not use any projection that wasn't supportive and would not be experienced as loving. In such a situation any abusive projection must die. Even that of God.

"It could be appropriate to use projections of ultimate reality in the form of a global Olympic god, but we have to choose carefully in tragic circumstances. Using the image of a god in that way, we could be saying, 'I am sorry your niece was hit by a car, but God in his infinite wisdom has better plans for her we cannot know—trust God knows what he is doing and your niece is in a better place. It's all part of God's plan that is hidden from us.' That image of God might be comforting to some religious people, but to many people it will feel abusive to suggest God manipulates our lives and enables catastrophes to happen for some secret divine purpose. Presenting ultimate reality in the form of an Olympic god manipulating our lives would be unfaithful to ultimate reality and would be abusive to grieving people. Religion's role will be to ensure such destructive projections are never used in such circumstances. Religion now has the duty to teach that."

That had been one of Rosalind's greatest puzzles growing up. In the end she had decided she must reject religion because it insisted God has a hidden agenda behind tragedy—God hurts people for some unseen greater purpose. She had revolted at that cruelty. No human would condone such actions. No wonder she'd rejected the whole thing. Curious that John seemed to agree with her about that.

With his next words it seemed he had almost read her thoughts.

He pointed out both religious and non-religious people are often under the illusion 'God' cannot have any meaning other than as a supreme being who tinkers with our lives.

"If that's the only meaning for 'God', then of course such images must be rejected. Used in that way, the projection of 'God' can be ridiculous if not outright abusive. It can imply the God of the entire universe doesn't care about individuals."

John saw her intense agreement. He saw her anger there, too. Something inside him leapt at her fierce commitment to the truth despite its implications for their own relationship. Her passionate atheistic and uncompromising rejection of God as an interfering cruel and arbitrary being placed her very close to ultimate reality. She was closer to God the more she rejected that abusive concept of God.

John continued. "Religious people can feel helpless and tongue-tied when trying to speak about God in the context of a tragic situation because they don't know the various projections of God are there to be used in appropriate ways depending on the circumstances. Religion's role now is to teach people how to move nimbly between the various projections of God so we can fully experience ultimate reality's profound love for us."

"I know it would feel weird, but couldn't we avoid all this complication by stopping using the projections and just refer to ultimate reality?" Rosalind suggested.

"That would be simpler," John agreed, "but dispensing with the image of God as a conscious being and substituting 'ultimate reality' won't help anyone. It would be inappropriate and inaccurate to say to someone in mourning, 'I am sorry you have lost your niece. I want to assure you we all live within ultimate reality and the deepest quality of ultimate reality is of intimacy, creativity, awe and fullness of life through death and resurrection understood through Jesus who is the projection we use to experience the Christ-process.' The person would wonder if we were in touch with reality at all and would certainly know we weren't in touch with theirs!

"Such a statement wouldn't be accurate because the question the sorrowing person would be asking in their grief is not, 'Is there a quality of love in our relationship with ultimate reality?' But, 'Is there an eternal lover who loves the one I loved? And knows that it hurts so much?' The answer is, 'Yes, the person you lost is in God's hands, as we all are at every moment, and God is even now re-creating them through infinite love. And God will do the same for all of us.' That may amount to exactly the same thing as saying, 'The deepest quality of ultimate reality is of intimacy, creativity, and full life in which we are all immersed forever,' but it uses the projection of a supremely loving God that more effectively expresses the intimate quality of ultimate reality in this person's circumstances."

It seemed to Rosalind there was something loving about choosing which projection of 'God' to use. There was an integrity in the medium being the message. It wasn't a way the speaker was getting power, but was giving power to the grieving person. That was impressive. It was only about how to support the grieving person; it was about the person in grief, not about the speaker. She knew grief. This process itself was loving.

Managing projections: praying in secular

This talk about grief and pain raised a question in Rosalind's mind.

"There's something personal I want to ask you. What I don't get is how you pray. I'm pretty sure, as a religious person, you pray for people who are sick or in grief. Don't you? Are you saying that's just a sham, you can simultaneously say you are praying for them to get better and not praying because God and all the other images are just projections? How does that work?"

"That's why we need all the projections," John replied. "The various projections aren't mistakes or immature imaginings. They are all real. But none of them are ultimately real. So, yes, I do pray for people that they get better, or for politicians that they lead more effectively toward policies of justice, or for my nephew just because I love him.

"To pray to God that someone gets better is to consciously use the projection of God as a local spirit who has the power to change things. But I have to consciously and deliberately enter into that projection, otherwise as you say, it's just a sham. The reason I can enter the projection with my whole heart is because it is really true—ultimate reality really does uphold patterns, and the patterns of health in my nephew or in politics are more to be desired than the breakdown of patterns that we call illness or political oppression. That's what ultimate reality is all about—endlessly emerging into physical patterns. And I want to team up with that ultimate reality the way animist cultures teamed up with surrounding spirits. Or the way ancient Greeks prayed to gods.

"So, I name that truth when I pray for someone to get better. It's not magic. I don't imagine they'll get better just because I prayed for them. As your colleagues so forcefully explained to me! But the truth is I want to align myself with the pattern-affirming quality of ultimate reality, I want to take a stand for their health, and I want to stand against being passively helpless in the face of sorrow or injustice to others. The truth is I'm not helpless, we are surrounded by ultimate reality that loves all of us more than we an imagine. And I am also telling the truth—I do want the person to get better, because I care. That sort of prayer is a way of loving. By doing it I am more like ultimate reality than if I didn't. And it might well have the effect of my getting more active in private or public to stand for justice and health for all.

"The same with praying by using the projection of God in the form of an Olympic god—ultimate reality lies behind the healthy patterns of our entire society—it makes sense for me to articulate that in the form of asking for justice—for increased healthy social patterns for everyone—as if I were asking a favour of a Greek god. And for my nephew—I try to see him from the perspective of ultimate reality—he's of immense, perhaps even cosmic, significance and I want to experience that, so I align myself with ultimate reality in upholding him in prayer.

"It's the same when I pray to God using the projection of a supreme being. To pray in that way is to see the world from a cosmic perspective and to experience the love that ultimate reality has for all existence to which it has given rise. To imagine a supreme being in love with all creation is an important way of experiencing that amazing quality of ultimate reality. And most importantly, imagining such a perspective breaks open my assumptions about the limits of what is possible and challenges me to see the world in new terms. That can be a highly creative way of praying. In this form prayer is not so much about asking for things, but of asking that I experience the world the same way ultimate reality does. That experience expands my perspective enormously and allows me to imagine new ways of embodying that life in my own."

"But," Rosalind objected, "what happens when people don't get better? Or leaders move us into exploitative policies? That's why so many people say they don't believe—it doesn't actually work. That's one of the reasons I can't take religious belief seriously. Nothing changes, no matter how much you pray."

John replied, "That's exactly why the projections have to be continually withdrawn and integrated. If we didn't withdraw the projection to which we pray, prayer would become a magic way of getting things done, even good things, that we couldn't get done otherwise. In the end, such prayer would be a lie. There will always be illness, and there will always be destructive greed in political and social leadership, but in prayer I insist on not aligning myself with those destructive policies and assumptions or agreeing they are normal or inevitable. It may be I who am changed, but indeed something changed. And of course, when a person does get well, or fair policies are introduced, I give thanks and rejoice, otherwise I'd have to isolate myself from their delight and have to take the attitude that their healing or fairness for everyone was of no significance and treat it as just random. That wouldn't be very loving or human or true!

"The same when just legal, financial and social policies are enacted—we must give thanks. Otherwise we might as well not care, and then we'd be deeply disconnected from ultimate reality. We aren't thanking some magic process; that's not what prayer is about. It's not a matter of indifference whether our society exploits those with less power—it matters very much because every

single person is an expression of ultimate reality, and when social policies
become more affirming of the poor so all can live with dignity, that's a matter
for rejoicing, not for saying it's all meaningless. A prayer of thanksgiving makes
that clear."

"As a believer, you think prayer isn't about getting things to happen?"

"No. It's more like just telling the truth."

"I'd never thought of prayer like that. I like the sense of freedom. You're not
trying to prove anything."

"Yes and no. No, I'm not trying to prove something about myself, or about
religion, or about God, or about prayer. I am trying to prove, or stand for, or
take a stand for, the absolute priority of upholding and nurturing patterns for
all the cosmos, but especially for the most vulnerable patterns—people, and
for the most vulnerable of those—people experiencing any kind of distress or
oppression.

"Prayer is hard work—I have to disengage any sense of wanting to get something out of it for myself, even at an unconscious level, and it takes work to see
people from the perspective of ultimate reality. In a way, prayer is just a form
of loving. And work. And it's no coincidence, I think, that the word used for
community prayer, 'liturgy,' is the Greek word for 'work.'

She paused.

"Loving is no small thing, I think."

"I think you are right," John agreed.

They were quiet for a bit.

Managing projections: the necessary failure of faith

Rosalind had been concerned all along about something else. And she cared
enough to raise it despite the discomfort it might cause John.

"As I said before, I doubt you'll get many people to follow a religion based
on believing in ultimate reality no matter how the projections we use for it
change for specific circumstances. It seems to me the only people who would
join such a religion would be philosophers who spend time thinking about
ultimate reality. Or people like you, thinking up these ideas about religious
projection. You'll end up with a church consisting of just you and one other
poor soul like you! I doubt people will really get a sense of loving, or meaning,
or purpose from the idea of ultimate reality. Even if ultimate reality is prepared
to sacrifice itself for us.

"How are religious leaders going to say the projected God they and their people have been worshipping isn't real, and the only real thing—ultimate reality—doesn't exist? I don't envy you that problem! That's got to be a tough sell to religious people!"

He had a sense she really meant it.

It *was* tough.

And good to be with someone who understood that, even if she was an atheist. Perhaps especially if she was an atheist.

"I think," John replied, "your concern about people not responding illustrates two issues facing religion in a secular context.

"The first is the importance of emphasizing the necessity of taking projections seriously. Knowing they are projections shouldn't prevent people from experiencing deep relationship with what the projections are presenting.

"And you raise a second very important issue.

"In secular society the worst possible sin an organization can commit is to fail at being popular and successful. We are so surrounded by advertising images of popularity and success that we can hardly imagine any group having value if it doesn't attract lots of people. But that attitude to success may be a way of distracting the public from noticing how empty are the meanings offered by our culture. The phrase 'It's hard to argue with success' isn't used to encourage people to question what's popular, rather it's intended to discourage people from questioning what's popular—don't waste your time questioning what everybody likes. But if the culture is hurtling toward the cliff of self-destructive consumerism encouraged by the projection that our planet wants us to fulfil every whim, as a cover-up for our sense of empty meaninglessness, then the small group who aren't joining that mass suicide becomes centrally important to human survival.

"A religion that's not driven by the need for success and popularity may provide the essential service of being an island of sanity within a culture organized around the insanity of unlimited consumerism, popularity, and self-interest as the supreme mark of success.

"That would be a role of profound importance, even if it were never 'successful,' because it would keep alive the awareness of the deep goodness and love that is the central quality of ultimate reality. For religion to accept such a role in our world would be an act of deep self-giving and sacrifice. It would also be an act of profound truth-telling. It would name the only way that humanity can have a secure future. Such a death of religion could be the hope of the world, the light of the world. A religion that learned how to serve well at the cost of not being popular would embody love in a way the rest of the world desperately needs to see embodied in a real community. Christianity in this new form could be that embodiment.

"But the issue isn't whether that radical understanding 'works,' or whether it makes a huge difference to society or whether lots of people join. The only question would be, does it tell the truth?

"A religion that did that would turn 'success' right side up, even if our society judged it to be turning the world upside-down.

"Our culture tells so many lies about where to find meaning that even a small group of people telling the truth would be transformative, maybe even revolutionary, because not being successful undercuts the biggest lie: you're nothing if not successful."

Rosalind was silent. If this were true it was frighteningly true. It was also self-evidently true. She doubted she would dare be part of it. But it made more sense than anything she'd ever heard.

She'd just heard a call to risky leadership and service, a call to love. A call to make science serve the fullness of life by naming the deep love in which the cosmos is grounded. And she was in a position to do that.

An invitation accepted

The muffins and the special coffee were all long gone.

"Time to get home," she said. "Fortunately, it's not far!"

At what level does she mean that? John wondered. Her home not far from his.

John took his heart in his hands. He'd been wondering when the right moment might be. If she had taken so much time with him already, maybe she might go further. If not ask her now, when?

"Just before you go, I had a thought."

She knew better than to joke about it this time

"How about a date?"

She had that sinking feeling. Part, *Just when you thought you knew what the relationship was about it turns into something quite different*; part, *Oh no, we're not going there*, part, delighted surprise, part, *What am I scared of, he's been great.* But what she said was, "That's so kind of you, and it would be great, but I really don't think so. No offence, but I'm really not into dating. Thank you anyway."

"Oh," John replied, "don't worry about that. We'd have plenty of chaperones. I was wondering about Sunday morning at church? Would you like to see how the idea of religion whose purpose is to self-destruct, and a God whose purpose is not to exist, could work in practice? I have an idea about how all this might make a lot of sense.

"We'd sit at the back. You can disguise yourself in a wig in case any of your colleagues are there—not that that's likely—and I'll whisper to you what's happening. How about it? As a research project?"

He was pretty sure that'd get her attention.

She paused.

It had.

She had thought she would have been spending Sunday morning sitting on her carpet, reading something light, with the sun streaming in. But she rather liked the idea of exploring this concept a bit further. His perspective on religion was so very different from what she was used to.

So, she thought maybe she would.

But if he didn't mind, she'd better get on now with preparing for a seminar.

Of course, he minded. But that was a very small sacrifice for what he'd get back.

Next Sunday they would be at church. And he would get to whisper in her ear.

Ultimate reality didn't get much better than this.

They parted easily, both very careful in light of their growing mutual comfort, to be sure there were no accidental touches. No signs of special care.

Which, of course, was a sign of special care.

Summary

Because everything arises from ultimate reality and participates in its basic processes, even religion and its projections must participate in the death and resurrection process.

So, religion must die to the belief that it exists to proclaim the literal reality of a supreme being called God. Instead religion must embrace its new role within a secular society of facilitating our embrace of all the projections upon God and then withdrawing and integrating them.

That underlying process is the way full life is offered to us. Religion must now support people in taking seriously whatever their projection of ultimate reality and then withdrawing it in order to receive its truth. That's to be lovingly nimble by loving people through appropriate projections.

In pastoral leadership, religion's purpose will be to support each person's projection, without judgement, in order to accompany them in their journey of withdrawing and integrating the truth of whichever projection they are experiencing.

Even religion itself must die to its desire for success and power. If religion is to be transparent to ultimate reality, enacting that path in its own life is essential. Such a path may be the only hope a secular society has for experiencing how a fruitful life into the deep future for this world could actually be lived.

Religion now has the humbling opportunity to become that path.

CHAPTER 19
Re-imaging Jesus

Scary worship

In an isolated community in the north in which I ministered, I was invited to attend an all-night worship service in which shouting and ecstatic experiences were to be expected. I'd heard about these sessions and accepted the invitation with curiosity and trepidation.

A hundred people gathered in a small hall. At first, singing and chanting were somewhat subdued but as the evening wore on, the music became louder and louder until it was deafening. People started moaning, some raising their arms and wailing, some screaming, many speaking in tongues. People were sobbing and praying, and leaders were working the crowd up into a frenzy, singing the same verses over and over again. "Jesus saved me! Jesus saved me! Jesus saved me!" was the theme of the songs, the ecstatic cries, and the moaned prayers. The emotional intensity was overwhelming.

The underlying message was repeated over and over: we are better than they are; the spirit of Jesus will enter us; miracles will happen; we've been lifted from failure nobodies into friends of Jesus. We are that special! Miracles will happen!

Thank you, Jesus! Thank you, Jesus! Thank you, Jesus!

And they did. People spoke in other languages, prophecies took place, people collapsed writhing on the floor, many declared how Jesus had changed their lives.

It was not an experience I could enter into even if I hadn't been self-conscious about my recent ordination into a sedate style of worship. Soon it became painfully obvious I was not a participant. In the course of a ranting address, a leader from outside the community declared that the Evil One was in their midst, and he could point out who the Evil One was, and it soon became pretty clear who that was. I was the only white person there. I was the only person who wasn't shouting about Jesus. I was identified as the devil. With the extreme emotional intensity of the crowded hall, I began to wonder if I were safe. At least in theory most of those present were my parishioners.

I was shaken at being the object of such intense feeling.

In the small hours of the morning the chanting began to slow down and gradually calm returned and people chatted to each other. "The Spirit really moved tonight!" was the repeated exclamation. Sweet tea and goodies were shared around, including with me. I left around three in the morning, making my way home, apparently no longer hated.

I wondered what the meaning of such primal religious experience could be. Was it Christian? Was there any integrity? Was it a manipulative power trip by some out-of-town leaders trying to collect money from the poorest inhabitants? Was it just emotional entertainment? Was it a religious language I simply didn't speak and so I missed whatever the point was?

The contrast with my ministry was disturbing in other ways. Each of my little churches might have ten people on a Sunday laboriously singing the same dull hymns year in and year out. Theirs had a hundred people in attendance—a quarter of the town's entire population—who poured out their passion in ecstasy for Jesus and claimed changed lives all night every night for a week. And indeed, there were some who had been released from the scourge of alcohol abuse.

I, too, had been ordained in the name of Jesus, and I, too, blessed people in the name of Jesus, and I too, struggled to understand how Jesus was central to my life. We both worshipped Jesus but was there anything in common other than the name?

On my walk home through the dark town that night, I was approached by someone I knew slightly who, quite drunk, staggered across the street to speak to me. The point she wanted me to be clear about was she was just as good as the religious people in the hall. And to prove it, she spoke to me in tongues. "See, I can do it, too; I'm as good as them," and she staggered off.

Part of me was relieved that others had doubts as I did; part of me was selfishly pleased that not all my parishioners were convinced by the emotional intensity of that worship; part of me was ashamed at my secret delight in finding someone who wasn't healed by this miracle-centred religion; and part of me knew another facet of a huge cultural tragedy had just unfolded before my eyes.

In the light of day and in a calmer frame of mind, it wasn't hard to understand what the point was. The event took place in a community, that, having experienced oppression, exploitation and racism, had become chaotic through escape into alcohol abuse, an escape enabled and encouraged for profit by whites like me, a community that knew too much of family violence, suicides, and death by house fire or catastrophic car crash. An entire community of people that had lost their dignity, power, hope, and meaning. Not unlike what is happening to power and meaning and hope within my own church tradition.

The way in which people of this oppressed community re-discovered their dignity and hope was through the experience of ecstatic possession. Members of the dominant culture never experienced such phenomena and that was proof that Jesus had chosen them, that Jesus was in the process of rescuing them from ignominy and self-loathing, that Jesus was giving them dignity and love. Jesus had done what no social worker had succeeded in doing: Jesus had removed their alcoholism. Because of Jesus they already lived in the wonderful world promised to all humanity—a world of dignity, joy, and fulfilment.

It all made perfect sense. As small groups of nomadic hunter-gatherers who were devastated by the arrival of an industrialized society that despised them as people without value, thereby excusing the theft of their lands, the First Nations projected onto Jesus all the dignity, hope, and self-confidence they had once known and desperately desired to regain. The destruction of their self-image and pride was so nearly complete that week-long all-night immersions in religious experiences of value and hope were the path by which to re-experience the dignity and hope that had always resided within them and still did. This projection of Jesus' raising them to ecstasy brought that truth to awareness.

I too was struggling with the arrival of a dominant culture—that of secular society—which had overwhelmed and devastated the religious experiences in which I had grown up. I was struggling with the complexities of theories about ultimate reality and finding a way of speaking about how humanity has been given back our dignity. I wasn't getting very far with that for myself, either.

When I left that part of the world some years after this experience, I was convinced the slide into total social and cultural annihilation was inevitable and before long the entire people would have died of alcoholism and despair. In spite of their commitment to Jesus, there really was no hope. I was quite sure of it. I had witnessed the end of their world and it broke my heart and I could do nothing to stop that tragedy.

When I visited those communities decades later, I was astonished to find many of the same people employed in steady work teaching classes in basic financial management, teaching primary health care, learning construction skills, many with their lives in good order.

A miracle had happened. No doubt the emotional frenzy of their all-night religious sessions in which they had made contact with their inner dignity had played a role in that healing. But there were no more all-night ecstatic meetings. As their culture withdrew the projection of the Jesus who redeemed them through writhing on the floor, they had come to own the dignity that had always been theirs. They no longer needed religious ecstasy to reassure themselves.

The Jesus who died had saved them.

Seems they were right all along.

The knife goes in

Early next Sunday morning John's phone rang.

The knife went in.

"Hi. Look, I'm really sorry about this, but I'm not sure about this morning. I hope you don't mind. It's…. well, I have a lot to get ready for that seminar I'm supervising tomorrow. And I don't feel ready to get into something like this so fast. I really appreciate your invitation. It's been great to be with you. But… I don't feel right about it, at least not yet. I know it means a lot to you. You understand?"

Sure, he understood. So, he said he did, but in a tone that implied he didn't, but that he was saying he did in order not to hurt her feelings.

"Sure. That's OK. Thanks for letting me know."

"See you. OK. Bye."

"Bye."

They both know what that "Bye" meant. She'd turned down his most intimate offer of connection. They'd both pretend the relationship could return to where it was, but they both knew it wouldn't. He'd taken the risk and offered. She'd said 'Yes,' thought better of it and finally said 'No.' He'd taken part in her passion. She'd refused to take part in his. There could be no return to the way things had been. She knew how much it meant to him. She'd made her decision. He'd not be prepared to be that vulnerable again.

Mustn't let that bother me, he thought as he drove to church.

Alone.

He was startled at the strength of his feelings. He'd anticipated the fun of sitting with her, the enjoyment of seeing her exploring a whole new world, the challenge of presenting to her things that were important to him while respecting her very different perspective, the chance to talk about her reactions afterwards. Yes, and the chance perhaps to feel her hair on his face as he whispered in her ear.

Damn.

Damn.

Damn.

Wandering and wondering in worship

As the service progressed, the disappointment hit John harder each time he remembered this was to have been the morning they were to have whispered together about what it all meant.

After all, he'd spent a day at her office, an entire evening at her lecture, and another whole day at her home, and then he'd generously had her over to his house. All he'd asked in return was one hour at church. He'd been totally flexible and open with her ideas; didn't she have an obligation to do the same in return? He should have realized right from the beginning this was the sort of behaviour you could expect from an atheist. They wouldn't know anything about caring or mutuality—of course; atheists don't believe in a loving God. He felt himself wishing he'd never met her. Or worse. That in some way he could hurt her. Perhaps he'd send a sarcastic note? Perhaps pleading and if she responded, turn her down? Then she'd know what it felt like.

Then something in the service mentioned Jesus on the cross.

He suddenly knew what that felt like.

Like nails going in. Like a knife going in.

After that he stayed alert, watching for images, feeling slightly guilty because he'd never examined a church service while it was in progress. Weren't you supposed to have nice religious feelings during the service, not be analyzing things, not being angry at your new friend? Who wasn't any more.

There were so many references to Jesus' suffering, pain and death. He'd never noticed how much of it had to do with real life. That part of his religion had always seemed depressing. Now it felt connecting. At least he could relate to Jesus.

Jesus got it. Pretty sure Rosalind didn't. But Jesus sure did.

John was so consumed by his grief and anger at Rosalind having refused him, that he missed most of the first part of the service and the first three readings.

But the fourth reading caught his attention.

Jesus and the big bang

The priest was reading the passage from the start of John's gospel. "Without him not one thing came into being."[1] It suggested Jesus had been present at, and was foundational to, the creation of the cosmos. John had never thought of it like that. The passage had always sounded like nice poetry, but the time spent with Rosalind and her colleagues had sensitized him to their worldview. If John, the gospel writer, thought Jesus was present at and central to the creation of the universe, that had implications.

Rosalind and her colleagues were fascinated by the physical processes of the universe, which inspired them and are foundational to the functioning of our culture. But if Jesus has no connection to those discoveries, then no matter how reasonable Christianity might sound, it will remain peripheral to scientists' interests as well as to our entire culture which is made possible by science. An interesting religious theory for those who like that sort of thing, but like any hobby, not of compelling or cosmic significance in the way that ancient John claimed it was.

If that other John, the gospel writer, said Jesus was central to the creation of the universe, maybe there was more in his idea than just an attempt to make Jesus look important. If that John were alive today, might he have included some references about creation that would have made sense to Andy the atheist or to Betty the biologist? Or to Charles the cosmologist? Or to Rosalind the rebel? Or maybe to himself? He wondered how that might work.

Most people, John knew, aren't interested in the detailed processes of the

---

1   John Chapter 1, verse 3.

early universe which brought everything into existence and without which we could not exist. For most people, the complex technicalities of that process prevent them from feeling connected to it. Yet complicated things don't have to be unconnected from us. My lover's body is immensely complicated yet I never say I can't relate to my lover because their body is unimaginably complex. John wondered if that could also be true of our relationship with the physical world and its processes.

Could we imagine the origin of the physical world, studied by science, as being, in some sense, simple? Simple, and therefore open to non-scientists experiencing an intimate relationship with the cosmos? John the gospel writer thought Jesus was an essential component of the creation of the universe and he knew nothing of modern science. John wondered if ordinary modern non-scientists could also relate to the origin of the universe through the image of Jesus.

John had learned from Charles that the origin of the universe may well have been a beautiful symmetry composed of nothing but multiple identical dimensions. But we exist, and the universe exists, only because that original symmetry died, and a lop-sided, but far more creative arrangement emerged in which some dimensions became space and at least one became time.

Why would that original beautiful and perfect symmetry have been broken? Would it be because mathematics, which is the form in which we experience pattern, already had imperfections built in? If there is no pattern in the emergence of prime numbers, and if mathematics necessarily contains inner contradictions then that might be the reason the original identical dimensions broke apart. The mathematics that they were made out of required that break. The sterile absolute beauty of mathematics died so that other things such as a universe, and we, could emerge.

If all the dimensions had remained spatial, there would have been no time, and the universe would have been locked in an unchanging and permanent solidity of physical dimensions. Without the dimension of time, nothing whatsoever would ever have happened. Only because the total symmetry of the early dimensions died, was it possible to have both space and time and things happening. Perhaps Jesus' death and resurrection could be an image by which we can grasp the necessary, and in some sense generous, death of that original perfect balance of mathematics, so that one dimension could be unbalanced and become time, which then made the cosmos and life possible.

Later, heat and light in the forms of photons were the only things that existed and they formed a beautiful and seamless, universe-wide flow of energy. But that perfectly smooth flow of energy degraded into discrete particles that marred the early perfection of pure seamless energy. If the original energy had remained in its pure form, we could never have come into being as physical bodies. Had that death of pure energy not happened, the universe would have consisted entirely of light, but there would have been no objects for the light to shine on—a universe of nothing but light would have been permanently dark. Again, the death of one process enabled the birth of something more wonderful. Jesus could be a projection enabling us to relate with gratitude to that dying of pure energy, and the rising of physical stuff.

As Charles had also explained to him, some of that pure light energy disintegrated and condensed into particles that formed simple structures; hydrogen atoms. The light now had something to illuminate. The universe at this point consisted only of uncountable myriads of utterly beautiful and utterly simple hydrogen atoms, each identical to all the others. Things could have remained that way forever—a virtually infinite and glorious dance of sub-microscopic particles all exactly the same. Nothing else. No structures, no stars, no processes of any significance. Just an infinite ocean of tiny billiard-ball particles colliding with each other for all eternity.

However, the same process of death happened yet again when that beautiful simplicity of a universe consisting of myriads of absolutely identical atoms was destroyed as these atoms clumped together. The original silky smoothness of the early universe died and became grainy and lumpy.

At the centre of those lumps, which we call stars, under the immense weight of uncountable billions of hydrogen atoms bearing down, some hydrogen atoms were crushed together and actually squashed inside each other. The deaths of those hydrogen atoms produced carbon atoms that were capable of connecting with one another in unimaginably creative combinations.

Up until that time there had been only straightforward interactions between hydrogen atoms bumping into each other and attracting or repelling, but doing nothing significant. The emergence of carbon atoms changed all that. Carbon atoms can link themselves together in long chains forming coordinated molecules with highly complex and convoluted shapes. These complex shapes allow an almost infinite repertoire of interactions with other enormous carbon molecules through a kind of three-dimensional jigsaw puzzle folding and refolding like live origami. It is those extraordinary three-dimensional shapes with their almost infinite repertoire of combinations that express themselves as life. It was the death of that utterly simple universe consisting only of tiny billiard-ball hydrogen atoms, that enables life to exist.

It dawned on John that the symbol of Jesus' death and resurrection could be a cosmic symbol of this universal process by which one stage of matter dies so a new one may be born. John thought that using the projected image of the dying and rising Christ, we could relate with gratitude, delight, respect, and joy to those processes through which the cosmos and we came to exist. That would feel good. John could imagine himself giving joyful thanks that it had all happened and had emerged as us. He wondered if his namesake, John the gospel writer, had been trying to say something like that in the terminology of his time. He suddenly felt a delightful closeness to that ancient John.

But closeness to Rosalind was the last thing he was feeling. That just felt like death.

Jesus and peace

A lot had happened in the service as his mind had wandered. He realized he'd missed the entire sermon, the forgiveness of sins and the cue to stand up. Everyone was already saying to one another, "The peace of Christ be with you."

Peace was also the last thing he was feeling. Besides pain, he was feeling anger. Certainly not peace.

People around were putting out their hands and wishing him peace. That really hurt. He felt like screaming.

The whole point of this worship was that Jesus had been executed by torture. At least that made sense to him. It seemed like an insult to Jesus to put your hand out and call his suffering 'peace.' If you're hurting, the last thing you want is for someone to tell you it's all right. "Its not all right!" he wanted to scream at them.

It had to be some kind of denial to say that Jesus was peaceful while being tortured to death. Either that, or this whole thing was some kind of self-deluding wishful thinking turning Jesus into an impossible disembodied spirit floating untouched outside the real world and its pain and brokenness.

John remembered the story about Jesus desperately asking God to make it stop. The last thing this dying Christ seemed to be was peaceful.

So what if Jesus wasn't peaceful?

John noticed Jesus' death is never presented as being passive. He is never described as having been accidentally caught up in the violence of the Roman empire. He is never shown struggling at the last moment to get away or being overwhelmed by the police and military. His death is always presented as deliberate, even planned on his part. In a strange way, especially in John's gospel, Jesus is in charge—he knows it will happen, insists to his disciples it must happen, and, in spite of their strong opposition, he deliberately journeys to the place where his death will inevitably happen.

John understood that Jesus was deliberately enacting a way of life in which patterns of consciousness have absolute priority. He was refusing to join a culture in which the threat of violence—the destruction of patterns—is the ultimate power. Could that be a kind of peace?

But cultures such as the Roman empire, with violence at its centre in the form of crosses planted across the world to discourage resistance, always respond to fundamental challenges such as Jesus' with more violence. When gentle people resist state violence, we assume the outcome will always be the destruction of the protester—in the end, violence always wins. Tank man in Tiananmen square. Even though we say violence is our last resort, we are always prepared to use it when all else fails. It's our fall-back position. Never love. But what if, John wondered, Jesus triumphed over the Roman empire not by passively resisting, not by preaching about the need to love each other, not by heroically but uselessly standing for a lost cause, not by inventing some superior technology, and not by inspiring fanatical fighters to defeat Roman violence by more violence?

Then by what?

It dawned on John that Jesus might have been deliberately and powerfully confronting violence with its only alternative. The alternative was peace no matter what the consequences. If he had been insisting on peace regardless of the consequences to himself, that was powerful. That would be to be in charge. That would be to have conquered violence without being violent. Otherwise violence would have conquered him.

What if he'd defeated violence by integrating violence into his own life as the joyful price of refusing to participate in violence and thereby triumphing over it? That would make sense of his suffering. It wasn't that he felt peaceful, but that he was enacting peace, not passively but by embracing the violence.

The alternative would be the one we so often use, to fight violence with more violence and so affirm violence as the ultimate solution. Whereas the power of violence is the ability to take away someone else's life, the greater power of this kind of integrative violence is the ability to give away one's own life. If Jesus was deliberately receiving violence into himself as a way of enacting the only alternative to violence, not passively but as a statement of victory, Jesus would remain aligned with ultimate reality.

Since that power incorporated the self-giving character of ultimate reality, it would be stronger than any violence. Such power would be stronger than the entire Roman empire. Stronger than nuclear bombs. Stronger, even, than John's own violence against Rosalind and against himself.

His stomach hurt as he realized that's what he wished he could to do with Rosalind—integrate his own externalized violence, but do the suffering himself and so respect her. But he doubted he would ever agree to pay that price, and was sure he couldn't actually deny himself the violence he wanted to carry out. He wanted to lash out at her.

Despair about himself was all that was left. More violence, now at himself.

Giving away one's security is what ultimate reality always does. If that's what the early Christians thought was going on, then Jesus would have been a window into the counter-intuitive quality of ultimate reality that is ready to offer up its own identity to protect ours. Then Jesus would be the projection by which we become aware of ultimate reality's commitment to love—a commitment that already lives in us and is presented to us by the projection of Christ. And as we withdraw that projection, we are able to enact such love ourselves. It would even mean that if a peasant in the ancient world could do that, so could John.

After all, if Jesus was incorporating ultimate reality, and John was an expression of ultimate reality, then maybe such a stance could be possible for him. Perhaps there was hope for him after all.

No wonder that ancient John had put Jesus at the centre of the big bang. Jesus' DNR, his death and resurrection, is present everywhere as the fundamental structure of reality. Always producing new life. Even now in himself.

John found himself wondering if that might intrigue Rosalind. She'd known violence when her family disowned her. He wondered what she'd make of Jesus' counter-intuitive embrace of violence.

Without noticing it, he had begun to care for her. He'd begun to withdraw the projection of his own violence upon her. That projection had demanded justice for the wound she'd inflicted on him, but now he had begun to withdraw that demand for retributive justice, and he'd begun to integrate the deep justice the projection had presented to him. That deep justice was already in him. By dying to making his own security the centre of their relationship, he had begun to enact the triumph of refusing violence and instead he'd begun to treat Rosalind with the justice of respecting who she wanted to be.

Even if that person no longer wanted to be with him.

John was becoming himself through being incorporated into the life of Christ. By allowing the projection of his own violence to be withdrawn and be integrated, he allowed deep justice to emerge.

He didn't know it yet, but what he wished for, but had despaired of—the ability to be at peace with Rosalind—had already begun. Because his projection was dying. Jesus' tragic death had become the image that allowed him to know himself. And be himself. Someone through whom the deep love of ultimate reality could flow.

Jesus and evolution

The priest was starting the first part of the long prayer, the centre of the entire service, which began with recounting the history of everything from the big bang onwards.

Would it be possible, John wondered, to relate Jesus to the whole sweep of biological history? Not just the tiny piece of human history in which he lived, but to the entire sweep of life on our planet? After all, his ancient namesake had said Jesus was there at the very beginning. That ancient John wasn't saying that Jesus had dropped in to watch as God did his creator thing, but that Jesus was the foundational process by which creation took place.

Then Jesus must be central not just to the big bang but also central to evolution.

John knew wolves hunt in packs and have developed social processes to ensure the pack hunts with efficient coordination. Individual wolves, though they may long to do so, do not successfully chase down prey much larger than themselves if they act alone. Wolves are far more successful if they coordinate their attack as a pack. But to do so they must submit to the discipline of cooperation, and resist their individual desires to attack at will.

Wolves learn that necessary cooperation by being nurtured within a social hierarchy structured in relation to the pack's alpha male and female wolves.

If members of the pack did not learn to coordinate themselves under the leadership of the alpha wolf pair, and lost the ability to recognize their own and other wolves' location on the pack's continuum of social status, their ability to hunt large prey as a pack would be lost. Without social discipline, the pack, and eventually the entire species, would die from the chaos of uncoordinated and therefore unsuccessful attempts at bringing down larger prey.

The structure of the pack hierarchy is essential. At the top of the hierarchy is the alpha male and female couple. In the middle are wolves of various ages and strengths. But at the bottom of the pack hierarchy lies the useless runt wolf in its pain and possible death from abuse by the more senior wolves. Which is all the rest of the entire pack. But much as we pity that hapless wolf, it has the indispensable role of anchoring the pack's social coordination from the bottom, as the alpha pair do from the top. Without that social hierarchy and its requirement that there be some wolf on the bottom rung, the pack would cease to exist.

The same thing, John knew, had happened when mutant black moths were born into the white 'Paper moth' species. Normally those rare mutants were easily seen by birds and were eaten and never reproduced. But when Nineteenth Century smog covered industrial cities in the UK, suddenly those occasional useless mutant black moths were less visible, the 'normal' white moths were eaten, and the black mutants became a new species. But those mutant, easily destroyed black moths were the means by which the moths evolved into a new species.

It suddenly struck John that nothing is more useless than a man dying on a cross in the Roman empire because he insisted on acting as a mutant, living on the bottom rung of society and finally being killed. John wondered if Jesus could be a projection by which we can relate to that runt wolf process and to parallel evolutionary processes leading to human consciousness. He remembered an ancient poem written centuries before Jesus, but applied to him by early Christians. The poem suggests ancient people may have had a hunch about this process:

> ...*he had no form or majesty that we should look at him, / nothing in his appearance that we should desire him. / He was despised and rejected by others; / a man of suffering and acquainted with infirmity; / and as one from whom others hide their faces / he was despised, and we held him of no account.*[2]

For us, John thought, the dying and rising Jesus *is* the process of evolution. Not a symbol of evolution, but in his dying and rising, he is the projection to which we can relate to the essence of evolution which created us. Using the

---

2   Isaiah 53:2b-3, NRSV.

projection of Jesus could be a great way of saying 'Thank you' for a process we didn't invent and that we would likely have refused to participate in, but which made us possible.

Jesus, God, and forgiveness

The priest had come to the middle part of the long prayer that focused on Jesus' actual death and how important it is.

John was back with the pain.

Damn it, she hadn't come.

But if she had come, John knew she would have pointed out that Jesus' death was the central focus of Christianity, and how pointless that was and how it made no sense to claim that a nice guy dying two thousand years ago could make any difference to anything. Let alone save the world. Even if he was God. Jesus dying for our sins? Give me a break, she'd say.

He knew exactly how she'd say it. He knew she knew it would be hard for him to hear. He knew she would honour him by telling the truth.

There it was again. *Jesus died for our sins. Jesus died for us. Jesus died. He takes away the sins of the world. For our sake he was crucified. On the night before he gave up his life for us.*

The more he thought about it, the less sense it made to him. He didn't get it, either. Just like Rosalind.

He knew what that was all supposed to mean. It was supposed to mean Jesus' dying made forgiveness possible. But in his mind Rosalind was present and he could hear her reaction—honestly, a peasant got executed in the ancient mid-east and that's supposed to make everyone forgive everyone else two thousand years later? Are you kidding?

John knew that unlike Judaism and Islam, in which prophets, or The Prophet (Peace Be Upon Him) speak for God, in Christianity Jesus is not a prophet speaking for God. In Christianity Jesus *is* God. So, when a culture withdraws the projection of God, as ours has, Jesus loses his entire point. That's why our secular culture has only a nostalgic respect for Jesus as a sort of ancient male Mother Teresa figure but no longer has any sense Jesus is of profound cosmic significance as Christianity has always claimed. John realized that's why, within our culture, the image of Jesus dying for our sins has died.

John saw that's why so much of Christianity is fighting a desperate battle to keep the idea of dying for our sins alive, because to lose that is to lose the whole point of Jesus. But the harder the religion tries, the more the whole idea seems preposterous. Christians are caught between believing in a grotesque or even abusive understanding of Jesus' death, or relegating Jesus to irrelevance.

But nothing could be further from the revolutionary origins of Christianity.

John knew what he was supposed to believe about Jesus' death. His death was the result of our deliberate sins—every time we do something wrong it is we who are nailing Jesus to the cross. Being nailed to the cross is Jesus volunteering to receive the punishment from God that humans ought to have received. Jesus' violent death then makes violence a way of life, just as the Roman empire claimed through their use of crucifixion. Violence works. No wonder so many people have rejected Christianity as, at best, nonsensical, and at worst, abusive.

No wonder Rosalind wanted nothing to do with it. For a moment John thought of stalking out of the service, just as she had already stalked out of his life. With integrity, he could do no other. Like Rosalind, John wanted nothing to do with such abuse. His anger at her had morphed into anger at God.

Then John remembered something he'd heard about a scholar, named Anselm, living in the medieval world a thousand years after Jesus. Anselm had discovered Jesus' death didn't mean much to most people of his time, either. It seemed so distant and irrelevant. *Just like our experience*, John thought.

John had heard that Anselm had thought up a story about Jesus' death that he hoped would make sense to medieval people. However, sadly over the years Anselm's story became twisted and abusive, but originally had been a brilliant explanation of what Jesus' death had been about.

In the medieval world in which immense disparity of wealth was the norm, it happened from time to time that a lowly, poverty-stricken serf would steal a golden cup from the manor house—an object that could be sold for a staggering amount of money. Everyone had heard stories of this happening. So, Anselm used such an incident to come up with the following explanation of Jesus' death.

When the thieving serf was caught, he would have no way of ever paying for the now melted-down golden cup. He could work his hands to the bone for the rest of thousands of life-times and make not the slightest dent in the financial loss incurred by his duke.

But much worse than that, his betrayal of the duke made the duke look incompetent, and that damage to the duke's reputation could never be removed even if by some miracle the serf could purchase a replacement cup. Even if some wealthy person took pity on the serf and bought a replacement for the duke, that would do nothing to repair the damage to the duke's reputation and his credibility as a leader. Even punishing the serf with torture and death would be pointless and leave the duke permanently the butt of jokes: He can't even keep his own peons in line!

In the medieval context, the importance of a duke's honour was not about a duke selfishly concerned about his personal reputation and prepared to execute a serf in revenge, the way twentieth century people understand this story. In the medieval world, there was widespread concern about how society could be kept stable, and dukes had a central role in ensuring local stability and peace. If a duke lost his authority over his underlings, his entire duchy could collapse into disorder and social chaos. It mattered a great deal to everyone that the duke's respect be restored and with that respect came the corresponding power to ensure good order.

However, the only way a duke's honour could be restored in face of such a theft was if someone of equal rank to the duke were to offer himself for capital punishment and so nullify the humiliation caused by the theft, thereby restoring the duke's public status and credibility. There was no point executing the serf—that would seal the duke's reputation for incompetence because such an execution would be pointless. But the duke's son offering to be executed had enormous implications. The duke would be restored to respect, and so order and life and a prosperous future would be assured for everyone.

Peasant people would have been astonished to hear Anselm's story about a duke's son volunteering his life to ensure their stability and peace. One could imagine peasants saying, for the first time, "Is that what Jesus' death is about? That's amazing! I'm in awe."

Anselm intended the story as a way to describe the significance of Jesus' death in terms ordinary people of his time would understand. He would have been horrified to find Christianity has interpreted his illustration to mean God needed to punish someone, and the generous Jesus was sent by his implacable father to receive our punishment of execution so humanity wouldn't be exterminated. That interpretation, which has become a widespread version of Christianity, took a clever medieval illustration and mis-interpreted it as an act of violence by God.

John wondered how such a misinterpretation could have become so nearly universal for Christians in the modern world. Perhaps, he thought, the violence lurking just beneath the surface of individuals, societies, and cultures around the planet may be so deep in us that we have projected that violence upon God because we couldn't bear to face the fact that such violence lurks within us. He knew that first hand. In his rage at Rosalind.

Jesus and resurrection

John caught some words in that long prayer, that after Jesus' death, he "rose again for us."

What on earth could that mean? Rosalind would have pointed out that just as Jesus dying has no effect whatsoever on us, the same is true of his resurrection. Even if we grant the impossible, that a dead body became alive with supernatural powers, that all happened a long time ago and has no effect today, and less and less as history marches on. Really, who cares? Many centuries from now, when Jesus is a hundred thousand years in the past, will anyone really think his coming back to life a hundred thousand years ago is central to understanding the cosmos? Of course not.

John wondered if there could be some other way of understanding Jesus' resurrection. A way that would be cosmic in scope and felt like really good news instead of some impossible mythical event from the distant past.

John had heard that one hundred and fifty years before Jesus, a group of faithful Jewish young men had been tortured to death for refusing to bow down to the Greek gods, who for the Jews embodied violence and oppression. Publicly defying empires and their gods was not likely to have a happy outcome, then as now. Telling the truth about injustice is never popular with those who act with injustice and violence.

Ever since the disaster of those young men's executions, Jewish thinkers had been wondering how God might even up the scales for the victims, whose only offence was to stand for justice against violent oppression. If God didn't enact some kind of justice for those young men cut down in the prime of life, God wouldn't be a God of justice. And if God isn't a God of justice, then violence and total destruction will ultimately win and that would be unthinkable. So, these ancient Jewish thinkers argued, there must be some way in which God must make up for those young men's lost years of living into ripe old age.

So what would a just God do?

Some Jewish thinkers proposed that sometime in the future God would restore those young men to life so they could enjoy the full length of life that would have been theirs if they hadn't been slaughtered in their youth for standing up against injustice, and that way they'd eventually die in old age having lived well. Anything else would be unjust.

A hundred and fifty years later, in Jesus' day, there was lively discussion still going on about this controversial proposal. The proposal wasn't primarily about miraculous biological repair for young men unfairly executed by torture, but rather a statement of certainty that the pattern-affirming quality of ultimate reality is deeper and more permanent than the violence and destruction wreaked on them by invading empires. The symbol of that expectation was young men restored to life so they could live full lives. It had to be real, and had to happen physically on this earth for justice to be carried out. Sometime God would give them their lost lives back, physically.

It made sense to John that ancient Jews could have applied that idea to Jesus. Proclaiming Jesus' resurrection meant they were claiming to have experienced the ultimate triumph of justice being enacted by pattern-affirming ultimate reality. They would have understood that God had ensured justice and fairness would reign in the entire world. They weren't thinking of an impossible medical miracle available only to Jesus, the way so much of Christianity thinks of it today.

If that's what Jesus' death and resurrection meant, it seemed to John that Jesus could again be an image for us of ultimate fulfilment. The claim of Jesus' resurrection would still be a statement that ultimate reality is ultimately victorious, not just for Christians but for the entire human race in all times from the ancient past into the far future, for all creatures, for the planet and indeed for the entire cosmos, because justice and pattern-affirmation is the nature of ultimate reality which underlies everything. Ultimate reality would be prepared to give its deepest self for the whole universe.

The Jewish followers of Jesus were using images from their day that made sense to them—God would gift long life to Jesus just as God would for those young warriors cut down in their youth.

But there was a difference when the early Christians applied that idea to Jesus: God would do the same for every person and every creature in all of history. John wondered if we might use the resurrection of Jesus as a projection claiming that ultimate justice is victorious always and everywhere even in face of the extreme violence of our times.

While part of him was dying to Rosalind's departure, and dying to his desire to inflict pain on her, part of him hoped that he might develop a deeper centredness and maturity through those deaths he was undergoing. But there wasn't much hope of that. His anger and rage at her was still hot.

But it was happening! The miracle just happened without his making it happen. He was starting to feel more calm and more respectful of Rosalind's decision. John was astonished. A kind of resurrection *had* happened to him. Without him even trying.

Jesus and consciousness, character, and culture

The priest had moved on to the final section of the prayer that longed for a fully complete world and asked for the Holy Spirit to make that happen.

He knew what Rosalind would think. "You want me to believe in a mysterious religious force that will make everything wonderful? Not likely!" He knew she wouldn't be saying it to be discouraging, but rather that she'd rather live in truth than illusion. She loved truth that much.

But John had no doubt Rosalind longed for global human fulfilment.

How could people become fully conscious, fully self-aware? Able to take themselves and others seriously? Able to look at themselves from the outside and see the triumph of ultimate reality's justice inside? And then act on that character?

He thought about how the gift of self-awareness is the foundational ability for that kind of love to happen.

Such self-awareness first arises for someone when as a baby they experience the whole world gathered around in the form of their mother. But through some disappointment, perhaps when their mother can't act instantly to meet the baby's need, the child becomes aware of being distinct from their mother. It is, no doubt, a disturbing discovery. But without going through the grief of losing the pre-animist projection of all-surrounding love, no human can become an adult. As a small child waits for their mother, they will substitute their imagination for the real thing and comfort themselves with the illusion their mother has arrived. Although it's an illusion, it's a foundational skill for planning and living a mature life in which patience is always required. Later, as the young child grows, she will become aware that the wider world is not as safe a place as she once imagined it to be. That will be another experience of the death of the animist projection of being constantly surrounded on all sides by kindly consciousnesses that will always look after her. It is a huge step in human maturity to accept that we are not always safe.

In turn, as young adults we die to the projection that we are each a wonderful complete person, and only through the death of accepting our embarrassing limitations can we move into the maturity and stability of more accurate self-knowledge. John was well aware that the process of dying to illusions about his own self in relation to Rosalind was still very much a work in progress.

John valued each of those projections that had taken him some distance along the road of his deepening adulthood. He didn't want to dismiss the earlier projections as infantile. Rather, he hoped that each projection would make an essential contribution to his deepening awareness of his self.

Through the pre-animist projection he could still enter into various kinds of ecstasy—emotional, artistic, or mystical—that are so important for a full life. Through the animist spirit projection, he could trust the reliable processes that science studies and that underlie our culture and by which Rosalind was so fascinated. Through the god projection he could appreciate his place in the wider world without an inflated sense of self-importance. Through the projection of God, he could chart a course for his future in relationship with a partner and with the planet.

That's the process, he realized, that makes human consciousness possible, and makes human culture possible and makes self-offering love possible. That dying and rising of projections is the process that makes us human.

It suddenly struck him what the prayer about asking for the Holy Spirit really meant. It meant we were asking for this Christ-process to become the normative character of humanity and of each of us.

He wished he could have said to Rosalind that the prayer asking for the Holy Spirit wasn't like a child asking Santa Claus for a happy world. To ask for the process to happen required the asker to commit to their own death and resurrection. To pray such a request was indistinguishable from enacting it. This wasn't a retreat into childish dependence upon an imaginary supreme being, or upon an imaginary friend called Jesus. This was asking to become the Christ. That would be to die to each projection and immaturity in turn so as to receive limitless life. That process of ever deeper maturing would never end.

The long prayer which had started with the creation of the cosmos and passed through Jesus' death and resurrection always concluded with that request; may we become Christs. That would be to live in the spirit of Christ. That would be to live in Holy Spirit.

What a difference that would make, John thought. We wouldn't be struggling with our failure to live up to some impossible standard imposed by Jesus, nor be ridden by guilt at having crucified Jesus, nor be failures because we hadn't responded to his suffering by becoming perfect. We would simply be rejoicing in the process for which ultimate reality made us. We'd be fully alive! The path of Jesus' death and resurrection already happening within us is always our path to maturity. We don't have to invent it, it's already built in! That would be good news.

That's exactly what had been happening in himself personally in relation to Rosalind. He'd toyed with returning to the projections. He'd have been happy to settle in turn for sex, for teamwork, for friendship, even for marriage. But something in him knew he'd never really be alive until he died to all his projections and stood naked, just himself, in front of her nakedness, just herself, and waited for her in silence with no projections clothing either of them. Just being who he was.

Then, in a flash he glimpsed how it all worked. If she accepted him, that could happen only when all the projections of their relationship had been withdrawn, and they would become a profoundly intimate and permanent couple.

Then they would begin the cycle of projections again from the beginning, but this time on the basis of the growth which they'd already received from each of the projections the first time around when they were just beginning to know each other.

In the second time around, the first projection would be their projection upon each other of being the totally embracing lover—the pre-animist experience of being surrounded with love. They would enact that physically in ecstatic joy and delight and would do so again and again. Infinitely more satisfying than the fantasy.

But that projection of being immersed in each other's infinite embrace would have to be withdrawn and die as the centre of their relationship, and they would begin to team up about their work together, discovering how their lives and styles would complement each other, and doing so by projecting the animist spirit of teamwork on each other. And when they had integrated that projection, they would create a long-term history together in which they would develop an entire culture of friends and relationships expressed through Olympic projections as culture-wide commitments within their social world. Over time, their entire history together would form a single story for which the projection of a single supreme God underlying their lives would express that experience.

Finally, their relationship that had originated in the accident of sharing a fence, a relationship that could well have happened with a different partner, would not itself be the point—even the Olympic projection, of being the most loving couple ever, and the monotheistic projection of being a permanent couple, would be withdrawn as the monotheistic projection of a single, guiding God died. There would be no more projections about their relationship.

Then they would just be an ordinary couple. Their meaning would be that in their particular struggles and formation of relationship patterns they would be expressing ultimate reality. That would be their purpose. To be completely ordinary. To completely express ultimate reality.

Then it would all be given again with new depth. Knowing the pattern of their joint life was an expression of ultimate reality, their love-making would move into the experience of souls touching. Their teamwork, their partnership, their commitment would all take on new depth. At every step they would be served by the death of one projection gifting them with its life so they could embody an even deeper projection.

Such an experience would take far longer than their lifetimes. It would be an invitation to infinite life. To infinitely deep life. To infinite love.

And that would only happen as they accepted the invitation to participate in the dying of each projection and the integration of each projection's gifts.

If Jesus were the projection by which we can relate to that infinitely life-giving process, then Holy Spirit would be the Christ-process in action.

John became clear this Christ-process wasn't some technique to attain personal or cultural maturity. Sort of an "If you suffer, you'll be more alive because there's no gain without pain." The openness to each death had to be total. Not a deal for him to get ahead, nor a technique to salvage his relationship with Rosalind, nor a security blanket to assure himself everything was somehow well.

It sounded wonderful.

But the truth was she'd left him.

That wasn't wonderful.

Only by fully accepting the fact that she'd turned him down, and this was the end of their relationship, could he ever enter another significant relationship.

He'd have to fully embrace this death so he could rise to intimacy with someone else.

But he didn't want a new relationship with someone else. He wanted Rosalind. And she didn't want him.

In his grief, he glimpsed the dreadful truth. He might come out of this more mature. That wasn't an outcome he wanted at all.

He just wanted her.

It really was death.

Something deep down in him knew the truth. Only by accepting the death of their relationship could he live. The alternative was to continue to live in an illusion and enter a deeper kind of death in which he would begin to die as a human. Refusing to die would guarantee his death as a mature person.

There really wasn't a choice. Like Jesus, he would have to walk deliberately toward the death of his relationship with Rosalind, despite parts of him that continued, like Jesus' disciples, to vehemently object. There was no other way forward.

Jesus: the projection of our self

John found himself walking absent-mindedly up the aisle to receive communion, almost at the end of the line. Looking imaginatively through Rosalind's eyes, and with some tears in his own, he actually looked at the piece of bread and at the wine before he swallowed them. Both were the result of evolution. He was eating evolution. Then he noticed the words being said to him and everyone. "The body of Christ. Keep you in eternal life." The dying and rising of the outcast individuals in every species is what has kept life evolving. And now, he realized, that process was physically feeding him. Just as it always had. He was being fed with death. In order to live. That was staggering.

The evolutionary implications could have been a way, John thought, that Rosalind's worldview and his could have converged.

But John knew that to go on imagining himself explaining things to Rosalind would be to succumb to his old projection of an ideal relationship with her. He wasn't going there again. To be really alive and not regress, he needed to accept her decision to walk her path without him. He needed to accept the death of their relationship, as she obviously already had.

As he returned to his seat, John recalled a phrase earlier in the service that had intrigued him. The third reading from Paul had included the phrase "....putting on Christ."[3] It always seemed to him to be a pleasant image, as if, when we were dressing up in our best Sunday clothes, we were somehow becoming Jesus. A comforting image, that we should all look good and loving and be nice to each other. A great ideal. But impossible to do, as he had discovered in his relationship with Rosalind.

But what if it wasn't about one's Sunday best clothes, but about putting on

---

3   Romans 13:14

the entire body of Jesus on the cross, as if Jesus were me? What if Jesus is the projection of our own true self?

We admire mature people who are ready to give up their own comfort to ensure the comfort of another, or even to give up their life to save someone else, or simply to give up their illusions about themselves in order to relate honestly to someone. That's how we all wish we were.

What if the purpose of Jesus is not to be an impossible example for us to emulate, but to be the projected image of our actual self already alive? If Jesus on the cross is a projection of the love we are capable of enacting, Jesus' significance is that in him we see our own self. As we withdraw that projection on Jesus, we could integrate it and find ourselves acting from the perspective that such love is simply natural for us.

What if Jesus is not an imaginary person from the distant past with super-human powers undergoing a terrible death by torture? What if his enthusiastic self-offering were the way I see, through projection, who I already am?

That makes all the difference, John thought, because for me to love that much wouldn't require a super-human effort far beyond my ability. It only requires me to say yes to what I have always been. That's the sort of Jesus our culture could affirm because that's the only style of personal or international commitment that can provide any hope for humanity. The hopes we are currently being offered—buy more stuff or vote for bigger bombs or just try harder to be nice or hope that everything will somehow work out—are hopes we all know are hopeless. Without another hope to offer as an alternative, there's not much hope.

As John sat in his pew, his gaze settled on a carving of Jesus on the cross. John found himself gazing at it. True, he was hurting that much right now. But there was more than that. Maybe it wasn't primarily about Jesus getting nailed to a cross long ago in a faraway land. He'd thought last week about offering himself to Rosalind without any pretense of being a good neighbour or even a good lover or a faithful partner. He'd realized none of that was left to offer. All he had to offer was his naked imperfect self. Painfully giving up all his self-centred projections. Just to care for her. Is that what the carving of Jesus symbolized? John himself?

Making no further contact to pursue her was the only way he could enact that care now. It was the only way to respect her. Giving her up was the only way left to respect himself. It was like turning the knife on himself. Like being his own priest at his own sacrifice.

The projections had all died.

That would be to be a Jesus, without Jesus' death having anything to do with violence or abuse or punishment or threat. It had everything to do with life.

That would be a liberating death.

He wondered if maybe it could happen to him. Not likely, he thought. But just maybe. After all, he could at least imagine it.

Thinking of Rosalind

After the service was over, he felt relaxed as he socialized at the coffee hour. Newly energized, a lot of things had begun to make sense as he had thought about Jesus and new ways of understanding his death and resurrection. This was something that might have made sense to Rosalind. He was smiling at that thought as he walked back to his car, reached for his keys and suddenly remembered. He got in, and just sat there.

She hadn't come.

He was surprised at how much it still hurt. It was as if all his insights during the service hadn't made any difference.

Then he wondered what she was feeling. It occurred to him she would be relieved not to have come. She'd given her life to her profession. He understood that, and he realized she'd never share his religious faith or his interest in seeing how it might connect to our culture. It was an odd feeling. Deep sadness; yet also a kind of relief that she'd be happy. He remembered the seminar she said she had to prepare. He hoped the preparation was going well.

If her absence this morning had contributed to her getting her work done, and if she felt satisfied after a morning's work, then he felt pleased. If she was happier never seeing him again, even though that felt like death to him, he'd be glad she was content. He started the car, but what he didn't notice was that he was smiling all the way home. It was a joy to give her back her freedom. Even if she never knew. Even if it hurt so very much. It was still his joy and his mature self coming to birth.

Despite the pain, something felt very right about making no further contact with her. He was startled how much that felt like honouring her. And honouring himself. The wounds remained, but a new life and stability had emerged.

The fact she still lived next door meant that his decision to not contact her was even more clear. It didn't arise from the convenience of not running into her. He'd continue to run into her almost daily as he passed her house. His new life emerging from the death of their relationship would be the more solid because he would have to own it every day. He had no choice. He'd have to own it.

Rosalind at night

As Rosalind went to bed that Sunday night after a satisfying day's work preparing her seminar, she was aware of something niggling at the edge of her consciousness. Something that hinted about something uncomfortable. She checked out her feelings. Yes, she was feeling conflicted about having told John she wouldn't join him in his religious practice. She knew he'd be hurting, but it wasn't that. She felt fine making what was the right decision for her. It was something else. If she could just put her finger on it.

So, she set her mind to wander. Sometimes that helped. She recalled John's delight when she'd told him about her shout of joy when she'd discovered the virus protein. She loved the *research*. She'd loved that *project*. It wasn't that. What was bothering her?

She was drifting off to sleep when it struck her. "*Research project.*" That's how he'd invited her to church. Go to church as a research project. What a weird thing for a religious person to say! Weird like light always going the same speed past you no matter how fast you go towards the light. Or away from it. Weird. Got Einstein thinking about how space works. Got her thinking about how ultimate reality works. Light and ultimate reality both totally different from what you'd think. Weird. The puzzlement that started every research project. "*Research project,*" he'd said. "*I wonder…*" she thought as she drifted off to sleep.

Summary

Jesus must die. Otherwise, if he just did something risky or caring, he wouldn't be the image of the process by which we must die to our projections about ourselves and those we love. That's the only way to truly love. And to truly live. That's the only way the Christ story can be told.

The irony is the age of disbelief enables religion to understand even more deeply how the symbol of the dying and rising Christ is central to all life—because that symbol of dying and rising must itself die to be a real symbol of what it symbolizes. Perhaps it is more than just ironical, perhaps this is the only way in which the Christ-process can be central everywhere, even in secular culture.

The basic process of all physical things, about which science has learned so much, works because one process dies and gives rise to another. Whether it is hydrogen atoms being crushed into helium atoms in the sun and so producing the immense heat that enables our life, or photons of light giving up their light in order that trees can make wood out of thin air, or whether it is creatures that are born mutant and then become the ingenious solution to a life-threatening change in the environment and so give rise to an entirely new species, at every level the physical processes of our universe all take part in this dying and rising process.

Just as the earliest Christians saw Jesus as the image of a cosmic reconciliation, and many Christians in our time see him as the image of how humanity escapes the punishment due to us, so our secular world is teaching people of faith to see Jesus as the projection through which we express awe and gratitude for the fact of existence and for the processes through which the cosmos, ourselves, and all life have arisen.

That's a way of understanding Christ that would be freeing and revelatory for our time. It's a projection that makes sense of science and of our selves, and carries no hint of vengeance, punishment, or abuse. The Christ, as the projection of cosmic and evolutionary processes, enables us to give thanks that they happened, gives us expectations about what sort of behaviour on our part will be consistent with the justice of deep reality from which we have emerged, and connects our own personhood and consciousness with the underlying processes by which the universe came to be.

Their discovery of Jesus' momentous significance drove the early Christians to leave the eastern shore of the Mediterranean and travel the known world. People of faith in our time wonder why the faith doesn't elicit the same transformative power today.

By learning the language of secularism and holding hands with that culture, we may be on the verge of experiencing that original power of Christ's significance. We may discover, within secularism, how to proclaim we've stumbled upon something that makes sense of our entire modern experience—from the mysteries of science and technology to the darkness of international power politics and even in the depths of our own psychology.

Making sense of things, finding meanings and connections, is the central human experience. To have a lens to offer people that makes sense of every aspect of modern experience will be a gift and a joy and a renewed source of purpose for the faith that will be as exciting and powerful and world-changing as was that of the first Christians. Perhaps even more so.

That's an immensely valuable skill in a time when so many simultaneous disasters loom large in our age.

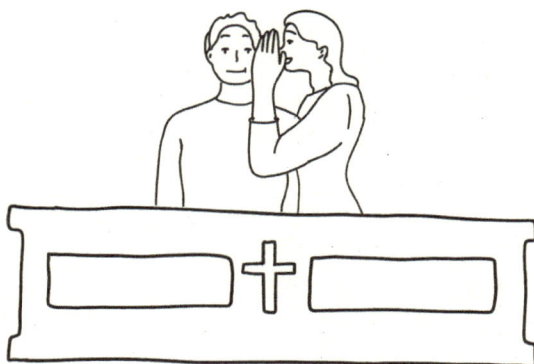

CHAPTER 20

The Secret Life of Priests:
Faith in Disbelief

It's Sunday morning and the service is about to start.

Church services are complex events. When you count all the roles that have to function smoothly in a public event on a Sunday morning there can easily be thirty or forty people, each with responsibilities — the choir, the musicians, greeters, welcomers, the building supervisors, the sound technicians, collection takers, three or four scripture readers, various kinds of servers, all sorts of people setting things up — the list goes on. To say nothing of the people who have undertaken the organizational preparation during the preceding week.

It's a live performance. You know what's supposed to happen, but it's like walking a tight-rope — the unexpected and unplanned can catch you out at any moment.

There has been a lot of busyness just before the service starts. Last-minute announcements, a quick consultation about how to provide for a role for which someone hasn't turned up, resolving two conflicting opinions about where people are to stand to give communion to the congregation, and a quick check with the organist so we both know when the communion hymn is going to happen. The clock is ticking. The play is about to start.

The mechanics are dealt with, and I am about to do something bizarre. It's still bizarre, even though I've done it close to four thousand times.

I kiss ultimate reality.

It's such an intimate thing that I try to do it in private.

It still sends shivers down my back.

It's a long, embroidered scarf called a "stole" with a cross half-way along. I kiss the cross on the scarf and then hang the scarf around my neck with the cross at the back of my neck.

From this moment on, for the next hour and a half, every word I say, every movement I make, every nuance of my voice, every thought I think, is to express ultimate reality and the way it is our source, as patterns of consciousness. About how its deepest pattern is to give up its pattern so we can have ours. That's why I wear the cross on my neck.

I'm to be, and to oversee, the enacting of that ultimate pattern.

I'm to think of nothing else for the next hour and a half.

That's hard work. By the time that hour and a half is over, wearing that symbol of ultimate reality throughout, I'll be exhausted. And full of adrenaline.

In the physical act of kissing a piece of cloth, I ground myself in the fact that this service isn't about me. For a change, I love something that isn't myself.

But what is really happening is the cross kisses me. Into my confusing world where everything clamours for attention and tries to make me succumb to my projection of myself as the universal saviour and the centre of every relationship, comes this extraordinarily simple symbol. I let it kiss me.

I need that kiss of ultimate reality so much. Without it, I'd be a sham leading the service. I'm a sham anyway, but ultimate reality kisses me, and its process of death and resurrection is what this service is about, so, dying to my projected image of me being the perfect priest makes the service possible.

How could I possibly lead anyone in that process unless behind the scenes I had already put on my own death?

If a hundred people came crushing through the door right now asking to be priests with me and kiss the stole and allow it to kiss them, I'd think it was perfectly normal. Who could resist this astonishing experience?

Surprised by joy

Sunday. Kneeling in his pew trying to say his prayers.

A week had passed since Rosalind had refused to join him at church. He hadn't called her. That would have been to intrude on her freedom. He had nurtured his sense she was happily getting on with her life. That made the ache bearable and gave it meaning.

He hadn't been able to pray properly for a long time. *What were you supposed to say?*

"Good morning, God. I'm here."

But God already knew that, and whatever God wanted, he was sure he wasn't supposed to be silly.

"Dear God, make Aunt Bessy well again."

It was a noble thought, but it felt like a child talking to Santa Claus, and it still sounded silly. He'd found lately if he could just be quiet deep down, even for a little while, he had a sense of something. Perhaps it was God having a sense of him. Who knows.

Anyway, be quiet.

There were the Smith twins: he could almost see Deborah through his closed eyes, trying to look calm as she came into church with twin wrigglers clutching at her dress and demanding she listen to them.

Focus on being quiet.

He could feel the quiet begin seeping in.

Clang!

It was old Mrs. Field's new aluminum cane, the one that looked as if it had been designed by her grandson smoking something he shouldn't be smoking. Swish-clunk-rattle went her purse, caught on the cane. Then, a concerned friend in a stage whisper directing another friend trying to retrieve the purse from under the pew.

Block it out. Be quiet.

Those two always chattering at the back. They have been coming for decades. They should know better.

Just block it out. Another silence. This time a long one. Perhaps one second long.

Pop!

The sound system being turned on. *How come a church, supposed to be a spiritual place, is noisier than rush hour in a subway station.*

Quieten the thoughts.

Getting frustrated.

People sliding in behind him and beside him.

Oh, give it up. A second and a half of real silence isn't bad. Better than some Sundays. At least I tried. Odd how much calm there could be in a second and a half of silence.

He opened his eyes, sat up, and reached for his leaflet.

"Hi," Rosalind whispered in his ear.

No.

No!

It wasn't supposed to happen that way. He was supposed to whisper in *her* ear. This was not at all what he'd had in mind. This was terrifyingly more intimate than he had expected, this was intimate beyond his most suggestive fantasies.

"Don't look so startled—they'll think you weren't expecting me. Telling them I was sitting with you was the only way I could escape that chain gang at the door from signing me up to polish something. You do this every Sunday? You have my deepest respect."

Heartbeat-delight-consternation-heartbeat. *Had she really come? Sinking-sensation, catch-my-breath.*

"Good morning, and welcome!" But it was the rector on his wireless mike.

What John said was, "Oh."

"Whooooosh" went Mr. James' hearing device because he had the receiver turned to his chest.

"Grampa, you've got it on backwards!"—one of the twins.

"What did she say, dear?" Mr. Field said to Mrs. Field.

"She said, 'Good morning', and it isn't a her. It's a him today. And your thing's on backwards."

"I like the hymns today, too, dear. I'm sure they won't be backwards," replied Mr. James, gently patient as always.

"Please note the processional hymn is number 397, not 793; sorry for the misprint in the leaflet."

"Pop!" went the sound system and the priest was gone.

We are so ordinary. Why can't it look even a little impressive when she comes? But he wasn't going to betray any embarrassment. He tried a smile. He moved along to give her more room. Whether she needed it or not. If she'd moved toward him in response, he'd have to make more space, and soon he'd have to start pushing people off the far end of the pew. She just looking pleased with herself.

"Where is this corrected hymn?" she whispered. He got her the hymn book.

"Hymn numbers, not page numbers."

"Where did he go? Have they forgotten something?"

"We're having a moment of silence." Wry smile.

"Ah," she whispered. "I see."

They weren't, and she did.

Thunderous roar from the organ. Everyone stood, she just a heartbeat behind. She snuck a look around. Everyone standing. Books open, full attention, lungs at the ready. This was well-organized.

Then from nowhere rows and rows and rows of people in pairs were coming down the aisle dressed in red and white. All very solemn. Some carrying things. Some singing, some just walking. The further back the more complicated the clothes. The last person all in blue.

"Why blue?" she whispered in his ear.

"Blue for being pregnant, like Mary—for this time of year we use blue to symbolize being pregnant with maturity, and with justice and in loving response to the needs of people."

"What's with his complicated clothes?"

"It's not the details of the clothes—they are supposed to be mysterious. The idea is we are in the presence of something wonderful, but beyond understanding. It's a way of getting at what the mysterious feels like. Sound familiar?"

It did.

Mr. Field never noticed they whispered behind him the whole service. But the twins thought it was cool that grown-ups could whisper in church and told their mom so. The young couples thought they were in love.

The leader who doesn't

As the procession makes its way down the aisle I walk at the very end. To show how humble I am. Nobody is fooled. We all know the important person comes last. But what isn't known is the person at the end has the least control over what happens. If the person at the front leading the procession gets the instructions mixed up and goes up the wrong aisle, the person at the end would look absolutely ridiculous keeping to the original plan all by themselves. The truth is, although I lead this congregation, I have no control over where the procession goes. Or, for that matter, the entire congregation. Whatever happens, I follow. And bless them.

I've often felt ambivalent about this business of processions and my coming at the end wearing the most elaborate robes. I have wondered if this actually undermines the fundamental proclamation that ultimate reality is equally present to everyone and death and resurrection are the foundational process of the cosmos. But at the same time, the order and dignity are a kind of ballet in which we non-verbally enact the mystery and infinite importance of ultimate reality. I simply take my part in the ballet. I know ultimate reality will have kissed all of us by the time the service is over.

Finally, we make it to the front of the church, and if the timing is right, the hymn ends shortly after and in the silence that follows I officially greet the congregation.

I look out over an enormous range of people — of all ages, of all economic backgrounds; some with extensive formal education, some with none. I see a longtime member there with a woman whom I've never seen before and I wonder if she is a visiting relative or something more.

I can tell, in that brief moment, the attitude of the congregation. For years it seemed as if my job was to find a way past their determined assumption that all they would hear would be the same old platitudes and their deepest commitment would be to keep on coming regardless of how pointless it all was. But in recent years it feels as if there has been a sea change — people are looking up expectantly, eagerly anticipating being exposed to something significant, to some deep energy; to being opened up to an enlivening experience that will provide them with foundation and direction and meaning for the week ahead.

And I get to tell them — my first words in the service — that they are loved. It's a ridiculous act by a person wearing peculiar clothes, who's a pretty poor lover himself, to tell them what they most want to hear. That they are loved. By ultimate reality. And, most incredible of all, I get to say it. And even more special: it is true.

I say,

"The grace of our Lord Jesus Christ...."[1]

Grace: from the word gratis, 'free.' There is a freedom in the process of death and resurrection we are commending to one another. That process of death and resurrection is the underlying reality of all relationships, and so it is

[1] The bold quotes are taken from *The Book of Alternative Services of the Anglican Church of Canada.* (Anglican Book Centre, 1985). p. 185 ff.

Lord of our lives.

"...and the love of God...."

Ultimate reality really does uphold us; it creates us without any obligation to do so and keeps us in existence by processes of which we scarcely have awareness despite all our research. It's about our relation to reality — it has gifted us with existence and self-awareness, so we start off by re-connecting with the fact that we are gifted by existing. That's to be loved.

"...and the fellowship of the Holy Spirit, be with you all."

It's possible that the direction we are going in relationships, in international affairs, in world history, can be congruent with ultimate reality — I am commending that direction to everyone.

Whispering, wondering, and wandering in church

Rosalind noticed the well-rehearsed back and forth dialogue. "Community building?" she asked in a whisper.

"Not exactly; more like, 'What's this community for?' More than just us having a nice time together. Are we about giving leadership in dealing with hunger, political priorities, standing up for those who can't? We are starting off by saying this service isn't about us, it's about us being the leadership of the human race in becoming human by being in touch with ultimate reality."

"And also with you."

"How'd you know to say that?"
"It's here in the book."
"But you don't have the book."
"I know it."
"You memorized the whole book?! Now I am impressed!"

It looks as if I'm saying it to the congregation and the congregation are saying it back to me, but the idea is ultimate reality is saying it to us — that we are to be free through death and resurrection, that ultimate reality is characterized by overflowing and unexpected events, that human community is called far beyond what it currently is. When we say it back, we are partly expressing our gratitude for ultimate reality being the way it is, and partly saying it to one another to encourage one another in those priorities.

"Almighty God, to you all hearts are open, all desires known, and from you no secrets are hidden,"

Ultimate reality is being imaged here as a supreme omniscient being who sees inside us. It doesn't matter that there is no such being. That's just a picture — the reality is much stranger than any supreme being. The intention is to focus on ultimate reality's connection to me personally. While the whole community needs to grow into maturity, I certainly need to do so myself.

John was glad she had no idea how much growing he had to do.

"So, in order to be clear this isn't just a generalized vague hope, it gets very personal — I am to imagine the whole of ultimate reality is focused on assisting me to grow. Not bad, eh?"

"Cleanse the thoughts of our hearts...."

The imagery is from an ancient culture in which ritual uncleanness was of primary concern in life — a person could be more objectionable because of omitting ritual than because of poor hygiene. But it makes sense as an image, because if my priorities — the thoughts of my heart — put me on a course that is opposed to my maturing or to the health of the human race, then that really is a kind of dirtiness. We want that to be removed.

"...that we may perfectly love you and worthily magnify your holy name...."

John whispered, "We want to love ultimate reality. That's not imagining a romantic relationship with ultimate reality, although sometimes it has been imaged in that way by mystics, but it suggests the desire to be like the one we love."

He hadn't guessed this about me, surely? wondered Rosalind. No, he's just talking about the service.

Odd, felt funny saying that; hope she didn't notice.

"Our desire is to be like ultimate reality—living deeply in death and resurrection, being free with ourselves, being generous with humanity, knowing this is our call as humans. Magnifying the name of ultimate reality is simply letting people know what it is like. There is a widespread unconscious assumption that reality is ultimately a great big zero, and we are just freak accidents—it would make a lot of difference if that weren't so."

Sure would, she thought.

"Glory to God in the highest...."

"Poetry for ultimate reality is unimaginable and really amazing!"

"....and peace to God's people on earth."

John whispered to her. "Peace means much more than just a quiet summer afternoon—here it is the equivalent of 'full life' being wished for all humanity. These are the words sung in the Christmas story by the angels when Jesus was born. The idea is that when ultimate reality is expressed in us, is given birth though us, we are fully alive—fully human—and therefore able to respond to one another in a way that would make our planetary humanity complete."

"You mean you really ask for that?"

"Oh, yes, we are quite serious about it."

She looked thoughtful.

"Free us from all that darkens and ensnares us, and bring us to eternal light and joy...."

"'Eternal' means more than infinitely long; more importantly it means infinitely deep. Our desire is for everyone to have light and joy without limit in their everyday life."

"I've known that," she said, "in moments of great joy in research."

"Exactly," he said.

And to himself, *Yes, exactly, and in my moments of self-discovery.*

Suddenly everyone sat down.

"How'd everyone know to do that?"

"Instinct—you get it from spending time with ultimate reality."

She paused for a heartbeat, wondering.

He just smiled. He'd got back at her for slipping in unawares beside him.

From this point on, for the rest of the first half of the service, there's really not much for me to do. I sit or stand while everyone else leads parts of the service — other people are reading the scriptures, leading the prayers, talking to the children. But I'm not off duty, even though I'm just sitting there at the front. What I am doing is symbolizing that ultimate reality delights in people exercising their full skills and being given the dignity of roles in life and leadership. The point is that the service isn't about me, or

348 Faith in Doubt

about my ideas. During this time when I do nothing, I'm one of the congregation. I am listening and praying along with everyone else. And I'm still wearing ultimate reality around my neck.

Someone reads a passage of scripture.

A long pause.

"Has someone forgotten something?"

"No. We are supposed to have time to let the meaning of the passage sink in during the silence."

"Sorry, what did you say?"

"Ha. Ha."

The choir stood up. So did she.

"We don't stand up for this one."

"Why not?"

"I don't know."

"I can see an opportunity for a research project—didn't you suggest that?"

Lovely chanting. A psalm.

Now someone else was reading.

"I didn't get any of that. What was he trying to say?"

"It's Paul. He was saying how astonished he was to discover that people who knew nothing about the Jewish God turned out to be full partners in that experience."

A nudge of her elbow. "So, Paul thought there was hope for atheists like me?"

The touch went right through his chest. He looked at her but didn't smile.

"I guess so." But, to himself, *I hope she doesn't think I'm trying to convert her. I care for her too much to want that. Please don't let her think that.*

He didn't notice the hymn had started, and she handed him the hymn book open at the right page. Her turn to smile.

Another reading. About the importance of Jesus dying and rising.

Then they sat down. The preacher preached. Some interesting analogies: when Jesus was born, the three wise men's gifts: myrrh symbolizing the presence of death as completion at the start and at the end of Jesus' life; gold symbolizing ultimate value; incense symbolizing worship and therefore ultimate importance. Ourselves as contemporary Jesuses; Herod's murders of children, and our experiencing destructive and constructive deaths; ourselves as each being ultimately valuable and of infinite significance.

She secretly thought, but of course never said, that her own small discoveries in biology might be of ultimate significance, and indeed, the pain of failure and the joy of subsequent discoveries were not unknown to her either.

John was very aware of the feeling of death he had experienced when he became committed to her fulfilment, and how that death had opened up into a new respect. And something about that ultimate value seemed exactly what he thought about her. He was proud to sit near her.

They sat in silence for a time, each pursuing their own thoughts. Each wondering whether they could ever share such thoughts with the other; and each deciding not to.

Everyone stood up. Both were caught off guard.

The congregation said the Creed together, the ancient summary of their faith. Later he would have time to suggest contemporary meanings for the ancient symbols.

Everyone sat down. This time she was ready, and sat too, proud that she had caught on. But then she found everyone was kneeling and went back to being confused. Prayers for places all over the world, even for non-Christian societies. She hadn't expected that. Prayers for all sorts of people she'd never heard of. Then prayers for families who'd had someone who had died. She caught her breath as her chest hurt—her father had died not long ago, and she'd had no one to tell how much it hurt.

I hope he didn't notice. And then hoped he did.

Then their sins were forgiven. She couldn't remember any that weren't just adolescent embarrassment, and felt relieved that perhaps, after all, this whole thing didn't mean much anyway. Then she realized what that would mean for him. She found herself hoping that, at least for his sake, having sins forgiven might mean something.

Then they all stood up. Taken by surprise, again, she'd expected to find a church service a passive experience and never imagined it would be so full of energy.

"I get it, the big advantage of being religious is you don't have to jog on Sundays." He smiled and felt understood.

"The peace of the Lord be always with you." **"And also with you."**

Chatter, laughter, turning around, hands clasped, walking out of pews.
"It's over?"
"Nope, only half-way through."

"You're kidding?"

He wasn't.

"So, what's going on?"

"It's street theatre. We are acting out, quite genuinely, the sense that we are delighted at being so loved, so at home in the universe, and so clear that our relationships and we ourselves and the world will be well in the end."

It was hard to say that, looking straight into her eyes.

And then he realized he was going to have to exchange the peace with her.

Not to do so, even if she didn't know it, would be unimaginably rude.

He held out his hand.

"Peace be with you."

"You're supposed to take my hand and say:

"And also with you."

She did. It stung. His hand. And his heart.

There they stood, as innocent as naked Adam and Eve, deliberately touching for the first time.

Everything around them went silent.

Then, **"Peace be with you! Peace be with you! Peace be with you!"** Little hands grabbing at their clothes.

It was one of the twins back from Sunday School waving her insistent hand in his face, determined to shake more hands than her twin brother. They were both relieved and delighted to see in the child's face the innocence that had been given them and snatched away in the same moment.

"What about that cute atheist nephew of yours? Who asks all the right questions? Is he here?"

"Yes. And his older sister is right up front with the priest. The priest told her to keep on asking great questions and experience the whole thing up close. So, she is. She has a role in the ceremony at the front. Who knows where that might lead. Thing is, when I told her some of my thoughts, she told me she'd already figured that out long ago. Said she became an atheist when she was six. Sort of put me in my place. Now she's taking it seriously."

Another hymn. She'd never heard the tune; the symbolism eluded her: and she didn't feel like being so close for a bit to whisper with him what it meant. But the repeated phrase, *Stars of the morning, dawn on our darkness and lend us thine aid* had a calming and reassuring sense.

And then someone passed a plate. Of course, always the money. From where she was standing, she could see it carried up to the front and then they prayed over it.

"You pray over money?"

"The idea is to commit the money for love, not for us."

Again, she was impressed.

Killing God Sunday by Sunday

We are now coming to the central part of the service, which is the enactment of, and our participation in, death and resurrection — the process by which everything came to exist. And the process by which we recover our existence and our meaning.

People have already laid on the table in front of me silver cups of wine and baskets of bread.

As I am standing waiting for the hymn to end and the collection to be carried up, I'm thinking about how parts of the service could have gone better. I'd forgotten to send the readers a clearer translation of a difficult passage; I should have had a special practice with them; I had preached the sermon and I'm frustrated about having accidentally omitted an illustration that would have made my point more clearly; and I suddenly realize I forgot to thank the people who put on the parish dinner last week. Darn. What a shemozzle. You'd think I could do it better after all this time.

And then that new server, the young niece of the long-time member I noticed earlier, very solemnly approaches me with a jug of water, a bowl, and a towel. She pours the water over my hands and it dawns on me that ultimate reality is pouring itself over me, the splashing water laughing up at me that I take myself so seriously, reminding me I'm not ultimate reality and it will look after the universe, and this congregation, and this service just fine without me self-centredly worrying about it.

I join in the laughter, realizing how silly it is for me to think I have to be responsible for everything and get everything right when ultimate reality underlies us all. Ultimate reality and I chuckle together at me in mutual affection. I smile, and hand the towel back to the young server who has no idea what I'm smiling at. She thinks it's because I like her. Which I do. She asks great questions.

And now I get to do what that bishop ordained me to do so long ago in the

Yukon. I get to press the congregation up against ultimate reality and what ultimate reality has done for us, and I read the account of how everything came to be — from galaxies to bodies to feelings to relationships. And I hold up the bread and wine and press the congregation up against the process of death and resurrection through which the cosmos, cultures, humanity, consciousness and all that is, was created and is even now being re-created. The process by which every single one of us here continues to exist.

I take an ordinary loaf of bread, made of ashes of stars, and hold it high and break it in half. I hold the broken pieces aloft in silence so everyone can see what has just happened. Then I put the pieces on the altar, the symbol of offering death through the sacrifice of animals and me the priest symbolizing that, and in silence I bow over that broken bread and the poured-out wine. Even though Jesus' death and resurrection is the ultimate symbol of that process, it's happening right now, every bit as two thousand years ago.

It takes me a while to take it all in. The stars that broke to form this bread. The species of grass that died that wheat could emerge. The brokenness in myself that miraculously led to growth. The death of illusions for everyone here. The dying of the womb-babe so it can become a child and be born. God, the ultimate reality, behind everything acting with unimaginable maturity to undergo death so we could be fulfilled. What a universe! What a source for all of us!

The same with the wine.

I stand in the silence to let it sink in. I am astounded every time.

God broken for us.

I sometimes worry someone will have to come and shake me so I don't go off in a haze of awe and forget to say the next words.

"The gifts of God for the people of God."   "Thanks be to God."

And then we all get to eat death and resurrection.

As I speak to every person, feeding them, often knowing something of their joys and pains, sometimes it's someone with whom I'm uncomfortable, but to each I say, "The body of Christ, keep you in eternal life;" in effect "Eat death and resurrection, the essence of ultimate reality, and live infinitely deeply." Over and over again. To elderly people, to someone in the final stages of cancer, to little children, to someone going through divorce, someone enraged, someone engaged, someone with their thoughts a million miles away, someone in profound silence, someone I've never seen before who doesn't quite know what she's doing but is with that longtime member I noticed. All being given unimaginably new life through the cosmic process of ultimate reality undergoing death and resurrection for them and in them all. I can hardly believe it myself, it's so extraordinary.

"You do this every week?"
"Some people think you should do it every day."
"You mean, commit yourself to that kind of depth every day?"
"Yes."

She began to understand why he did this. If only it wasn't so religious, if you didn't have to be so weird, she could imagine doing that.

We actually digest the bread and the wine. The molecules of bread and wine seep into our circulatory system within seconds, and if a person wanted to, they could be tracked travelling into every capillary in our bodies. Every piece of me, from my brain, to my skin, to the tips of my toes ends up with some of the atoms of the food that took on the meaning of Jesus as death and resurrection. It's a startling thought that everything from my hair to my toe nails are made, in part, of atoms from that food.

John continued his whispering, "I think death and resurrection is the central dynamic of evolution. And that is only what is happening at the level of biology. At the level of personality and relationships, parallel things are happening. The dying and rising, the de-throning of ego in order to love, the death of immaturity and the development of maturity, all arise from ultimate reality. And in the communion, I receive those processes from ultimate reality."

She had heard the biology before, and of course knew it better than he. But she had never, since her high school days, thought about being so aware of the processes that were taking place in her own body whenever she ate. There was nothing new in the explanation, but the idea of deliberately, week after week, exposing oneself to the significance of what was going on, was startling. Part of her didn't want to expose herself to that. Part of her was fascinated, wondering what the experience would be like.

Seduced by a dead God

Suddenly she had a decision to make. The things he had been whispering to her made so much sense. But to say she believed them, that wasn't at all sure. Part of her wondered what it would feel like, to be symbolically so open to the process of death and resurrection. Part of her wondered what people would think.

In a flash, she understood that this was her death. It had always been so important to be right that sometimes it was a burden. She was being faced with dying to that certainty and launching out into the unknown. But what about him? Would he be offended? After all, it meant so much to him.

And then it was obvious. He was preparing to step around her, gently and unobtrusively, but quite clearly not expecting her to go as well. Then the moment was upon her. She must throw caution to the winds.

"Would it be alright if I came?"

He was dumbfounded. He knew that many in his tradition would not approve since she wasn't baptized. Was his desire to say yes motivated mainly by his feelings for her? And then he saw the courage and the risk her question entailed and found himself amazed to see a glimpse of her experience of death and resurrection—the very process he had been whispering about. He was in awe of her.

"Yes," he said, as if it were simply matter-of-fact.

"The body of Christ, the bread of heaven, keep you in eternal life."

And she thought of the energy of the stars, of our sun, of the elements of the big bang, of the whole process of death and resurrection in evolution entering her and coursing through her body. And a glimpse of new and more difficult deaths that might lie ahead. And of un-guessed-at new life.

"The blood of Christ, the cup of salvation, keep you in eternal life."

Blood. Sin. Shake off the old meaning. Drinking alcohol so as to be uplifted past the dashed expectations of all those difficult times growing up, all the relationships that might have been, her own loneliness, all being somehow not removed but transformed. Small though the sip was, she felt the warmth of it in her stomach. It was quite a hope if her inward darkest parts could be transformed like that.

"Go in peace, to love and serve the Lord."

Announcements.

The person who'd read one of the scriptures was speaking.

"Hi everyone! Great service, eh? But the fun's only just begun. Next is coffee hour! Anyone who's here for the first time, I've got my eye on you—can't hide from me! You have to have coffee ta get a ticket to get outta here! Tickets cost ya—just have to tell my sweetie you liked her coffee! Catch you next door!"

I'm half out of role, shaking hands, trying to respond to comments about the weather, figure out if someone wants to linger, decipher cryptic remarks about someone's aunt, try to remember if I'm free for a committee the Thursday after next at 2.30 p.m.; there's John with that lady — maybe I can connect with them at coffee, but by the time I've responded to all the issues of shaking hands, they've long gone.

They did the required socializing.

The reader and his wife were serving coffee. Polite as could be.

"Hi, John, good to see you. And who's that with you?"

"Rosalind."

"Come here often?" A twinkle in his eye.

"Here's your coffee. Goodies down the line, help yourself. You don't socialize, I'll report you to the brass polishers!"

They both laughed.

"We'll socialize if it kills us!"

"Who's your minister? The priest person? I liked his sermon."

"Him? I thought you might. I heard he went to boarding school and became an atheist. Maybe one day I'll hear the rest of the story."

"I got the sense he was talking to me in between all the other people."

"So, whadya think?"

"It was. Interesting. Needs a lot of translating. Whispering was OK."

"That all? Free lunch unbutton your lips? If you don't have a seminar to prepare?"

"Cancelled. Lucky for you. Since the universe is the ultimate free lunch, who am I to refuse?"

Holding hands

Over lunch she proposed a translation of all those prayers so ordinary people could understand them.

He proposed, too. But not a translation.

He waited in silence, seeing her for the very first time. Present to each other without projections.

Whatever she replied, he knew it would be right.

She just reached out her hand.

And he held it.

Summary

In order for us to grow in the pattern of ultimate reality's death and resurrection, and so be really alive, we need to participate at least weekly in the projections that enable us to experience that pattern.

Liturgical worship is not a gathering of like-minded people who support one another in the faith. Rather, it is a carefully designed process by which to expose humanity to the basic process of death and resurrection by which we become mature personally and politically and cosmically.

Those with responsibility to enable that process must themselves participate, during the liturgy, in the process of death and resurrection. John and Rosalind find the same happens to them.

Then ultimate reality, God, Jesus, the Christ-process, death and resurrection, become our life and our hope.

Ultimate reality doesn't get much better than that.

A Peek Behind the Scenes

In western culture, science and faith are longing to hold hands, even if they don't entirely know it yet.

Both need the other so badly.

In a culture dominated by the certainties of science, religion finds its central beliefs to be uncomfortably uncertain. Science has made certainty and accuracy the touchstones of truth, and much of religion has bought into that assumption. No wonder in some religious communities doubt is the ultimate sin and the religious response to science's challenge is a fanatic emphasis on the factual accuracy of the Bible.

One religious response to religious uncertainty is to invent evidence to provide the longed-for certainty—from Noah's Ark theme parks with ridiculous dioramas of humans cavorting with dinosaurs, to the equally ridiculous claims that only in religious community can people be fully human and happy.

With the rise of science, the divine authorship of the Bible and the accuracy of its historical descriptions are called into doubt, and fundamental beliefs such as the Trinity or the divinity of Jesus turn out to have originated within the cultures in which they were formulated as responses to particular issues of the day.

Historical research shows Christian missionary work was as much driven by desire for power and control as by desire to share God's love. Worse, Christianity's global success was possibly due as much to the impressive technology that western culture and the expansion of European empires brought with Christianity, as to the truth of the proclamation of Christ as saviour of the world. Missionary 'success' turns out to be much an illusion. We'd bought into the illusion that we were all about loving. It turns out it was very much about making us look good.

Faith has a second unhealthy response to the almost universal acceptance of scientifically certain truth. Faith sometimes prides itself on holding beliefs for which there is no evidence, and makes that a central article of belief. Indeed, 'faith' is often understood to be the ability to hold beliefs regardless of evidence to the contrary. The extreme nature of such claims is itself evidence that religion remains deeply uncomfortable about the uncertainty at its core.

Religion would love to have the certainty that is science's stock in trade.

Of course, religion is projecting this sense of absolute certainty upon science. Science has no such certainty, the whole scientific project is about moving beyond current inadequate understandings. But as with all projections, projections are the first step in discovering that the projected quality is already present in the one doing the projecting. That would imply there is a certainty at the heart of religious faith that faith is not yet prepared to own.

What might that certainty be at the heart of religious faith?

The certainty at the centre of faith doesn't consist in scientific knowledge of the mechanics of physical processes, or in the factual accuracy of scripture, or they psychology of religious practice, but is about the characteristics of the source from which the physical cosmos has emerged. Those characteristics are as certain and credible as anything in science because as we have seen they are deducible from scientific knowledge.

The certainties to which religion has access are that order, pattern and creativity emerge throughout the cosmos. Personhood, consciousness and responsibility emerge naturally from, and as a consequence of, that basic order, pattern, and creativity. Because preserving patterns is so fundamental to life and especially to conscious life, it's clear why people so urgently crave connections and meaning, and why the highest moral action is to value another's life, or pattern, more highly than one's own. The implication is that such a quality must in some way be inherent in the source of the cosmos. The certainty at the centre of faith is the character of our underlying source: ultimate reality.

It will be painful for religion to withdraw the projection that science has certainty, and faith only has a *faux* faith-based certainty, but when faith does withdraw the projection, it will be able to integrate this new kind of certainty into a wonderfully vibrant life in which certainty will be its stock in trade.

So, religion looks across the table and in humility reaches a hand out to science, longing to receive the certainty that is so central to the practice of science.

Then something extraordinary happens.

A parallel but opposite desire is happening within science.

What science aches for is exactly what religion is already good at.

Scientists in all fields find themselves in utter amazement as well as in humility at what they are discovering.

Awe is everywhere in science.

At the scale of the cosmos, not long ago there was speculation about whether there might be planets around other stars. Then one was discovered, then hundreds. And now thousands, some of which are not very different from this planet. In the very recent past, it was pure conjecture to speculate if there could be other conscious, thinking beings out there. Suddenly that has become a very real, scientifically credible possibility.

The possibility that consciousness emerges throughout the universe is an astonishing and world-changing discovery—it is not just another intriguing fact uncovered by science. When the real possibility of consciousnesses around other stars sinks in, it will radically transform humanity's image of ourselves. What does it mean if consciousness is sprouting throughout the cosmos and we are just one local manifestation? There is no scientific way to approach what that means. Religion, however, specializes in dealing with the deeply mysterious, and with meaning. That's mystery at the cosmic level for which science has no vocabulary.

At the opposite end of the awe scale from cosmology is microscopic DNA. When DNA was discovered not much more than seventy years ago, it seemed the genes of DNA coded for all the physical processes of our bodies, rather like the blueprint for a building or the circuit diagram for an electronic device. But ninety-nine percent of the DNA turned out not to be part of genes and seemed to do nothing and so was relegated to the status of 'junk' DNA left over from ancient and now useless genetic processes that had been mindlessly and uselessly copied ever since. But now we know this 'junk' DNA is not junk at all but has an essential role in modulating our genes. Billions of interactions going on between genes and 'junk' DNA turn those genes on and off in response to internal and external conditions. Even now that the human genome has been mapped, it is unclear whether we will ever fully understand the process because of the unimaginable complexity of the interactions between the various parts of our DNA and our genes.

At either end of the size scale, science gives rise to astonishment, awe, and wonder.

But science has no vocabulary of its own with which to express that experience of awe and mystery in the discoveries science is making.

Another, second, mystery is confronting the practice of science.

The more science we throw at nature the more nature becomes unknown. Science is rightly proud of the explosion of knowledge with which it has gifted humanity in the past hundred or so years. However, that explosion of knowledge has been accompanied by a strange phenomenon. In every sphere of research each advance in knowledge results in an exponential increase in the unknown. The naïve belief, at the end of the nineteenth century, that before long we would know everything, has been turned on its head—the more we know, the more we encounter the unknown. It would be laughable in our day for any scientist to imagine that a few more discoveries will complete our knowledge of any discipline. Exactly the opposite is the case. Every advance in knowledge gives rise to scores of new questions, each of which, when examined, leads to scores of more unknowns. The more science succeeds the more the unknown expands exponentially faster.

If the questions multiply faster than the answers, does that mean that science is leading us into a kind of cosmic ignorance? The more we know, the less we know. What does that mean? Ultimate scientific despair? How can science respond to that strange contradiction at its heart?

Science is also facing a darker kind of problem.

The theory of science is that it is driven by the search for pure knowledge without personal bias or desire for personal gain. But in practice, scientific research is increasingly driven by motives of profit and political power. A significant portion of professional scientists, perhaps up to half, do research into how to kill humans more effectively through the production of ever more sophisticated military equipment. Yet to kill people is to destroy the most complex patterns we know of in the cosmos, an activity contrary to the basic scientific commitment that is to investigate the ubiquitous emergence of pattern, much less destroy patterns, especially the most complex of which are us. At the same time, much of science has allowed itself to be hijacked into the production of trinkets in the form of the latest electronic gadgetry. Equally concerning is the scientific production of drugs that provide profit but are not medically necessary, yet redirect money and research away from dealing with basic illnesses from which much of humanity suffers and for which healing could be easily available. Without that distraction of profit, basic illnesses could be cured in less profitable parts of the world.

Finally, science is the one activity that has made possible the destruction of our world, either by lightning-fast nuclear disaster or through gradual strangulation by climate collapse.

How can science respond to those internal contradictions from a scientific perspective? On what basis can science judge itself? Science believed for a long time that it had finally freed humanity from illusions of blind obedience to antiquated moral and ethical laws. Yet it finds itself inextricably yoked to evil and has become handmaid to disaster. How is science to deal with this problem at its heart?

No wonder science gazes longingly across the table and sees exactly what it craves—the ability to understand and express and integrate the awe and humility that science is encountering at every turn. Science also longs for the deep experience with meaning and ethics and hope that is religion's stock in trade.

As we have seen, projections are about what already lies within us. It's not that religion has a corner on mystery or ethics and that science is hard, unimaginative and unethical but accurate. But by projecting expertise about issues of awe and ethics and meaning onto religion, religion may become the projection by which science can own and incorporate its own expertise about awe and rejection of falsity. After all, those skills are already foundational to the scientific process.

It's no wonder science might want to reach back across the table to an outstretched religious hand.

At the very least, science needs to articulate awe and stand with ethics against the seduction of power in order to prevent science from destroying our planet. In turn, faith needs credibility, supplied by science, to articulate the character of the underlying source of the cosmos that has given rise to humanity and our consciousness and to everything that science studies.

Each has exactly what the other needs.

It wouldn't be an exaggeration to suggest that in this secular age, ultimate reality is drawing both communities together into a deeper pattern in order that each should become more meaningful and life be more abundant on this planet.

If they both accept the touch of the other, there's no knowing what may be born from that union.

Life itself, and indeed the future of our planet, depend on the outcome of that hand-clasp.

Let us hope they are each sufficiently seduced by the other that they can divest themselves of their projections and stand naked, each just their-self to the other's reality.

Then a miracle may happen as each allows their projection on the other to die, and as each integrates the other's gift.

Who knows what might happen then.

It's not impossible that John and Rosalind might draw on their respective gifts to address the climate collapse which threatens both faith and science, and indeed all life on this lovely blue dot. But that will take dying to more projections and rising to even deeper life together.

Science and faith would then dance together the Christ-process of giving life through dying to death and rising to life. So might Rosalind and John. Christ, the projected image of ultimate reality, would then be all in all.

Glossary

Animist. A culture in which people experience conscious beings living in various significant objects. These beings are usually called "spirits" and they often direct the behaviour of animals or natural phenomena. It is possible to communicate with the spirits and they with us.

Christ-process. The process by which objects and people are transformed by ceasing to be what they used to be and becoming more significant. Jesus, in his role as a projection for that process is called The Christ. 'The Christ-process' refers to the universal process of death and resurrection which enables the emergence of matter or the emergence of maturity.

Faith. Sometimes used to mean the effort required to believe in something that cannot be proved. However, the original meaning of the word was closely connected to the Greek word for 'trust.' In this sense, to have faith in God is not to convince oneself there is a God even if that can't be proved, but to trust in God's love being ultimate.

God. Depending on the culture in which the word is used, it can mean an invisible directing force, a conscious but invisible being, an infinite supreme being who creates and rules the entire universe, or as in this book, a projected image enabling us to experience our relationship with ultimate reality.

Integration. I behave in a new way on the basis of knowing that the qualities I previously only saw in someone else are really part of me.

Occam's razor. The principle that when there are two possible explanations for something, the simpler explanation is more likely to be accurate. Occam was a medieval scholar and this insight became known humorously as Occam's razor because it shaved off unnecessary complications from the face of competing explanations.

Olympic gods. Olympic gods were experienced in classical Greek and Roman culture as super-human beings who lived on Mount Olympus in Greece and who had their own extensive society among themselves. They could interact with individual humans and with entire nations if they chose to do so. By prayer and expressions of loyalty, humans could persuade gods to act on our behalf to influence behaviour or change the course of history.

Planck. Dr. Max Planck, a German researcher, measured the size of quantum particles and the time it takes them to do whatever they are doing. The Planck distance is a billionth of a billionth of a centimetre and the Planck time is a billionth of a billionth of a second. Anything that is larger than the Planck size or exists for longer than the Planck time behaves in normal ways. Anything smaller than the Planck size behaves in ways that make no sense to us, such as being in multiple places at once, or arriving before they left where they started from, or simply stopping existing, or starting existing for no reason whatever.

Pre-animist. A hypothetical culture in which people experience everything as conscious—rocks, blades of grass, animals, and people are all aware of themselves and make decisions about their behaviour. We don't know if such a culture ever actually existed but there are suggestive parallels in human development.

Projection. I attribute characteristics of myself (sometimes desirable and sometimes undesirable) to someone else, without realizing the qualities are part of me and not necessarily present in the other person.

Quantum particle. Take any physical object and cut it down to its very smallest pieces, a billionth of a billionth of a centimetre wide. That's very small! It doesn't matter what you started with, the tiniest parts will be identical to the tiniest parts of everything else. These tiny parts are very strange indeed. They seem to exist outside of time and space. They can end up where they are going before they left where they started. Each particle seems to exist everywhere in the universe simultaneously and might become physical literally anywhere at all, and at any time in the past or future. There is no reason at all where or at what time they appear. They are called quantum particles and all physical objects are made of nothing but quantum particles.

Religion. A cultural way in which members of a culture relate to unseen beings who have important roles in our lives.

Resistance. Without realizing it, I prevent myself from discovering that certain undesirable qualities I see in someone are actually a part of me.

Schrödinger equation. Dr. Schrödinger was an Austrian researcher who devised a formula that predicts exactly how likely it is for a quantum particle to move to any particular time or place. Any quantum particle could, for no reason at all, suddenly move 10,000 years in the past, or move instantly to the other side of our galaxy, or much further. The Schrödinger equation will tell you how many quantum particles you would have to watch until you found one that did that, but there is no way to know ahead of time which one will do it.

Schrödinger's cat. Schrödinger proposed an intriguing imaginary experiment to demonstrate the bizarre behaviour of quantum particles. In the imaginary experiment a cat is exposed to a quantum process which will kill the cat if the process occurs. Because the process is quantum, the quantum particle is both present and absent at the same time. That means that during the quantum time a quantum particle might appear and kill the cat, but it might not appear and the cat will live. Schrödinger point was that since quantum particles are everywhere and nowhere at the same time, that means the cat must be both alive and dead at the same time! However, when we take a look at the cat, the indeterminate process is over and we will find the cat either alive or dead because the quantum particle appeared or didn't. Real experiments are still being done, never on cats, but on submicroscopic particles and indeed this bizarre behaviour is being observed. It actually happens, although nobody pretends to understand it.

Science. In the modern world, science is a method, using mathematics, to measure how things or people behave. It relies on methods such as the ability for anyone anywhere to do the same experiment and get the same results.

Ultimate reality. A way of speaking about God. Traditional ideas about God have one drawback—they can make God seem like a very big, even infinite, thing or consciousness that exists within the universe. 'Ultimate reality' refers to what gives rise to existence, but isn't limited to being inside existence. If ultimate reality invents existence, or is what existence emerges from, then everything that exists shares in whatever qualities ultimate reality has. Other terms have been used for the same thing: "Ground of Being," "Being-itself," "Power of Being," or "Abyss of Being." Nobody knows how to describe this; it's just a way of trying to point to something that's beyond knowing in itself. We only know the effects ultimate reality has on us.

Withdrawal. I allow myself to recognize that the qualities I saw in someone else are really part of me. After I've 'withdrawn' a projection, I'm able to accept that what I'd projected onto someone else is actually in me, and I then integrate its truth into my self-understanding and into my behaviour.

ABOUT THE AUTHOR

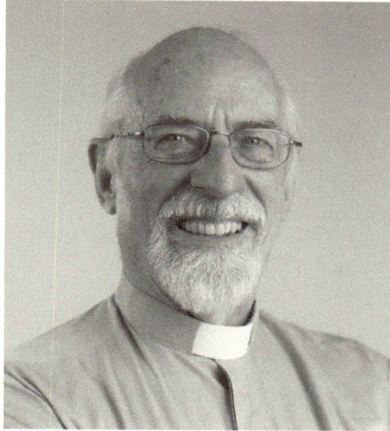

Photography by Sean Pullen

REVEREND DR. HAROLD MUNN, B.A., M.DIV, D.MIN, DD., has led congregations ranging from tiny churches in Canada's far north to All Saints' Cathedral in Edmonton, Alberta. He is an associate of the international Society for Ordained Scientists, and has received awards for his writing.

In addition to the cross-cultural experience of being a priest in secular culture, Harold has lived in, or in close proximity to, many cross-cultural contexts, teaching science in East Africa; with miners in northern B.C.; with oppressed women in Edmonton's inner city; with First Nations villages in the Yukon, on the Naas River, and on Vancouver Island; in Victoria addressing homelessness, addictions, and mental health issues; and in prisons outside Vancouver. He has been active in movements opposing nuclear war, supporting social justice, and urging action to address climate collapse.

Rev. Munn lives on the campus of UBC, Vancouver, with his wife of fifty years. They have two adult sons and four grandchildren whom he claims can be scientifically proven to be the most delightful grandkids in the world.